D0719646

Violence

Also by Richard Bessel

Germany 1945: From War to Peace (2009)

(ed., with Claudia Haake), *Forced Removal
in the Modern World* (2009)

Nazism and War (2004)

(ed., with Dirk Schumann), *Life after Death:
Approaches to a Cultural and Social History of Europe during
the 1940s and 1950s* (2003)

Germany after the First World War (1993)

*Political Violence and the Rise of Nazism. The Storm Troopers in
Eastern Germany 1925-1934* (1984)

Violence

A Modern Obsession

RICHARD BESSEL

**SIMON &
SCHUSTER**

London · New York · Sydney · Toronto · New Delhi

A CBS COMPANY

First published in Great Britain by Simon & Schuster UK Ltd, 2015
A CBS COMPANY

1 3 5 7 9 10 8 6 4 2

Simon & Schuster UK Ltd
1st Floor
222 Gray's Inn Road
London WC1X 8HB

www.simonandschuster.co.uk

Simon & Schuster Australia, Sydney
Simon & Schuster India, New Delhi

A CIP catalogue record for this book
is available from the British Library

Hardback ISBN: 978-0-74323-957-8
eBook ISBN: 978-1-47112-600-0

The author and publishers have made all reasonable efforts to
contact copyright-holders for permission, and apologise for
any omissions or errors in the form of credits given.
Corrections may be made to future printings.

Typeset in the UK by M Rules
Printed and bound by CPI Group (UK) Ltd, Croydon, CR0 4YY

Contents

Introduction

Violence, it seems, is on everyone's mind. It is constantly in the news. It is ever present in popular entertainment. The subject of violence has given rise to an enormous historical, sociological, and philosophical literature; it is regarded as a fundamental problem affecting social, political and interpersonal relations. Human history, so it seems, is often understood as a history of violence. The violence may be planned and deliberate or it may be an eruption of uncontrolled passion; it may be lauded or it may be condemned; it may be overt or it may consist largely in the threat. But it appears never to be out of the frame. Violence, Michael Geyer has written, 'has a lot in common with dirt':

Much as the latter is misplaced matter, the former is misdirected energy. [...] Both are basic facts of human life. They seem random and arbitrary, yet they are by-products of ingenuity and end results of great ambition. Much effort is expended to clean them up. Indeed, such efforts are considered essential to the well-being of individuals and communities. Pollution, to use the technical term for dirt, is just as intolerable as violence. Both threaten the very existence of society or community. Nevertheless, violence – much like pollution – comes back time and again, because society and community, in generating bonds of belonging and the security of social conditions that maintains them, are unimaginable without them. Like dirt, violence may not be what you want, but it is what you get.[1]

Yet violence, like dirt and pollution, is a matter of perception as well as of fact. The exploration of the history of violence therefore should not be limited to describing various manifestations of what some might assume to be an unchanging feature of the human character and condition. Attempts to measure violence are as frequent as they are problematical. Violence is not a constant, nor are perceptions of violence. If violence is 'misdirected energy', it follows that we have a sense of what *properly* directed energy is.

This book is about perceptions of violence in the modern, western world. It does not aim to measure violence – an undertaking so complicated and subjective that it is probably destined to fail – but rather to discuss a remarkable shift in attitudes towards violence, a shift that has affected politics, warfare, legal codes, social life, culture and private interpersonal relations. This shift has occurred against the background, on the one hand, of a conviction that we have lived through a period of quite extraordinary violence and, on the other, of a heightened sensitivity towards violence to the point of obsession. This shift, how it came about and what its effects may be, provides the subject of this book.

The heightened sensitivity towards violence in recent decades has rested on the widespread belief that our world is more violent than ever – a belief that seems more to reflect how people perceive their world than it is based on what actually may have been seen. Expressions of the belief that the contemporary world is uniquely violent are legion. In his foreword to the 2002 World Health Organization's *World Report on Violence and Health*, Nelson Mandela began by observing: 'The twentieth century will be remembered as a century marked by violence. It burdens us with its legacy of mass destruction, of violence inflicted on a scale never seen and never possible before in human history.'[2] This is an observation with which many if not most people probably would agree. The century recently ended is regarded widely as the most violent in human history, and not without cause. During the twentieth century at least 100 million people met violent death in wars, forced removals and campaigns of genocide. It was a century that saw the formation and prolifer-ation of what Christian Gerlach has termed 'extremely violent societies';[3] it was a century whose most enduring images are the mushroom cloud of the atomic bomb dropped on Hiroshima and the gates of Auschwitz. In a public lecture presented at Columbia University on 12 March 2002 and published in the *Boston Review* a few months later, Charles Tilly began with the assertion:

> More collective violence was visited on the world (in absolute terms, and probably per capita as well) in the twentieth cen-tury than in any century of the previous ten thousand years. China's Warring States period, Sargon of Akkad's conquests, the Mongol expansion, and Europe's Thirty Years War were times of terrible destruction. But earlier wars deployed nothing comparable to the death-dealing armaments and state-backed exterminations of civilians characteristic of twentieth-century conflicts.[4]

Tilly, who died in 2008, had spent much of his career as a his-torical sociologist charting patterns of collective violence through the centuries. In his lecture, delivered in the shadow of the attack on New York's World Trade Center (just a few miles from where Tilly spoke), he articulated the widely held view that, in terms of violence, we have lived in the worst of times, that the twentieth century was *the* century of violence.

Even more explicit about the violent character of the twentieth century is the American psychologist David G. Winter, who in 2000 looked back on the century just ended:

The twentieth century turned out to be not so much the 'American Century' (as Henry Luce claimed in a 1941 magazine essay)[5] but rather the violent century. We have had world wars, colonial wars, civil wars, ethnopolitical wars, guerrilla wars, wars of national liberation, police actions, ethnic cleansing, low-intensity conflicts, total wars, and small-scale teenage 'wars' fought in the corridors and playgrounds of American public schools. In this century, perhaps 100 million people have died from high explosives, machine guns, land-mines, torpedoes, poison gas, gas chambers, saturation fire-bombing, biochemical agents, napalm, people dropped into the sea from helicopters, and nuclear weapons. The twentieth-century techniques of mass production work not only for automobiles and food, it seems, but also for death.[6]

Similar assessments emerged in western Europe, not least in Germany (which contributed more than its share of the violence of twentieth-century European history). There the left-wing academic and public intellectual (and former doctor) Till Bastian introduced his book, *The Century of Death* (published in 2000), with the declaration: 'In view of the facts, we know this [...] only too well, this twentieth century [...] was hardly the best but certainly the most bloody era of human history.'[7] For Bastian, as for so many people, the key question is: 'How could it possibly have come to that?' This is a question that has concerned many people, and not only in Germany.

Niall Ferguson, whose approach is rather different than that of Till Bastian, based his book and television series *The War of the World* on a similar premise: 'The hundred years after 1900 were without question the bloodiest century in modern history, far more violent in relative as well as absolute terms than any previous era.'[8] For Ferguson, too, the question is how to explain this: 'What made the twentieth century, and particularly the fifty years from 1904 until 1953, so bloody?' His answer – that the huge eruption of violence arose from the tensions along the tectonic plates between the world's great empires at the outset of the twentieth century, where 'dark forces' were able to 'conjure up ethnic conflict and imperial rivalry out of economic crisis, and in doing so negate our common humanity [...] forces that stir within us still', and 'leaders of apparently civilized societies were able to unleash the most primitive murderous instincts of their fellow citizens'[9] – may be open to criticism, and the Freudian assumptions that seem to lie behind it are left rather undeveloped.[10] Nevertheless, the question is important, and reflects a need to understand the outbursts of deadly violence that occurred in so many regions of the world during the twentieth century.

What is interesting about such assessments is not simply whether, measured on some yardstick of violence, we really do live in the worst of times, but the fact of their expression. They reflect a widespread conviction that the twentieth century was an age of unprecedented violence, not just in terms of its quantity but also of its quality, and that this represents the undermining of civilization and a return of barbarism.[11] Civilization is commonly assumed to involve the control and suppression of violent instincts and passions, and the terrifying upsurge of violence during the first half of the twentieth century is often regarded as the negation or even collapse of civilization.[12] The thinker most associated with the idea that the control of violence through codes of behaviour, restraint and self-restraint amounted to a 'civilizing process' was the German-Jewish sociologist Norbert Elias – whose own life was seared by the eruption of deadly violence that emanated from his homeland in the middle of the twentieth century, which drove him into exile and claimed the life of his mother.[13] That eruption of violence amounted to a 'civilization break',[14] a rupture in human development, which many regard as having been the defining feature of the century just passed.

As a result of that twentieth-century 'civilization break', in particular the murder of the great majority of the Jewish population in German-occupied Europe during the Second World War, modernity has been equated with violence on a new level.[15] A typical assessment in this vein is the description of a recent research project on the history of violence and foreign occupation in the 'age of extremes':

> With the advent of modernity, the phenomena of violence, war, and foreign domination have taken on a qualitatively new dimension. Since the beginning of the twentieth century the industrial and technical revolution has opened up hitherto unknown possibilities to the planners of future 'total wars'. With the development of the railway network the shifting of large masses of people – deployments of one's own troops as well as deportations – became possible for the first time. The enhanced range and destructive power of new weapons abolished the separation of front and home front. Ethnic and social tensions that accompanied the birth of nation states in the nineteenth century introduced ideological aspects into armed conflict to an ever greater extent.[16]

Some of the assumptions upon which this description rests may reveal a rather myopic view of history: those who lived through the Thirty Years War during the seventeenth century or the Revolutionary and Napoleonic Wars of the late eighteenth and early nineteenth centuries probably would have been puzzled by the idea that a 'separation of front and home front' had existed only to be 'abolished' in the twentieth century.[17] Nevertheless they often frame our contemporary views. Mark Mazower has pointed to the prevalence of such assessments of the last century, noting:

> The twentieth century is increasingly characterized by scholars in terms of its historically unprecedented levels of bloodshed. 'More human beings had been killed or allowed to die by human decision than ever before in human history,' Eric Hobsbawm has written. For Isaiah Berlin, the twentieth century was 'the worst century there has ever been'. Genocide, ethnic cleansing, and the killing of unprecedented numbers of civilians both in wartime and through acts of massive political repression have all contributed to what Charles Maier has described as an epoch of 'moral atrocity'.[18]

The horrors of the first half of the twentieth century – a large proportion of which took place in Europe and were perpetrated by Europeans[19] – have cast a long, dark shadow over the recent past and our understanding of that past. Whether articulated explicitly or not, we are aware that our immediate past has included war and murder on an unprecedented scale. The contemporary world, it would seem, has been more violent than ever.

Yet not everyone agrees. Most prominently, the Canadian-born Harvard psychologist Steven Pinker has asserted that, in fact, 'violence has been in decline over long stretches of history, and today we are probably living in the most peaceful moment of our species' time on earth'.[20] In his recently published magnum opus (with the subtitle 'The Decline of Violence in History and its Causes'), Pinker (who is not exactly known for his modesty) claims that his book 'is about what may be the most important thing that has ever happened in human history. Believe it or not – and I know that most people do not – violence has declined over long stretches of time, and today we may be living in the most peaceable era in our species' existence.'[21] The catalogue of horrors that disfigured twentieth-century history notwithstanding, Pinker argues that people are becoming less violent, not more:

> In sixteenth-century Paris, a popular form of entertainment was cat-burning, in which a cat was hoisted in a sling on a stage and slowly lowered into a fire. [...] Today, such sadism would be unthinkable in most of the world. This change in sensibilities is just one example of perhaps the most important and most underappreciated trend in the human saga: violence has been in decline over long stretches of history, and today we are probably living in the most peaceful moment of our species' time on earth.
>
> In the decade of Darfur and Iraq, and shortly after the century of Stalin, Hitler, and Mao, the claim that violence has been diminishing may seem somewhere between hallucinatory and obscene. Yet recent studies that seek to quantify the historical ebb and flow of violence point to exactly that conclusion.[22]

According to Pinker, and contrary to much popular opinion, 'we have been getting kinder and gentler'. Of course, that rather depends on who 'we' are considered to be. Kindness and gentleness might be easier to exhibit in contemporary Sweden (leaving aside Kurt Wallander's Ystad) than in the Democratic Republic of the Congo or in Syria. And evidence that there has been, as Pinker observes, a 'change in sensibilities' is not necessarily evidence that 'violence has been diminishing'. However, what Pinker's assessment and those of people who regard ours as 'the most bloody era of human history' have in common is an intense, almost obsessive interest in violence as a historical topic.

The German historian Habbo Knoch distilled the position when – introducing a collection of essays assembled under the title *Violence and Society* – he asserted that 'whoever speaks about history and therefore about society [...] cannot remain silent about violence'.[23] In recent decades countless historical, sociological and psychological studies have been published on the theme of violence. Numerous journals have been devoted to the subject in various forms, ranging from the *Journal of Interpersonal Violence*, the *Journal of School Violence*, *Violence against Women* and the *Journal of Family Violence*, to *Terrorism and Political Violence* and the *International Journal of Conflict and Violence*. Throughout the western world research institutes have been established with the aim of investigating the practice of violence and the control of violence – from the Centre for the History of Violence at the University of Newcastle in New South Wales and the Peace Research Institute in Frankfurt, to the Institute on Domestic Violence and Sexual Assault at the University of Texas at Austin and the *Centre de recherche interdisciplinaire sur la violence familiale et la violence faite aux femmes* situated in the universities of Montréal and Laval in Québec.

Particularly in the United States, violence has become a hot topic for academic study, against a background of intense public concern. For example, the programme of the Center for the Study and Prevention of Violence at the University of Colorado Boulder asserts that 'violence in America has reached epidemic proportions' and that 'today all Americans are touched directly or indirectly by violent acts'; 'in response' the Center 'was founded in 1992 to provide informed assistance to groups committed to understanding and preventing violence, particularly adolescent violence'.[24] This neatly expresses what has become a fundamental assumption of much recent research into violence:

that violence 'has reached epidemic proportions' and that understanding the causes of violence is necessary to prevent it. This reflects a widespread conviction that violence is 'inherently undesirable',[25] a profound social evil that both needs to be combated and can be checked. While violence itself may or may not have 'reached epidemic proportions', the development of academic centres to carry out research into violence certainly has.

In recent decades people in many western societies have become increasingly and acutely sensitive to violence, refusing to accept or condone behaviour that in earlier times had been widely tolerated. Political violence is regarded as illegitimate; domestic violence is regarded as intolerable; armed forces proclaim that 'peace is our profession' (the motto of the United States' Strategic Air Command, which was responsible for America's nuclear deterrent from 1946 to 1992). This comprises a profound shift in mentalities, and one that shapes expectations of politics, the military, public institutions and interpersonal relations. Whether or not Steven Pinker is correct in asserting that 'today we may be living in the most peaceable era in our species' existence' and that this may constitute 'the most important thing that has ever happened in human history', we have witnessed a transformation in *attitudes* towards violence, with profound consequences for our political, social and personal lives. It may be debated whether we really 'have been getting kinder and gentler', but we do live in a world where being kinder and gentler increasingly is regarded as admirable and where violence is routinely condemned.

This shift in attitudes has a history, and many of the changes in public sensibilities have their origins in the Enlightenment of the late eighteenth and early nineteenth centuries. Within the frame of Enlightenment ideology that gave value to the individual, to individual rights and to the pursuit of individual happiness, new grounds arose for limiting and opposing violence. Campaigns against torture, against slavery and against the death penalty gathered support, and at least in some bourgeois circles wife-beating became less acceptable. Nevertheless, although campaigns against torture and slavery achieved important successes during the nineteenth century, it was not until 1948 that their aims received international recognition when prohibitions against slavery and 'torture or [...] cruel, inhuman or degrading treatment or punishment' were incorporated into the United Nations Universal Declaration of Human Rights. Although violence against the individual attracted increasing censure, it was not really until after the Second World War that there was a truly broad challenge to the legitimacy of violence *per se*.

But what do we mean by violence, and how has that changed? From a 'common-sense' perspective, what comprises 'violence' seems obvious: war, murder, massacre, assault, rape, physical attack – perhaps verbal aggression, intimidation and threats as well. Indeed, current definitions of violence do not restrict themselves to physical violence. According to the *Oxford Dictionary of English*, violence is not limited to the use of physical force 'intended to hurt, damage, or kill someone or something', or even 'intimidation by the exhibition of such force'; it also extends to 'strength of emotion'.[26] Especially with regard to 'domestic violence', the concept of violence is conceived broadly. *The New Oxford Companion to Law* notes: 'Most current definitions now extend beyond physical violence. Types of behaviour identified as constituting domestic violence range through murder, rape, assault, indecent assault, and destruction of property to threats, belittling, isolation, deprivation of money, and harassment.'[27] That is to say: it is not necessary to lay a finger on someone in order to have committed an act of violence. Threats, harassment, deprivation of money, even belittling someone, can also be regarded as violence.

Other contemporary definitions of violence are equally

expansive. The World Health Organization, for example, has recently referred to violence as 'the intentional use of physical force or power, threatened or actual, against oneself, another person, or against a group or community, that either results in or has a high likelihood of resulting in injury, death, psychological harm, maldevelopment or deprivation'.[28] Thus 'violence' is not limited to the application of physical force or the inflicting of physical damage, but extends to the 'threatened' use of force and action that may cause 'psychological harm' or 'maldevelopment'. The definitional leap is significant, not just because it goes beyond violence as something physical but also because it is necessarily subjective. As long as violence is defined as something physical, it can be measured relatively objectively: common sense suggests that either one is stabbed, shot, beaten or one is not. However, what may constitute 'verbal force' has less clear-cut definitional boundaries. What may be perceived as threatening or violent verbal behaviour to one person may not be so to another; what in some cultures may be regarded as threatening may not be so in another. Thus violence becomes that which is violence in the eye, or ear, of the beholder.

The commentary provided by the World Health Organization to its 2002 definition of violence demonstrates the extent to which the concept of violence has expanded in recent years:

> The inclusion of the word 'power', in addition to the phrase 'use of physical force', broadens the nature of a violent act and expands the conventional understanding of violence to include those acts that result from a power relationship, including threats and intimidation. The 'use of power' also serves to include neglect or acts of omission, in addition to the more obvious violent acts of commission. Thus, 'the use of physical force or power' should be understood to include neglect and all types of physical, sexual and psychological abuse, as well as suicide and other self-abusive acts.

This definition covers a broad range of outcomes – including psychological harm, deprivation and maldevelopment. This reflects a growing recognition among researchers and practitioners of the need to include violence that does not necessarily result in injury or death, but that nonetheless poses a substantial burden on individuals, families, communities and health care systems worldwide.[29]

Here violence is understood to include intimidation, threats, 'all types' of 'psychological abuse', actions that result in 'psychological harm, deprivation and maldevelopment' and actions that do 'not necessarily result in injury or death'. Of course, all these manifestations of violence are to be combated.

Increasingly, the *perceived threat* of violence has been included in the definition of violence, particularly where violence against women is concerned. In the Declaration on the Elimination of Violence Against Women, adopted by consensus by the United Nations General Assembly in December 1993, violence was defined as 'any act of gender-based violence that results in, or is likely to result in, physical, sexual, or psychological harm or suffering to women, including threats of such acts, coercion or arbitrary deprivation of liberty whether occurring in public or private life.'[30] This signals an important extension: the inclusion into a definition of violence of the *threat* of actions that are likely to lead to not just physical but also psychological harm or suffering, either in public or private. Violence and the damage that it may cause do not necessarily have to be physical; violence is not just something that causes actual harm, whether physical or psychological, but also something that 'is likely to result in [...] harm'. This shift in focus has developed in the context of growing global concern about violence against women, and the conviction that such violence constitutes a violation of human rights[31] – itself a relatively new concept that developed in its modern sense with the American and French Revolutions of the late eighteenth century. The right to a life free of violence thus extends beyond a right not to be hit to a right not to be threatened or psychologically harmed.

While the extension of the concept of violence beyond physical harm indicates a heightened sensitivity towards violence, it would be wrong to assume that the inclusion of threat and coercion into the definition was completely novel to the late twentieth century. In fact, definitions of violence from over two centuries ago were not limited to physical confrontation but also extended to the emotions. In his *Complete Dictionary of the English Language*, published in London in 1789, Thomas Sheridan defined violence as 'strength applied to any purpose, an attack, an assault, a murder, outrage, unjust force, eagerness, vehemence, injury, infringement, forcible defloration.'[32] Eleven years later Nathan Bailey offered a similar definition of 'violence' in his *Universal Etymological English Dictionary*: 'Vehemence, boisterousness, eagerness, earnestness, force or constraint used unlawfully, oppression, outrage.'[33] Here violence was defined as a matter more of an emotion than of an exclusively physical act. This was reflected in later definitions as well. For example, the American *Webster's Revised Unabridged Dictionary* from 1913 defined 'violence' as follows:

1. The quality or state of being violent; highly excited action, whether physical or moral; vehemence; impetuosity; force.
2. Injury done to that which is entitled to respect, reverence, or observance; profanation; infringement; unjust force; outrage; assault.
3. Ravishment; rape; consturpation. To do violence on, to attack; to murder.[34]

Here too the definition of violence extends beyond physical acts and assault to 'injury done to that which is entitled to respect' as well as to 'vehemence' and 'impetuosity'.

What these definitions have in common, while at the same time distinguishing themselves from understandings of violence that coalesced during the second half of the twentieth century, is not the extension of the definition beyond physical violence; it is the perspective from which violence is defined. Earlier definitions of violence took the perspective of the person being violent, whether or not the violence is physical – the perspective of the person who commits or attempts an assault or a murder, or who demonstrates violent emotions ('eagerness', 'vehemence'). More recently it is the perspective of the victim that has come to the fore. Violence no longer is just a matter of 'murder, rape, assault, indecent assault, and destruction of property', but has extended to 'threats, belittling, isolation, deprivation of money, and harassment'. How threats, belittling or harassment are understood is determined not necessarily by a supposedly objective observer but through the perception of the alleged victim.

This shift is significant, and points to the increasing importance of empathy in our understanding of violence. Empathy is seen as the enemy of violence: 'empathy is anathema to killing, to torture, and to the waging of war'.[35] If we can empathize with other human beings, can imagine ourselves in their place and be aware of their feelings, then, it is assumed, we are inhibited from doing violence to them. The corollary of this has been to identify more with the alleged victim, less with the alleged perpetrator. Both in academic debate and in public discussion, empathy has become an important feature of modern perceptions of violence; in order to understand violence one needs to empathize with the victim. In one of his many essays about understanding the murder of European Jews during the Second World War, Omer Bartov has articulated this widely accepted opinion clearly: 'Listening to the voices of victims, Jewish or not, is crucial to the kind of empathy that brings with it a modicum of understanding.'[36] Bartov's assertion not only reflects the shift in the recent historiography of the Shoah, away from a focus primarily on the perpetrators and towards one that focuses increasingly on the experience of the victims;[37] it is also symptomatic of a broader trend of stressing the importance of empathy with victims in our approach to violence. In particular, feminist approaches to understanding domestic violence, in both the historical and the contemporary contexts, tend to identify with the objects of violence.[38] Only by understanding how those on the receiving end have felt can we achieve a 'modicum of understanding'.

The amplification of empathy has occurred as personal security has increased. It may be that empathy is a luxury that we can now afford. Compared with their counterparts during the first half of the twentieth century, in the second half of the century people in many parts of the world – most obviously in Europe – came to live safer and more secure lives, much less threatened by violence. Nevertheless, declines in everyday violence, at least in western societies, or more effective control of potential violence, are not necessarily read as indications that people are becoming less violent. Sometimes the response has been quite the opposite: the fact that violence may not be overt and out in the open, so the argument goes, that does not make it any less dangerous or despicable. Indeed it seems that possible declines in the threat of violence have been accompanied by a heightened concern about violence. In relatively peaceful and secure societies, the threat of violence may be all the more frightening.

Furthermore, at least until the collapse of the Soviet Union and the end of the Cold War, relatively pacified societies were haunted by the spectre of thermonuclear war. At the beginning of the 1980s, at a time when millions of people in Europe generally and in Germany particularly were desperately concerned about the possibility of a violent confrontation between NATO and the Warsaw Pact, Ute Volmerg (who then was working with

16

the Hesse Foundation for Peace and Conflict Research in Frankfurt, and who subsequently became a 'conflict advisor' and director in the Dharma Centre for Spiritual Development in Schaffhausen), observed:

> In the Middle Ages robbery, murder, mutilation, rape and oppression were daily occurrences; today we have the paradoxical situation, that in our daily lives we indeed feel more secure than people in former times, but we live in the immediate vicinity of potentials of violence and destruction of incomprehensible dimensions. [...] The horror is banned from public sight, placed in bunkers, buried and surrounded with barbed wire fences, it is hidden in the depths of the oceans, in space and in the desert, and where the launch platforms and rockets cannot be concealed for practical military reasons they are disguised so they cannot be recognized.[39]

This assertion was characteristic of its time, a comment on and a reflection of the strange environment of the Cold War, in which (at least in the prosperous West) remarkably peaceful societies lived under the threat of nuclear catastrophe. Nevertheless, the general message was that even where life may have become more peaceful and secure, there was no cause for complacency. Even where the threat of violence was not so visible, in societies that increasingly came to regard it as anathema, it continued to give rise to tremendous concern and anxiety.

While human history may be in large measure a history of violence and while wars and violent political upheaval have long been prominent subjects for investigation, the systematic study of violence as an analytical category has been undertaken by historians and social scientists only in the past few decades.[40] What is more, the recent flood of analyses of violent incidents, violent behaviour and aggression, has emanated mostly from societies that, in relative terms (both relative to other societies and to their own pasts) have been rather peaceful and whose members' daily lives have been, for the most part, rather free of violence.[41] Violence seems to have become a preoccupation in almost inverse proportion to its presence in our lives; the people who write about it live lives remarkably free of the phenomenon about which they write.

This paradox frames the subject of this book. The intention here is not to document or to quantify violence, but rather to understand the causes and effects of a remarkable contemporary concern about, even obsession with, violence in the modern world. Thus the focus on western Europe and North America, where this phenomenon appears to have been most pronounced. Certainly people in Asia, Africa and Latin America too have been deeply concerned about the causes and effects of violence on their lives. However, the story of the modern obsession with violence is in large measure a western story. The history of violence is not just about acts of violence and aggression; it also concerns how we see, understand and react to violence and to the perceived threat of violence. In this sense, too, human history is in large measure a history of violence.

I

Spectacle

On the evening of Saturday, 24 March 1962, the boxer Emile Griffith knocked out Benny ('The Kid') Paret in a fight for the world welterweight championship in New York City's Madison Square Garden. It was the third time that the pair had contested the welterweight championship, and it was broadcast live on nationwide television in the United States. After nearly being knocked out himself in the sixth round, Griffith landed a right hook in the twelfth, sending Paret onto the ropes, where he remained as Griffith kept hitting him until the referee, Ruby Goldstein, stopped the fight. On the following day, Robert Teague in *The New York Times* described what millions had seen on their television screens as it happened:

> Whatever it was that Griffith was thinking about last night, it certainly was translated into something akin to savagery. After the ten rights to the face had failed to do the job, he began alternating the rights with left hooks. [...] Paret sagged but would not go down.
>
> Goldstein finally made his move but had difficulty restraining Griffith. When the referee finally pulled the attacker away,

Paret slid slowly down the ropes and to the canvas. He lay on his back unconscious for about eight minutes while the physicians worked on him. He was still unconscious when carted to his dressing room.[1]

According to a later commentator, 'Paret slipped to the canvas like a *Titanic* going stern-first into the dark water, sliding towards oblivion, seemingly in slo-mo, shocking by his total animal unconsciousness a nationwide TV audience'.[2] Griffith regained the title that he had lost to Paret at their previous meeting. Paret never regained consciousness, and died ten days later.

The broadcast was a shock to millions of television viewers (including this author, who as an adolescent saw the fight on television that night). They had tuned in to watch a spectacle of controlled violence – with rules, with a referee, with an outcome from which both contestants were expected to recover without long-term effects. They had not tuned in to watch one man kill another. On the following Monday, *The New York Times* editorialized, under the heading 'The Manly Art':

> The tragic conclusion of the Emile Griffith-Benny (Kid) Paret world welterweight championship fight in the Madison Square Garden ring makes us wonder whether it is not time to toll the bell on the savage 'sport' called professional prize-fighting. [...]
>
> This is the Saturday night pleasure of a civilized people? [...] Spare us the reminder that there are deaths in other sports, including football. At least these others are not man-to-man licensed mayhem promoted for profit, where the sole inspiring ideal is to bring the opponent to the canvas, beaten to an insensibility that will arouse the crowd to huzzas.[3]

Letters to the editor concurred. One correspondent, Abbie L. Gottlieb, wrote:

It does indeed seem inconceivable that in this day of supposed civilization people are entertained by seeing two men punch each other until one or the other becomes unconscious.

We look back with horror on the ancient Roman gladiatorial contests, we have outlawed public executions, have organizations for the prevention of cruelty to animals and to children. Let us now pass a law prohibiting man's brutality to man and depriving the public of the sadistic pleasure derived from seeing one man, for financial gain, inflict severe pain, if not injury or death, on another.[4]

Cries reverberated for a ban on professional boxing. US Congressman Abraham Multer (a Democrat from Brooklyn) introduced legislation to prohibit the broadcasting of boxing matches on radio and television; a call was raised in the Danish parliament for a ban on professional boxing in Denmark; the Vatican admonished boxers and fight promoters not to forget the fifth commandment, 'Thou shalt not kill'.[5]

The Griffith–Paret fight was not the first widely publicized boxing death, nor was it the first to provoke public concern. Perhaps most famously, in Cleveland on 24 June 1947, Jimmy Doyle was knocked out in a welterweight title fight in front of more than 11,000 spectators by 'Sugar' Ray Robinson – often credited with being the greatest boxer of all time – and died the following afternoon. It was the first time that a boxer had died as a result of injuries suffered in a world-title championship fight.[6] However, it was television that gave the Griffith–Paret fight its resonance. On that Saturday night in 1962, not thousands but millions had watched a spectacle of violence that was supposed to provide entertainment, and not overly bloody entertainment at that, after which the performers would collect their rewards and then go about their lives. The violence of the boxing ring was supposed to be subject to clear rules of engagement and to be aborted before either of those in the ring suffered serious injury. It was not supposed to end in death. These expectations, shattered that night, reflected the idea that the violence of sporting spectacle had become more spectacle than violence. Spectators generally do not now attend sports events in the hope or expectation that the violence on display will end in death.

Abbie Gottlieb was right: it was not always thus. We do 'look back with horror on the ancient Roman gladiatorial contests, we have outlawed public executions, [and] have organizations for the prevention of cruelty to animals and to children'. Our modern gladiators, professional boxers, are not expected to kill people. The 'Queensbury rules for the sport of boxing', first published in 1867, and the professionalization of boxing transformed the sport from the 'quite brutal' activity that had been popular at local fairs and religious festivals in early eighteenth-century Europe.[7] Our understandings and sensibilities about what constitutes public entertainment and the place of violence in that entertainment have changed. The contrast between contemporary spectacles of violence in the western world and those staged in past times and in other corners of the world is remarkable. Spectacles of violence in ancient Rome were famously public, performed before crowds that expected to see men and beasts put to death in huge numbers and performed with a view to confirm and reinforce the existing social and political order.[8] That was public entertainment, and entertainment with a purpose: the maintenance of social stability and the reinforcement of the social order through public displays of lethal violence.

Few things illustrate this shift in sensibilities more clearly than the evolution of capital punishment. Until the nineteenth century, executions in western countries were performed widely in public (in staged events that have been described as 'theatres of horror' or 'theatres of cruelty'),[9] often before crowds of people who 'in great multitudes flocked to the place of execution'.[10] The crowd was assembled for entertainment, but not just for

22

entertainment. At a time when the state was incapable of effective policing and the idea of sentencing people to prison for specific periods had not yet gained currency, public executions served to symbolize and reinforce the power of the state in front of its subjects, and to deter crime.[11] Executions were designed 'as displays of civil and religious authority and order, as a "spectacle for Men and Angels"'.[12] The public spectacle of violence buttressed order in societies where the state was too limited to exert day-to-day control over its subjects.

The ritual of public execution served not only to reinforce the social order and the power of the state; it also could serve as a 'quasi-religious popular festival' that on the one hand restored 'a world that had been violated by a crime' and on the other celebrated 'the religious sacrifice of a penitent sinner'.[13] The presence of the crowd could be an important element of a quasi-religious process whereby a convicted criminal in effect might retrieve his honour and thus achieve a sort of reintegration into society as a 'remorseful sinner'.[14] In early modern Europe such violence had to be displayed in order to be effective. The religious meanings may seem rather distant today, and the abolition of executions as public spectacle may reflect a secularization of western societies, as well as the growth of an effective state, over the past two centuries. But they were meaningful to those who performed and observed them, in societies of believers where violent punishments were not subcontracted to state institutions that performed them behind walls, out of the public gaze.

Public executions were not without their dangers for public order, however. The crowd could, and often did, get out of hand. In Rome during the early Empire, public rituals of execution probably led to violence elsewhere in the city; and in early modern Europe executions could pose a serious challenge to political authority.[15] During the modern era this changed. At least in the western world, executions came to be performed behind closed doors – a process described (for the United States) as 'a major transformation from a large and rowdy public spectacle to a hidden and tightly controlled ritual'.[16] Pieter Spierenburg, who has investigated executions in Europe over the centuries, notes that from the middle of the eighteenth century 'confidence in public punishment began to crumble'. However, it took another century before public execution began to be abolished in Europe – a slow process that largely reached its conclusion towards the end of the nineteenth century.[17]

How did this come about? What caused the 'repugnance to the sight of physical punishment' to spread and intensify? The change in attitude towards public spectacles of punitive violence occurred as the modern nation state was established and extended its bureaucratic reach into society. For Spierenburg the transformation 'comprised changes which took place both on the ideological and on the institutional level', and consisted of 'at least three phases': 1) 'the quest for legal and penal reform which began during the Enlightenment'; 2) 'the rise of confinement to a more prominent position within the penal system and the emergence of the penitentiary'; and 3) 'finally, and only after the rise of the penitentiary, [...] the abolition of public punishment'.[18] This 'transformation of repression' was not due simply to political and legal changes but was a consequence primarily of a 'fundamental change in sensibilities' that preceded the abolition of public executions. Disgust at the spectacle of public executions and punitive violence reflected a diffusion of Enlightenment-based middle-class sensibilities in the western world, sensibilities that simultaneously underpinned the crusade against slavery and campaigns to abolish torture.

Nineteenth-century reformers who campaigned for the cessation of public execution were also concerned about the conduct of an unruly, uncivilized and irrational crowd. In the wake of the Revolution in France, fear was expressed in Britain that public executions constituted a 'festival of blood calculated to shock or brutalize the feelings of man [and to] encourage ferocious habits in the people'.[19] In December 1847, the *Liverpool Mercury* reported about a petition to spare two convicted murderers public execution in Kirkdale, asserting that 'familiarity with the spectacle of violent death feeds the brutality which would lead to the commission of murder'.[20] The belief that civilization required the abolition of public execution occupied an important place in the arguments of English reformers.[21] When moving a 'Bill to permit Capital Punishments to be carried out under certain regulations within the interior of Prisons' in the House of Commons on 6 March 1866, John Hibbert (Liberal MP for Oldham) observed that 'at the commencement of the present century criminals were hung, one might say, in droves; there were then no less than 160 crimes subject to capital punishment', and he 'could not avoid referring to those times when the pillory was a public punishment, when culprits were hung in chains, and whipping was resorted to as a means of correction'. Relaxing 'the rigour of the law' meant, rightly in his opinion, 'doing away with the few remains that were left of the barbarism of a past age'.[22]

The spectacle of public execution reflected 'the barbarism of a past age', and the advance of civilization required that the practice be stopped. In the parliamentary debate of early 1868 on the 'Capital Punishment within Prisons Bill', such arguments played a prominent role. (This discussion took place shortly before the last man to be hanged publicly in England – the Irish Fenian Michael Barrett, who killed fifteen people when blowing up the wall of Clerkenwell Prison in an attempt to free other Fenians held there – was executed outside Newgate Prison, on 27 May.) Speaking in the Commons in March 1868, Edward Knatchbull-Hugessen, Member of Parliament for Sandwich, claimed: 'Making even the fullest allowance for exaggeration, any person who read the newspapers could not doubt that the scenes which really did take place at public executions were a disgrace not only to civilization but to our common humanity.'[23] In April 1868 William Gregory, MP for Galway – no opponent of capital punishment *per se* – claimed that 'the time had, in his opinion, arrived when public executions ought to be abolished. They were not in accordance with the spirit of the age. They were barbarous and, he believed, demoralizing'; they would, he felt, instil greater awe 'if they were conducted within the precincts of the gaol'.[24] The point was not to do away with punishment, but to abandon a practice – execution as public spectacle – that had come to be considered 'barbarous and demoralizing' and a 'disgrace not only to civilization but also to our common humanity'. It was not violence *per se* but violence as public spectacle that was regarded as 'objectionable and horrible'.

Similar attitudes surfaced in the United States. During the 1830s a number of states in north-eastern America – Rhode Island in 1833, Pennsylvania in 1834, and New York, Massachusetts and New Jersey in 1835 – abolished public hangings (before any countries in Europe had done), and by 1849 fifteen states had done so.[25] The birth of the modern prison paralleled the campaign against public execution; as penitentiaries were built, the gallows was moved indoors and the crowd excluded from the proceedings.[26] Concerns in the United States were similar to those on the other side of the Atlantic. There the public execution crowd was 'typically described as uncivilized, irrational, and ignorant' and 'vulnerable to the violence displayed', and 'came to be viewed as a political challenge of sorts' to the authority of those staging the event.[27]

On the European continent the practice faded as well. In Vienna, the last public execution took place in the same year as in England, in 1868; and in most German states executions were performed within prison walls from the 1850s onwards. In the Netherlands, the last public execution – a hanging in Maastricht – was carried out in 1860 (and the death penalty was abolished completely ten years later).[28] In France, however, public executions continued to attract substantial crowds in the early twentieth century, and the last public execution in France – the beheading of the German-born convicted murderer Eugen (French: Eugène) Weidmann – took place at Versailles shortly before the Second World War, in June 1939.[29] (Afterwards the French president banned future public executions due to shock at the 'hysterical behaviour' of the spectators.) However, Weidmann's death did not quite mark the end of public execution in Europe. The Second World War led to a last wave of the practice. In German-occupied Europe many real and imagined enemies of Hitler's 'New Order' were executed publicly during the war in order to intimidate subjugated populations, and immediately after the war a last spate of public executions on the continent were carried out against Germans and their collaborators in eastern Europe.[30] Perhaps the most remarkable public execution at the time was that of Arthur Greiser, the former Nazi *Gauleiter* (governor) of the 'Warthegau' in western Poland. Greiser was hanged in July 1946 for 'crimes against humanity' amidst the ruins of the Citadel in Poznań, in front of a crowd of 15,000 Poles. According to one account, the spectators watched the execution 'in intense silence', and tickets had been printed to give their holders a place in the front rows, closest to the hanging.[31] According to another, 'a picnic atmosphere prevailed, there were children among the observers, and vendors sold ice cream, soft drinks and sweets. After the execution, people fought over pieces of the hangman's rope.'[32] The spectacle provoked criticism from intellectuals and the Church, and was the last public execution in Poland. Indeed, it marked something of a spectacular end to public execution in Europe.

Public execution and its demise have not been limited to spectacle organized by the state. The frequency of popular, vigilante violence was also reflected in the shift in attitudes about public execution – something that can be seen in the transformation of how lynching was regarded over the course of the twentieth century. Especially (but by no means exclusively) in the American South, lynchings – particularly (but by no means exclusively) of African-Americans by Americans of European descent – were a regular occurrence during the late nineteenth and early twentieth centuries. Although many of these murders involved small groups of men killing their victims away from public gaze, others assumed the character of ritualized public spectacle, which served to enforce a system of apartheid through terror:

> To intimidate and warn other blacks, lynchers sometimes paraded their victims, either before or after they were killed, in black areas. Many lynchings took place at the spot on which the alleged crime had taken place. Fire might be used to torture victims, but fire also helped to expiate the harm done to the ritual order – as we can see in those instances in which lynch mobs killed their victims in one place and burned their bodies in another – at the site of the crime, perhaps, or in a town square.[33]

The spectators were not just passive bystanders, as the burning at the stake of a black tenant farmer, Henry Lowry, demonstrated. In January 1921, over 500 onlookers assembled near Wilson, Arkansas (along the Mississippi River, north of Memphis, Tennessee) – 'a great crowd [consisting of] every able-bodied man from Wilson, a crowd from Blytheville and surrounding towns', according to the *Arkansas Democrat* – and watched as Lowry was chained to a log, had petrol-soaked leaves placed around his feet, and was set alight. A reporter from the *Memphis Press* described the scene:

> Inch by inch the negro was fair cooked to death. [...] Every few minutes fresh leaves were tossed on the funeral pyre

until the blaze had passed the negro's waist. As the flames were eating away his abdomen, a member of the mob stepped forward and saturated the body with gasoline. It was then only a few minutes until the negro had been reduced to ashes.[34]

This account, published in a city newspaper that had engaged in an editorial crusade against lynching,[35] is a description of what now seems a terrifying but far-off world. It was a world in which lynching was 'a community ritual dedicated to the perpetration of white supremacy':

Usually applied to the accused black rapist or murderer, the macabre ritual included the following aspects: (1) Ample notice of a day or two so that whites from neighbouring areas (or from areas even further away) could stream into the site of the lynching by train, buggy, or car to join local whites in witnessing the lynching. Railroads sometimes ran special trains and frequently assigned extra cars to regular trains to accommodate the demands of lynch-minded crowds. (2) The lynching itself thus became a mass spectacle with thousands of whites, in gatherings up to as high as fifteen thousand persons, participating as spectators. (3) The doomed victim was burned at the stake – a process that was prolonged for several hours, often, as the black male was subjected to the excruciating pain of torture and mutilation (frequently initiated by the masculine relatives of the wronged white in the case) climaxed, ordinarily, by the hideous act euphemistically described as 'surgery below the belt'. (4) Nor did the obscenely sadistic ritual end with the death of the victim. Souvenirs from the body, taken in the course of the mutilation process, were collected, and picture postcards of the proceedings were sold (sometimes for years thereafter) by enterprising photographers.[36]

We may be fascinated and horrified by such behaviour, which rightly has attracted the attention and condemnation of historians, but the history of lynching in twentieth-century America is not just a history of violence and terror. It is also a history of the disappearance of the practice. Looking back over the history of lynching in the United States since the late nineteenth century, it becomes apparent that it was a phenomenon of a particular time, and that time has passed. One may speak of a 'lynching era' during the last two decades of the nineteenth century and the first three decades of the twentieth.[37] Thereafter, the practice slowly declined. According to statistics of lynchings in the United States between 1882 and 1968 compiled by the Tuskegee Institute, in only one year before 1900 did the total number of lynchings fall below 100 (96, in 1890); after 1901 it never again exceeded 100, but until 1922 it remained above 50 in every year but one (38, in 1917); after 1923 it never again exceeded 30; and from 1945 through 1968 there were 26 recorded victims of lynching altogether.[38] Lynching was overwhelmingly a phenomenon of the Old South: of the 4,742 victims between 1882 and 1968 recorded by the Tuskegee Institute, 3,442 (i.e. more than two thirds) were black and 2,343 (i.e. roughly half) were killed in Alabama, Georgia, Louisiana, Mississippi and Texas. (No lynchings were recorded in four states, all of them in New England: Connecticut, Massachusetts, New Hampshire and Rhode Island.)

What changed over the course of the twentieth century? During and after the First World War, and as hundreds of thousands of African-Americans turned their backs on the South and headed north in the 'Great Migration', public opinion in the United States began to shift increasingly towards a condemnation of lynching. Indeed, in July 1918 President Woodrow Wilson, a Democrat from Virginia not exactly noted for his concern for African-Americans, had publicly condemned lynching. A few months earlier, in April 1918, an Anti-Lynching Bill was introduced by the Republican Missouri Congressman Leonidas C. Dyer, into whose Congressional district many African-Americans fled from the racial violence that had left more than forty people dead in East St Louis in 1917. Dyer's bill aimed to make lynching a federal crime and to make 'any State or municipal officer' who failed to make reasonable efforts to prevent a lynching liable to criminal prosecution. A revised version of the bill passed the House of Representatives in January 1922 and, although the Senate failed to pass it due to a filibuster by Southern Democrats,[39] its introduction and near success (as well as its prior inclusion into the Republican Party platform in 1920) revealed the extent to which sensibilities were changing.

As public opposition to lynching grew and its frequency declined, the nature of the crime also appears to have undergone a change. Lynchings became less likely to be public spectacles of violence – that is, 'ceremonial racial murders characterized by white mobs, manhunts, chases, torture, mutilation, and the public display of the victim's remains'.[40] More typical as the practice became less frequent was the notorious case of two black teenagers kidnapped by four white men from the Leon County Jail in Florida in the early hours of 20 July 1937 and shot near a highway about three and a half miles out of town soon thereafter. In the words of Florida Governor Fred Cone, this 'was not a lynching – it was murder'.[41] Cone understood the difference: this was not lynching as public spectacle; it was murder committed away from public gaze (although placards had been left near the bodies with messages such as: 'Negroes, remember you may be next').

Public lynchings were increasingly an embarrassment. Concern was expressed, particularly in southern states, about the negative image created by well-publicized lynchings. Local and regional newspapers took stands against the practice; local law enforcement officers displayed a growing commitment to curb vigilante activity;[42] and during the brief period in the 1920s when it emerged into the mainstream of small-town, white Protestant American politics, the Ku Klux Klan looked to political activity rather than overt violence to spread its message and increase its influence.[43] Public acts of vigilante violence did not cease altogether, but they met with mounting disapproval. The lynching in Florida in October 1934 of Claude Neal, a 23-year-old African-American accused of raping and murdering a young white woman, proved a milestone. Neal had been seized by a mob of 100 men from jail in Brewton, Alabama, and taken to the scene of the crime in Marianna, Florida (about 150 kilometres distant), where 'a crowd of several thousand persons' ('made up of men, women, children and babies in arms'), gathered to see the lynching.[44] There he was tortured, castrated, stabbed and shot, in a pre-planned spectacle of violence. This murder attracted nationwide media attention and such fierce public condemnation that 'local Southern leaders had to state openly their opposition to lynching to save face, if for no other reason'. Lynchings continued, but they became less frequent and much less likely to be committed openly: 'By the 1940s ritualized public executions were a thing of the past, and lynching practically disappeared altogether during the 1950s.'[45]

After the Second World War the climate of public opinion changed rapidly. What has been described as a 'wave of racial violence that swept across the South in 1946'[46] attracted national – and international[47] – attention and condemnation. It also outraged President Harry Truman, who in December 1946 justified the creation of the President's Committee on Civil Rights by noting that 'we have just ended a bloody conflict to vindicate and preserve human rights' and yet 'we have seen in the few months past several of the most abhorrent instances of mob vengeance in the history of our nation'.[48] In 1947 even Strom Thurmond, then governor of South Carolina (and in 1948 the 'Dixiecrat' candidate for the presidency, and later long-serving conservative senator from South Carolina), felt moved to assert that such 'mob rule is against every principle for which we have so recently sacrificed so much, and we expect to combat it with the same determination'.[49] And on 2 February 1948 Truman gave a speech before the United States Congress devoted entirely to civil rights (the first time that ever had been done), in which he urged 'a specific Federal measure [...] to deal with the crime of lynching – against which I cannot speak too strongly'.[50] Violent public behaviour that had been tolerated by so many before the Second World War (and that had been widely accepted before the First) now was roundly condemned. Of course, inter-ethnic violence did not cease, and the American civil-rights struggles of the 1960s were accompanied by reprehensible violence, but no longer was lynching accepted as public entertainment.

The transformation in American attitudes towards the spectacle of public lynching is evidence of a remarkable cultural distancing from violence in public life. However, to argue that violence as spectacle has become less accepted in the western world may seem at odds with received popular wisdom. Is our culture not saturated with violent spectacle? Perhaps people no longer clamour for public executions or gather to watch ritual lynchings, but do they not spend inordinate amounts of time watching violent spectacle on modern media ranging from film and television to video downloads and computer games? Has not the average British or American child – or, for that matter, the children in many countries in Europe and elsewhere who are exposed to violent American 'action films' and television programmes – already seen thousands of simulated deaths on television and other electronic media by the time they reach their teenage years?

The choreographed violence to which children become exposed has given rise to numerous calls to protect children from violence on television and to restrict when violent programming may be broadcast. These calls have been buttressed by alarming, if rather imprecise, statistics about the amounts of violence seen on television by children. Already in 1951, a survey in Los Angeles of television programmes for children 'revealed, among other things, that: (1) 70 per cent of all programmes televised for children during the survey week [the first week in May] were based on crime; (2) 800 major crimes were portrayed on children's programmes during this single week; (3) the average child in the television home saw death inflicted by violence more than forty times during the survey week'.[51] In the late 1980s, it was claimed that the average American child had observed '18,000 killings before graduating high school'.[52] In 2001 it was asserted that, 'by the time the average American child graduates from elementary school, he or she will have seen about 8,000 murders and about 100,000 other assorted acts of violence (e.g. assaults, rapes) on network television'.[53] (Even more acts of violence may be added to the total if one includes what is depicted in children's cartoons, from *Bugs Bunny* to *The Simpsons*.) Introducing a discussion of 'Mass Media Effects on Violent Behaviour', the sociologist Richard Felson, a specialist in the social psychology of violence, offered a series of observations with which many people would probably agree:

Watching violence is a popular form of entertainment. A crowd of onlookers enjoys a street fight just as the Romans enjoyed the gladiators. Wrestling is a popular spectator sport not only in the United States, but in many countries in the Middle East. People enjoy combat between animals, e.g., cock fights in Indonesia, bull fights in Spain, and dog fights in rural areas of this country [i.e. the United States]. Violence is frequently depicted in folklore, fairy tales, and other literature. Local news shows provide extensive coverage of violent crimes in order to increase their ratings.[54]

Yet is it really true that 'a crowd of onlookers' today 'enjoys a street fight just as the Romans enjoyed the gladiators', when the latter performed in grandiose spectacles of violence that often resulted – and were expected to result – in death? Contemporary commercial entertainment – for example, film – that is saturated with staged violence, has a very different quality from that of spectacle where violence is real and lethal. There is a huge difference between computer-generated flames and real fire, between a staged death and a real killing. People in recent decades may have viewed increasing quantities of simulated death and fake blood, but this does not seem to have been paralleled by enthusiasm for participating in ritual murder or viewing real blood. It is one thing to watch a scripted and staged spectacle of violence, in which the spectators can be confident that no one will come to serious harm; however, as reactions to the televised pummelling of Benny Paret suggest, it is quite another to watch someone being beaten to death.

In recent years it is not just real violence against the person that has gone out of fashion, but violence against animals as well. Cockfights and dogfights have been outlawed, and in late twentieth-century America even a pigeon shoot could provoke mass protest: for protesters against the United States' largest pigeon shoot, in Hegins, Pennsylvania, the shooters represented 'predatory, phallocentric rapists who promoted violence for its own sake' and as a result of the pigeon shoot, according to a placard carried by a protester in 1991, 'children learn to kill'.[55] Such disquiet has not been limited to urban middle-class Americans. Elsewhere concerns about animal welfare and distaste for the public killing of animals have also gained strength. Among the most striking examples are changing attitudes towards bullfighting in Spain, where in July 2010, the legislature of Catalonia voted to ban bullfighting from the beginning of 2012, making Catalonia the first region in Spain to ban this violent spectacle.[56] (Bullfighting had been banned on the Canary

Islands in 1991.) According to the International Movement against Bullfights, these spectacles are 'barbaric shows, and relics of the Dark Ages'; 'bloody "spectacles" such as this [...] should be prohibited in any civilized society'; 'the savagery of this "cultural demonstration" [*manifestación cultural*] is only comparable to gladiator fights'.[57] In Catalonia, at least, the popular appeal of bullfighting is on the wane; the spectacle of a bull being killed in front of thousands of spectators is losing its appeal.

To return to the Griffith–Paret fight with which this chapter began: the apparent paradox of the reactions to that fight, to that spectacle of violence, lay in the fact that the millions of people who watched Benny Paret being beaten to death on live television and were shocked by what they had seen had probably also viewed thousands of simulated killings and woundings in film and on television. Yet they knew the difference between acting and killing, between make-believe violence and violence in real life. Real violence is genuinely shocking; it is not entertainment. Lynda Johnson Robb, the elder daughter of President Lyndon Johnson, expressed sentiments shared by millions of people who, after the assassination of John F. Kennedy, watched the fatal shooting of Lee Harvey Oswald on live television: 'You couldn't believe it. This was not pretend.'[58] It might be argued that the huge amounts of violence staged on film and television have taken the place of actual violent spectacle where real people suffer real injury and die a real death. There can be little doubt that during the second half of the twentieth century the nature and extent of acceptable on-screen violence were redefined, as restrictive codes governing permissible sex and violence were loosened. In the United States after the revision in 1966 of the 'conduct injunctions' of the film industry's Production Code Administration (established in 1934), violence on film became more intense, extreme and graphic – as evidenced in mainstream Hollywood offerings such as *Bonnie and Clyde* (1967), *A Clockwork*

Orange (1971), *Dirty Harry* (1971), *The Godfather* (1971), *Carrie* (1976), *Alien* (1979) and *Rambo* (1982). Film censorship was replaced by film classification – in the UK the British Board of Film Censors (established in 1912) became the British Board of Film Classification in 1985 – and film-goers around the world flocked to watch the violent adventures of Sylvester Stallone, Chuck Norris, Jean-Claude Van Damme and Arnold Schwarzenegger.[59] Yet however much blood and gore in films may have aroused public concern (a reflection of continuing sensitivity about violence), and however disturbing might be the image of Arnold Schwarzenegger punching through the stomach of a punk in an opening scene of the first film of the Terminator franchise – we knew it was fake.

Real killing as public spectacle is something quite different. In early 2001 the journalist Jason Burke reported what he had witnessed in Kabul, when Afghanistan was under Taliban rule:

> The first execution I saw was in August 1998. All the executions in Kabul take place in the football stadium, and I sat high in the concrete terraces, buying endless small glasses of green tea from a hawker as I waited for the amputations – which precede most Taliban executions – to start. A crowd of around 5,000 had filed quietly through the tunnels and onto the stands. Lessons from the Koran were being read aloud over the public address system and people sat and talked and bought nuts and sweet biscuits and cold kebabs. There were no women present but many boys.
>
> Just after three o'clock two men were led into the centre circle of the pitch by a group of Taliban soldiers and made to lie on their stomachs. Their arms were tied behind their backs. For a few minutes, a group of white-coated surgeons huddled around them. The stadium was quiet but for a low murmur of conversation and the cries of the hawkers. Once a hand and a foot had been cut from each of the men tied up on

the grass, the white coats retired and the amputees were led away. Later, in the street outside, I saw a Taliban soldier holding the severed hands above his head to keep them away from some children who were jumping up to try and touch them.

Soon another man was brought out from the cab of a pick-up truck that had been driven onto the centre circle. He was made to squat in front of one of the goals. He had no blindfold or hood and I could see lank, dark hair and thin features. The soldiers had tied his hands behind his back though he made no attempt to escape. His movements were awkward and sudden. As I watched him fidget, a mullah at the side of the pitch took a microphone and, through the static, announced that the condemned man was a convicted murderer who was to be punished, according to the principle of an eye for an eye, by the brother of his victim. There was a short pause and some discussion among the soldiers.

Then a man took a kalashnikov from one of the Taliban, and aiming it awkwardly, pulled the trigger. Six or eight rounds rattled out in a sharp, loud burst and the muzzle of the weapon jerked upwards and to the right. The condemned man, still squatting, shuddered and spun round as the bullets hit him, seemed to hold himself upright for a moment and then toppled over onto his side. I saw him turning his head, craning his neck as if looking for something he had left behind. The crowd were on their feet shouting, then there was another short burst of fire and the body shook again. There were long shouts of 'Allahu Akbar'. The small pool of blood was mopped up with rags and, fifteen minutes later, two football teams filed out and started warming up.[60]

To our sensibilities such practices are deeply shocking. They are regarded as evidence of barbarism, and served to justify the American-led military intervention that resulted in the initial overthrow of the Taliban regime in Afghanistan in late 2001, after the terror attacks in the United States. However, it should be remembered that, not all that long ago, not completely dissimilar practices were common in Europe. As Pieter Spierenburg has noted, when tabulating the frequency of public executions in Amsterdam in the late seventeenth and eighteenth centuries, 'any resident of Amsterdam could have witnessed many executions during his lifetime'.[61] Physical punishments that in western countries today would not be sanctioned behind prison walls, let alone applied in public, were once meted out routinely in public. Public humiliation through the application of violent sanctions was an integral, accepted part of punishment. Malefactors had to be seen to be punished, physically, on their bodies.[62] But sensibilities have changed. Now, as Pieter Spierenburg notes, in the West 'most people have merely a vague sense of public physical punishment as a thing of the past'.[63] And they are shocked when it occurs in the contemporary world.

II

Religion

In recent years there has been an upsurge of interest in the relationship between religion and violence. This interest has been spurred by the spread of Islamic terrorism, and its incursion into the western world, over the past couple of decades. More than that, the apparent growth of religious fundamentalism among adherents of a number of faiths has called into question once-confident assumptions about a (western) world in which Enlightenment values of individualism and rationality had triumphed. The belief in our progress towards an increasingly non-violent, secular world no longer appears so robust. The 'return of religions' in recent decades has cast doubt on the idea of a forward march of secularization – on the thesis, popular during the 1950s and 1960s, that the modernization of society would inevitably lead to the decline of religion. Instead, Peter Berger has asserted that 'it is precisely this key idea that has turned out to be wrong'; more recent discussion has been of a 'desecularization of the world' and of 'post-secular society',[1] in 'a world characterized by religious resurgence rather than increasing secularization'.[2] As Madawi Al-Rasheed and Marat Shterin observe in the introduction to their recent volume on

41

'religiously motivated violence in the contemporary world': 'It was only recently that the link between faith and violence looked like a thing from the past.'[3] It now seems very much a thing of the present.

The growing prominence of religious fundamentalism and its public association with violence, in the western as well as the non-western world, seems to have shifted our focus and altered our understanding of the place of religion in society and of the relationship between religion and violence. During the twentieth century, traditional mainstream religious faiths and organizations in the western world made strenuous efforts to associate themselves with peace and non-violence, and to condemn violence as unethical and contrary to reason and justice. The religiously inspired violence of earlier times appeared far removed from contemporary mainstream understandings of religious faith and theology. Yet at the same time, during the twentieth century there occurred some of the most terrible instances of violence ever committed against people defined by their religious faith and identity. Recent upsurges of religiously inspired violence, frequently but by no means exclusively associated with Islamic fundamentalism and, more generally, in countries with largely Muslim populations,[4] pose a challenge to the idea that religion necessarily is about peace and that religious authorities are necessarily committed to non-violence; and in recent years religiously inspired violence – for example, in South Asia, in Africa, in the Middle East, and in the terrorist attacks that have spilled over into the western world – has aroused great concern.

One response to this uncomfortable juxtaposition has been to argue that true religion is the religion of non-violence. The position was put clearly and succinctly by Archbishop of Canterbury Robert Runcie when he stated in his widely noted sermon in St Paul's Cathedral on 26 July 1982, in the immediate aftermath of the Falklands War, that 'it is impossible to be a

Christian and not to long for peace'.[5] Even more explicit was Cahal Daly, who became the Roman Catholic Archbishop of Armagh and Primate of All Ireland in 1990, when he asserted in 1972 that 'non-violence is not the coward's way. Its model is Christ.'[6] It was Daly who is credited with drafting one of the most dramatic pronouncements of Pope John Paul II, coming less than a year after the beginning of his pontificate: on 29 September 1979 (only a month after the killing by the IRA of eighteen British soldiers at Warrenpoint and the assassination of Lord Mountbatten), Pope John Paul II declared to a crowd of roughly 300,000 people at Drogheda, about halfway between Dublin and the border with Northern Ireland:

> I proclaim, with the conviction of my faith in Christ and with an awareness of my mission, that violence is evil, that violence is unacceptable as a solution to problems, that violence is unworthy of man. Violence is a lie, for it goes against the truth of our faith, the truth of our humanity. Violence destroys what it claims to defend: the dignity, the life, the freedom of human beings. Violence is a crime against humanity, for it destroys the very fabric of society. I pray with you that the moral sense and Christian conviction of Irish men and women may never become obscured and blunted by the lie of violence, that nobody may ever call murder by any other name than murder, that the spiral of violence may never be given the distinction of unavoidable logic or necessary retaliation. Let us remember that the word remains for ever: 'All who take the sword will perish by the sword'.[7]

If true religious faith is non-violent, violence cannot legitimately be justified in the name of religion. Lord (Jonathan) Sacks, then Britain's Chief Rabbi (officially the Chief Rabbi of the United Hebrew Congregations of the Commonwealth), addressed the matter in a House of Lords debate in December 2011 about the persecution of Christians in the Middle East committed in the name of Islam and intensified in the wake of the 'Arab Spring': 'The tragedy of religion is that it can lead people to wage war in the name of the God of peace, to hate in the name of the God of love, to practise cruelty in the name of the God of compassion and to kill in the name of the God of life. None of these things brings honour to faith; they are a desecration of the name of God.'[8] Speaking at Assisi on 27 October 2011, Pope Benedict XVI made a similar point:

> The post-Enlightenment critique of religion has repeatedly maintained that religion is a cause of violence and in this way it has fuelled hostility towards religions. The fact that, in the case we are considering here [i.e. terrorism], religion really does motivate violence should be profoundly disturbing to us as religious persons. In a way that is more subtle but no less cruel, we also see religion as the cause of violence when force is used by the defenders of one religion against others. The religious delegates who were assembled in Assisi in 1986 wanted to say, and we now repeat it emphatically and firmly: this is not the true nature of religion. It is the antithesis of religion and contributes to its destruction.[9]

He ended his speech with the declaration that 'the Catholic Church will not let up in her fight against violence, in her commitment for peace in the world. We are animated by the common desire to be "pilgrims of truth, pilgrims of peace".' True religion does not motivate, promote or affirm violence – 'the antithesis of religion' – but fights against it. Again, true religious faith is one that rejects violence; the approval and promotion of violence in the name of faith is a 'desecration of the name of God'.

Where does this leave Islam? How have western religious observers assessed the relationship of the Muslim faith to violence in the wake of the upsurge in terrorism often committed in the name of Islam in recent years? Here too we see the tendency to regard proper religious faith as essentially non-violent. In the United States shortly after the attacks of September 2001 the Catholic journalist Peter Steinfels, who wrote a bi-weekly column entitled 'Beliefs' in *The New York Times* from 1990 until 2010, observed: 'Authentic Islam, the world has been told repeatedly in recent days, condemns terrorism, rejects violence against innocent civilians and advocates peace. The message has come from many of the highest Muslim religious authorities, from American Muslim organizations, from the Pope, from the president and from many others.'[10] In Germany, Hans-Jochen Jaschke, the Auxiliary (Catholic) Bishop of Hamburg (and someone who has been outspoken in his support for Israel), wrote in the newspaper *Hamburger Abendblatt* of the invoking of the name of God by perpetrators of the 2001 terrorist attacks in the United States: 'They thereby profane the name of God. They misuse it for their perverse conviction. [...] We must not permit criminals to justify their actions in the name of God, call for Holy War and promise the deluded a reward from God. For God's sake, no!'[11] In the West at least, it is assumed that God is as sensitive about violence as we are.

Of course, not all people of faith, even in the West, have been unequivocal in condemning violence. Evangelical Protestant Churches in the United States, for example, have set aside the idea of Jesus as a pacifist and Christian traditions of non-violence with regard to wars, offering support for American military campaigns in the interests of preserving freedom and combating evil.[12] At the same time militant religious opponents of abortion in the United States have explicitly defended the use of violence in their campaign, which has included attacks on abortion clinics and the murder of abortion clinic staff. Thus the 'Army of God', which has been active in the fight against abortion since the early 1980s, has affirmed 'the justice of taking all godly action necessary to defend innocent human life including

45

the use of force' and asserted that 'whatever force is legitimate to defend the life of a born child is legitimate to defend the life of an unborn child'.[13] Nevertheless, evangelical churches too have reflected the general sensitivity towards violence at least in the domestic sphere, condemning violence in interpersonal relations and everyday life. According to the Saddleback Church, a major evangelical congregation in California that 'wants to help prevent domestic violence and offer support to those who need help [...] There is no excuse for abuse.'[14]

Arguments surrounding religion-based attitudes towards violence, and the embrace of violence in the service of what its perpetrators regard as a righteous cause, have not been limited to evangelical Christians. In Israel, Jewish messianic politics, which grew in strength as Jewish settlements were established in the territories conquered during the Six-Day War, injected an element of religiously inspired violence into Israeli public life that had been absent before 1967. This culminated in the murder by Baruch Goldstein of twenty-nine Muslim worshippers in Hebron in February 1994 and the assassination of Yitzhak Rabin by Yigal Amir in November of the following year – outrages motivated by opposition to the signing of the Oslo Accords in 1993 as well as by religious conviction.[15] It might be tempting to dismiss these murders as something that emerged solely from the peculiar conditions within post-1967 Israel. However, this violent messianic politics originated in part in the New York Jewish community during the late 1960s, where Rabbi Meir Kahane founded the Jewish Defense League and affirmed the role of 'violence if necessary to defend the Jewish community'.[16] However, such expressions were no more accepted by the American Jewish mainstream than the campaigns of the 'Army of God' have been by most American Protestants, and in 1969 members of the Jewish Defense League were described by the president of the Union of American Hebrew Congregations, Rabbi Maurice Eisendrath, as being 'no different from whites carrying robes and hoods, standing in front of burning crosses'.[17]

To highlight such condemnations of violence by mainstream religious leaders is not to suggest that their predecessors had approved of or condoned violence before the mid-twentieth century, but rather that violence *per se* had not necessarily attracted the unequivocal, high-profile response that it has in recent decades. Contrast the uncompromising position taken by Pope John Paul II with regard to sectarian violence in Ireland with the willingness of the Vatican to reach agreements with the Italian Fascist and German National Socialist governments in 1929 and 1933 respectively. In Italy, the signing of the Lateran Accords in February 1929 between the Holy See and the Italian government led by Benito Mussolini (and approved by the Italian parliament in June of that year) was aimed at overcoming outstanding issues and mutual hostility that had arisen after the Kingdom of Italy invaded the Papal States in 1860 and occupied Rome in 1870 (and that had kept successive popes confined to the Vatican in voluntary exile since 1870). It gave Mussolini what has been described as 'the most resounding political triumph of his career'.[18] The violent nature of Fascism was not addressed directly, but it clearly was in evidence. In 1928 the Vatican newspaper *L'Osservatore Romano* had reported incidents of Fascist violence aimed at the *Federazione Universitaria Cattolica Italiana* at a number of Italian universities.[19] And when (speaking in the Italian Senate) Mussolini addressed the vexed question of the role of the Church in education, he asserted that it was the state's job to educate the country's youth as it saw fit: 'We are intransigent. If the modern world were not that world of wild wolves we all know, [...] we could do without educating youthful generations in our own way. I refer, since I do not like hypocrisy, to the warlike education of our youth.'[20] While Pope Pius XI reacted stubbornly to Mussolini's assertion of the state's pre-eminence with regard to education, and while

47

he condemned the Fascist theory of the totalitarian state and its cult of violence, these concerns did not prevent the Vatican from signing an accord with a government headed by an avowed atheist and an advocate of violence – a man whom the Pope had described as 'the man of Providence'.[21] After all, according to the Pope, Fascism stood for 'order, authority and discipline, none of them contrary to Catholic ways of thinking'.[22]

Parallel observations may be made of the *Reichskonkordat* that the Vatican signed with the German government in July 1933, less than six months after Adolf Hitler had become Reich Chancellor and by which time he had consolidated his dictatorship. The violence of the National Socialist movement was no more a secret than that of the Italian Fascist movement had been. During the early months of 1933 a wave of Stormtrooper violence had terrorized the opposition, broken the back of socialist labour movement, targeted the country's Jewish population, and on occasion attacked supporters and leading members of the Catholic Centre Party and the Catholic youth organization.[23] Of course, the Catholic Church was concerned to protect itself as far as possible from threats to its interests posed by the new dictatorship, and in the years that followed, Pope Pius XI remained critical of National Socialism – most notably with his 1937 encyclical *Mit brennender Sorge* (*With Burning Concern*), which made his alarm at developments in Germany very clear. Yet although (as Pius XI noted in his 1937 encyclical) the Vatican had had 'many and grave misgivings' when it agreed to the 1933 Concordat,[24] it had agreed. The overriding concern was to secure the position of the Catholic Church in National Socialist Germany, not to take an unequivocal position against violence.

While the agreements made by the Catholic Church with the inter-war Italian and German governments became an embarrassment after the Second World War, less than unequivocal stands against violence continued to be taken during the second half of the twentieth century. The Catholic Church faced a particular challenge when confronted by the violence of the military dictatorships established in South America during the 1960s and 1970s. In Chile, while Cardinal Raúl Silva Henríquez, the Archbishop of Santiago, voiced outspoken opposition to Augusto Pinochet and the human-rights violations of the military regime, more conservative bishops greeted the coup of 11 September 1973 for having rescued the country from Marxism; and when Silva retired in 1983 the Vatican chose one of the bishops who had spoken in favour of the 1973 coup, Juan Francisco Fresno, to succeed him.[25] Equivocal Catholic attitudes concerning violence also arose on the other side of the political divide in Latin America, from supporters of the 'liberation theology' of the 1960s and 1970s who felt that, faced with the exploitation, repression and institutionalized violence of conservative and right-wing regimes, 'counterviolence' and indeed guerrilla war were legitimate and justified in order to achieve revolutionary social transformation.[26]

Of course there were other church leaders in Latin America who rejected violence as a tool for political activism, believing – as expressed by one Columbian bishop interviewed in March 1972 – that political action necessarily led to violence and that 'violent action is never appropriate for us'.[27] However, it was particularly in Europe, in the wake of the terrible destruction of human life during the Second World War and against the background of the threat posed by nuclear weapons, that the rejection of violence was more categorical, as representatives of religious organizations sought to mobilize internationally for peace and an end to violence. It was here that heightened sensitivity towards violence was most evident among religious figures.

This can be seen clearly in the campaigns of the World Council of Churches (WCC), which was formed in Amsterdam in 1948 by representatives of 147 churches and which by 2006 included 349 churches in 170 countries with a membership numbering some 550 million people, roughly half of them in Europe. The WCC has regarded one of its main purposes as 'affirming peace' and 'promoting just peace',[28] and has called for 'ecumenical engagement by the churches in light of inter-personal, economic, environmental, military and other forms of violence in society, in families and even in the church.'[29] In 2001 the WCC launched its 'Decade to Overcome Violence', assert-ing: 'The goals of overcoming violence and building a culture of peace imply spiritual, theological and practical challenges for the churches which touch them in the centre of what it means to be a church'. Among its stated goals were 'challenging the churches to *overcome the spirit, logic and practice of violence*; to relinquish any theological justification of violence; and to affirm anew the spirituality of reconciliation and active non-violence.'[30] The duty of Christians was to work for peace and reconciliation.

The efforts of the WCC form only one part of the initiatives to combat violence in the name of religion since the Second World War. Others include the World Conference on Religion and Peace, which grew out of efforts by representatives of various religious organizations during the 1960s and which began a series of world conferences, the first of which was convened in Kyoto in October 1970. This led to the formal establishment of 'Religions for Peace', an 'action-oriented organization' that aimed to further peace through international interreligious dia-logue, working for conflict transformation and reconciliation, human rights, disarmament and peace education, and whose membership included religious leaders from various faiths ranging from the Bahá'í faith, Buddhism, Confucianism, Hin-duism and Shinto to Islam, Reform Judaism and Orthodox, Protestant and Roman Catholic Christianity.[31] As the twentieth century drew to a close, religious denominations and inter-denominational and multireligious bodies (such as the World

Council of Churches) increasingly 'prepared themselves for and assumed proactive peacemaking roles'.[32]

But are religious organizations deceiving themselves when they declare such lofty aims? Whatever their intentions or pretensions, established religious institutions, religious leaders and theologians no longer either legitimize wars or mediate their settlement. That role has fallen to the United Nations, where the Security Council determines the legitimate grounds for military intervention (e.g. the 'responsibility to protect' and, if necessary, 'to take collective action' in cases of genocide, crimes against humanity, etc.).[33] Church leaders no longer are in fact the highest authority with regard to sanctioning 'just wars'. As international diplomatic forums have assumed this role, religious leaders have become relegated to the status of principled bystanders, who admonish people and states to behave morally and peacefully while the hard decisions are taken elsewhere. This perhaps granted western religious institutions the luxury of issuing principled statements against violence and declaring their readiness to assume peacemaking roles, but it also meant that the repeated calls by religious leaders for peace during the war-scarred twentieth century were destined to be ineffective.

Such well-meaning but ineffective calls for peace surfaced throughout the previous century. During the First World War, Pope Benedict XV made passionate but unsuccessful appeals and proposals to the belligerents to bring the conflict to an end: 'The first words which We, as Supreme Pastor of souls, spoke to the nations and their rulers were of peace and love. Our counsel was affectionate and insistent, both as father and friend, but it was not listened to.'[34] Pope Pius XII (who as Eugenio Pacelli had negotiated the *Reichskonkordat* with the newly installed Hitler government in 1933, whose reluctance to speak out directly against Nazi atrocities has been the subject of controversy for decades, and who was motivated by a deep anti-communism)[35] appealed for peace during the Second World

War, to no greater effect.[36] His pontificate had been dominated by the Second World War and the Cold War, but when he died in October 1958, he was heralded as a 'crusader for peace' and as 'the Pope of Peace'.[37] After 1945, clergy were prominent in peace movements and campaigns for the control or abolition of nuclear weapons. In 1959 and 1960, when the British anti-nuclear campaign was gathering unprecedented support, religious groups such as Christian Action and the Friends Peace Committee were actively involved in the public mobilization to 'Ban the Bomb'.[38] Yet the bomb was not banned. From the late 1970s, the Interchurch Peace Council (the IKV, a grouping of nine churches founded in 1966, which aimed to examine issues of war and peace, inform the wider public and urge appropriate action) played a prominent role in revivifying the campaign for disarmament in the Netherlands.[39] During the early 1980s, when the movement for nuclear disarmament again reached a peak of activity across Europe, it was the former Roman Catholic priest, Bruce Kent, who played a leading role in the Campaign for Nuclear Disarmament in the UK, serving as the organization's chair from 1977 to 1979 and as its General Secretary from 1980 to 1985. Yet nuclear disarmament was not achieved. In April 1983, the German Catholic Bishop Conference proclaimed, in a statement characteristic of its time, that 'today war is less than ever a means to achieve political goals. It must never be! [...] Today this goal, to prevent every war, is no longer a matter of debate for us.'[40] Yet they could not prevent any war. What they did do, however, was reflect the heightened sensitivity with regard to violence that increasingly was characteristic of western public and political culture.

The religious message of peace and non-violence proved perhaps more effective in socialist eastern Europe than in the capitalist democratic West. Prior to the collapse of the Communist regimes, clergy in eastern Europe were prominent in peace and disarmament campaigns during the 1970s and the

1980s. In the German Democratic Republic, for example, the Protestant Church cautiously supported the nascent peace movement; church figures supported peace seminars, 'peace weeks', peace prayers in churches and the idea of 'social peace service', and they helped to launch what became the 'Swords into Ploughshares' campaign (although church leaders proved unwilling to back these campaigns fully for fear of endangering their accommodation with the state).[41] During the last decade of state socialism in eastern Europe, concern about conscription and nuclear arms spilled over into overt pacifism and political opposition, even when that meant challenging both church and state hierarchies. Lazlo Kovacs, a young Catholic priest at the time, expressed this in strident terms when he addressed some 700 young Hungarians in the village of Hajós in the summer of 1981:

> If we are Christians, we must not take the oath that would compel us to kill. And if we refuse to kill, we must also refuse military training for licensed murder ... We must suffer blows, jail if need be – and we must not hit back. We must preach to the violent, the way Jesus did ... For those who fail to bring up their children in this spirit, religion is – as Marx said – opium only, never mind how many times they take communion.[42]

While his uncompromising opposition to military service was rewarded with immediate suspension from the priesthood, Kovacs voiced sentiments that had considerable support among church congregations. In eastern Europe, as in the West, pacifists looked to the churches for support, and religious faith and religious groups helped to undermine the militarized socialist states of eastern Europe, most notably in Poland and the German Democratic Republic.

Religious organizations raised their voices against violence in other spheres as well. In the United States the National Council of Churches (NCC, which had been established in 1950 and which stood 'at the centre of the churches' efforts to support the Civil Rights Act of 1964')[43] proclaimed in its policy statement of November 1993:

> We live in a climate of violence. Violence is everywhere: in city and suburb, in mean streets and quiet lanes, in private conversations and public media. Our society knows violence through abuse and rape, rising crime rates and diminished trust. We acknowledge that the climate of the psychological violence of words, as well as physical violence, breeds fear and rapidly escalating concerns for personal security. This in turn leads to more violence and contributes to society's tightening cycle of violence.[44]

Media violence was condemned not just because it was destructive of society, but (the NCC concluded) 'because it is in contradiction to our basic beliefs'.

Another area in which churches became involved was in campaigns to prevent sexual violence and to support its victims. In the late 1980s, in an account of the work of the Center for the Prevention of Sexual and Domestic Violence (founded in Seattle in 1977 and now named the Faith Trust Institute), Marie Fortune, an ordained minister in the United Church of Christ, and Frances Wood wrote:

> Common as this violence was, it was seldom addressed by religious institutions or leadership. That was in 1977. Ten years later, things are different. Sexual and domestic violence are no longer secrets in society, the church, or the synagogue, thanks to the women's movement and the efforts of many, including the Center for the Prevention of Sexual and Domestic Violence.[45]

Increasingly, violence in all areas of human interaction came to be regarded as anathema, and church organizations regarded it as their religious duty to be at the forefront of campaigns against it.

In the western world at least, the dream was of a world without violence – a modern enlightened world in which 'civilized life also should be a civil life, in which warlike characteristics and needs are not simply forbidden by religion and morality but can be stilled and moderated and diverted into sporting or economic competition'.[46] In the wake of the worst outbreak of organized violence that the modern world had seen, after the profound shock of Nazi genocide and of the atomic bombing of Hiroshima and Nagasaki,[47] and under the cloud of possible nuclear annihilation, religious leaders strove urgently and obsessively for a world without violence. The advent of nuclear weapons led in Britain to changes in the attitudes of 'a wide array of British churchmen, including many who had been stalwart proponents of the war effort hitherto'.[48] Archibald Walter Harrison, president of the Methodist Conference, expressed a widely held view when he declared in September 1945: 'We believe that ultimately world peace is the fruit of Christian life and work; therefore there rests upon the Church at this moment a tremendous responsibility to lead, and not to follow, public opinion and political action.'[49] This perhaps was rather woolly, and perhaps nothing tangible came of it (Harrison himself died the following January), but it was typical of the way many Christian leaders understood their mission. Religion was equated with peace and non-violence. God was on the side of the meek.

Such sentiments were not just pious hopes expressed by clergy. It should be remembered that the end of the Second World War in Europe was accompanied by something of a mainstream religious revival, not least in Germany. After the catastrophe of National Socialism, total defeat in war and the huge loss of life, homes, communities and much of their built environment, people flocked to the churches. The churches in turn could regard themselves, perhaps paradoxically, as the 'victor among the ruins', a memorable phrase used to describe the Catholic Church, 'with its proud processions through cities destroyed by war', in western Germany.[50] Both Protestant and Catholic churches emerged from the wreckage left by National Socialism and war strengthened in their belief in the correctness of their positions and in their importance, and convinced that it was both necessary and possible to achieve a 're-Christianization' of society.[51] The horrors that Germans had just experienced (and inflicted on others) demonstrated what happened when religious teachings were ignored; as the German Catholic bishops asserted on 23 August 1945, in their first joint pastoral letter after the war; 'an era of pure secularism has collapsed and left us with an enormous expanse of ruins'.[52] The ruins were moral as well as physical, and 're-Christianization' and rolling back the tide of secularism meant the condemnation of the violence of the National Socialist regime and the conflict it had unleashed. Religious leaders asserted, as articulated in the Declaration of the Council of the Protestant Church in Germany – the 'Stuttgart Declaration of Guilt' – of 19 October 1945, that they had 'fought in the name of Jesus Christ through long years against the spirit that found its expression in the National Socialist rule of violence'.[53] The shock of violence in 1945 appeared to provide mainstream churches an opportunity to build a new, Christian Germany and Europe, and to attract a greater following among people who had been confronted with the horrors of the violence that resulted when they failed to heed religious teachings.

Germany was not the only country where the Second World War and fears of atomic catastrophe sparked an upsurge in religious activity. In the United States during the immediate post-war years there were substantial increases in church

membership, a veritable church building boom, and the recruit-
ment of large numbers of new clergy.[54] While this post-war
religious revival in the US contained a strong element of Cold
War anti-communism – the idea of a religious West confronting
a godless ideology[55] – it also unfolded in the shadow of violence, past and (potentially) future. According to the influential
theologian (subsequently president of the Union Theological
Seminary in New York) John C. Bennett, writing in 1946: 'We
live in a world that is appalled by the horrors of war and its
aftermath, with more baffling problems than our forefathers
could have imagined, and we are haunted by fears of an even
greater catastrophe.'[56] In Britain, too, the attraction of the
churches and of religious faith was enhanced in the wake of the
war, as the post-war years saw what Callum Brown has
described as 'the greatest church growth that Britain had experienced since the mid-nineteenth century'.[57] The shock of the
violence of the Second World War left millions of people receptive to a religious message, and after the horrors of the early
1940s peace and non-violence appeared an essential element of
religious conviction.

While mainstream religious expression in the West reflected
heightened concern to promote peace and non-violence in the
wake of the catastrophes of the 1940s, in recent years the spectre of religiously inspired violence has appeared increasingly
threatening. Once thought of as a phenomenon whose time
had passed, in an increasingly secular and rational (and therefore non-violent) western world, religious violence has become
a hot topic. Modernization theory once posited a world in
which non-violent conflict resolution comprised a central element of modernity.[58] Violence inspired by fundamentalist
religious faith would have no place in such a world. But that is
not how things turned out, and the consequence has been a
new obsession with religious violence. In the introduction to
his recent exploration of violence and Judaism, Robert Eisen

(whose academic specialism had been Medieval Jewish philosophy and whose interest in the contemporary relationship
between religion and violence stemmed from his shock at and
reaction to the terrorist attacks of September 2001 in the United
States) has written:

> Few topics have received as much attention in recent years as
> religious violence. It has been examined from innumerable
> angles in every outlet of the popular and academic media.
> Books, newspaper editorials, television documentaries, and
> movies have steadily bombarded us with analyses of every
> aspect of this phenomenon. And no wonder. In the wake of
> 9/11, the western world awoke to a new reality, one in which
> religious violence had taken centre stage. The problem had
> been simmering under the surface for years, even decades, in
> regions and cultures throughout the world, but only after this
> momentous event did westerners begin to realize that it
> involved them as well and that it had the capability of
> destroying everything they held dear. As a result, the problem
> of religious violence has become one of the most – if not *the*
> most – pressing issue of our time.[59]

This lent increased credence to the idea that religion – in particular, monotheistic religion – is inherently violent.[60] Following
Arthur Schopenhauer's assertion that 'it is only to monotheism
that intolerance is essential',[61] many observers have regarded
religious intolerance as a collorary of monotheism. Religious
faith appears antithetical to reason, the enemy of violence; irrational, unverifiable belief is its friend. Such a view received
apparent confirmation in the 2001 terror attacks in New York
and Washington, in the wake of which there has been a flood of
studies by historians, political scientists and religious-studies
scholars that focus on 'the peculiarly violence-prone nature of
religion'.[62]

Yet the conviction that religion can and should be equated with non-violence remains strong. The assumption that (monotheistic) religious faith by its nature necessarily encourages violence has been challenged, and dismissed as a 'myth [that] helps to construct and marginalize a religious Other, prone to fanaticism, to contrast with the rational, peace-making, secular subject'.[63] Religious violence and secular violence, it is asserted, cannot be separated so easily from one another. Some argue that, although religion and violence may be linked, the precise connection nevertheless remains tenuous and too complicated to allow straightforward conclusions to be drawn.[64] And for some, violence inspired by religious faith makes it all the more important to reinforce the message that the essence of religion is peace, not war and violence.

To many in the West, religiously inspired violence has appeared to come from beyond the western world and to be a throwback to the past. Europe witnessed more than its fair share of religious violence over the centuries. During the French Wars of Religion of the late sixteenth century, terrible violence was inflicted by Catholics against Protestants and vice versa. The years between 1562 and 1572 have been described as 'the golden age of the religious riot throughout France',[65] famously culminating in the St Bartholomew Massacre in Paris in August 1572, which led to three days of slaughter resulting in some 2,000 dead and the elimination of much of the Protestant nobility that had provided the leadership of Huguenot armies.[66] Further east, the Khmelnitsky massacres of 1648–1658 left tens of thousands of Jews (some estimates are in excess of 100,000) dead in southern Ukraine – a bloodbath that continued to be a reference point for violence against Jews into the twentieth century, when far worse occurred. However, we now tend to think of deadly clashes between different faith groups as something that occurs away from the western world, along religious fault lines between Islam and Christianity (e.g. in the Central African

Republic and Nigeria), between Sunni and Shia Muslims (e.g. in Iraq, Syria and Lebanon), or between Islam and Hinduism (e.g. India). Yet, violence between adherents of different religions involves more than religious faith and religious difference: it has many overlapping causes beyond simply religious intolerance and hatred; and it may be understood better as communal violence than as religious violence *per se*.[67] This has been no less the case in outbursts of violence between people of different religious faiths in South Asia[68] than, for example, in the recent 'Troubles' in Northern Ireland.

How can we explain the contrast between the recent identification of religion with non- or anti-violence discussed above and the sorts of religious violence that once so scarred the European continent – between cultures in which religion is assumed to embody a message of non-violence and peace and cultures in which 'warriors of God' (i.e. Catholics during the French Wars of Religion) left their victims' bodies mutilated, eyes torn out, noses cut off, disembowelled, dismembered, genitalia displayed and naked corpses dragged through the streets?[69] One place to look for an answer is in the distinction between societies and cultures that have not tolerated a plurality of belief and societies and cultures where the coexistence of different faiths has been accepted as legitimate. Gradually, with the separation of church and state over the past two centuries, plurality of religious belief increasingly became accepted, at least in much of the western world. Important milestones along this road were the First Amendment of the United States Constitution adopted in 1791 (which prohibited Congress from enacting any law 'respecting an establishment of religion, or prohibiting the free exercise thereof'), the Catholic Emancipation Act of 1829 in the United Kingdom (which permitted Catholics to vote and to sit in the UK Parliament), and the emancipation of European Jews (beginning with the reforms of Emperor Joseph II in Austria in the late eighteenth century and with the French

Revolution). In Europe one country after another saw the separation of church and state: Ireland in 1869, France in 1905 (initially in 1791, but church and state were reunited in 1801), Geneva in 1907, Portugal in 1911, Germany in 1919, Wales in 1920, Spain in 1931.[70] Following the separation of church and state and the establishment of constitutional guarantees of religious freedom, and with the recognition of religious faiths whose adherents had previously been discriminated against, there emerged in western Europe and North America what might be regarded as a marketplace for religions. (In eastern Europe, by contrast, religious nationalism remained more powerful.) In theory at least, religion became a matter of choice, which removed the basis for state campaigns of religious violence. And again, in theory at least, as various competing religious denominations could be tolerated, religious faith no longer was a legitimate ground for killing or something to be forced upon someone at the threat of violence.[71]

In practice, however, there remained one particularly prominent target of religious violence in nineteenth- and twentieth-century Europe: Jews, primarily but not exclusively in eastern Europe. Waves of pogroms took place in the western provinces of the Russian Empire (the main centres of Jewish settlement at the time) in 1881 and again in 1903 and 1905; explosions of antisemitic violence occurred in Poland and Lithuania during the First World War; and violence against Jews in Ukraine between 1918 and 1920 during the civil wars that followed the Bolshevik Revolution claimed tens of thousands of lives.[72] German rule in Europe during the Second World War created a favourable environment for extreme anti-Jewish violence – not just for the systematic genocide that brought death to millions, but also for local violence by non-Jews against Jewish communities, a phenomenon described graphically by Jan Gross in his account of events in Jedwabne on 10 July 1941, when residents of that small town in north-eastern Poland murdered hundreds of their Jewish neighbours while the recently arrived German occupiers stood by.[73]

This is not the place to explore in any detail the histories of either the pogroms of the late nineteenth and early twentieth centuries or the mass murder of Jews in German-occupied Europe during the Second World War. However, the history of the persecution and murder of Jews in Europe over the past century and a half also reflects the changing relationship between religion and violence. While the pogroms in the Russian Empire during its last decades, and to a more limited extent those elsewhere in Europe, were often popular outbursts of violence triggered by what might be described as traditional allegations of blood sacrifice (albeit often aided and abetted by the Tsarist police),[74] the campaigns of mass murder during the Second World War were fuelled primarily by racist ideology, committed by and through the state, and also drew on economic and opportunist motivations rather than religious zealotry *per se*. The targets of the Shoah may have been singled out by their religion (conceived of in racial rather than strictly religious terms), but they were essentially victims of ideological, political and ethnic violence. Religious violence in the strict sense of the term – violence motivated by religious faith – had been superceded by ethnic and racial violence directed against people identified with a particular religious faith.

Nevertheless, religiously motivated violence did not disappear completely in Europe during the twentieth century. There still were echoes from an earlier age. Despite the efforts of the German National Socialist regime, not all of Europe's Jews were killed during the Second World War, and violence against Jews did not come to an end with the German surrender in 1945. In Poland there was a recurrence of pogroms in the immediate aftermath of the war, beginning with violent outbursts in Rzeszów in June 1945 and in Kraków in August of the same year, and culminating in the terrible events during the following summer in Kielce, in south-central Poland, on 4 July 1946.[75] The 1946 pogrom in Kielce, which had been the site of a pogrom in November 1918 as well,[76] took a familiar course: it began with accusations that Jews had kidnapped a young Polish boy and with rumours of the ritual murder of children, was instigated in large measure by the police, and ended with mob violence that claimed the lives of forty-two Jews housed in the town after having survived the German onslaught during the Second World War. The Kielce pogrom, which provoked ambivalent responses within Poland at the time,[77] turned out to be the last major incident of its kind in Europe. This is not to suggest that antisemitic prejudice, and with it anti-Jewish violence, disappeared in Europe. However, it appears with hindsight that the events in Kielce marked something of a turning point, in the sense that they marked an end of rather than a return to earlier forms of religious violence.

On a continent where religious violence once was the extension or inversion of religious ritual and regarded as a supposedly necessary struggle against heresy and impurity,[78] and where during the first half of the twentieth century terrible violence was aimed against Jews, churches are now expected to be forces against violence. Established Christian churches have come to see their role as advocates of peace and tolerance, of a gospel of non-violence, as religious toleration and reconciliation have become the ideal. As Manfred Kock, then chair of the Council of the German Protestant Church organization EKD (*Evangelische Kirche in Deutschland*) asserted in 1999: 'Our churches must be places in which Christians give witness with their utterances and deeds, with their prayers and their labours, to how powerful is non-violence. Our communities must become places where non-violence is practised and learned.'[79]

This understanding of the role of mainstream religion in the West has come about in part as a reaction to the explosions of violence that occurred in Europe during the first half of the twentieth century: two world wars, brutal civil wars and campaigns of forced removal and genocide. More generally it reflects the development of pluralist and relatively secularized societies. For centuries, religious conflict framed political and cultural life in Europe. However, toleration of religious difference has increasingly become the ideal, and mainstream religious institutions reflect this.[80] This has been accompanied by an evolution of religious institutions into organizations committed to campaigning for social justice and subjecting government policies to moral scrutiny.[81] A modern society is seen as one in which disputes are settled without violence, and modern religious institutions in pluralist and largely secular societies have adapted to their cultural surroundings. Although the growth of religious fundamentalism may be viewed as a reaction to modernization and apparent secularization in western societies,[82] and may indicate a narrowing of the cultural distance between the West and the rest, this has not (yet) altered the place of traditional religious institutions. In pluralist societies, religious denominations have to compete in a marketplace of ideas where religious affiliation has become largely a free choice. Religious violence has no legitimate place where religious pluralism is respected. Pluralism has allowed religion to be decoupled from violence. This has not occurred everywhere in the West, as recent conflict in Ireland and Bosnia have shown at great cost to their inhabitants. However, in general, mainstream religious institutions have reflected increased sensitivity towards violence and have displayed a remarkable commitment to non-violence. After the explosions of violence during the first half of the twentieth century, and in societies that had become both remarkably prosperous and remarkably peaceful and had embraced a pluralism of religious belief, sensitivity towards and rejection of violence became the dominant response of organized religion in the western world.

III

Revolution

Much of what we associate with revolutionary violence – violence unleashed by or in the service of revolutionary political transformation – stems from the French Revolution: the Terror, the fanaticism of the Jacobins, the massacres, the executions by guillotine, the eruption of violence and the 'genocide' in the Vendée. Indeed what we associate with the very idea of 'revolution' arises from how we imagine what occurred in France in the late eighteenth century.[1] The revolutionary nature of the violence stemmed not only from its ferocity or its roots in a secular ideology pursued with seemingly religious zeal, but also from the fact that it was affirmed both by its leaders and by its supporters. This was a violent new politics that George Mosse has described as 'the politicization of the masses. [...] The age of modern mass politics had begun.'[2] The attack on established hierarchies and privilege, the popular involvement in revolutionary violence, and the ferocity of counter-revolutionary responses heralded a new epoch in the history of violence – linking the French Revolution of the late eighteenth century not only with the Russian Revolution but also with the failed German Revolution (particularly with the counter-revolutionary bloodshed that followed it) and with the fascist revolutions in Italy and Germany in the twentieth century.

If the French and Russian revolutions have provided the benchmark for modern revolution, there are grounds for postulating, as does Arno Mayer, that 'there is no revolution without violence and terror; without civil war and foreign war'.[3] This may be true for more recent upheavals beyond the European continent, for example the revolution that gave birth to the People's Republic of China in 1949; consequently, war and peasant insurrection have been seen as distinguishing characteristic ingredients of revolution. However, such generalizations do not always fit the facts, even in the 'Third World',[4] and since the middle of the twentieth century ferocious violence has not been necessarily a central characteristic of revolution in the western world. If we define revolution as the collapse or overthrow of one political order and its replacement by another, it follows that revolution does not necessarily have to be violent. The sorts of revolutionary transformations that one associates with 1789, 1848, 1871 and 1917 in Europe, now appear largely to be a thing of the past in the developed western world. Introducing his book *The Furies*, Mayer begins with Hannah Arendt's assertion that 'freedom has been better preserved in countries where no revolution ever broke out'. Looking back from a vantage point at the end of the twentieth century, he observes: 'The grand romance and the great fear of the French and Russian revolutions have given way to the celebration of essentially bloodless revolutions for human rights, private property, and market capitalism.'[5]

This is the view from Europe and North America. Since the Second World War, violent revolutionary upheaval is something that has occurred elsewhere: in China in the late 1940s, in Cuba in 1959, in Iran in 1979, in the Arab world in the 1950s and more recently in 2011. Attempts at revolutionary transformation, successful and unsuccessful, are not themselves consigned to the past in the West, but the ready acceptance of violence as part of these revolutionary upsurges does appear to be so – at least for now.

In their different ways, the two major waves of post-war revolutionary upheaval in Europe – the protests of 1968 and the largely peaceful revolutions of 1989 that toppled Communist regimes across eastern Europe – suggest this conclusion. The wave of student protest in France, West Germany, the United States and elsewhere that goes under the rubric of the events of 1968 has often been viewed as carnival,[6] despite the violent rhetoric that occasionally accompanied the unrest and despite the violence (but almost no lethal violence) of confrontations with police (in particular with the CRS in Paris, which quickly came in for public condemnation).[7] In Paris, student protesters looked to historical precedents when erecting their street barricades. Romain Goupil, at the time a teenage Trotskyist and an organizer of the *Comités d'actions lycéens* (High School Action Committees) in the French capital, recently looked back on the events of 1968 and placed them clearly within the tradition of revolutionary violence:

We were the heirs of eternal revolt and we did not understand why our parents had stopped. We wanted to have a revolution as it happened in Russia. We were the direct heirs of 1917. [...] We built barricades as if we had always built barricades. As if we were in 1830, 1848, 1871, 1968. The only thing to do was to build barricades, that was it. We saw ourselves as insurgents.[8]

The forces of 'order' responded accordingly, and CRS and police units proceeded violently when clearing the barricades in the early morning hours of 11 May 1968 – an action described (with a measure of hyperbole) by the German news magazine *Der*

Spiegel as a 'battle without quarter'.[9] Yet when compared with what had occurred on the streets of East Berlin in 1953 or in Budapest in 1956, the events of 1968 in Paris did seem more like theatre – 'the baby-boom generation's coming-of-age party', as it was once common to view it[10] – than a fundamental challenge to political and economic structures. In France, West Germany and the United States, the events of 1968 may have comprised 'the greatest protest mobilization of the post-war period';[11] some young protesters may have chanted the names of Chairman Mao and Ho Chi Minh and looked approvingly at the Chinese 'Cultural Revolution' of the late 1960s; and some demonstrators hurled cobblestones at police and police clubbed some demonstrators. However, the protests did not descend into revolutionary violence in any way comparable to what occurred in some eastern European cities during the 1950s, to say nothing of what had happened during the Russian Revolution of 1917 and the years that immediately followed it or during the French Revolution of the late eighteenth century.[12]

In his best-selling account of the French Revolution, *Citizens*, Simon Schama places revolutionary violence at 'the centre of the story. [...] In some depressing unavoidable sense, violence *was* the revolution itself.'[13] The ferocity of the revolutionary violence of both the French and Russian revolutions stemmed from a determination to purge and purify society and the body politic. Alexis de Tocqueville observed that the French 'had the air of tending to the regeneration of the whole human race'.[14] In this sense, the revolutionary violence of the modern period, beginning with the French Revolution, took up where the religious violence of the early modern period (e.g. during the French Wars of Religion) had left off. According to Caroline Ford:

> Like the violence of the sixteenth century, revolutionary violence ostensibly played a purifying role, ridding society of contagion and pollution, and it also assumed a distinctive

corporal form in terms of mutilation and torture. The enemies of the revolution – aristocrats, priests, and emigrés –
were demonized and animalized in public rhetoric, carica-
ture, and print, as the Huguenots had been. While the
language of purification and de-humanization was abundant
in revolutionary discourse, it was justified in terms of the
rights of the nation as a collective body.[15]

The rhetoric of 'enemies of the people' that had to be eliminated,
of the need to create a new society cleansed of the reactionary
and the degenerate, drove the ferocious violence of revolutions
from the French Revolution of the late eighteenth century
through the Russian, the Chinese and the Iranian revolutions of
the twentieth century. When one needs to purify the nation, to
rid society of pollutants and parasites, and to do this in the
name of the people, there can be no concessions. Revolutionary
democracy, and utopian revolutionary movements that aim to
construct pure societies – and this goes for the racist utopia of
German National Socialism as well as the socialist utopia of
Leninist and Stalinist Communism – contain the impulse to
uncompromising violence.[16]

Revolution both rested on violent upheaval and unleashed
violent behaviour, as normative constraints dissolved and violence became the default response to real and perceived threats.
The overthrow of the old order, and the actions of the revolutionaries, triggered resistance, which in turn provoked those
associated with the revolutionary regime – both its leadership
and its supporters in the provinces who often acted more or
less at their own initiative – to become more extreme in applying
violence and terror to defend the revolution as they understood
it. In many (but not all) places this fuelled an escalation of
violence, 'a common logic of a proliferation of competing dis-
courses about the revolution that leads inexorably, in a spiral
development, to massacre'.[17]

Massacre there was, most famously during the war in the Vendée during the years of the Terror, 1793 and 1794. The crushing of the popular insurrection of the largely peasant, conservative population of this maritime region in the west of France led to what has been described as 'one of the most atrocious single massacres in the whole of French history'.[18] Anger at the persecution of the churches by a self-professed atheist regime – the attacks on people going to mass, the exiling of clergy who refused to swear allegiance to the new Civil Constitution, the confiscation of church property, and the order to close the churches in March 1793 – and resistance among the rural population to military conscription led to the insurrection of March 1793. Within weeks the rebels in the Vendée had formed a Royal and Catholic Army and engaged in a sort of guerrilla war – to be cut down savagely by the armed force of the revolutionary state, which sent the 100,000-man strong Army of the West to crush the rebellion. Following the rout of the insurrectionists in the autumn of 1793, a wholesale massacre took place, after which General François Joseph Westermann, commander of the Army of the West in the battle, allegedly reported to the Committee of Public Safety:

> The Vendèe is no more [...] According to your orders, I have trampled their children beneath our horses' feet; I have massacred their women, so they will no longer give birth to brigands. I do not have a single prisoner to reproach me. I have exterminated them all. The roads are sown with corpses. At Savenay, brigands are arriving all the time claiming to surrender, and we are shooting them non-stop [...] Mercy is not a revolutionary sentiment.[19]

According to Maximilien de Robespierre: 'The revolutionary government owes its good citizens all national protection; to the enemies of the people it owes nothing but death.'[20] The rapid defeat of the Vendée insurrection was followed by a campaign of 'pacification'; the Committee of Public Safety then ordered General Louis Marie Turreau (who later served under Napoleon as French ambassador to the United States) to use his forces to 'exterminate the brigands to the last man'.[21] Turreau's appropriately named *'colonnes infernales'* systematically worked their way across the Vendée, rounding up villagers and killing them – bayoneting them, bludgeoning them, shooting them, burning them alive. Tens of thousands of civilians – including women, children and the aged and infirm – were slaughtered; crops were confiscated or burned; farms and villages destroyed. Nearly one in six of the population of the Vendée were killed and nearly a fifth of the housing stock destroyed in a campaign to eliminate the capacity of the region to provide a base from which to resist the revolution.

The quintessential expression of the violence of the French Revolution was the Terror of 1793 and 1794. Its leading protagonist was Louis Antoine de Saint-Just, who alongside his friend and political ally Robespierre was the moving spirit of the Terror, urging the execution of Louis XVI and drafting the radical constitution of 1793. Saint-Just saw the Terror as required to defend the ideals of the revolution and to cleanse the Republic of its enemies, and proclaimed that 'it is necessary to rule by fire those who cannot be ruled by justice'.[22] Those who refused to submit to revolutionary rule had thus placed themselves outside the law and therefore condemned themselves to death. The key concept was that of 'enemy of the people', introduced with the 'Law of 22 Prairial' (the *'loi de la Grande Terreur'*). 'Enemies of the people' were defined as 'those who seek to destroy public liberty, either by force or by cunning'. The net was cast very wide: it included 'those who have instigated the reestablishment of the monarchy, or have sought to disparage or dissolve the National Convention', 'carried on correspondence with the enemies of the Republic', 'sought to create scarcity in the Republic', 'supported the designs of the enemies of France', 'deceived the people or the representatives of the people, in order to lead them into undertakings contrary to the interests of liberty', 'sought to inspire discouragement', 'disseminated false news in order to divide and disturb the people', or 'sought to mislead opinion and to prevent the instruction of the people, to deprave morals and to corrupt the public conscience'. The penalty 'provided for all offences under the jurisdiction of the Revolutionary Tribunal' was death.[23] Not only was this a recipe for liquidating just about anyone that the Revolutionary Tribunal might choose to eliminate, it also envisaged popular involvement in the orgy of revolutionary violence, noting that 'every citizen has the right to seize conspirators and counter-revolutionaries' and 'is required to denounce them as soon as he knows of them'. The law had its effect, and in the weeks that followed the introduction of the *'loi de la Grande Terreur'*, the numbers of people executed daily in Paris increased more than five-fold, from an average of five per day in Germinal to twenty-six per day in Messidor.[24] Even though the direct threats to the revolutionary regime (the uprising in the Vendée, the threat of foreign invasion, the food shortages in Paris) had faded by the time the law was passed, the revolution had been overtaken by its own violent logic. The Terror did not last long before it devoured its leading protagonists: Robespierre and Saint-Just were guillotined in July 1794 (Thermidor). But it did reveal the violent potential inherent in revolutionary upheaval. Revolution, it seemed, was at its core about violence.

Subsequent revolutionaries often sought inspiration and precedents in the French Revolution, and viewed enemies of the revolution through the prism of the late eighteenth and early nineteenth century in France. During the 1840s, radicals across Europe looked to the earlier French Revolution for inspiration and symbols; demonstrators in Paris in 1848 were guided by Jacobin precedents of 1793, as barricades were erected and street fighting in Paris during the 'June Days' left 1,500 combatants dead and as a further 3,000 captured insurgents were shot by forces defending the republic born of the insurrection in February.[25] When the Paris Commune was declared in the wake of the Franco-Prussian War, violence in defence of the revolution was justified with reference to the events of the 1790s – as in the call reprinted (from the newspaper La Sociale) in Paris on 1 April 1871 in the Journal Officiel of the Commune:

> The royalists of the Assembly are trying to raise armies in the provinces ... As yet they have only a gang of policemen, ex-municipal guards, and the Pope's zouaves; as generals, they have the infamous Ducrot, Vinoy the Bonapartist, the Catholics Charette and Cathelineau, who have risen against the revolution in 1871, as did their forefathers against that of 1793, and who will have the same fate today as the latter had eighty years ago.[26]

The Commune of 1871 may have been 'the "dusk" of a revolutionary period [within France] that began in 1789',[27] but it did provide a point of reference for subsequent revolutionaries, notably in Russia. In 1921, Trotsky judged that while 'the Commune was weak. [...] We have become strong. The Commune was crushed. [...] We are taking vengeance.'[28] However, it was primarily to the French Revolution of the late eighteenth century that Russia's revolutionaries in the early twentieth century looked for historical precedents. The leaders of the provisional government after the February Revolution that toppled the Tsar 'saw themselves as re-enacting that French Revolution on Russian soil'; 'La Marseillaise' became the anthem of their revolution; and political groups were often given labels taken from the French Revolution (with the Bolsheviks being referred to, and seeing themselves as, Jacobins).[29] The Bolsheviks often viewed their revolution through the prism of the French

Revolution, which had demonstrated (according to Trotsky) that the transition of the revolution from one stage to another 'is accomplished through civil war'.[30]

While the French Revolution offered precedents, it was in the twentieth century that revolutionary violence reached a peak. The Russian Revolution combined features that had been present in the French Revolution more than a century before: a political leadership committed to the use of violence, civil war and foreign military intervention, and an upsurge of popular violence in the absence of effective state control over the countryside. Lenin shared the belief (held by the Russian Social Democratic Labour Party and the Mensheviks as well) that violence was called for in the struggle against the autocratic Tsarist regime. He justified the use of revolutionary violence in theory long before he had the opportunity to apply it in practice, refusing to reject terror as it might be perfectly suitable or even essential to the revolutionary struggle and believing that a successful revolution would necessarily involve violence and that violence would be necessary for the dictatorship of the proletariat to function. In Lenin's eyes, revolution was war.[31]

When he achieved power, Lenin put theory into practice. He did so in a country that had already been subjected to terrible violence during the war against Germany and Austria-Hungary and in which millions of people in its western provinces had been removed forcibly from their homes, and where many of the Bolsheviks' desperately poor and ill-educated supporters proved more than willing to attack those they felt had kept them in poverty. This proved a toxic mix when the Bolsheviks were fighting for their survival in a civil war. What distinguished the Bolsheviks from their political rivals on the left were not so much the differences in their economic and social programmes as their readiness to resort to violence. Over sixty years ago, the Jewish biographer of Lenin, David Shub, emphasized the Bolshevik leader's 'utter ruthlessness'. One hair-raising example that Shub cited was a telegram sent by Lenin to the Nizhni Novgorod Soviet on 9 August 1918 (shortly before he was shot and nearly killed by Fanny Kaplan on 30 August), in which the Bolshevik leader wrote:

In Nizhni Novgorod there are clearly preparations for a White Guard uprising. We must gather our strength, set up a dictatorial trio and institute mass terror immediately; shoot and ferret out hundreds of prostitutes who get the soldiers drunk, former officers, etc. Not a moment of delay. It is necessary to act all-out. Mass searches, execution for concealment of weapons. Mass seizure of Mensheviks and other unreliables.[32]

A few days later Lenin demanded a merciless struggle, 'the last decisive fight', against the kulaks:

Ruthless war on the kulaks! Death to them! Hatred and contempt for the parties which defend them – the Right Socialist Revolutionaries, the Mensheviks, and today's Left Socialist Revolutionaries! The workers must crush the revolts of the kulaks with an iron hand![33]

Violent orders were put into violent practice, as revolution and war created the context for a fundamental breakdown of normative constraints on civilized behaviour. It was violence, more than the degree of social and economic change, that defined Lenin's revolution.

The clearest sign both of the willingness of the Bolsheviks to engage in revolutionary violence and of the importance of their reading of the French Revolution was the creation of the Cheka within weeks of the October Revolution. The Cheka – the All-Russian Extraordinary Commission for Struggle against Counter-Revolution and Sabotage – was established in early December 1917, directed by the Polish Communist Felix

Dzerzhinsky and headquartered from March 1918 in the former
offices of Lloyd's Insurance Company in Lubianka Street in
Moscow. For Dzerzhinsky the task of his new organization was
to conduct a merciless struggle against the revolution's internal
enemies – a war 'face to face. A fight to the finish', that required
'determined, hard, dedicated comrades ready to do anything in
defence of the Revolution'.[34] The Cheka grew rapidly, to become
in effect a state within a state; in an echo of the Terror of the
French Revolution, the 'extraordinary' fight against counter-
revolution became a central feature of the new revolutionary
regime. Cheka units were established in regions where the
Bolsheviks were in control; denunciations, arrests and summary
executions of real and alleged counter-revolutionaries and
'bourgeois elements' multiplied; and by the summer of 1918
revolutionary terror had descended on the areas under Bolshevik rule. In December 1918, *Pravda* printed the advice of a
leading Cheka official, who instructed:

> Do not demand incriminating evidence to prove that the pris-
> oner has opposed the Soviet government by force or by
> words. Your first duty is to ask him to what class he belongs,
> what are his origins, his education, his occupation. These
> questions should decide the fate of the prisoner.[35]

That fate often was death. In the summer of 1918 an amateurish
anti-Bolshevik uprising (in Moscow, on 7–10 July) and assassination attempts by Left Socialist Revolutionaries (including the
murder of the head of the Petrograd Cheka and the shooting of
Lenin – who narrowly escaped death – at the end of August)
provided the catalysts for an escalation of terror. As Peter
Holquist has noted, 'the Bolsheviks gladly took advantage of the
opportunity that their competitors had so conveniently provided them'.[36] Mass arrests and mass executions followed, not
just of Left Socialist Revolutionaries but also of people assumed

guilty of being counter-revolutionaries by virtue of their station in life: former officers, priests, lawyers, doctors, prosperous farmers, members of pre-revolutionary governments. Arbitrary arrest, sadistic torture and summary execution became the order of the day; people were killed not because they had necessarily done anything themselves but because of who they were. The Cheka also executed Tsar Nicholas II, who had been taken prisoner (initially in quite luxurious surroundings), on orders from the Party leadership in Moscow, at Ekaterinburg in July 1918. As with the French Revolution before it, the violent logic of the Russian Revolution led to the execution of the last monarch of the old regime. And it was not just Nicholas Romanov who was murdered but also his family and the servants in his entourage (and other members of the Romanov family were murdered in the northern Urals). Trotsky asserted: 'We must put an end once and for all to the papist-Quaker babble about the sanctity of human life.'[37]

In the Civil War context of 1919 the violence in the name of the revolution extended further, to campaigns of mass terror against whole peoples. A prime target was the Cossacks, who were uniformly, but often mistakenly, viewed as counter-revolutionaries, with the Don region in southern Russia imagined as a Cossack Vendée. For the Bolsheviks, 'counter-revolution was no longer revealed through any concrete counter-revolutionary act; counter-revolutionary was simply what the Cossacks were'.[38] In a seeming echo of the French revolutionaries during the Terror of 1793, in January 1919 (when the policy of de-Cossackization was announced officially) the Bolshevik Central Committee called for a 'merciless struggle' against the Cossacks, stating that it was necessary 'to conduct merciless mass terror', and declaring that 'no compromises, no half-way measures are permissible'.[39]

Executions followed; revolutionary tribunals operated without regard for evidence, and there was no right of appeal; and over the next two months thousands lost their lives in an officially sanctioned campaign of violence and terror. Of course, the brutal treatment of suspect ethnic or social groups was not exclusive to the Bolsheviks or to revolutionary regimes in general – one thinks, for example, of the policies of forced removal conducted by the Tsarist regime and directed primarily against Germans and Jews in the western provinces of the Russian Empire during the First World War[40] – but couching this brutality within revolutionary rhetoric and revolutionary logic was neither accidental nor inconsequential. Mercy was not a revolutionary sentiment.

While precedents for the revolutionary violence and terror of the Bolsheviks may be found in the French Revolution, the Bolsheviks went further. Unlike their Jacobin predecessors, they were not defeated quickly and their terror regime did not come to an abrupt end. In the Soviet Union the revolutionary violence that began with the Cheka became institutionalized under Stalin, with the campaign against the kulaks and the waves of terror during the 1930s and 1940s claiming hundreds of thousands of lives, as the Cheka metamorphosed into the GPU, then into the NKVD (and eventually into the KGB), and the 'Lubianka' became a place of execution and a synonym for terror. Peter Holquist has observed: 'Unlike the violence of its predecessors and competitors, Soviet violence was not a temporary and extraordinary tool intended for use only during a circumscribed period of civil conflict. Rather, for the Bolshevik party-state, political violence was a regular and calculated programme.'[41] In so far as the Soviet Union under Stalin was a revolutionary state, it was a state based upon the liberal use of violence and terror.

Of course, the violence that accompanied and followed the October Revolution was not committed solely by Bolshevik revolutionaries. For one thing, the revolution and the subsequent civil war that followed provided a context conducive to violently settling old scores, to acting upon old hatreds – as calls among the Don peasants in late 1918 for the 'extirpation of the Cossacks *in toto*' illustrate.[42] The terror was not simply driven from above by people committed to a violent political ideology, but also was driven from below, by ferocious popular hatred against the nobility, the wealthy, the landowners, the Church. Already during the autumn of 1917, as state authority was disintegrating in the vast Russian countryside, peasants seized and destroyed estates, plundered livestock, and attacked landowners as well as government officials. One peasant in Tambov was recorded as asserting in September 1917: 'You think this is done by hooligans and vagrants and drunk ragamuffins, but you are mistaken. This is not vagrants and ragamuffins, but people drunk from hunger.'[43] This too was revolutionary violence – popular violence that arose from a combination of long-held grievance, a crisis of food supply and opportunities for direct action that a revolutionary situation and the disintegration of state authority had created. The Bolsheviks may have organized terror and violence, but they did not do so in a vacuum. Orlando Figes has argued that 'there is no doubt that the Terror struck a deep chord in the Russian civil war mentality, and that it had a strange mass appeal. [...] People even called their daughters Terrora.'[44]

For another, the terror of the Bolsheviks' opponents, the Whites, paralleled and in some instances surpassed the terror of the Reds themselves. The military campaigns of the Whites during the Civil War in southern Russia and Ukraine were accompanied by horrible violence. Certainly the willingness of Lenin and the Bolsheviks to resort to violence was a key factor in making the revolution so bloody after their relatively bloodless success in the autumn of 1917. The consolidation by the Bolsheviks of their revolution between October 1917 and March 1918 was a matter not just of military victories but also of violent campaigns against those they defeated; and the treatment of

White volunteers captured by the Reds was characterized by beatings, torture and execution. However, the Whites were no less bloodthirsty than the Reds, and were keen to exact revenge for the violence that their enemies had meted out against them. White generals were as extreme in their exhortations to violence as were their counterparts on the Bolshevik side, and repeatedly told their men to take no prisoners and that 'the more terror, the more victories'.[45] One White guard member described what occurred during the 'Ice March' of the Volunteer Army through the Kuban in southern Russia in the winter of 1918:

> Our first company, while going on the attack against the Reds, came under heavy machine gun fire. Those taken prisoner, the dead and the wounded officers were stripped of their clothing and subjected to humiliations and torture: their eyes were gouged out, their tongues were cut out, nails were driven into their epaulets, and barely but still alive, these officers were buried. And we avenged those atrocities. In this battle, four officers were killed; however, the losses of the 'comrades' reached 150, and most of these were shot (executed).[46]

The head of this expedition, Colonel Drozdovskii, told those under his command that 'we live in a terrible time, when man is becoming an animal. These unbridled hooligans understand only one law: an eye for an eye, a tooth for a tooth. But I would propose two eyes for one, and all teeth for one'.[47] Anton Ivanovich Denikin, the general who succeeded Lavr Kornilov as commander of the White forces in southern Russia after the latter's death and who nearly succeeded in toppling the Bolsheviks, later wrote from exile:

> Four years of war and the nightmare of revolution did not go by without consequences ... All those dark sides of existence which surfaced during the war were further emphasized

during the revolution because of a general increase in lawlessness and the rudderless government, and the lack of prosecution of crimes committed and the general indifference toward criminal acts laid a fertile ground for criminal elements which penetrated into the army as well ... Many developed a particular type of psychology consisting of a double standard of morality, the first pertaining to himself and his own, and the second pertaining to others.[48]

The revolutionary upheaval and civil war also provided the context for a terrible upsurge in antisemitic violence, that Richard Pipes described as 'the worst violence the Jews had suffered since the Cossack Hetman Bohdan Chmielnicki had ruled this region [in Ukraine] nearly three centuries earlier'. This anti-Jewish violence began in Ukraine under German occupation during 1918, and in 1919 the violence escalated; the victims were numbered not in the dozens or hundreds, but in the tens of thousands. The presence of people of Jewish background among the Bolshevik leadership fed antisemitic prejudice. Vicious pogroms were unleashed and military units fighting against the Reds attacked Jews, with Cossacks serving in White ranks at the forefront; synagogues were desecrated, property destroyed, and Jews robbed, raped and murdered. One witness to the pogrom in Kiev in October 1919 (in which nearly 300 people were killed) described the streets of the city as being 'in the grip of medieval terror'.[49] Revolution and civil war opened the gates to unspeakable violence during 'a terrible time when man is becoming an animal'.

It was not only regions that had constituted the Russian Empire that were engulfed by violence in the wake of the First World War. The success of Russian revolutionaries in overthrowing the Tsarist autocracy and the subsequent Bolshevik capture of power inspired left-wing revolutionaries and their supporters to attempt to seize power across Europe and beyond.

These attempts at revolution were all failures, but they managed to unleash substantial violence in what had seemed orderly and peaceful societies before 1914, and they led to an epidemic of paramilitary violence across Europe after the First World War.[50]

Among the more prominent attempts at revolution occurred in Hungary, where there initially were parallels with what had taken place in Russia. In the end, however, it was counter-revolution that triumphed. The establishment in Budapest of a Soviet Republic in March 1919 under the leadership of Béla Kun (who had joined the Bolsheviks following his release from a prisoner-of-war camp in 1917, returned to Hungary in November 1918, and was to meet his end in Stalin's purges in 1938) opened the gates to revolutionary and counter-revolutionary violence. After the failure of an anti-Communist coup attempt, Kun organized a Red Terror through secret police, revolutionary tribunals, and revolutionary squads that executed hundreds of people. Worse came after Kun's Soviet Republic fell to the forces of Admiral Miklós Horthy at the beginning of August 1919. White Terror followed Red Terror in 1919 and 1920, during which Horthy's 'National Army' (the 'White Guard') carried out a campaign of torture and summary executions of suspected 'Reds'. (Particular targets of the Hungarian White Terror were Jews, who were associated with the Soviet Republic; Kun himself was of Jewish background.) The revolutionary unrest in Hungary also spilled over into Slovakia, which had been part of the Hungarian half of the Austro-Hungarian Empire and where a third of the population was Hungarian. There, Communists established a very short-lived Soviet Republic in the summer of 1919 on the back of a military campaign by the forces of Béla Kun, and there too they 'tried to establish their political power by means of intense fear produced by the systematic use of violence'; hundreds of people were jailed without charge, and liberal use was made of the death penalty.[51]

It was in Germany that the most significant of the failed revolutions triggered by the First World War occurred. There, imperial rule collapsed in November 1918, in a revolution remarkable initially for its lack of bloodshed. However, Germany's November Revolution was followed by months and then years during which the once well-ordered country was overwhelmed by revolutionary and, especially, counter-revolutionary violence. Attempts by the revolutionary left to take power – an abortive Communist rising in Berlin in January 1919 and the establishment of a succession of radical left-wing regimes in Munich following the abdication of Bavaria's Wittelsbach monarchy – aroused fears of impending chaos. However, it was in the counter-revolutionary onslaughts by the German military and, especially, by *Freikorps* units in the service of the socialist-led government under Friedrich Ebert (who was horrified at events in Russia and overestimated the threat posed by the left in Germany) that hundreds were killed. These included Rosa Luxemburg and Karl Liebknecht, brutally murdered in Berlin in January 1919, and perhaps a thousand people who lost their lives in the White Terror after the suppression of the 'Soviet Republic' in the Bavarian capital. During the following three years, Germany witnessed an epidemic of counter-revolutionary violence, with hundreds of people falling victim to political murder.[52]

Left-wing revolutionaries did not shy away from violence either: in 1921 the communist-inspired 'March action' in the industrial region around Mansfeld and the giant Leuna chemical works in central Germany included arson, bank robberies, bomb attacks on public buildings and violent confrontations with police, before government troops suppressed the uprising at a cost of 145 dead and an unknown number wounded.[53] Nevertheless, although revolutionary and counter-revolutionary bloodshed left hundreds dead in post-1918 Germany, the extent of the violence was limited when compared with what had occurred in Russia. The German state did not disintegrate; revolution did not triumph; civil war remained latent rather than out in the open.

Although its extent and intensity varied according to circumstances in different countries of post-1918 Europe, the violence of the revolutionary and counter-revolutionary waves between 1917 and 1923 was a transnational phenomenon. The First World War had unleashed violence across the European continent and weakened the ability of old-regime states to contain challenges to their existence. The story of revolution during the first half of the twentieth century belongs very much to what is often described as the most violent century ever. During the second half of the twentieth century, however, something changed, at least in Europe. The change did not come at once, nor did it arrive uniformly across the European continent. But it came.

In the immediate aftermath of the Second World War, revolutionary political and economic transformations were carried through in eastern Europe. Capitalist economic systems were abolished and replaced by centralized state socialism, and one-party dictatorships clothed as 'people's democracies' were established from Berlin to Sofia. In some instances these transformations were accompanied by outbreaks of violence – for example, intimidation and street fighting in Romania in the run-up to the parliamentary elections of November 1946 (which gave the Communists a majority), and a minor civil war in Poland when the activities of the Soviet NKVD in 1945 provoked armed resistance in the countryside that continued for nearly three years. However, the post-war eastern European socialist revolutions, such as they were, were essentially imposed from above and they owed their success to the victorious Red Army and to Soviet power. During the next four decades, what had begun as a revolutionary transformation in eastern Europe evolved into a bureaucratized and immobile political system with the lid kept on by ever-expanding secret police forces. While popular risings in socialist eastern Europe during the 1950s (in the German Democratic Republic and Czechoslovakia in 1953, in Poland and Hungary in 1956) were suppressed with the aid of Soviet armed force, during the second half of the twentieth century the era of substantial revolutionary violence in eastern Europe ended. The collapse of eastern European state socialism and one-party dictatorship towards the end of the century was a revolutionary transformation, but it was not accompanied by much violence. Quite the opposite.

Against the background of what had occurred during the first half of the twentieth century, the revolutions that took place in eastern Europe in 1989–1991 are remarkable. The revolutions that unfolded as the Soviet bloc disintegrated did not descend into orgies of violence as did the French Revolutions of 1789 and 1871 or the Russian Revolution of 1917; nor did they provoke counter-revolutionary violence as had the failed revolutions in Europe after the First World War. The earlier revolutions were products of war and civil war and led to war and civil war. By contrast, the European revolutions of 1989 marked the end of a very peculiar war, the Cold War, and were followed in most of the post-socialist states by an absence of violent conflict.

The revolutions that brought down the socialist dictatorships of eastern Europe were (with the exception of the events in Romania in December 1989) intentionally non-violent. They produced no counterparts to Robespierre or Lenin. Many of the unlikely revolutionaries of 1989 were inspired by the politics of non-violence. As the eastern European socialist regimes crumbled, their (relatively limited) recourse to violence contributed to the erosion of their legitimacy. Violence by the state became illegitimate not only in the eyes of the broad population but, increasingly, in the eyes of state and party functionaries themselves, and non-violence had become revolutionary. The Czech

'Civic Forum' and the Slovak 'Public against Violence' were formed in November 1989 partly in reaction to heavy-handed police action against a student-led march in Prague – what was referred to as the 'massacre' of 17 November 1989.[54] The participants in the 'Monday Demonstrations' in the German Democratic Republic during the autumn of 1989 were exponents of non-violence, and in a political system characterized by police repression and a comprehensive militarization of society, the politics of non-violence were revolutionary. This was a European revolution of a new type. The attraction of the revolution lay precisely in the commitment of its leading figures to non-violence and the non-violent manner in which it developed. The general absence and rejection of violence was fundamental to its development and success.

Calls for non-violence occupied a prominent place in the protests of the revolutionaries of 1989, and their commitment to non-violence appears to have inhibited the forces of the socialist states of eastern Europe (which still had massive capacities for violence at their disposal) from opting to drown popular protest in a sea of blood. In the German Democratic Republic, the Communist leadership did not opt for violent repression to save their regime when faced with growing street protest in the autumn of 1989. In Estonia, the 'Singing Revolution' that had begun in 1987 with mass demonstrations involving the singing of national hymns forbidden under Soviet rule – peaking when 300,000 people (a quarter of the entire Estonian population in the country) took part in a song festival in Tallinn in September 1988 – ended after Estonians acted as human shields to protect the radio and television stations, and the country regained its independence without bloodshed.[55] In Czechoslovakia the Communist regime dissolved in the 'Velvet Revolution' of November 1989, after which two members of the Slovak movement 'Public Against Violence' (*Verejnosť proti násiliu*, VPN, formed in November 1989, that aimed to be a 'society-wide movement' open to all citizens who rejected violence)[56] – Vladimir Meciar and Marian Calfa – were elected Slovak and Federal Premier respectively. (Petr Pithart of the Czech counterpart to the VPN, the Civic Forum, was elected Czech Premier.)

The end of state socialism and the recovery of independence was accompanied by violence in Lithuania, where in January 1991 Soviet troops, called in to suppress Lithuania's move to independence (declared the previous March), killed fourteen protesters and wounded hundreds more who were defending the television tower and the parliament building in Vilnius. The crowd responded non-violently, however, linking arms and singing, and on 2 February the Lithuanian parliament passed a resolution stating:

> We are convinced that in this decisive period of trial Lithuania has only one effective and undefeatable weapon, expressive of our Baltic and Christian culture – that of non-violent protest, of people's self-control and calm endurance. [...] We urge all to resist provocations of the foreign troops, to refrain from any acts of physical resistance so desired by the enemy.[57]

The Lithuanians, like their Baltic neighbours, drew on a long tradition of non-violent rhetoric, and were rewarded. Lithuanian independence was recognized internationally in the following summer. Bloody revolution in Europe had been succeeded largely by 'velvet revolution', in which people took to the streets to oppose violence rather than to exercise it.

Perhaps the best-known example of the rejection of violence during the revolutions of 1989 is 'the peaceful revolution', 'the gentle [*sanfte*] revolution' that brought an end to the German Democratic Republic. The popular opposition that grew in the GDR during 1989 was marked by what Mary Fulbrook has described as 'the very peaceful, positively non-violent, character of the demonstrations'.[58] This is neither to assert that the demonstrators were always non-violent nor to suggest that the East German state security forces (the Stasi) hesitated to employ strong-arm tactics before their power evaporated in late October and November 1989. Indeed, before the demonstrations had grown to such dimensions that physical intimidation short of shooting into the crowds was no longer an option, members of the Stasi regularly roughed up demonstrators and led them away into custody. On 4 October 1989, when special trains carrying GDR citizens who had sought asylum in the West German embassies in Prague and Warsaw passed through the main railway station in Dresden on their way to the West, they were greeted with violent protests of others who also wanted to leave for the Federal Republic. The security forces responded with violence and mass arrests, beating many of those taken into custody, and on the afternoon of 5 October units of the National People's Army were called in. However, although each soldier had been given ammunition, they were ordered not to shoot.[59] The tide was turning, but the possibility of a violent crackdown had not vanished. Günther Jahn (at the time First Secretary of the Socialist Unity Party in the Potsdam District) made clear before a meeting of the 'leading cadres of the District [Potsdam]' on 13 October that, while violence was to be employed 'only in the most extreme emergency', 'if it must be, our hand will not shake'.[60]

Nevertheless, when the existence of the East German Communist system, of 'real-existing socialism', hung in the balance, the hand did shake. As long as the demonstrations remained relatively small, leather-jacketed members of the Stasi had been willing and able to beat up demonstrators, arrest them and carry them off to prison. Non-lethal violence had been employed routinely to intimidate the opposition. However, when the revolutionary moment arrived and the survival of the regime was at stake, the security forces did not open fire. The reluctance of the East German Communist state to resort to open violence owed much to the broad commitment to non-violence by those on the streets, where the demonstrations were characterized by placards and exhortations against violence. The demonstrators sought not the violent overthrow of the East German regime (which probably would have provoked a violent response and condemned their movement to failure), but rather its peaceful replacement. The repeated calls for 'no violence' served a dual purpose: to dissuade the state from resorting to violent repression, and to dissuade the demonstrators themselves from engaging in behaviour that would provoke violence from the other side.

The commitment to non-violence was both principled and tactical. On the one hand, democratic revolution could be achieved only if the state were drawn into dialogue and dissuaded from violent confrontation, and it was of great importance that support and institutional cover for oppositional activity came from the churches, which were committed to non-violence, organized public prayers for peace and urged dialogue with representatives of the regime. On the other hand, had violence erupted, the police, the Stasi and the army would have had an excuse to unleash overwhelming force, and the demonstrators knew it. This helps to explain the lengths to which the demonstrators went to maintain discipline and to prevent attacks on state property, including that of the Ministry of State Security.[61]

Given what had happened in Beijing during the previous June, when violent repression crushed opposition to Communist rule, it may seem surprising that the East German dictatorship did not resort to violence in the autumn of 1989 but instead succumbed to a non-violent revolution. What inhibited the East German leadership from unleashing lethal violence to maintain their rule? It is clear that the option to send in the tanks was considered in October 1989, as the demonstrations grew in size and strength. The regime was preparing for a showdown, and the preparations were ominous: 'People's Police' units were placed on alert, supplied with truncheons, water cannon and ammunition; units of the National People's Army were put in a state of readiness and specially equipped to intervene; locations (army barracks, etc.) were prepared to hold oppositionists who would be arrested *en masse*; special forces of the Ministry of State Security were sent to Leipzig and 'prepared for the arrest of the ring-leaders [and] for engagement in special tasks [*Einsatz zu besonderen Aufgaben*]'.[62] Erich Honecker, still in post as General Secretary of the Socialist Unity Party and Chairman of the GDR State Council, continued in mid-October to urge that the demonstrations be broken up forcibly. But this did not happen. Although it was considered, the East German Communist leadership did not opt for a 'Chinese solution'.[63] On 16 October, 120,000 people took part in the Monday demonstration (up from 70,000 the week before, itself the largest unofficial demonstration in the GDR since the uprising of June 1953), and on the following day Honecker was dismissed abruptly by his Politburo colleagues. Unable to call upon the Soviet Union to intervene in order to save their crumbling political system and unwilling to send in the tanks on their own, Honecker's erstwhile colleagues rejected the violent defence of 'real-existing socialism'. Once it became clear that the threat of violence was lifted, the numbers of those on the streets grew even greater: the next Monday demonstration in Leipzig, on 23 October, attracted a crowd of roughly 300,000 people. When theatre workers applied to hold a pro-democracy rally in East Berlin's Alexanderplatz on 4 November, official approval was granted and half a million people gathered (with the demonstration broadcast live on East German radio and television). 'The masses united under the motto "no violence"';[64] the 'peaceful revolution' became unstoppable.

In an open letter to Erich Honecker, published in the news magazine *Der Spiegel* in early 1991, Egon Krenz (Honecker's successor as General Secretary of the Socialist Unity Party) wrote: 'I want to say openly: had we not carried out at the top the change [*Wende*] that long since was underway on the streets, there most probably would have been a civil war.'[65] In the end, the East German leadership were not willing to wage civil war; neither those in office nor those on the streets proved keen to unleash violence. The first successful revolution in German history was essentially bloodless. At the end of the twentieth century, revolution in the heart of Europe succeeded not through violence but through the renunciation of violence. As one police officer in Dresden (where the police had used considerable violence against demonstrators in early October 1989) put it in 1990: 'Believe me, hardly any of us likes to hit people. And all have wives and families who prefer to know that their people are healthy at home rather than in the barracks beaten black and blue. In future we really want only to protect peaceful citizens.'[66]

The East German 'peaceful revolution' of 1989 provided a catalyst for the rapid disintegration of state socialism across eastern Europe. Essential to this transformation was the evaporation of fear. The violent suppression of the uprising of June 1953 in the German Democratic Republic had scarred a generation, leaving those who experienced it reluctant to risk their lives a second time, and in Czechoslovakia 'the representatives of the 1968 generation [...] were always constrained by the fear of a repetition of the bitter year of their youth'.[67] It thus seems hardly coincidental that the largely peaceful revolutions across eastern Europe occurred when younger generations, who had not experienced as adults previous repressions of attempts to shake off the Communist system, came of age. The state no longer intimidated as it had done previously. The key moment came with the realization that one could challenge the socialist dictatorship without applying or provoking lethal violence. In Estonia, where (ultimately successful) protests against environmentally damaging phosphorite mining during the 1980s had been followed by the singing demonstrations that eventually accompanied Estonian independence, one activist later reflected: 'I realized that now it was the time [...] There was the experience that something already had been achieved, phosphorite mining had been stopped. That was the first experience [...] that you can go to the streets, you can demonstrate, and nothing happens, no repression will follow.'[68] In Prague in mid-November 1989, a few days after police had brutally dispersed a student demonstration, there were mass demonstrations involving some 200,000 people to protest against the violence. As one observer put it: 'all the shrewd "soldier Schweiks" absorbed one very specific lesson from the East German example: if enough people assemble, under the new circumstances the police don't dare shoot'.[69] What followed was Czechoslovakia's Velvet Revolution, which brought the playwright Václav Havel, a man committed to non-violent politics, to the presidency of his country. According to the Czech novelist and playwright Ivan Klíma: 'For those who still believe in the power of culture, the power of words, of good and of love, and their dominance over violence [...] the Prague revolution must have been an inspiration.'[70] The role model for the revolutionaries of 1989 was not Che Guevara or Mao Tse-Tung, but Martin Luther King Jr.[71] This was a very different concept of revolution than that propagated by the Jacobins of the late eighteenth century or by Lenin in the early twentieth. It seemed that, as Timothy Garton Ash has argued, '1989 has supplanted 1789 as the default model of revolution: rather than progressive radicalization, violence and the guillotine, we look for peaceful mass protest followed by negotiated transition'.[72] This is, of course, a rather Euro-centric perspective and, as Garton Ash admits, it 'has taken a battering of late, not only in Ukraine but also in the violent fall that followed the Arab spring'. However, it describes how revolution came to be understood widely in the western world at the end of the twentieth century.

In the developed states of late twentieth-century Europe, revolution could be successful if it remained essentially non-violent. In the absence of open warfare, and in states that had been able to construct huge and seemingly effective security apparatuses, probably the only way to bring them down was *not* to turn to violence. In the peculiar context of late twentieth-century Europe, revolutionary violence had become counter-productive. After the extreme violence of the first half of the century, after two world wars (in both of which the majority of the casualties had been European) and after the violence committed by the most murderous dictatorships that the world had ever seen, there was a widespread conviction that such things must not be repeated. This was reflected in the pronouncements of European churches, in the rationale for establishing what eventually became the European Union, and in the repeated assertion by the states of the socialist bloc of their 'peace-loving' nature.[73]

In addition, the extraordinary increase in material prosperity during the post-war decades meant that millions of Europeans, not only in the West but also (if to a lesser extent) in the East, had a great deal to lose from violent upheaval and little to gain. At the same time, the presence of large and effective police and armed forces and modern communications networks meant that violent uprisings could be suppressed more easily than had been the case in less developed and largely rural countries, e.g. late eighteenth-century France or early twentieth-century Russia, where the forces of 'law and order' had been, by late twentieth-century standards, thin on the ground. In these circumstances, revolutionary violence had neither much chance of success nor much popular support – as the abject failure of the would-be revolutionaries in the German Red Army Faction and the Italian Red Brigades demonstrated during the 1970s.

Successful revolutions involve the dissolution of the power of the state, the crumbling of its legitimacy and the break-up of its sovereignty. Revolution occurs when the writ of the state no longer holds, when its servants no longer obey its orders, when its power evaporates, and when alternative centres of power parallel and overtake those of the old regime. This is roughly what occurred in France at the end of the eighteenth century and in the Russian Empire during the First World War, and to some extent in much of eastern Europe during the late 1980s and early 1990s. However, in late twentieth-century Europe the state did not really dissolve, although its authority certainly did; the huge apparatus of the modern state – from its educational institutions and welfare administrations through to its criminal-justice and its regulatory apparatus – did not disappear. Consequently, there was not an institutional void of the sort that created space for violence in earlier revolutions.

Much of the violence surrounding revolutionary upheavals has stemmed not so much from the initial event as from the reactions to it – from counter-revolutionary campaigns and efforts by revolutionary regimes to defend themselves against the real and imagined forces of counter-revolution. The ferocity of the reaction often contributed to the violence as much if not more than the revolution itself. In both the French and Russian Revolutions resistance to revolutionary transformation, both internally and from outside, fuelled the violence that followed the initial political upheaval (which, compared to what came thereafter, was not terribly bloody). Each was followed by a reign of terror, which revolutionaries regarded as necessary for the defence of the revolution against those who sought to reverse it, whether the nobility and the wealthy classes of France and the Russian Empire or the external armies that waged war on the revolutionary regimes. Each was 'revolutionized' by war,[74] and each was followed by ferocious civil war. By contrast, during the late twentieth century in Europe there were no substantial domestic interests willing in the end to prevent or reverse by force the overthrow of the old socialist dictatorships, no armed resistance by the cadres and functionaries who had administered 'real-existing socialism', no attempt by armed forces from abroad – i.e. the armed forces of the Soviet Union, itself in slow meltdown – to crush revolution. Thus, in the peculiar revolutionary context of late twentieth-century Europe, ferocious counter-revolutionary violence did not materialize.

Another important contrast may be found in the relationship of organized religion to revolution, and to revolutionary violence. In both the French and Russian Revolutions, atheist regimes attacked the hegemonic churches of the respective countries, the Catholic Church in late eighteenth-century France and the Orthodox Church in early twentieth-century Russia. If one wanted to overthrow the state, one had to do away with the hegemony of the church and dismantle its considerable privileges, which inevitably involved making far-reaching social as well as political changes and which inevitably provoked fierce resistance. As Arno Mayer points out, 'nothing could have been more divisive than the instant desacralization of high politics; disestablishment of the state church; dispossession of ecclesiastical property; and emancipation of religious minorities'.[75] Not surprisingly, the clergy were hostile to the revolutionaries; country priests urged peasant resistance; and Pope Pius VI and the Orthodox Supreme Patriarch Tikhon respectively excommunicated Jacobins and Bolsheviks. (In an encyclical in early 1918, Tikhon castigated the hatred and cruelty unleashed by those he called 'the monsters of the human race'.)[76] For their part, revolutionaries and their supporters among the population at large turned on priests, with a ferocity fuelled by ideological hostility towards organized religion as well as by the resistance of the clergy to the revolution. In Bolshevik-controlled Russia, churches were raided and plundered after the October Revolution, and hundreds died while participating in religious processions or trying to protect church property. The Bolshevik regime and the Orthodox Church in effect were at war, and after worshippers violently resisted a raid on a church in March 1922,

Lenin issued the chilling order that 'we must now give the most decisive and merciless battle to the Black Hundreds clergy and subdue its resistance with such brutality that they will not forget it for decades to come'.[77] Of course, religious institutions and clergy have not always been in the counter-revolutionary camp, as the marriage of parliamentarianism and Puritanism in the English Revolution of the seventeenth century and the role of militant Shiites (who regarded obedience to the secular state as equivalent to idolatry) in the Iranian Revolution of 1979 have demonstrated.[78] However, these two types of revolution – those driven by militant atheism and those driven by militant religious faith – have had an important ideological characteristic in common: a millenarianism – secular in the former, religious in the latter – that justified and fuelled violence.

In this the revolutionary transformations of the late twentieth century in Europe were of a different character. Unlike in the French or Russian Revolutions, the clergy were agents for revolutionary change; unlike in the English or Iranian Revolutions, they were committed to non-violence. Most prominently in the German Democratic Republic and in Poland, the churches had been involved deeply in movements that eventually toppled socialist regimes. These were churches that preached peace and non-violence, and that challenged a militarized socialist state that had threatened violence against dissenters; they supported and reinforced revolutionary movements in their reluctance to engage in violent action. Thus organized religion served to reduce the likelihood of violence in revolution, not to increase it.

Ultimately the most important contrast between the non-violence of 1989 and the violence of the earlier French and Russian Revolutions was probably the role of external armed force. Foreign powers attempted to reverse and defeat the French and Russian revolutionary regimes militarily, attempts that served in both cases to increase the bloodshed as counter-revolutionary violence within the country was augmented and abetted by interventions of armed forces from outside. In 1989 in Europe quite the opposite occurred: the foreign power that many had expected would intervene militarily to crush the revolutionary challenge and to preserve the old regimes, the USSR, refrained from doing so. Eastern European regimes that in the final analysis had been dependent for their continued existence upon the military backing of the Soviet Union suddenly found themselves without support. The French and Russian revolutionary regimes had survived by defeating the military interventions of foreign powers; the political transformations that emerged from the revolutionary events of 1989 owed their existence and survival to the absence of foreign military intervention.

Can a revolution be non-violent and still be a revolution? Some think not. Peter Holquist, writing about the upheavals in Russia between 1914 and 1921, asserts that 'the foundation of all new political entities requires violence'.[79] In his examination of the French and Russian Revolutions Arno Mayer is equally clear: 'there is no revolution without violence and terror'.[80] Consequently, Mayer is contemptuous of the view that 'in this day and age the only genuine and virtuous revolution is said to be one in which at best limited violence, well short of terror, is used to force the establishment of a *Rechtsstaat* to guarantee individual rights, political freedoms, private property, and free-market capitalism'.[81] Leaving aside his well-founded scepticism about the 'promiscuous use' and trivialization of the term 'revolution' when it embraces 'every single aspect of contemporary society, economy and culture', Mayer's observation of how the term is employed 'in this day and age' is to the point: at least in the West, 'revolution' is no longer necessarily associated with violence. In developed and relatively prosperous modern states, with highly developed state bureaucracies and mainly secular societies in which organized religion no longer sits at the centre of power, 'revolution' could be largely non-violent.

97

Thus the peculiar conditions found in the western world during the second half of the twentieth century provided the basis for a new understanding of revolution, one that was successful because it largely eschewed violence rather than embraced it. This does not mean that human nature has changed, that we now necessarily pay more attention to 'the better angels of our nature', as Steven Pinker would have it. The revolutionary violence that erupted in the wake of the revolutions in China in 1949, in Iran in 1979, and in the Arab world in 2011 and thereafter should make one think twice before embracing such a conclusion. However, at least within the western world, in the peculiar context of the second half of the twentieth century, revolution and violence were not necessarily bound up with one another. One could be non-violent and be a revolutionary at the same time.

IV

Politics

In the night of 9–10 August 1932, shortly after midnight, a band of drunken National Socialists brutally murdered a Communist sympathizer, Konrad Pietczuch, in his home and in front of his mother, in the Upper Silesian border village of Potempa. Although Pietczuch was but one of dozens of people who met their deaths as a result of political violence during the dying days of the Weimar Republic, the killing attracted tremendous attention across Germany. The notice paid to the Potempa murder stemmed not only from the extraordinarily vicious nature of the crime; it also resulted from the fact that it was the first case to fall under emergency anti-terror legislation just passed by the German government, legislation that introduced the death penalty for political murder and that came into force at midnight on 10 August 1932.[1] The resulting trial, before a special court in the Upper Silesian mining town of Beuthen (on the border with Poland), provided the occasion for tumultuous scenes. When the death sentence was pronounced on five of the accused, the leader of the Silesian Stormtroopers organization, Edmund Heines, jumped up in court and shouted that 'the sentence is the signal for the German uprising!' He then left the courtroom to give an inflammatory speech across the street, after which an angry crowd of Stormtroopers and sympathizers went on a rampage through the town. Politically inspired violence continued in and around Beuthen for days; police were attacked; shop windows were smashed.

The National Socialist leadership, aware of the need to keep their more violent supporters on board despite mounting frustration with the strategy of pursuing a 'legal' path to power, voiced support for the convicted murderers. Hermann Göring telegraphed to tell the condemned men that they were not murderers but had defended their 'lives and honour', and that he was sending one thousand *Reichsmarks* to their families. The 'Chief of Staff' of the Stormtroopers' organization, Ernst Röhm (who was to meet his death in the 'Blood Purge' of 1934), went to Beuthen to express solidarity with the convicted murderers and visited them in prison. And Adolf Hitler sent a telegram declaring his 'unbounded loyalty' to the condemned men, who the Nazi Party leader described as his 'comrades': 'From this moment on your freedom is a question of our honour. The struggle against a government, under which this [sentence] was possible, [is] our duty.' The leader of the largest and most popular political party that Germany had ever seen thus declared his solidarity with a band of convicted murderers. In just over five months, he would be called upon to head the German government.

By expressing his solidarity with murderers, Hitler risked losing popular support among respectable public opinion, and the negative publicity that the National Socialists received for this and other acts of political violence and terror committed in early August 1932 hurt them at the polls in the following November (when they lost roughly two million votes as compared with their total in the *Reichstag* elections at the end of July). Nevertheless, the damage proved limited. Within the Stormtroopers' organization the ostentatious show of solidarity by the Party leadership had its desired effect, and the fact that the leader of Germany's largest political party publicly identified with a band of drunken murderers temporarily reduced but did not fundamentally undermine its electoral support. In Germany during the early 1930s, aggressively violent politics and the acceptance and indeed glorification of violence in politics did not repel large sections of the public. Even if they did not necessarily glory in political violence, the millions who voted for the National Socialists during the early 1930s were not put off from supporting the Hitler movement by its violent rhetoric and actions. The fact that the National Socialists did not shrink from violent confrontation with the left, particularly with the German Communists against whom they portrayed themselves as fighting a defensive struggle with a dangerous adversary, may have attracted support from people who were pleased to see Communists attacked but were not prepared to engage in physical violence themselves. Such reactions helped to underpin the popularity that Hitler enjoyed among Germany's middle classes and conservatives once he became Reich Chancellor, not least as a result of the brutal suppression of the left (and especially of Communists, who were arrested in their thousands and many of whom were killed) in early 1933.[2] Political violence directed against an opponent widely regarded as violent and threatening and in an apparent defence of order attracted considerable popular approval.

The Potempa murder was a striking indication, but only one among many, that politics in Germany had become more violent during the 1920s and 1930s than they were before the First World War. After the war, violence became a prominent feature of German political life; people came to expect that political activity would involve violence, even if they did not all necessarily welcome it. When viewed from the early twenty-first century, however, the evidence of contemporary reactions to the Potempa murder appears to have come from a strange, foreign world. By the late twentieth century it had become almost inconceivable that the leader of a major political party in the West could endorse such violent, murderous behaviour and largely maintain popular support. Politicians in the western world now routinely condemn political violence, not support it, and political involvement and elections are not generally marked by explosions of political violence (although this certainly does occur elsewhere in the world). Since the Second World War the expectation that elections will be accompanied by violence and intimidation has largely been conspicuous by its absence, at least in the West. The legitimacy of the political process rests with its non-violent nature. We tend to take it for granted that politics should (and will) be largely free of violence, and to view the political violence that accompanied the demise of the Weimar Republic with fascination and horror.

For all the attention that the aggression of the Hitler movement has received, it would be a mistake to assume that violence began suddenly to feature in political life only after the First World War. Popular politics had often been violent politics. As Manuel Álvarez Tardío has observed recently, violence surrounding elections 'was by no means a child of the inter-war period. Even prior to the widespread adoption of universal suffrage, the increasingly competitive nature of elections had prompted violence of varying degrees and character.'[3] Politics in the second half of the nineteenth century was punctuated on occasion by serious violence, even in countries that we usually consider to be well ordered. For example, during the 1868 general election in England, physical attacks were made on candidates and their supporters, with claims that 'Liberal agents from London [...] organized and paid "flying columns" of 200–300 men armed with bludgeons who drove off Conservative voters from polling places', and the mayor of Stalybridge near Manchester testified that his borough 'lay under a perfect reign of terror'.[4] Violence often accompanied elections in nineteenth-century United States, and antisemitic rioting spread across France in 1898–9, at the time of the Dreyfus Affair. However, what occurred during the first half of the twentieth century was quantatively and qualitatively different, and the remarkable upsurge in political violence across Europe after 1918 cannot be explained without reference to the First World War.

Following the longest period of peace among the European great powers in their history, the 1914–1918 war led not only to the collapse of multinational empires but also to the erosion and indeed the destruction of communities, social structures, economic stability and political frameworks. It did not just lead to revolution and revolutionary unrest; it also eroded normative constraints that had increasingly helped to limit violence in politics during the nineteenth century. It undermined the authority of states and their ability to suppress political violence, and opened the door to violence on an extraordinary scale. Welcoming the new world of violence precipitated by the Great War, Ernst Jünger wrote in *Der Kampf als inneres Erlebnis* the oft-quoted passage:

> This war is not the end but the beginning of violence. It is the forge in which the world will be hammered into new borders and new communities. New forms want to be filled with blood, and power will be wielded with a hard fist. The war is a great school, and the new man will bear our stamp.[5]

The First World War was a catalyst not only for the destruction of political and social systems and established hierarchies but also for the creation of a new world of violence – and of politics in a new and violent key, that remains shocking to those who regard overt violence in politics as fundamentally illegitimate. In the early nineteenth century, Carl von Clausewitz famously described war as 'merely a continuation of politics by other means'.[6] In Europe in the first half of the twentieth century, it seemed as though the relationship had been reversed: politics had become a continuation of war.[7]

The post-war upsurge in political violence owed much to the revolutionary upheavals that arose as a result of the First World War, most notably in Russia and Germany. The Russian Revolution and the success of Lenin's Bolsheviks (who, as noted above in Chapter III, distinguished themselves from their competitors not least by their embrace of violence) brought a radical ideological agenda to politics across Europe, inspiring revolutionary unrest and violent reaction. Attempted revolution provoked violent and bloody response, and created a climate in which political violence became a feature of public life in many European countries. During the two decades that followed, squads of political soldiers allied with and supported political movements, violent confrontations punctuated political rallies and marches, physical attacks on political opponents became frequent, and the glorification of political violence among political movements on both the left and the right became commonplace. Across the European continent, the First World War was followed by a wave of paramilitary violence that has been termed 'war in peace' – an apposite description of domestic politics in a new and violent key.[8]

It is tempting to attribute the upsurge in political violence after the First World War to a brutalization of millions of soldiers caused by their combat experiences – that the war brutalized post-war domestic politics.[9] Certainly considerable numbers of ex-soldiers proved unable or unwilling to return to peaceful, civilian life after their return from the war; and many veterans of the Great War emerged in the ranks of Mussolini's Fascist squads, in *Freikorps* units, in the formations of the German National Socialists, or in the Austrian *Heimwehr*. Yet millions more returned home after the war to build a peaceful life as civilians. Politics became more violent, but this was probably due less to a transformation of soldiers' characters as a result of their experience of combat than to developments that followed from the war: defeat, revolutionary unrest and fears of revolution, a disintegration of effective state control of civil society, and the territorial settlements following the demise of multinational empires that proved to be recipes for ethnic and political conflict.

Violence thus became a prominent feature of domestic politics in numerous countries after the First World War, from Italy and Germany to Ireland, Poland and Turkey.[10] In many respects, the classic example of the violent politics of post-war Europe was that which occurred in Italy, where the Fascist leader Benito Mussolini came to power in 1922. Violence has long been regarded as 'a fundamental ingredient', as 'the actual substance' of Italian Fascism,[11] which developed as a paramilitary movement in the wake of the First World War. As Wolfgang Schieder pointed out decades ago, Fascism aimed not 'to convince or defeat its opponents, but to destroy them'.[12] The determination to smash opponents characterized the rise of the Fascist movement between 1920 and 1922 in response to the labour unrest of the immediate post-war period – the *biennio rosso* (the 'two red years' of 1919 and 1920) that marked the post-war apogee of Italian revolutionary socialism and echoed in new circumstances the sort of violent social protest that had been common in Italy before the war.[13] The Fascists advanced in northern and central Italy during the early 1920s, spreading violence and terror, with *spedizione punitive* of the *squadristi* against socialist targets: large numbers of Fascists – sometimes as many as 500 – would arrive in a village at night, locate the most prominent local socialists and then beat or kill them.[14] According to a newspaper correspondent in January 1921:

Every day punitive expeditions go out. The Fascist lorry arrives at a certain village aiming at a certain *capolega*. First they talk. Then, either the *capolega* gives in, or violence takes the place of persuasion. It almost always happens that the negotiations achieve their end. If not, it is the turn of the revolver.[15]

The Fascist campaigns of violence in 1921 and 1922 were largely successful in breaking the socialist leagues and, increasingly, challenging the power of the state. Political violence attracted support; intimidation worked. As Fascism began, so it remained: a politics of violence. Paul Corner has pointed out that 'throughout the *ventennio* – the twenty years of the regime – the politics of Fascism were always the politics of the bully; the Blackshirts never left anyone in doubt that violence against opponents was an acceptable method of action, a constituent part of Fascist "style", something frequently and proudly described as "exquisitely Fascist."'[16] The Fascist *squadristi* viewed violence not simply as a means to an end, but rather as a 'value on which to base the conduct of one's life'.[17] More generally, as Michael Ebner has shown, 'ordinary' political violence remained central to Fascist rule and repression in Italy throughout the two decades of Mussolini's dictatorship: 'Fascists and police, according to official sources, regularly "killed", "beat", "clubbed", "punched", "slapped", "kicked", "hit", and otherwise used spontaneous "force" and "acts of violence" against citizens.'[18] Violence, Ebner observes, was 'central to the ideology and practice of Fascism':

> The Fascists viewed violence as a vital force capable of bringing about a moral and physical regeneration, or 'reclamation' (*bonifica*), of the organic nation. Violence, for Fascists, was not merely a strategy or technique for achieving political goals, but also a 'positive' formative experience in its own right. In many ways, Fascists compensated for their relative ideological and programmatic vacuity by ascribing immense transformative power to interpersonal and military violence.[19]

Over and above this, violence was viewed as transformative: 'On perhaps no other issue was Mussolini so consistent: violence, inflicted *by* and *upon* his people, would transform the Italians from a bunch of undisciplined, chattering "mandolin players" into fearsome, conquering warriors.'[20] Such an aspiration appears both repellent and absurd today, but while Fascism failed to turn the Italian people into a nation of fearsome warriors, its ideology of violence did prove attractive to significant numbers of people in the wake of the First World War.

The affirmation of violence trumpeted by Italian Fascists was mirrored by their counterparts north of the Alps. Like Italian Fascism, German National Socialism was a politics of violence. It glorified violence, whether that be the violence of war or the violent pursuit of power within Germany; and its origins as a political movement lay in the violent domestic politics of the immediate post-war years, when numerous *politische Kampfbünde* (political fighting leagues) made a mark on German politics in a way that had had no parallel before 1914. While violence erupted on occasion when strikes were put down (as in the Ruhr in 1912, when clashes left several miners dead),[21] politics in Germany had not featured huge amounts of violence in the years before the First World War. However, the end of the war and the revolution of 1918–9 saw bloody confrontations across the country. In Berlin, unrest on the streets and left-wing challenges to the Social Democratic-led government were put down with force in early 1919, and in the Berlin *Blutwoche* ('Blood Week'), clashes between armed workers and *Freikorps* units led to the death of at least 1,200 people. In Munich, the suppression of the short-lived Bavarian Soviet Republic at the beginning of May 1919, when army and *Freikorps* units entered the city and ousted the Communist revolutionaries from government, saw deadly fighting, and hundreds were arrested and summarily executed in a campaign of terror that left at least 600 and probably more than 1,000 people dead.[22] In the Ruhr region, the violence peaked with the struggle of a workers' 'Red Army', which fought against *Freikorps* troops and for some weeks controlled a considerable area during the 'Ruhr War' that followed the collapse of the Kapp-Lüttwitz Putsch attempt in March 1920. That same spring, armed formations of workers fought against *Freikorps* in central Germany after the Kapp Putsch. And in the following year a Communist attempt at rebellion in the industrial region of Halle, Merseburg and Mansfeld was crushed by police and army units.

In addition to these explosions of violence, the early years of the Weimar Republic were marked by the assassination of numerous political figures, almost all of them on the left. These included not only Rosa Luxemburg and Karl Liebknecht (both killed in Berlin in January 1919) but also the Bavarian socialist revolutionary Kurt Eisner in Munich in February 1919; the Independent Socialist Hugo Haase, who was shot in Berlin on 8 October 1919 and died of his injuries on 7 November; Matthias Erzberger, the Catholic Centre Party politician (who had signed the armistice with the Allies in 1918) who was killed by two members of the right-wing death squad *Organisation Consul* at Bad Griesbach in the Black Forest on 26 August 1921; and Walther Rathenau, the Jewish Foreign Minister who was gunned down near his home in Berlin-Grünewald, also by members of the *Consul* organization, on the morning of 24 June 1922. This was only the prominent tip of a huge iceberg: more than 350 people were murdered in this epidemic of violence in Germany between 1919 and 1922, the 'four years of political murder' that comprised the early years of the Weimar Republic.[23]

The violence on Germany's streets during the early 1930s, as the National Socialist movement became the largest political movement that Germany had ever seen and organized hundreds of thousands of young men in its 'storm sections' (*Sturmabteilungen*, SA), did not reach the scale or intensity of the clashes in the immediate aftermath of the First World War.

Nevertheless, it was frightening enough, with countless confrontations as Stormtroopers battled with Communist and Socialist sympathizers on the streets, at political rallies, in taverns, in organized attacks and as a result of chance encounters. 'Every appearance of the SA was accompanied by violence, whether as the threat of a gathering of people prepared for violence [or] as concrete, physical violence in fights in halls or on the streets.'[24] They were meant to be intimidating, and they were. Marches through what was regarded as enemy territory were staged in order to challenge opponents and provoke violent confrontation. Joseph Goebbels famously wrote in an account, first published in 1932 and reprinted many times subsequently, of the rise of the Nazi movement in Berlin: 'The SA-man wants to fight, and he has a right to be led into battle. His existence only wins its justification by fighting. The SA without a fighting tendency is absurd and pointless.'[25] Such posturing not only struck a chord with the hundreds of thousands of young men who joined the movement's 'storm sections' during the early 1930s; it also met with the apparent approval – or at least the toleration – of supporters of the NSDAP from among the bourgeois electorate.[26] Through their violent street politics they could raise both the spectre of civil war and fears of a return to the chaotic events that had followed the collapse of the Empire in 1918, as well as appeal to a desperate desire for order.

The embrace of political violence in Weimar Germany was not a one-sided affair. The Communists encouraged violence as well, and much of their appeal to their proletarian supporters in Germany's urban slums lay in their willingness to use their fists when confronting their opponents: 'Smash the Fascists Wherever You Find Them!' was the cry that accompanied the substantial growth in support for the Communist Party during the early 1930s.[27] The willingness to provoke violent confrontation led to one of Weimar Germany's bloodiest incidents, when

German Communists in Berlin challenged a prohibition by (the Social Democratic-led) police on open-air demonstrations in 1929. The Communists, determined to demonstrate on May Day, responded to the ban with defiance and made standing their ground a matter of pride and principle: 'In the current situation any falling back in the face of reaction, any tactic of cowardly capitulation in the face of reaction represents a betrayal of the working class.'[28] The police, for their part, were prepared for confrontation, and had conducted training exercises for 'street and house-to-house fighting' in those proletarian districts of Berlin where the actual clashes later took place.[29] The result was the notorious *Blutmai* ('Blood May') of 1929, during which thirty-three civilians were killed and another 198 injured in five days of street warfare.[30] (The police, who were responsible for much of the violence, lost one dead and had forty-seven injured.)

During the early 1930s, with the explosive growth of the Stormtroopers organization, the Communists intensified their struggle against their political enemies on the right, and Berlin remained the frontline: in April 1931 the Communist Party newspaper *Die Rote Fahne* published a list of taverns in Berlin where formations of Stormtroopers were based, complete with addresses and telephone numbers, and claiming that 'self-defence is the right of all who are attacked'.[31] According to contemporary analyses by the Prussian Interior Ministry for the second half of 1932 and January 1933 (that is, until Hitler was appointed Reich Chancellor at the end of that month), Communists were classified as the 'attackers' in 38–45 per cent of confrontations and National Socialists in 32–42 per cent.[32] The Social Democrats, many of whose young male supporters joined the formation *Reichsbanner Schwarz-Rot-Gold*, also did not shy away from violent political confrontations (although the above-mentioned Interior Ministry analyses pointed to the *Reichsbanner* and the Social Democratic 'Iron Front' as 'attackers' in only about 6–10 per cent of incidents). Parties across the political spectrum found it necessary to organize squads to protect their rallies, and dozens of people were killed and hundreds injured in political clashes as the Weimar Republic disintegrated. Violence had become a ubiquitous feature of German politics.

In many respects, the Italian Fascist movement had provided a model for German National Socialists, and the violence of the two movements' strong-arm formations invites comparison.[33] Both Italian Fascism and German National Socialism were products and expressions of the new, violent politics in Europe that followed the First World War. Both applauded violence, which was welcomed rather than avoided. In both cases political violence was conceived first and foremost as a challenge to the left, and in both cases violence in the service of militant anti-communism did not fundamentally repel and indeed served to attract bourgeois support (despite the hostility to bourgeois attitudes often expressed by the squads). In both cases, violence served to promote group integration and was an expression of it, focusing the aggression of groups of predominantly young men against political enemies. Both drew upon an ideal of manliness, an expression of the perceived need to stand one's ground, to confront the enemy, to avenge attacks – a logic that provoked violent responses and thus made political violence self-perpetuating.[34] And in both cases, the politics of violence was rewarded, as the Italian Fascists and the German National Socialists were able to achieve power and establish brutal dictatorship.

While it was in Germany and Italy that Fascist movements which embraced violence both as a tactic and as a positive value actually captured power, the upsurge in organized political violence in inter-war Europe was by no means limited to them. Paramilitarism 'remained a central feature of inter-war European political cultures'.[35] It could be seen across the continent, from the legionnaires of the Romanian Iron Guard, the

Hungarian Iron Cross, and the Croatian Utasha in central and eastern Europe to Léon Degrelle's Belgian Rexists and the French *Croix de Feu* in western Europe. A frequent component of this violent politics was antisemitism, which overlapped with anti-Communism and was shared widely among the populations of Europe. As noted in Chapter III, the worst of the antisemitic violence occurred in the east, during the civil war that followed the Russian Revolution, when Jews (often equated with hated Bolsheviks) were subjected to appalling brutality; in pogroms in Ukraine between December 1918 and December 1919 between 50,000 and 60,000 Jews lost their lives.[36] If one can speak of a brutalization of civil society after the First World War, this is where it most clearly occurred.

Antisemitism continued to fuel violence in politics in eastern Europe throughout the inter-war period, and not just in Germany and Austria. In Poland, for example, during the economic crisis of the early 1930s, the nationalist 'Great Poland Camp' born of the National Democratic movement and founded by Roman Dmowski, turned to an extra-parliamentary politics that consisted largely of physical attacks by members of fighting squads, particularly against Jews.[37]

Important as they were, antisemitism and the effects of the First World War were far from the whole story, as the case of Spain suggests. In Spain, from which Jews had been expelled centuries earlier and which remained neutral during the 1914–1918 conflict, political violence had 'ebbed and flowed with the opening and closing of elections' during the late nineteenth and early twentieth centuries.[38] The violence increased with an upsurge in anarchist agitation ('propaganda by deed') at the end of the nineteenth century,[39] and flared up repeatedly after 1918. The years from 1918 to 1920, the so-called *trienio bolchevique* (the 'three Bolshevik years', 'which, as has sometimes been pointed out, was neither a *trienio* nor *bolchevique*'[40]), saw substantial unrest in the rural south. In the summer of 1923, violence by anarchists and communists played an important role in the collapse of the parliamentary system and helped to pave the way for the establishment of General Primo de Rivera's dictatorship by military coup in September of that year. However, the most significant surge in political violence was that which disfigured the Spanish Second Republic, proclaimed in 1931. During the early years of the Second Republic, to the end of 1933, the violence stemmed in the main from anarchist insurrections and the police response (which left over 200 people dead). The election campaign in the autumn of 1933 saw hundreds of instances of political violence that claimed the lives of thirty-four people,[41] and in 1934 the October workers' insurrection in Asturias led to the deaths of some 1,500 people. In 1936 dozens were killed in the campaign for the elections in February, and after the election victory of the Popular Front and again shortly before the outbreak of the civil war in July, waves of violence between left and right resulted in hundreds of deaths.[42]

The significance of the violence in Spanish politics during the 1920s and 1930s lies not just in the numbers of people who lost their lives, but also in the vocal support that violent politics elicited. Speaking at the *Teatro de la Comedia* in Madrid on 29 October 1933, when the right-wing Falange (the *Falange Española de las Juntas de Ofensiva Nacional Sindicalista*) was founded, José Antonio Primo de Rivera proclaimed that if Falangist aims were 'to be achieved in some cases by violence, then we do not halt before [committing] violence',[43] and in the first issue of the party newspaper of the Falange, he asserted that 'violence can be legal when employed for an ideal which justifies it'.[44] Perhaps more important than active support for political violence was the acceptance of it as civil war drew closer – that (as Manuel Álvarez Tardío observes of the bloody 1936 election campaign), 'at a time when political violence had become so commonplace, it is possible that a total of almost 100 dead or seriously injured did not, in itself, have a great impact on public opinion'.[45]

In republican France as well, political violence found its advocates and apologists. There the Dreyfus Affair had sparked widespread rioting at the end of the nineteenth century and, in the immediate aftermath of the First World War, left-wing militancy and strike action led to violence, including serious street-fighting in Paris on 1 May 1919.[46] During the inter-war period a number of extra-parliamentary leagues, which may or may not be characterized as 'Fascist', were active in French politics. These included the *Action française* (established before the First World War) and its youth movement the *Camelots du roi*, the *Jeunesses patriotes* (founded in 1924), and the ultra-nationalist *Croix de Feu* (the largest of the leagues), which was founded in 1927 and which drew its support in the first instance from among war veterans, organizing perhaps as many as 700,000 men in its paramilitary formations by 1935. The *Croix de Feu* and its leader Colonel François de la Roque took a seemingly ambivalent attitude towards violence, combining aggressive rhetoric with expressions of respect for legality while maintaining that its stance was essentially defensive and stopping well short of condemning violence.[47] Yet the *Croix de Feu*'s activities did spark violence, and violence was (as Kevin Passmore argues) 'central to the self-definition and political practice of Croix de Feu militants'.[48]

Although the political violence in France was less extensive than that which had occurred in Italy and Spain, nonetheless the unrest grew during the mid-1920s, as meetings were disrupted and fighting led to casualties, most notably in April 1925 when conflict between Communists and the *Jeunesses patriotes* left four people dead and many injured.[49] The most significant and best-known instance of political violence in inter-war France occurred during the following decade, however: with the anti-parliamentary rioting that followed demonstrations by right-wing leagues in Paris in February

1934, fourteen demonstrators attacking parliament were shot dead by police.

The violence of February 1934 was one occasion among many, albeit the most prominent, of political violence in France during the 1930s. Political meetings became the stage for ritualized conflict over who would control space, and there were numerous confrontations between rival political activists, often involving firearms. Serious incidents also took place in Brest and Limoges in 1935 and in Clichy in 1937. In Lille, brawls between rival groups became so frequent that the police referred to an 'atmosphere of battle',[50] and the French press on both sides of the political divide labelled the atmosphere in Paris as one of 'civil war'.[51] While the violence was not on the scale of that which accompanied the rise of Italian Fascism and German National Socialism, it became expected as part of political activity in inter-war France.

Britain seems an exception. By mid-twentieth century, the British, or at least the English, had come to regard themselves as essentially non-violent, and British politics was not marked by levels of political violence comparable to those seen in Italy or Germany after the First World War. Nevertheless, election campaigns before the First World War had frequently involved street fighting between supporters of opposing parties, and 'in truth the political elites were remarkably tolerant of violence when they thought they might have the upper hand' – although this stopped short of lethal violence: 'Killing or maiming an opponent was simply not "done".'[52] In 1919, serious rioting broke out at Victory Day (19 July) parades, most notably in Luton, where at the subsequent trial of the ringleaders, the public prosecutor attributed the violence to 'Bolshevism, anarchy, drunkenness and animality'.[53] Furthermore, as Adrian Gregory has pointed out, 'English self-congratulation over the lack of a post-war *Freikorps* mentality needs to be heavily qualified by the observation "except in Ireland"'.[54] The 1926 General Strike was accompanied by some violence, as were Communist attempts to organize the unemployed in the early 1930s. Nevertheless – to cite Gregory once again – 'to write of political violence in inter-war Britain is, in any normal terms, to discuss a striking absence'.[55]

Some insight into this 'striking absence' may be gathered from the failure of British Fascism. During the 1930s Britain did not completely escape the rise of the radical right and its affinity with violence. In October 1932, Oswald Mosley founded the British Union of Fascists (BUF), which 'adopted all the main techniques of the German Nazis and appeared, for a time, to be capable of emulating their success'.[56] However, Britain's Fascists ultimately proved unable to gain a mass following, and the failure of Mosley's 'spectacular but ineffective assault on democracy'[57] was due in no small degree to his embrace of violence. While the perception that the BUF always, or even necessarily, provoked the violence that surrounded their activities has been challenged,[58] the black 'Action' uniforms and the aggressive posturing of Mosley's supporters were hardly designed to create a peaceful impression. During the mid-1930s, Communists in particular sought to disrupt BUF rallies by organizing disturbances that sometimes led to severe injuries. As Philip Piratin, a Jewish Communist activist and leading opponent of Mosley in London's East End (and from 1945 to 1950 the Communist Member of Parliament for Mile End) proudly put it, 'we had taken steps to ensure that [...] they would not be able to hold their meetings'.[59]

Two well-publicized incidents ultimately undermined the political fortunes of the British Union of Fascists: the violence directed by blackshirted stewards against hecklers at a BUF rally attended by 15,000 people at Olympia on 7 June 1934, and the 'Battle of Cable Street' on 4 October 1936, when a march by the now openly antisemitic BUF through a largely Jewish area in London's East End was met by a huge number of Jewish, socialist and Communist demonstrators and developed into a running battle that included the police and left at least seventy people injured. The first cost Mosley the sympathy of some conservatives and the support of Lord Rothermere and his *Daily Mail*, which subsequently turned its back on the Fascist leader;[60] the second led the government to pass the 1936 Public Order Act, which prohibited 'the wearing of uniforms in connection with political objects' and 'the maintenance by private persons of associations of military or similar character' and restricted political activity that threatened violence.[61] By the time the Public Order Act came into force in 1937, however, the BUF was already in decline. Mosley's Fascists became associated increasingly with practices regarded as 'foreign' and 'alien' to Britain, which relegated them to the fringes of British political life; and the overwhelming majority of the British public proved unwilling to support a movement associated with political violence.

While the United Kingdom may have been something of an exception, the upsurge in political violence in inter-war Europe presents a remarkable contrast to what occurred during the latter part of the twentieth century. In most of the European continent and in North America, the sorts of political violence that had been prevalent in inter-war Europe – involving large numbers of people and tolerated and even approved by many more – were conspicuous largely by their absence. Of course there were exceptions, notably in the immediate aftermath of the Second World War; and the outbursts of home-grown terrorism in the 1970s in Germany and Italy, as well as the violent campaigns waged by paramilitary groups in Northern Ireland and the Basque country, demonstrate that not all was peace and sweet reason even in Europe during the second half of the twentieth century. Nevertheless, the general context in which politics was conducted had altered significantly, and diminished the sources of and scope for political violence.

The Second World War saw the defeat of countries that had been in the grip of political movements with ideologies that glorified violence. After the Second World War there were fewer genuinely multinational states in Europe (and the most multinational, Yugoslavia, broke up in a series of bloody wars in the 1990s). During the second half of the twentieth century, therefore, European states were stronger internally and, on the whole, more stable than they had been in the years after the First World War, and consequently enjoyed greater legitimacy. The Cold War division of Europe lent an appearance of permanence to political structures from the 1950s through the 1980s, until eastern European state socialism collapsed. And the western world enjoyed a period of unprecedented economic growth – the 'thirty glorious years' (a phrase used to describe the development of France from 1945 to 1975,[62] but which might be applied to much of western Europe) – that led to vastly improved living standards for the mass of the population and gave Europeans a much greater stake in maintaining political stability. These changes provided the context for a diminution of political violence and an increased intolerance of violence in politics. This is not to argue that political violence completely disappeared or that it no longer found admirers. However, parties and movements that perpetrated and/or tolerated political violence generally found themselves at the fringes of politics in the western world, not at the centre.

One may respond to this assertion by observing that nevertheless, in many countries, violence and intimidation have dominated the political process during the second half of the twentieth century and the early years of the twenty-first. Even a cursory reading of newspapers from the second half of the twentieth century and the early years of the twenty-first reveals huge numbers of reports of violent politics, often in Africa, Asia and Latin America. Violence remains an oft-repeated and oft-expected feature of election campaigns in various states around the world. Accounts, for example, of the elections in Bangladesh in January 2014, where dozens of people were killed during a bitter campaign,[63] or recent spates in Mexico of 'threats, assaults and sometimes outright killings [of candidates for public office] by criminal gangs, political rivals and other opponents',[64] testify to the continuing prevalence of political violence in the contemporary world. A recent description of how 'many politicians have taken advantage of rampant poverty and unemployment to recruit young men, who intimidate and even kill their opponents' supporters',[65] from a report filed in January 2003 (ahead of the elections of that year) about political violence and elections in Nigeria, contains disturbing parallels with what occurred in parts of Europe (e.g. Italy, Spain and Germany) before the Second World War.

Of course, violence did not vanish altogether from politics in Europe or North America either, but remained a serious public concern in a number of states. Prominent among these has been Italy, where violence became a worrying feature of politics during the 1970s, with the terror campaigns of the *Brigate Rosse* (Red Brigades) on the left and of the *Ordine Nero* (Black Order) on the right. These organizations posed a serious threat to public safety and security and committed some spectacular acts of violence and terror – culminating in the kidnap and subsequent murder of former Prime Minister Aldo Moro by the *Brigate Rosse* in March 1978,[66] and the bombing of the Bologna Main Railway Station on 2 August 1980 which was attributed to the neo-Fascist terrorist organization *Nuclei Armati Rivoluzionari* and which resulted in the deaths of eighty-five people. This period saw public displays of support for political violence in Italy, including demonstrations in September 1977 in Bologna, where 'at least ten thousand voices shouted "Viva Curcio"' (for Renato Curcio, the co-founder of the *Brigate Rosse* and at that time in prison), and in a school in Rome the announcement that a local

119

Christian Democratic leader had been attacked 'was greeted with applause'.[67] Curcio himself asserted that the revolutionary protest movement of the Italian extra-parliamentary left had enjoyed the active support of thousands of people and the admiration of many more.[68]

Nevertheless, the murder of Aldo Moro and the Bologna bombing overwhelmingly shocked the Italian public, and marked the beginning of the end for the politics of open violence. In Bologna, the station bombing was followed by mass demonstrations against the violence in the Piazza Maggiore in the centre of the old city, and the murder of Aldo Moro led not only to more concerted and successful police action against the Red Brigades but also to the distancing of other left-wing organizations from Red Brigade terrorism. It is revealing that both the Italian Communist Party (PCI) and the neo-Fascist Italian Social Movement (MSI) were concerned during the 1970s to distance themselves from the violence of the extreme left and the extreme right. In contrast to the rise of Mussolini and the Fascist movement in the 1920s, the path of the MSI (subsumed into the National Alliance under Gianfranco Fini in 1995) into government with Silvio Berlusconi was not through an affirmation or glorification of political violence. 'The planners of the "Italian civil war of the 1980s"'[69] were destined to be disappointed. Few were prepared to follow them down the path of violence.

In Spain, too, the attraction of political violence faded. With the re-establishment of Spanish democracy in 1976, in the wake of the long-awaited death of Francisco Franco, political organizations and the wider public largely turned their backs on violence. While democratic Spain continued to be plagued by political violence, this was much less prolific than during the Second Republic of the 1930s and had much narrower bases of support. According to Stanley Payne, writing in 1990:

Broad consensus soon developed in a large part of public opinion, and – apart from the Socialist dalliance with military conspirators in 1980 – all major and nearly all minor political groups have firmly rejected any tactic of violence. [...] Since 1976, violence has been limited to small fringe groups: the Basque ETA, which enjoys the support of only a small minority in two very distinct provinces without counterpart in the rest of Spain; the Spanish terrorist extreme left (FRAP and GRAPO), without any real electoral support at all; and tiny groups of the extreme right, equally bereft of political backing.[70]

ETA continued its campaign of terror, which claimed the lives of some 800 people, for four decades, before it too moved away from violent tactics. In 2011, ETA declared an end to its armed campaign, and in a remarkable scene at the beginning of 2014, roughly seventy recently released prisoners from the Basque separatist group read a statement in which they expressed regret at having carried out acts of violence.[71] It may be that the shock of the violence of the Spanish Civil War and the severe repression under Franco in the years that followed,[72] followed by the stability of Spanish democracy within the European Union, served a function similar to that performed by the extreme shock of violence in Germany as a result of Nazism and war.[73] Or it may be that changed attitudes elsewhere in western Europe proved infectious, that in a European community where political violence was condemned almost universally, it was no longer possible to assert (as the tourism slogan during the 1960s had it) that 'Spain is Different'. Whatever the cause, and despite its tortured history, in this regard Spain came to conform to a wider European pattern.

The political violence and terrorism in parts of continental Europe during the 1970s – most prominently the Red Army Faction (the Baader-Meinhof group and its successors) in West

Germany and the Red Brigades in Italy – were offshoots of the student radicalism of the late 1960s that had spun off into a violent politics of fantasy in the 1970s. Hopes that violent actions would somehow spark revolution, that the radicals could be urban guerrillas able to attract popular support among the working class, proved completely illusory, and the path of violence led to their isolation, suppression and dissolution in the 1980s. Although the security problems that these terrorist groupings posed during the 1970s were hardly trivial, we should not overlook that in the end the most important feature of their history was their complete failure either to attract broad popular support for their violent politics or to succeed in any but their most limited objectives. While their actions comprised a significant outburst of political violence in Europe a generation after the end of the Second World War, it is their lack of resonance and their failure that ultimately are most important in understanding their place in the politics of violence during the second half of the twentieth century.

Mainstream politics and successful politicians rejected violence. Violence in politics did not completely disappear in the West during the late twentieth century, but its status changed. No longer did political parties manage to mobilize large numbers of men in strong-arm squads. No longer did political leaders of major parties, at least in Europe, identify with political violence as Adolf Hitler had done in the wake of the Potempa murder in August 1932. After the Second World War it became almost unthinkable for a leader of a mainstream political party to proclaim solidarity with street fighters and defend the actions of murderers.

Where does this leave violence in politics in North America? The First World War did not constitute a fundamental break in American politics as it had done in Europe. Paramilitary politics did not gain traction in the United States after the war; the structure and rhythm of the American political process were not interrupted fundamentally by the war; and much of the American population enjoyed a degree of material prosperity during the 1920s far greater than that enjoyed by the vast majority of Europeans.

Yet there were some parallels with developments on the other side of the Atlantic. One American political scientist, keen to calculate correlations between war and various categories of public violence in the United States, has asserted that 'the empirical evidence indicates that World War I is associated with a strong (603 per cent) increase in political violence' in the US, and that 'the post-World War I years [were] charged with a statistically significant (290 per cent) increase in political violence'.[74] This is seen largely as 'the result of actions taken by government agencies and other status quo groups against leftists, farmers and pacifists protesting the war and selective service laws', and 'due, in large part, to the sustained concern of national administrative elites with repressing groups or individuals espousing communist, socialist or anarchist views'.

While this reflects a rather different understanding of political violence than that committed by fascist strong-arm squads in inter-war Europe, and although the issues that provoked political violence in the United States may have been different to those in Europe, it suggests that violence was far from foreign to American politics during the first half of the twentieth century. It was not unknown for elections in the US to be marred by violence and intimidation, not least in order to prevent non-whites from exercising their right to vote. A most distressing case occurred in November 1920 in Florida, where white supremacists prevented African-Americans from voting in what has been described as the bloodiest election day in modern American history: in the worst of the violence, African-Americans who attempted to vote in Ocoee (near Orlando) were driven out of the town, their houses burned and dozens were killed.[75] More generally, the explosive growth of the Ku Klux Klan during the mid-1920s demonstrated a broad underlying tolerance of violent politics. (For a short time the KKK became a mass organization with four to five million members, with support not just in the South but also, and especially, in the Midwest, where in many towns it was able to organize a substantial proportion of the entire – white, Protestant – population.)[76] And, as has been noted in Chapter I, lynching continued to be a frequent occurrence in the American South during the 1920s.

While extreme outbursts of political violence largely disappeared in the United States after the Second World War, during the 1950s and 1960s advocates of civil-rights campaigns were often targets of vicious and sometimes fatal attacks.[77] Nevertheless, this should not lead us to assume that there was uniform support or tolerance for brutality and violence against civil-rights activists, even in the segregated American South. Looking back from his vantage point of the early twenty-first century, Joseph Luders points out: 'Forgotten among the memories of the harassment, beatings and murder of peaceful demonstrators are the differing responses to protest across the South. While all southern states met NAACP desegregation lawsuits and civil-rights demonstrations with various forms of legalistic repression, few seemed to countenance widespread white violence or police brutality against civil-rights protesters.'[78] Business and political elites often realized that violence in their communities would generate negative publicity and have negative economic consequences, and they had an interest in reaching peaceful compromise.[79] Without this realization among some, although certainly not all, of the opponents of the civil-rights movement, it would have been far more difficult for the campaign to succeed. The non-violent tactics of Martin Luther King Jr could meet with success only where people were ultimately unprepared to resort to or to tolerate violent politics.[80]

Nevertheless, not everyone active in the American civil-rights movement was prepared to maintain a commitment to non-violence, and in the second half of the 1960s calls for violent responses to the hostility and repression faced by African-Americans grew louder. Yet for all the publicity and concern they aroused in the late 1960s, calls for violence did not generate broad support or lead to much success. The short history of the Student Non-violent Co-ordinating Committee (SNCC), which was established in 1960 and whose activist volunteers played a leading role (and sometimes risked their lives) as the 'shock troops'[81] of the desegregation campaigns in the American South, provides a prime example of the trajectory from non-violence and rapid growth to an embrace of violence and political oblivion.[82]

SNCC's 'Statement of Purpose', originally adopted in 1960, began with the unequivocal statement: 'We affirm the philosophical or religious ideal of non-violence as the foundation of our purpose, the presupposition of our faith, and the manner of our action.'[83] However, influenced by the violence that often met campaigns with which SNCC volunteers were involved and by impatience and disillusionment with government responses to demands for full civil rights, by the mid-1960s SNCC activists were turning away from the organization's initial non-violent creed and towards a militant ideology of 'Black Power'. White staff and volunteers were removed from the organization and funding from contributors fell steeply,[84] while a new leadership – first Stokely Carmichael as chairman in 1966 and his successor H. Rap Brown a year later – embraced violence, with Brown famously proclaiming at a news conference in July 1967 that 'violence is necessary. It is as American as cherry pie'.[85] (Brown subsequently converted to Islam in prison, and today is serving a life sentence for the shooting of a policeman.) In July 1969, SNCC dropped 'non-violent' from its name, becoming the 'Student National Coordinating Committee',[86] by which time the organization was withering. By the early 1970s it had largely ceased to exist.

One disillusioned former SNCC activist described the civil-rights movement at the end of the 1960s as mired in 'self-absorption and self-delusion with its ultra-romantic notions of armed revolution succeeding in urban America'.[87] The embrace of violence may have had some appeal in the heated atmosphere of the United States in the late 1960s, but in a functioning democracy it soon proved a path to political oblivion – as did the embrace of violence during the 1970s in western Europe by terrorist groupings, which also found themselves mired in 'self-absorption and self-delusion' and in 'ultra-romantic notions of armed revolution'.

The violence that met the civil-rights campaigns during the 1950s and 1960s, and the unrest that erupted in many American cities between 1964 and 1970, aroused tremendous concern about levels of violence in American politics and public life. A prominent expression of this concern was the establishment by President Lyndon Johnson of the 'National Commission on the Causes and Prevention of Violence' in June 1968, following the wave of urban rioting that had spread across the United States and the assassinations of Martin Luther King Jr and Robert Kennedy. (The commission was disbanded at the end of 1969.) In the autumn of 1971, Lloyd Cutler, who had been a member of the commission, noted that he and other former members 'felt that in the various areas of violence we covered there has seen little if any abatement', voiced concern about 'a substantial rise in terrorism as seen in the polarization of young blacks, in the prison uprisings, and in the ambush shooting of policemen', and asserted that if the then present trends were to continue 'we are going to make Belfast look like nothing in another decade'.[88] There may have seemed grounds for such pessimism in the early 1970s. In fact, however, in the decade that followed, Cutler's prediction did not come true. America's cities did not 'make Belfast look like nothing', and if violence threatened the health of urban America it was in the shape of violent crime, not of political violence. Nevertheless, Cutler's comments should be taken seriously not as a prediction but as a reflection of the fears about violence in American politics during one of the country's more turbulent periods.

So where are we now? Fears about violence remain, but political violence is not something that attracts support or threatens America's stability. It is perhaps a sign of the times that the Ku Klux Klan, which has been associated with racist violence for much of its history, has sought recently to participate in 'Adopt-A-Highway' programmes in various places in the United States.[89] This has been, according to one critic (speaking about an application by the Klan to 'adopt a highway' in Union County, Georgia in 2012), 'another attempt by the Klan to somehow portray itself as a kinder, gentler group rather than the terrorist organization that it has historically been'.[90] An organization once notorious for burning crosses, intimidating political opponents and promoting racist violence now wanted to demonstrate its members' willingness to be good citizens by picking up litter along America's highways. It seems that neither the Klan nor its opponents want to be identified with violence. While concern about political polarization may have grown in the United States in recent years, political violence remains taboo. The American journalist Adam Serwer recently summed up the position well:

Political violence in the United States has never been more illegitimate. There was a time when a member of Congress could walk into the Senate and beat a political rival senseless and walk away unmolested. The South was once a place of unrestrained terrorist violence conducted with the tacit approval of local authorities. Even when those authorities were brave or responsible enough to press charges, securing

127

guilty verdicts would be difficult because of a local culture willing to accept crimes committed in service to white supremacy. We live in a time where no major political movement would be willing to openly justify such behaviour.[91]

The political violence that had been prevalent in many parts of the United States until the second half of the twentieth century arose to a large degree from the apartheid regime in place in the American South, a system that was a legacy of slavery and civil war and that really was dismantled only after the Second World War. In this it differed from the sorts of political violence that flourished in Italy or Germany during the inter-war years. Nevertheless, Serwer's observation about political life in America appears apposite for much of Europe today as well: political violence has never been more illegitimate.

Certainly there have been people and groups who in recent decades have looked upon violence favourably as a tactic for achieving political ends, who have regarded collective violence as a 'form of protest, a quest for justice'[92] or as an expression of 'real grievances over underlying social, economic, and political issues'.[93] However, mainstream political and public opinion has stood overwhelmingly against this violence, and few serious political figures in the West now would seek to justify political violence in a democracy. The dominant view seems to be that 'Violence is Our Enemy' – the title of an article by the writer and political activist George Monbiot in *The Guardian* on 1 May 2001, commenting on the violent May Day demonstrations expected in London at that time and aiming his fire at 'anything-goes direct action' which supposedly had displaced 'non-violent direct action'.[94]

How can we explain the apparent decline of political violence and the clear decline in its attractiveness, at least in the West? A few years before his death, the historical sociologist Charles Tilly wrote in his book, *The Politics of Collective Violence*:

With two major qualifications, collective violence generally declines with democratization. Democratic regimes, on the average, harbour less collective violence than undemocratic regimes. Broadening of political participation, extension and equalization of political rights, regularization of non-violent means for making claims, and increasing readiness of third parties to intervene against violent resolution of disputes over claims all dampen the processes that generate violent contention.[95]

Leaving aside the difficult matter of how to quantify and compare violence in different countries, democratic or otherwise, the characteristics that Tilly identifies seem to have been important in shaping attitudes towards political violence. They have helped to create an environment and a public sphere in which violence and threats of violence are less likely to be considered necessary and less likely to be tolerated or condoned. As non-violent political behaviour becomes more legitimate and offers better chances for achieving aims, political violence becomes relegated to the fringes. Consequently, political violence is not tolerated or affirmed, but feared and rejected.

However, democracy in and of itself is insufficient as an explanation, for the outbreaks of widely tolerated political violence in post-First World War Italy, in the Spanish Second Republic and in Germany's Weimar Republic all occurred in countries where a democratic constitution was in place. Other factors need to be considered as well:

Prosperity. The decline in the prominence and the acceptability of violence in political life in the western world after the Second World War coincided with one of the most remarkable increases in economic well-being that the world has ever seen. The poverty and desperation that afflicted tens of millions of people in the first half of the twentieth century were, to a considerable extent, mitigated in the second half of the century. Nevertheless, poverty alone cannot explain levels of political violence, as in most European countries politics was more violent in the early twentieth century than they had been in the late nineteenth, when incomes had generally been lower. It also is a matter of how material resources are distributed, and of levels of unemployment. The mass unemployment during the inter-war period that left millions of young men with large amounts of time on their hands but without perspectives for developing a career or establishing a family, was not replicated in Europe and North America after the Second World War. Political violence largely involved young men, and the remarkable economic growth and increasing prosperity during the second half of the twentieth century allowed young men more easily to fill their time constructively and peacefully, in employment and in family life.

Stability. Alongside economic prosperity, western Europe (like the United States) enjoyed a remarkable degree of political stability during the second half of the twentieth century. (In a peculiar sense eastern Europe did as well, from the imposition of Soviet-style Communism until its collapse in 1989–1991.) This contrasted starkly with Europe after the First World War, as well as with many countries in Asia, Africa and Latin America through the second half of the twentieth century. Political violence has thrived in environments in which mass politics developed during a period of flux and when state structures were new and unstable. As Hannah Arendt observed, 'violence appears where power is in jeopardy'.[96] Where an underlying consensus about how politics should be conducted is lacking and where confidence in the strength and stability of political institutions is weak, political violence becomes more easily accepted and thus more likely. In this regard Weimar Germany resembled 1980s Turkey or Egypt after 2011 more than it did the Federal Republic of Germany since the 1950s.

Legitimacy. Political and constitutional stability both rests upon and reinforces legitimacy, whereas political violence is both a challenge to political legitimacy and a symptom of its absence. Political violence in Europe during the first half of the twentieth century erupted most prominently in countries where the legitimacy of political and constitutional systems was contested (e.g. in Germany), and it found little acceptance where the state enjoyed broad legitimacy (e.g. in Britain). Hannah Arendt drew the distinction between power, which rests on legitimacy, and violence, which 'can be justifiable, but [...] never will be legitimate'.[97] Where a political system is powerful and enjoys legitimacy, violence finds no legitimate place.

Pluralism. Not only the legitimacy of the state and the political structure but also the perceived legitimacy of competing political views, ideologies and organizations is necessary for an environment in which political violence does not thrive. Just as Italian Fascism aimed not 'to convince or defeat its opponents, but to destroy them', so most perpetrators of political violence have been unwilling to accept the legitimacy of their opponents' opinions. The success of non-violent politics rests ultimately on the acceptance of political pluralism. Political violence is the enemy of pluralism and pluralism is the enemy of political violence.

These factors not only distinguish attitudes in Europe during the second half of the twentieth century from those during the first, but also often frame how politics in the 'rest' has come to be regarded in the West. Political violence is often seen as endemic to Africa, the Middle East and South Asia, not to Europe and North America.[98] While they may be a product of a Euro-centric myopia, perceptions of difference in behaviour and attitudes with regard to political violence colour the ways in which the 'rest' have been perceived and understood in the western world, often as a backward and uncivilized domain where violence still plays a central role in politics. The broad rejection of political violence that emerged in the western world as a consequence of a set of fortuitous (and quite possibly reversible) circumstances that arose after the terrible bloodshed of the Second World War thus is read as a measure of progress in politics. In this way, changes in the attitudes towards political violence have framed not only how people in the West regard politics in their own countries and themselves, but also the ways in which they have come to view the nature of politics else-where.

V

War

It is one of the most famous and oft-quoted interviews of an American soldier. On the evening of 24 November 1969, while the trial of Lieutenant William Calley for his role in the massacre at My Lai of March 1968 was underway,[1] the newscaster Mike Wallace interviewed Paul Meadlo on nationwide television. The story of the massacre had been publicized just a couple of weeks before by the investigative journalist Seymour Hersh (who subsequently won a Pulitzer Prize as a result). Meadlo had been a member of 'Charlie Company', which had been sent in December 1967 to Vietnam and in January to Quang Ngai Province, where it formed part of a unit deployed to put pressure on the Viet Cong in an area of the province referred to as 'Pinkville'. The company was commanded by Captain Ernest Medina, and among its platoon leaders was the 24-year-old Lieutenant William Calley. Meadlo, who lost his foot in a landmine explosion on the day after the massacre, described to Wallace how on 16 March 1968 the unit had rounded up Vietnamese villagers in the village of My Lai and killed hundreds of men, women and children:

A. [...] And we all huddled them up. We made them squat down, and Lieutenant Calley came over and said, 'You know what to do with them, don't you?' And I said Yes. So I took it for granted that he just wanted us to watch them. And he came back about 10 or 15 minutes later, and said, 'How come you ain't killed them yet?' And I told him that I didn't think you wanted us to kill them, that you just wanted us to guard them. He said, 'No, I want them dead.' So—

Q. He told this to all of you, or to you particularly?

A. Well, I was facing him. So, but the other three, four guys heard it, and so he stepped back about 10, 15 feet, and he started shooting them. And he told me to start shooting, I poured about four clips into the group.

Q. You fire four clips from your ...

A. M-16.

Q. And that's about – how many clips – I mean how many ...

A. I carried seventeen rounds to each clip.

Q. So you fired something like sixty-seven shots ...

A. Right.

Q. And you killed how many? At that time?

A. Well, I fired them on automatic, so you can't – you just spray the area on them and so you can't know how many you killed 'cause they were going so fast. So I might have killed ten or fifteen of them.

Q. Men, women and children?

A. Men, women and children.

Q. And babies?

A. And babies.[2]

This was one of the most famous exchanges of the Vietnam War era, and one that found its way onto the most famous anti-war poster of the time: 'Q: And babies? A: And babies.' It has been described as 'the question that changed America'.[3]

The shock at this revelation was widespread, and at the end of the interview Mike Wallace formulated the unanswerable question:

Q. Obviously, the thought that goes through my mind – I spent time over there, and I killed in the second war, and so forth. But the thought that goes through your mind is, we've raised such a dickens about what the Nazis did, or what the Japanese did, but particularly what the Nazis did in the Second World War, the brutalization and so forth, you know. It's hard for a good many Americans to understand that young, capable, American boys could line up old men, women and children and babies and shoot them down in cold blood. How do you explain that?

A. I wouldn't know.

Reflecting on his visit to the Meadlo house in rural Indiana to investigate the massacre, Seymour Hersh wrote of Paul Meadlo's mother: 'She looked at me, and she said – very angry and very low – she said, "I gave them a good boy and they sent me back a murderer." [...] And the bottom line is, this is what war is.'[4]

The massacre at My Lai, the trial and conviction of William Calley, and the televised interview with Wallace, thrust America's Vietnam War into the public consciousness with even greater intensity than had been the case hitherto. The American news magazines *Time* and *Newsweek* made the massacre their cover story, and in the week after the Meadlo interview was broadcast, *Life* magazine published a lengthy feature article on 'The Massacre at Mylai', which included numerous disturbing photographs by Ronald Haeberle of the corpses of the Vietnamese victims.[5] Of course, by that time America's military campaign in Vietnam had already become deeply divisive, provoking massive popular protest and leading to President Lyndon Johnson's decision not to seek re-election in 1968. The Tet Offensive launched by the North Vietnamese and the Viet Cong at the end of January 1968 had severely dented confidence in the United States that the war could be won. The violence of the war and the suffering it was causing had been widely reported, with journalists enjoying an access to the battlefield that was unprecedented.

Nevertheless, results of opinion polling conducted in April 1971 suggest rather ambivalent feelings about the perpetrators and cast doubt upon the idea that the publicity given to the My Lai massacre suddenly altered Americans' attitudes about the violence unleashed during war. Seventy-eight per cent of respondents to a telephone survey conducted for President Nixon across the United States disagreed with the decision of the military court to find Calley guilty of murder and to sentence him to life imprisonment, while a mere 7 per cent agreed; 51 per cent thought that Nixon should free Calley and a further 28 per cent thought that the President should substantially reduce his sentence.[6]

My Lai was not unique. Massacres of civilians and of prisoners have been a feature of war. They occurred in the First and Second World Wars, in the Russian Civil War, in the Yugoslav wars of the 1990s, and they are occurring in the Syrian Civil War as I write. What made the My Lai massacre noteworthy was the extraordinarily wide exposure that it received at the time, the effect that it had on public discussion in the country whose soldiers were guilty of the atrocity, and the way the reactions to it reflected contemporary attitudes about military violence.

War is violence. Those who volunteer or are conscripted to make war become practitioners of violence. Their job is to apply violence against those defined as the enemy, to wound and kill, to disable and destroy. This has been a persistent feature of warfare, from ancient times to today. So one may ask: what, if anything, has changed over the past century? Have the world wars, the explosion of military violence during the first half of the twentieth century, and the depressing catalogue of military conflicts since 1945 made a significant difference to the ways in which military violence has been regarded and applied? Obviously, the answers to such questions depend on where one looks. However, there are indications – such as the shock at the murderous violence committed by American soldiers against Vietnamese civilians in 1968, as expressed by Mike Wallace and Paul Meadlo's mother – that attitudes indeed may have changed.

Towards the end of the twentieth century, some historians – notably Joanna Bourke and Niall Ferguson in their discussions of British soldiers during the First World War – attracted considerable attention by writing of soldiers' enjoyment at participating in lethal violence. Ferguson put it bluntly: 'Many men simply took pleasure in killing'; 'Men kept fighting because they wanted to.'[7] Coming after numerous studies of the experiences of soldiers of the Great War which tended to view them as the objects rather than as subjects of violence, Bourke and Ferguson challenged the dominant conception of soldiers – at least of those who fought on the Western Front during the Great War – as victims of horrific violence. They may have been reluctant to admit it publicly, but quite a few soldiers no doubt shared the feelings of the French veteran of the First World War who wrote in 1936:

At times, I [...] who have never punched anyone, who loathes disorder and brutality, took pleasure in killing. When we crawled towards the enemy during a raid, a grenade in our hand and a knife in our teeth, like cut-throats, we felt fear in our gut, and yet an ineluctable force urged us on. Taking the enemy by surprise in his trench, jumping on him, enjoying the terror of a man who doesn't believe in the devil yet suddenly sees him dive to the ground! That barbarous, horrendous moment had a unique flavour for us, a morbid appeal; we were like those unfortunate drug addicts who know the magnitude of the risk but can't keep themselves from taking more poison.[8]

Although soldiers tend to be decorated for acts of sacrifice rather than for success at killing, as Joanna Bourke put it in the opening sentence of *An Intimate History of Killing*: 'The characteristic act of men at war is not dying, it is killing.'[9]

Such a thesis is not completely new. In 1970, the American philosopher Glenn Gray (who had been a member of a counter-intelligence unit during the Second World War and who had witnessed fighting at that time in Italy and southern France) claimed that 'many men both hate and love combat' and experience the 'delight of destruction [...] thousands of youths who never suspected the presence of such an impulse in themselves have learned in military life the mad excitement of destroying.'[10] And it is worth remembering that nearly two centuries ago Carl von Clausewitz wrote of 'a hostile feeling that is kindled by the combat itself; for an act of violence which anyone commits upon us by order of his superior, will excite in us a desire to retaliate and be revenged on him, sooner than on the superior power at whose command the act was done. This is human, or animal if we will; still it is so.'[11]

Nevertheless, the supposition that 'many men simply took pleasure in killing' during the First World War may need to be qualified somewhat, since at least on the Western Front almost all of the fighting and killing was the result not of face-to-face combat but rather of impersonal and anonymous destruction at a distance due to artillery and machine-gun fire.[12] Artillery shelling was directed not at individuals but at areas on a predetermined grid, and even machine gunners did not necessarily aim at individual soldiers.[13] (Roughly three quarters of the French and German soldiers – and presumably of the British soldiers as well – who were wounded during the First World War were wounded by artillery fire, and about 16 per cent by infantry ammunition; just 0.1 per cent of the injuries were caused by sabres, daggers and bayonets. These percentages can be taken as indicative of causes of death as well as of injury.)[14] As Benjamin Ziemann has observed, 'the artilleryman's activity was marked by the invisibility of the enemy'.[15] However, for the purposes of the argument presented in this book, perhaps more important than the degree to which the joy-of-killing thesis is correct is the discomfort that it arouses. The notion not only that war is about killing but also that those who engage in the violence may actually take pleasure in the act, has become difficult to face. The conclusion may be correct in many cases, but we don't like it.

It is noteworthy that the First World War – and particularly the war on the Western Front – has occupied so prominent a position in arguments put forward about soldiers' reactions to the violence of war. Although roughly half the armies, the fighting and the casualties of the First World War were not in the trenches of Flanders and northern France, and although even in the West it was the periods of a war of movement (in the war's first few months, and in the spring of 1918) that saw armies taking the highest casualties,[16] the horrors of trench warfare provided ample evidence that war was not to be applauded but to be condemned. Given what occurred in 1916 at Verdun and the Somme, where hundreds of thousands of men were killed or wounded in battles where there was almost no gain in territory, it could hardly be otherwise. Thus the First World War in the West seems to have become the benchmark for understanding what modern war came to signify during the twentieth century: mass violence and senseless sacrifice. It also marked the point where, in retrospect, those who fought came to be regarded

overwhelmingly as victims of violence. Violence became brack-
eted with victimhood, both in the popular imagination and in
much of the historiography.[17]

The place of the First World War in our understanding of military violence and of attitudes towards violence and war needs
to be examined critically. In an interview that was published in
2002 and that stressed the huge casualties resulting from a succession of civil wars after the Second World War, Charles Tilly
pointed to the 'shifting patterns of violence' as a result of war
over the course of the twentieth century.[18] He asserted, correctly,
that 'over the century as a whole, the proportion of war deaths
suffered by civilians rose startlingly'. However, the starting
point given for this shift – the First World War – needs to be considered in context. Tilly based his claim upon the assertion by
Simon Chesterman, in a volume edited for the International
Peace Academy (now the International Peace Institute, and
linked to the United Nations), that 'in World War I only 5 per
cent of all casualties were civilians: in World War II that number
was 50 per cent; and in conflicts through the 1990s, civilians
constituted up to 90 per cent or more of those killed, with a high
proportion being women and children'.[19] This observation,
while it draws attention to the ferociously violent nature of civil
wars during the second half of the twentieth century, raises
important questions with regard to the use of the First World
War (or of the two world wars together) as a baseline for meas-
uring wartime violence.

First, the history of violence in war obviously did not begin
with the First World War. This makes it problematical to use the
1914–1918 conflict as the baseline for analysis, since patterns of
death and killing were quite different during the nineteenth
century and earlier. Then, civilian casualties comprised a substantial proportion of the deaths caused by war. During the
Thirty Years War, the total population of the Holy Roman
Empire may have declined by 15–20 per cent, perhaps by as

much as a third; while relatively few civilian deaths were caused directly by violence, it was disease that proved the great scourge, and even among soldiers 'disease proved more potent than muskets, swords and cannon' and 'it is likely that three men died of disease for every one killed in action'.[20] During the Napoleonic Wars of the early nineteenth century, as well, large numbers of civilians met their deaths and more soldiers lost their lives to disease than were killed in combat. For example, during the campaigns on the Iberian Peninsula and in southern France between Christmas 1810 and May 1814, 8,889 British soldiers were killed in action or died from their wounds, while 24,930 succumbed to disease.[21]

This not only distinguishes the First World War on the Western Front from the wars of the nineteenth century and earlier, it also points to a profound change in the nature of warfare in the twentieth: that a far smaller proportion of soldiers succumb to disease – leaving, obviously, a greater proportion to succumbed to acts of violence. (Here, however, one should note that the influenza epidemic of 1918 caused millions of deaths around the world, some of them soldiers.) In this sense, perhaps, the wars of the twentieth century can be said to have been more violent than earlier wars, even if the proportion of the total population in combatant countries killed during both the First and the Second World Wars was less than it had been during the Thirty Years War in the seventeenth century.[22]

Second, the assertion that only 5 per cent of all casualties were civilians in the First World War is wrong. Civilians comprised perhaps a third of the dead of the 1914–1918 conflict.[23] The claim that 'the proportion of war deaths suffered by civilians' was only '5 per cent in World War I' seems based on a typically narrow view of that war, a view that focuses on the fighting along the largely static Western Front, where relatively few civilians came into the firing line. On the Eastern Front things were very different. There, armies moved across vast distances in what at times was a war of movement; there, disease was a greater cause of mortality among both soldiers and civilians; and there, millions of people were torn from their homes in brutal campaigns of forced removal.[24] Thus civilian populations in eastern Europe found themselves at far greater risk of death or injury than did their counterparts in the West. This is far from marginal to an understanding of violence and the First World War, since roughly as many soldiers fought and died in eastern as in western Europe. It is all too easy to forget, and most people at least in the West have forgotten, that of all the combatant powers it was the Russian Empire that lost the most people in absolute numbers and it was Serbia that lost the most people relative to its population during the First World War.

Third, the horror and massive bloodletting during the 1914–1918 conflict followed a time when many people had hoped that the violence of war could be and was being brought under control. What may be regarded as the modern anti-war movement had its origins in the years before the First World War, with the publication in 1889 of Bertha von Suttner's novel *Die Waffen nieder! (Lay Down Your Arms!)*, with the awarding of the Nobel Peace Prize from 1901, and with an upsurge in anti-war agitation in the decades before the catastrophe of 1914.[25] Only a few years before the 'guns of August' began firing, international treaties had been negotiated and signed by representatives of the world's 'civilized nations' in the Hague. The Hague Conventions of 1899 and 1907 laid out protocols for the 'pacific settlement of international disputes' and laws for the conduct of war, on the basis that 'the right of belligerents to adopt means of injuring the enemy is not unlimited'.[26] In 1910, Andrew Carnegie established the Carnegie Endowment for International Peace (with a contribution of $10 million), which may not have succeeded in preventing war in 1914 but which funded important studies of its effects and which continues to provide a leading think tank dealing with questions of war and peace. Even though armed conflict had in fact broken out on every continent during the years just before and just after the turn of the century, it seemed that one might imagine a world in which (as Carnegie described in an address in 1905):

> Non-combatants are now spared, women and children are no longer massacred, quarter is given, and prisoners are well cared for. [...] There is great cause for congratulations. If man has not been busily striking at the heart of the monster War, he has at least been busily engaged drawing in some of its poisonous fangs. Thus even in the savage reign of man-slaying, we see the blessed law of evolution increasingly at work performing its devine [sic], making that which is better than that which has been and ever leading on to perfection.[27]

A decade later a horrible mockery would be made of these fine words: instead of the 'poisonous fangs' of war being drawn in, soldiers would be killed in Flanders by poison gas (which had been explicitly prohibited in the Hague Conventions). The juxtaposition of hopes that the world was becoming less violent through the acceptance by civilized and enlightened nations of legal codes to control the violence of war on the one hand with the slaughter of the First World War engaged in by those self-styled civilized and enlightened nations on the other was deeply disturbing.

The First World War, in the trenches of the Western Front at least, was a new type of war: a conflict where relatively few men died in hand-to-hand combat, where killing largely took place at a distance and where the deadly violence tended to be impersonal. It was war in an industrial age. Killing and wounding in this way was relatively easy to do – as John Mueller has written, 'men generally tend to find killing each other at long range less repugnant than up close'[28] – and the result was shockingly large numbers of casualties. This not only added to the horror with which warfare was subsequently regarded, but also has been seen to usher in a new era of mass violence and mass killing. Outlining the arguments offered in his book, *Murder in our Midst*, Omer Bartov told the Millersville Holocaust Conference in 1997:

> [...] the First World War had introduced to the West a wholly new concept of war, which in turn had far-reaching consequences for the understanding of human society and man's ability to control violence and improve humanity – or at least those parts of humanity deemed valuable. This is what I have termed 'industrial killing', namely the mechanized, impersonal and sustained mass destruction of human beings, organized and administered by states, legitimized and set into motion by scientists and jurists, sanctioned and popularized by academics and intellectuals. To be sure, there were some precedents to industrial warfare before the Great War, and the concept of total war was aired in some quarters prior to 1914. Yet I argue that it was first and foremost the mass slaughter of the trenches which had a direct and long-lasting effect on Europe – and subsequently on much of the rest of the world – and that therefore the Great War is crucial to our understanding of many of the characteristics of modern war and genocide as well as their popular perception and representation.[29]

This argument rests upon the 'industrial warfare' in the West rather than the horrors that accompanied the First World War in the East (which included the forced removal of millions of people and outbursts of violent antisemitism, foreshadowing even worse to come roughly a quarter of a century later). It reveals the enduring importance of a particular understanding of the violence in the First World War.

Bartov seeks to spotlight 'a crucial and largely neglected connection between the Great War and the Nazi attempted genocide of the Jews' during the early 1940s. More common has been to regard the First World War as the prime example of the wanton destruction of life in modern war. Particularly in Britain, the military dead of the First World War came to be viewed as victims of horrible, needless violence, of futile campaigns waged by generals whose callousness and stupidity led to the deaths of hundreds of thousands of their soldiers. Kenneth Morgan put it well when he observed in a lecture in July 1996: 'The First World War is, irredeemably it seems, associated with tragedy and disaster, with the mass slaughter of the trenches during the war, and cynical betrayal by the "hard-faced men" in the aftermath of the peace. It is seen not just as slaughter, but as senseless slaughter, conceived in dishonour.'[30] Rather than being hailed as the hero who won the war, Field Marshal Douglas Haig (Commander of the British Expeditionary Force from 1915 until the end of the war) came to be regarded as 'the butcher of the Somme'; rather than being an object of continuing adulation (as still evidenced at his state funeral in 1928), Haig posthumously came to be regarded increasingly with anger and even hatred for having pursued a military strategy that delivered hundreds of thousands of brave men to their deaths.

The costly war of attrition on the Western Front led to a change in perceptions and assessments of military violence not only in Britain. In Germany, Erich von Falkenhayn, Chief of the General Staff from the stalling of the German offensive in September 1914 until the end of August 1916, had been a protagonist of a strategy of attrition. Falkenhayn was the architect of the Battle of Verdun, with its aim of bleeding the French into defeat, and the failure of his strategy at Verdun led to his replacement by Paul von Hindenburg.[31] What the Battle of the Somme was for British memories of the First World War, Verdun arguably was for French and German memories, and it continues to be regarded 'as one of the greatest, most costly and most senseless battles not only of the First World War but of the entire history of armed confrontations'.[32] Both for the French and for the Germans, the Battle of Verdun (which claimed the lives of roughly 700,000 soldiers altogether) became the symbol of the horror of the trench warfare of the Western Front: the memory of Verdun is the memory of the senseless 'battle of attrition', whatever the actual merits or otherwise of the military strategy that led to it in 1916.[33] Today the ossuary at Douaumont, built with privately raised funds and American aid and where the remains of those Verdun dead who could not be identified are buried, remains a strange, eerie monument to a military conflict that had left only death, sorrow and hollowed-out society in its wake. Not by accident did François Mitterrand and Helmut Kohl choose the site for their famous hand-holding display of Franco-German reconciliation in September 1984. If there was one site that was fitting to confirm to the French and the Germans that the violence of war was senseless, it was Verdun.

Not only in Europe did the war of attrition lead to a widespread conviction that the military effort had led to a senseless waste of life. Similar reactions arose in the outposts of the western world in the Antipodes, in reaction to the decision to send ANZAC troops to land on the Gallipoli Peninsula in April 1915, in a campaign that proved an ill-conceived and costly failure. After eight and a half months of fighting, during which roughly 200,000 troops from Britain and the dominions and perhaps 300,000 Turkish soldiers lost their lives (and large numbers became seriously ill), the invasion force was withdrawn, ending an operation 'which did not shorten the war by a single day'.[34] Looking back in July 1927 on the Gallipoli campaign, *The Times* judged that 'it will ever be a warning to statesmen with ideas on war'.[35] (It should be noted, however, that this is a rather western-centred perspective, as the battle has been regarded rather differently by Turks – as a victory achieved under the leadership of Mustafa Kemal, who became the first president of the post-war Republic of Turkey.)[36]

The tragic and costly Gallipoli campaign played a significant role in the emergence of Australian and New Zealand identities separate from the 'mother country', and is commemorated in both countries on 25 April, ANZAC Day, the day of the initial landing in 1916. According to Peter Hoffenberg, the Great War 'offered a radical departure for the Australians [...] particularly so with combat on the Western Front and at Gallipoli on the Dardanelles, understood as a narrative of violence, war and catastrophe, both tragic and egalitarian'. As in western Europe, in Australia, too, memory of the conflict became framed in 'general myths about the Great War's stunning futility and limitless casualties'.[37] Violence and war came to be associated not so much with heroism as with loss – something that one can still sense when visiting the huge, sombre 'Shrine of Remembrance' overlooking the city centre of Melbourne and containing 'Books of Remembrance' with the names of more than 89,000 soldiers from the State of Victoria.

The sense of loss is also reflected in the motif chosen for memorials to the dead of the First World War not only in Whitehall in London but also in Sydney, Auckland, Toronto, Hong Kong and Singapore: a cenotaph – an empty tomb, a monument to someone whose body is elsewhere. The memorial reflects the void left by war. If there was meaning in the violence of the First World War, it was found not in the celebration of battle but in the mourning of loss.[38] The cry was 'War Never Again!', as pacifism gained adherents, particularly in France and Britain. In France during the 1930s, Eugen Weber tells us, 'children who once were stuffed with ideas of martial glory were now being taken, class by class, to see anti-war films and then invited to put down their impressions.'[39] Of course, pacifism and pacifist movements were not invented in 1918. However, in the wake of the First World War and reinforced by the conviction that the 'war to end all wars' had in fact been an exercise in senseless slaughter, anti-war sentiment enjoyed a new strength and visibility.

Even in Germany, where (despite a growth in the membership of pacifist organizations after the First World War) pacifism found little appreciable echo in the politics of the Weimar Republic, anti-war sentiment was not insubstantial.[40] Although historians have tended to focus on the paramilitary formations that affirmed war and violence in Germany after the First World War and that have been regarded as the 'vanguard of Nazism', the story in fact is rather complicated. During the Weimar period, the largest organization of war veterans specifically *as veterans* was the Reich Association of War Disabled, War Veterans and War Dependents, which had been founded by Social Democrats, the membership of which in 1922 was 830,000 (double the number of the men who had been organized in all the *Freikorps* combined), and which counted itself 'among the opponents of new wars'.[41] During the 1930s, after the Nazi dictatorship had extended its control over public expression in the media, memories of the First World War still evoked fears about a politics that affirmed war and violence and that threatened to plunge the country into another conflict. When conscription was re-introduced in March 1935, there was considerable disquiet among sections of the German population who had experienced the last war and dreaded the prospect of the next. According to reports collated by the Social Democratic Party in exile through its network of informers in the country, reactions were 'very mixed', ranging from enthusiasm among young people (and among some of their elders who believed that this way 'the youth would finally learn discipline and order again') to fears about a new war; veterans of the Great War in particular, it was reported, had made veiled comments that 'they are not keen to experience the years 1914–1918 again'.[42]

The well-known anti-war motifs in the prints and drawings of Käthe Kollwitz, Otto Dix and George Grosz were not without their context, and struck a chord among at least some strands of popular opinion. Particularly provocative was the establishment by the anarchist-pacifist Ernst Friedrich of an International Anti-war Museum in Berlin in 1924, and the publication by Friedrich of the photographic narrative *Krieg dem Kriege!* (*War against War!*).[43] Friedrich, who had been a conscientious objector during the First World War, published photographs that had been censored by the German government during the conflict. The result was a book that sold 70,000 copies within a few months of its initial printing and then went through ten editions. By 1930 it had been translated into more than forty languages,[44] and it remains an iconic collection of anti-war propaganda.

To be sure, Friedrich's efforts did not go uncontested. Calls were made by nationalist organizations for the book to be banned, and when images from it were displayed in the window of Friedrich's bookshop a police raid followed and the offending material confiscated. Other bookshops that displayed the book faced similar measures, and in the years that followed, organizations on the right countered with their own, affirmative images of the war – images that focused on the drama of battle and the technology of war. Nevertheless, the sorts of images published by Friedrich continue to frame the ways in which military violence has come to be regarded in the wake of the First World War. According to Dora Apel:

> Friedrich's visual strategy depended primarily on an identification of the viewer with the humanist image of the suffering soldier as a universal subject. Like other pacifists, he attempted to convey a picture of war that called forth visions of mutilation and meaningless death, shattered identity, and the devastating consequences of modern military technology. Pacifists attempted to lay bare the horrors of combat and the

hypocrisy of militarist rhetoric and construct a national collective memory that would serve to galvanize the population into opposing and preventing future wars.[45]

The focus was on the individual and his body, the soldier as victim of military violence, not its perpetrator. Such images may have been attacked in the heated political atmosphere of the Weimar Republic, but over the course of the twentieth century, images and understandings of military violence (like other forms of violence) have been drawn increasingly from the perspective of the victim of violence rather than of its perpetrator.

In many respects the shock arising from the violence of the Second World War – of deaths that surpassed in number even those of the 1914–1918 conflict, of the 'war of extermination' on Germany's Eastern Front, of bombing campaigns that killed hundreds of thousands of civilians, of campaigns of genocide that extinguished the lives of millions – was even greater than that arising from the First. Not only the vast numbers of people involved, but also the fact that so many of the dead were civilians aroused deep concern. A reflection of this concern was the attempt after the Second World War to extend the legal framework governing conflict to include civilians, with the ratification of the Geneva Convention of the Protection of Civilians in 1949. This extension both reflected and enforced a changed attitude towards violence and war, in the wake of the shock of 'total war' and genocide in the Second World War. Although the 1949 Geneva Convention had its origins in ideas that had coalesced in the nineteenth century, and although the laws of war have been ignored routinely in conflicts since – in civil wars (e.g. in Yugoslavia and Syria) and in anti-colonial wars of national liberation (e.g. in Namibia and Algeria) – the recognition after the experience of the Second World War 'that civilians should be protected from the actions of aggressor states' marked an important development in how the violence of war has been regarded internationally.[46]

When looking back at the Second World War, it is not just the quantity of lethal violence that is so shocking but also the mentalities that accompanied it and helped to make it possible. Military leaders expressed views and committed their troops to operations that are deeply disturbing. Among the most extreme examples is the behaviour of German generals during the last days of the Reich in 1945. Following the failure of the Ardennes Offensive in the west and the success of the Red Army's offensive of January 1945 in the east, at a time when Germany's military position was obviously and utterly hopeless, Wehrmacht commanders repeatedly committed their forces to suicidal battles that could result only in massive casualties and catastrophic defeat. Defending their country against invasion became synonymous with destroying it. Cities and towns were declared 'fortresses' to be held to the last; military units were committed to battles where they could only be annihilated. In early March 1945, orders were given, for example, for the defence of Berlin, stipulating that 'every block of flats, every house, every storey, every hedgerow, every shell-crater ... [be defended] to the last man and the last bullet'.[47] By this point there was no chance of avoiding total defeat, and yet the military leadership displayed a continuing commitment to boundless violence and a callous disregard for the lives of the soldiers under their command and of the civilian population.

On 16 April 1945, a mere three weeks before the German surrender, representatives of the International Red Cross made a proposal to provide safe zones for the civilian population in Berlin during the battle that was about to take place for the German capital. This was turned down flatly by Wilhelm Keitel, the Chief of Staff of the German Armed Forces High Command, with the words: 'Rejection, because [it is] only an attempt to discover if the will to resist still exists!! Agreement would be the first step towards becoming soft.'[48] The National Socialist regime did not become 'soft', but instead condemned the people still in Berlin to a hopeless last-ditch battle that would leave nearly 100,000 German soldiers and an even greater number of German civilians dead and the city in ruins. In order to demonstrate that this time round there would be no dishonourable surrender as allegedly had occurred in November 1918, and to set a supposedly glorious example for future generations, a violent end was embraced in what has been described as a 'choreography of the downfall' and a 'strategy of self-annihilation'.[49] The National Socialist regime and its armed forces were determined to apply violence without limit, to fight to the very end, to sacrifice their own soldiers, to condemn the country's civilian population to violence on an unprecedented scale.

The embrace of violence displayed by German military commanders during the Second World War may have been extreme, but they were not alone in accepting levels of violence in war that seem shocking today. At times, reservations were expressed – as when General Douglas MacArthur responded to a request to approve American air attacks during the battle for Manila in February 1945 by asserting that to bomb 'a part of a city occupied by a friendly and allied population is unthinkable. The inaccuracy of this type of bombardment would result beyond question in the death of thousands of innocent civilians.'[50] Nevertheless, one should not overemphasize the contrast. In fact, British and American air forces had already bombed 'a friendly and allied population' in France for years (causing more than 53,000 deaths);[51] American aircraft had already bombed parts of Manila; and while MacArthur was leading the operation to drive the Japanese from the Philippines, American planes were engaged in the fire-bombing of Japanese cities (where most houses were made of wood, and thus highly combustible) – a campaign that culminated with the dropping of atomic bombs on Hiroshima and Nagasaki.

We are acutely aware of the devastation caused by the atomic bombs, but the toll of the conventional attack on Tokyo on the night of 9–10 March 1945 was even greater (and far greater even than that caused by the fire-bombing of Hamburg by British and American forces in July 1943). On that night, American incendiary bombs destroyed sixteen square miles of the Japanese capital, killed between 80,000 and 100,000 people, and made over a million people homeless. The victims were, in the words of Major General Curtis LeMay, the man who master-minded the attack, 'scorched and boiled and baked to death'.[52] Altogether, perhaps 400,000 people were killed in Japan as a result of the bombing. Bonner Fellers, a brigadier general and an aide to General MacArthur, wrote in a confidential memoran-dum in mid-June 1945 (i.e. before the atomic bombs were dropped on Hiroshima and Nagasaki) that the bombing of Japan constituted 'one of the most ruthless and barbaric killings of non-combatants in all history'.[53]

At the time, however, public comment in the countries pur-suing the bombing campaigns was supportive. As bombs were falling on German cities, with terrible consequences for the civilian population, *Time* magazine wrote approvingly of a cam-paign in which the goal was 'to destroy cities, industries, human beings, and the human spirit on a scale never before attempted by air action', and Arthur Harris – the 'Air Officer Commanding in Chief' of the Royal Air Force Bomber Command and from 1943 'Air Chief Marshal' – expressed himself in unambiguous terms when he asserted in December 1943 that 'it is not enough to admit that devastation is caused by our attacks, or to suggest that it is an incidental and rather regrettable concomitant of night bombing. It is in fact produced deliberately.'[54] Harris argued bluntly with the British Air Ministry for acceptance that the aim of the bombing campaign was 'the obliteration of German cities and their inhabitants'.[55] To utter such statements, to accept the violence of war in such candid terms, is almost unimaginable today, at least in Britain and the United States, and they would have met with horrified reaction before the outbreak of the Second World War. But they accurately described the bombing campaign against Germany after the shift in 1941 to a strategy aimed at destroying working-class housing in Germany's cities and to killing Germany's workers.[56]

According to the Italian cultural historian Giovanni Rebora:

> Only after the Second World War did Europeans agree that war was no longer a question of honour and that there was no particular glory in bombing unarmed people from on high. Not everybody understood this, but the suffering and real hunger experienced by civilian populations (not to mention those in concentration camps and gulags) were more real and certainly worse than anything suffered by the populations of the Middle Ages and the Early Modern period.[57]

It may be questioned whether the suffering experienced by civilians during the twentieth century in fact was 'worse than anything suffered by the populations of the Middle Ages and the Early Modern period', and if it seems 'more real', that may be because it is closer to us, within living memory. Also, before the outbreak of the Second World War, targeting of civilians by bombing had in fact been widely condemned; aerial bombing had been prohibited explicitly by the Hague Conventions of 1899 and 1907, and after the First World War numerous calls were made to outlaw bombing, but such qualms were swept away in the heat of war.[58] However, Rebora is right to observe that attitudes towards such violence have changed: there is a huge difference between the sorts of things said by those responsible for the bombing during the Second World War and, for example, the statement by George W. Bush on 19 March 2003, announcing the start of the military campaign against Iraq, that 'coalition forces will make every effort to spare innocent civilians from horror'.[59] Michael Knights asserted in 2003 that 'there is now no such thing as an "enemy civilian"'.[60] That would have been news to Arthur Harris (and to the British or American public) during the Second World War.

The history of the bombing war shows that the boundaries of acceptability of military violence against civilians shifted fundamentally during the Second World War, and it is deeply disturbing to us that 'Britain and the United States, liberal democracies which self-consciously occupied the high moral ground during the war, and had both deplored bombing before 1939, ended up organizing strategic bombing campaigns that killed around one million people in Europe and Asia'.[61] Once people, both the decision-makers and those who carried out the orders, found themselves engaged in a brutal conflict, acts of violence were accepted in the interest of winning the war that in peacetime had been unthinkable. When he was interviewed in 2000 for what became the award-winning film *The Fog of War*, former US Secretary of Defense Robert McNamara reflected on the firebombing of Japan, of which he had been a major architect:

I think the issue is not so much incendiary bombs. I think the issue is: in order to win a war should you kill 100,000 people in one night, by fire-bombing or any other way? LeMay's answer would be clearly 'Yes'. [...]

I don't fault Truman for dropping the nuclear bomb. The US-Japanese War was one of the most brutal wars in all of human history [...] kamikaze pilots, suicide, unbelievable. What one can criticize is that the human race prior to that time [...] and today [...] has not really grappled with what are, I'll call it, 'the rules of war'. Was there a rule then that said you shouldn't bomb, shouldn't kill, shouldn't burn to death 100,000 civilians in one night?

LeMay said, 'If we'd lost the war, we'd all have been prosecuted as war criminals.' And I think he's right. He, and I'd say I, were behaving as war criminals. LeMay recognized that what he was doing would be thought immoral if his side had lost. But what makes it immoral if you lose and not immoral if you win?[62]

How we might respond to McNamara's thought-provoking question reveals much about how the violence of war has come to be regarded since the end of the Second World War. Today most people probably would answer that there is no difference, that an immoral act of war is just that, regardless of whether one is on the winning or the losing side. In recent decades it has become much more difficult to apply selective moral standards. The increasing sensitivity towards violence witnessed across the western world has left less space for moral relativism.

Like McNamara's thoughtful, even tortured reflections, transformations in mentalities in the principal countries that lost the war demonstrate how much perspectives changed after 1945. The idea that one could desire war and that one would continue fighting almost for its own sake was met with incredulity after the conflict, and in the years that followed came to be rejected utterly in Japan and Germany. In the spring of 1946, a British occupation officer addressed representatives of the city council in Bochum when they met for their first sitting after the war and informed the assembled Germans that 'no normal person' wanted war, and that therefore no country where the will of the people was reflected in their government would start a war.[63] This statement may have reflected the often uncritical and self-satisfied opinions held by many Britons in the wake of the war,[64] as well as an understanding of the violence at the heart of German National Socialism, but it also indicates a changing attitude towards war and violence. Something that once had been regarded as obvious, namely that states start wars, became something that no 'normal' person would welcome. Following the shock of the violence at the end of the

Second World War, attitudes changed. Today the extreme, exceptional nature of the fanaticism that helped to fuel the violence of the Second World War is a cause of fascination, precisely because it seems at odds with values and modes of behaviour that we tend to accept and take for granted.

The extent of the change in attitudes after the Second World War was nowhere more apparent than in Germany, where the aggressively violent and militaristic ideology of National Socialism was succeeded during the second half of the twentieth century by a growing aversion to military service. In the autumn of 1951, although a narrow majority of West Germans favoured the re-formation of a national army, opinion polling indicated that nearly half of the population (and more than half of former *Wehrmacht* soldiers) expressed their approval of conscientious objection.[65] Whereas only a few thousand young West Germans had applied for conscientious objector status during the late 1950s and early 1960s, in 1980 the figure jumped to 54,193 and in 1998 it had reached 172,024; by the beginning of the 1990s roughly two in five of the men called upon to perform military service in Germany refused and opted instead for *Zivildienst* ('civilian service').[66] By the end of the twentieth century not only was conscientious objection widely accepted in Germany, but attempts to denounce those who performed alternative service as cowards and shirkers found little resonance.[67]

Further evidence of heightened sensitivity towards violence in recent decades has been the growth and resonance of peace movements in western Europe, Japan and the United States since the Second World War.[68] Of course, campaigns for peace did not emerge suddenly in 1945. The roots of modern peace movements extend back at least to the 'peace churches' that emerged from the Protestant Reformation, especially the Mennonites and the Quakers (Society of Friends, who emerged from the English Civil War during the seventeenth century to call for the renunciation of violence in social relations). During the nineteenth century, peace societies grew on both sides of the Atlantic, in the US and the UK,[69] and the slaughter of the First World War was followed by an upsurge in pacifism in the United Kingdom and France and concern that such violence not be repeated – something reflected in the high hopes accompanying the Paris Peace Conference of 1919 and the establishment of the League of Nations.[70] Nevertheless, the growth of armies of 'anti-warriors' since the middle of the twentieth century has been a remarkable phenomenon. These have encompassed the protests across the world against America's Vietnam War during the 1960s and early 1970s as well as the global movement for nuclear disarmament that emerged after the Second World War and that reached a peak during the early 1980s, when millions of people in North America, Asia, Australia and western Europe (as well as in the Soviet bloc) demonstrated for a nuclear arms freeze and against the deployment of American missiles.[71]

Despite the efforts of anti-war movements, peace obviously did not descend upon the world after 1945. After the end of the Second World War, western nations soon rearmed and became involved in one military conflict after another. However, during that time, attitudes with regard to military violence and how wars ought to be conducted have changed not only in public discussion but also among the military. Concern to limit their own casualties has been particularly evident within the American armed forces. For example, during the Korean War, in December 1952, the American Eighth Army issued an order 'to make every effort to reduce combat losses to an absolute minimum consistent with the proper performance of the Army's current combat missions', prohibiting among other things raids on enemy positions except to capture prisoners.[72] Upon leaving military service, General Frederick Weyand, the last commander of US military operations in the Vietnam War during 1972 and 1973 and US Army Chief of Staff from 1974 until his retirement from the army in September 1976, observed of 'the American way of war': 'We believe in using "things" – artillery, bombs, massive firepower – in order to conserve our soldiers' lives. The enemy, on the other hand, made up for his lack of "things" by expending men instead of machines, and he suffered enormous casualties.'[73]

The ability and determination to use 'things' in order to preserve the lives of one's own soldiers also meant that an increasingly large proportion of armed service personnel have been involved not in combat operations but in a vast array of support roles. As modern war fighting has become more complex, a steadily smaller proportion of the armed forces are exposed regularly to combat (although those that are so exposed then face violence no less intense than their counterparts in the wars of the first half of the twentieth century). According to a 2002 study of post-combat syndromes among British soldiers over the course of the twentieth century, 'the proportion involved in actual fighting fell over time as the numbers in combat-support roles has risen. [. . .] Of the First World War pensioners 73.4 per cent [had been in combat], of the Second World War sample 52 per cent, while only 19.8 per cent of the Gulf War sample had seen action.'[74] A decade after the end of the Vietnam War, a disillusioned former American sergeant, who had been wounded in early 1970, 'a foot soldier, a "Grunt"', as he called himself, described what he had seen in Vietnam:

The American Armed Forces operated with a huge logistical tail. For every Grunt in the field, there were approximately seven men in the rear supporting him. These included cooks, clerks, supply people, maintenance men, truck drivers, military policemen, entertainment personnel, headquarters' staffs and men running PXs. [. . .] Thus, out of a total of 549,000 Americans [in Vietnam at the peak of US strength in 1969], there were at best 70,000 infantrymen.[75]

Of course, logistics have played an increasingly important role in war fighting over the course of the twentieth century (and the First World War marked a watershed in this regard – 'the first true, modern war' in which millions of men had to be supplied with vast amounts of materiel, from ammunition to food).[76] However, it was with the West's wars of the late twentieth century that the projection of force – the application of violence – consequently became the task of a relatively small minority of soldiers at war.

The idea that the armed forces should use 'things [...] in order to conserve our soldiers' lives' contrasts sharply with how their human resources had been treated by military commanders at the Somme and at Verdun in 1916, at Stalingrad in 1943, or at Berlin in 1945. The observation that during the twentieth century the United States military was concerned to develop tactics designed to minimize American casualties while directing overwhelming force against the enemy reflects two things: the enormous material resources that the Americans have had at their disposal, and the growing reluctance to accept American casualties and to put American soldiers 'in harm's way'. The reluctance to expose one's own soldiers to lethal violence is not limited to the Americans, and reflects an important shift generally in political and military attitudes with regard to the violence of war. Indeed, by the 1990s arguments had been advanced that 'democracies' concern with military casualties had become a phobia, with military operations being undertaken if there was only a risk of zero or a few military casualties', especially in the United States.[77]

Despite the reluctance to expose their soldiers to the risk of death and injury, the United States and its allies did go to war repeatedly from the 1990s onwards, and did take casualties. Nevertheless, the recent military campaigns conducted by western forces in Iraq and Afghanistan have been striking for the low levels of casualties suffered and the high levels of concern expressed about those casualties.

Altogether, 4,487 American soldiers (19 per cent of whom died due to non-hostile causes) were killed in Iraq between 2003 and the end of 2011, when American forces withdrew from the country; 32,223 were seriously wounded.[78] (In the same period, 179 British soldiers were killed, as were 139 soldiers of other coalition forces.)[79] These are remarkable numbers. They are quite small not only when set against the numbers of Iraqi casualties (which have been estimated at over 100,000 civilians and 55,000 insurgents) but also when compared with the huge numbers of military casualties that the western democracies took during the world wars (to say nothing of the millions of Soviet, German, Japanese and Chinese dead during the Second World War) or even the 58,220 American service personnel killed in the Vietnam War (of whom 40,934 – about 70 per cent – were killed in action).[80] Ten years of fighting in Iraq left behind a number of coalition dead that was less than a quarter of the dead that the British Army had suffered on the first day of the Battle of the Somme.

Hardly less remarkable than the low numbers of military deaths in Iraq is the ratio of dead to wounded: for American forces this was roughly 1:7.4 (or about 1:8.9, if one strips away the 19 per cent killed by non-hostile causes such as motor-vehicle accidents). By way of contrast, among the German armed forces during the First World War the ratio of dead to wounded was roughly 1:2.36.[81] Huge resources have been devoted to treating the wounded, with the vastly improved medical facilities put in place by the western forces in Iraq and Afghanistan, a reflection both of medical advances and of the extraordinary lengths to which the Americans and the British went in order to safeguard the lives of their soldiers. While not determined to avoid casualties at any cost, they had become very 'sensitive to casualties to the extent that they do not want to pay a greater price for an objective at stake in military conflict than is necessary'.[82] This reflected a 'casualty sensitivity' that had grown from the 1970s, in the wake of the Vietnam War.[83] Edward Luttwak, a prominent critic of the new, exceptionally casualty-averse way of war, wrote in 1994 that 'it is not hard to guess what would have happened to President [George H. W.] Bush and his administration if the casualties of the Persian Gulf venture [of 1991] had reached the levels of any one day of serious fighting in either world war.'[84]

As Luttwak was keen to point out, this was not limited to the United States. Referring to the reluctance of Britain, France and Germany to commit ground forces 'to resist aggression in the former Yugoslavia', he asserted that 'no European government was any more willing than the US government to risk its soldiers in combat. Of Japan, literally nothing need be said on this score.' Luttwak extended his critique even to the former USSR, referring to what he described as 'the inordinately prudent tactics of Soviet ground forces' in their failed intervention in Afghanistan.

This casualty phobia contrasts not only with the mass violence of military engagements during the two world wars, but also with military tactics of non-western countries that have neither had to contend with a democratic public sphere nor have possessed the military technology that might enable them to conserve their own soldiers' lives. In some respects the fighting tactics of non-western armies remained more like those of the French, German and British armies of the First World War and the Soviet Army of the Second, and the military confrontations of the Iran–Iraq War of the 1980s bore greater similarity to those of the First World War than to the American-led invasions of Iraq in 1991 and 2003 (the first of which cost coalition forces only 340 dead).[85]

The contrast also can be seen in the history of the Korean War when, after an initial war of movement up and down the Korean Peninsula, the conflict developed into static trench warfare which was reminiscent of the Western Front during the

First World War and in which American forces faced 'a series of brutal, human wave offensives by the Chinese [...] which American firepower butchered'.[86] The results were reflected in the respective casualty figures: while the Americans lost 54,246 soldiers (of whom 33,629 were battle deaths) during the Korea conflict and the South Koreans lost about 47,000, estimates of Chinese dead are in the region of 400,000 and of North Korean military deaths roughly 215,000.[87] The difference in willingness to accept casualties was expressed clearly by Ho Chi Minh when he remarked to a French general on the eve of the First Indochina War that 'you will kill ten of our men, but we will kill one of yours, and in the end it is you who will tire'.[88] In the end neither the French nor the Americans were prepared to take massive casualties in Vietnam. Ho Chi Minh's forces were, and they won.

In recent years there has been much discussion about war weariness in western societies. In the United States, the Vietnam War left behind a widespread aversion to military engagement, and more recently the wars in Iraq and Afghanistan again have undermined public support for foreign wars. In the United Kingdom, whose armed forces have been involved in repeated military conflict since the Second World War ended and where the engagements in Iraq and Afghanistan also have led to war weariness, the Ministry of Defence has become increasingly concerned about a growing reluctance on the part of the public to see British troops involved in war – a reluctance, we were told in January 2014, that 'is influencing the next two strategic defence reviews'.[89]

In addition to war weariness, after deployments together lasting for more than a decade in Iraq and Afghanistan, another factor has been cited, one which the UK shares with most contemporary western states: a perceived 'resistance in an increasingly diverse nation to see British troops deployed in countries from which UK citizens, or their families, once came'.

It may be that a willingness to engage in war is dependent, among other things, on a shared sense of (national) identity (something that, by the way, may have played a role in the determination of German soldiers to continue fighting and killing during the final months of the Second World War). Cultural diversity, something that most western countries now have in common, may undermine support for war fighting and the acceptance of the violence that inevitably follows from it.

In the early years of the new millennium a significant gap appeared to develop between the US and the UK on the one hand and continental European countries (most notably, Germany) on the other with regard to willingness to go to war. As the oft-repeated cliché of recent years goes, Americans supposedly are 'from Mars' while continental Europeans supposedly are 'from Venus'.[90] According to this view, whereas Europeans sought to escape a violent and bloody past by distancing themselves from military conflict, the United States, unencumbered by such a past, has been prepared to accept military conflict to defend its (and Europe's) interests. In the last few years, however, the differences may have narrowed, and it may have become more difficult to argue, as Robert Kagan has asserted, that 'it is time to stop pretending that Europeans and Americans share a common view of the world, or even that they occupy the same world'.[91] Although Americans and Europeans may have disagreed on whether military intervention in Iraq and Afghanistan had been the right thing to do, there was basic agreement with regard to the intervention in Libya (in which no western power proved willing to risk the lives of its soldiers).[92] More generally, the western world as a whole seems increasingly to be 'from Venus'. The divide seems not so much between the Anglo-Saxon countries and other western nations, but between the West and the 'rest'.

The second half of the twentieth century saw a transformation in how armies in the developed world fought wars, from combat involving mass armies of conscripts to wars involving comparatively small numbers of professional soldiers. In most developed countries, mass conscripted armies have become a thing of the past. The model of a mass conscript army still may hold for the Democratic People's Republic of Korea, but it no longer does so for the United Kingdom, Germany, France or the United States. This in turn has meant that a much smaller proportion of the population possesses experience of life in the military or of war. Societies have become more civilian, more distanced from military violence (which has become the job of a relatively small number of trained professional soldiers). Compared with the populations of Europe and North America two or three generations ago, and compared with the inhabitants of countries where large numbers of men still find themselves conscripted into the armed forces, the lives of most people in western countries now are far removed from experience of military life and violence in war. At the same time, our understanding of the purpose of armed forces has evolved, whereby their primary task is regarded not to exercise violence so much as to prevent it. The purpose of armed force is supposed to be preserving the peace rather than making war. Ministries of war have been renamed ministries of defence, and military organizations proclaim that 'peace is our profession'.

In February 2014, Massachusetts Senator Elizabeth Warren delivered the Whittington Lecture at Georgetown University in Washington. Her theme was 'Collateral Damage, National Interests, and the Lessons of a Decade of Conflict', and she articulated a view that says a great deal about how war fighting has come to be regarded in the early twenty-first century:

> We take pride in the way that our service members conduct themselves, but some people assume that when the shooting starts, military law, domestic law, and international law are

165

left behind. The reality is the opposite. Law is an integral part of American warfare. Our soldiers learn basic legal proce- dures as part of their training. Military lawyers are embedded into our fighting units, working alongside commanders to evaluate the legality of even the most sensitive decisions.

We follow the law because our national values – and our national interests – demand it.

Under the laws of war, we have an obligation that requires our military to distinguish between civilians and combat- ants – and to attack only combatants. But the laws of war are realistic. The laws recognize the possibility of collateral damage and therefore require us to weigh the military advan- tage gained from an attack against the humanitarian costs incurred. In other words, the laws of war require us to con- sider not just expedience, but also humanity.[93]

Warren's comments reflect a sober assessment of the tactics and strategy that her country's military used in the wars it fought in Iraq and Afghanistan and against a global terrorist threat. At the same time, they are revealing of contemporary attitudes towards the use of force and violence in war. These attitudes are a world away from what lay behind the military practices of Imperial Germany, described by Isabel Hull as 'absolute destruction' (including the 'gratuitous destruction' during the First World War that was 'understood by the Supreme Command as "military necessity"'),[94] or the sentiments expressed by those responsible for the bombing campaigns of the Second World War, not to mention the crimes committed by William Calley in Vietnam in March 1968 (for which he received only minimal punishment). Today we expect that, even in war, the use of violence be gov- erned not solely by expediency 'but also humanity'. Such a view may be the product of a society that enjoys the luxury of safe dis- tance from the violence of war. But it also reflects a sensitivity towards violence that has become symptomatic of our age.

VI

Women and Children

I n December 1997, sixty-year-old Ana Orantes appeared on a television talk show in Andalusia and spoke about the beatings she had endured at the hands of her husband over the course of their forty-year marriage. She had been unable to get a restraining order against her husband, who a few days after her television appearance beat her again, doused her with petrol and set her alight, burning her alive. Although Spain had made habitual violence against a family member a crime with changes to the Penal Code in 1989, not until after the murder of Ana Orantes and the media attention it received did domestic violence become a major topic of discussion in the Spanish media and a subject of attention by leading politicians. Spain's Socialist Party (PSOE) leader, José Luis Rodríguez Zapatero, made a point of visiting women's centres and refuges, and after the PSOE election victory in 2004 the new government passed the *Ley Integral contra la Violencia de Género* (Comprehensive Law against Gender-related Violence). From a subject that had met with a 'culture of tolerance' during the Franco dictatorship and the early post-Franco years, 'gender violence' became a prominent public concern and (according to a judge of the Superior

Court of Justice of Andalusia) 'a priority of the Spanish political agenda' by the beginning of the new millennium.[1]

Recognition of the serious nature of domestic and sexual violence may have come relatively late to Spain, but it was part of a general trend. Such violence has come increasingly into the public spotlight, and recent studies have exposed and confirmed its extent as never before. In the United States, probably the most influential country in this regard (and certainly the source of the most literature on the subject), in 2010 the 'National Intimate Partner and Sexual Violence Survey', which was based on over 16,000 interviews with both women and men, revealed that 'nearly 1 in 5 women (18.3 per cent) and 1 in 71 men (1.4 per cent) in the United States had been raped at some point in their lives'; 'more than half (51.1 per cent) of female victims of rape reported being raped by an intimate partner and 40.8 per cent by an acquaintance'. The violence referred to was not limited to sexual penetration: 'About 1 in 4 women (24.3 per cent) and 1 in 7 men (13.8 per cent) have experienced severe physical violence by an intimate partner (e.g. hit with a fist or something hard, beaten, slammed against something) at some point in their lifetime', and 'nearly half of all women and men in the United States have experienced psychological aggression by an intimate partner in their lifetime (48.4 per cent and 48.8 per cent, respectively)'.[2] More broadly, the survey found that 'more than 1 in 3 women (35.6 per cent) and more than 1 in 4 men (28.5 per cent) in the United States have experienced rape, physical violence, and/or stalking by an intimate partner in their lifetime.'

This confirmed, in a national, government-sponsored study, a phenomenon that had attracted increasing attention from researchers over the previous three decades. In what was the first comprehensive study of the practice of marital rape, based on interviews conducted with a random sample of 930 women in San Francisco in the early 1980s, Diana Russell found that 14 per cent of the 644 women in the sample who had ever been married had been the victim of rape or attempted rape by their husbands or ex-husbands.[3] In the late 1980s, it was estimated in the United States that between 10 and 14 per cent of married women experienced rape within marriage.[4] In 1991, a study of 2,291 adult working women in Cleveland found that a fifth said they had been raped; and in an earlier study of 3,187 women at thirty-two colleges the comparable figure was 15 per cent, four fifths of whom said that they knew the rapist.[5]

In the United Kingdom at about the same time, Kate Painter undertook a study that involved questioning 1,007 women in eleven towns across Britain in August/September 1989 about marital rape, to find that 140 (14 per cent) testified to having been 'made to have sex when refused consent/threatened/or had violence used'; the total number raped 'at some time by some man' (i.e not just within marriage) was 239 – almost a quarter of the sample.[6] According to Painter, 'almost half of all rapes involved threats and/or the use of physical violence: 36 per cent (51) of victims had been threatened with violence and raped; 31 per cent (43) had been physically assaulted and raped'. Marital rape also was not an isolated act of violence: Painter noted that '"one-off" rape was unusual'.[7] Rape tends to be but one element in the violence that is inflicted on the cohabitee; those who are raped have often been battered as well.[8]

Disturbing though the findings of such research are, they may not reflect the full extent of violence that takes place in the private, intimate sphere. In the introduction to her monograph on marital violence from the mid-seventeenth century to the mid-nineteenth century, Elizabeth Foyster observes:

Domestic violence does not yield evidence that can be readily translated into reliable numbers or statistics. Even today, when domestic violence is a crime, and we have a professional police force and modern systems of recording crime, we cannot be certain about the numbers of people it affects. [...] Whereas most historians agree that domestic violence was likely to be reported if it became so severe that death was the result, the extent of the more common and non-lethal forms of domestic violence is unknown. As a result we can make no confident assertions about whether the levels or incidence of domestic violence have increased or decreased over time.[9]

This caveat needs to be kept in mind when considering claims about trends in domestic violence, and indeed about the extent of violence at any one time. While surveys such as those cited above have gone a long way towards exposing the extent of domestic and intimate violence, they are probably less exact than the apparently hard statistics suggest. How people respond in such surveys depends not just on their lived experiences of violence, but also on their willingness to reveal or admit those experiences to others and, in the case of 'psychological aggression by an intimate partner', by their perceptions of what aggression is and how much of it is required to cross the threshold of what is considered to be violence, perceptions that are subjective and shaped by cultural norms and expectations. Nevertheless, they do reflect a heightened concern about such violence. For it seems clear that, whether or not in fact there has been more or less violence behind closed doors in the private household and in the bedroom, recent decades have witnessed a marked rise in public concern about private violence. Rape within marriage has generated a substantial literature in recent decades – a sign of its diminishing acceptability no less than of its frequent occurrence.[10] At the end of the twentieth century, an American researcher, discussing the theme of 'Wife Rape: A Social Problem for the 21st Century' and introducing a journal issue devoted to marital rape, was able to observe: 'In the past thirty years, we have seen a proliferation of research on (roughly in order of their emergence as social problems) child abuse, rape, battering, child sexual abuse, elder abuse, date rape, and lesbian battering. Hundreds of journal issues and books have been devoted to these forms of violence – and rightly so.'[11] The flood of studies of domestic and sexual violence published over the last few decades may or may not be evidence of increases in the frequency of such violence – although they do indicate that it is much more common than many had believed – but it certainly is evidence of increased awareness and sensitivity about domestic and sexual violence.

Surveys of public opinion reflect this. A recent report, based on interviews with 26,800 European citizens across all the countries of the European Union in February and March 2010 revealed that 98 per cent were aware of domestic violence as an issue (up from 94 per cent in the previous survey taken in 1999), and 86 per cent said that domestic violence is unacceptable and always should be punishable by law (up from 63 per cent in 1999).[12] What had often previously been hidden away, what people – both victims and perpetrators – had tended not to mention in public, has become a major topic of public discussion and concern.

In this, as in so many areas concerning the public understanding and discussion of violence, the early 1970s appear to have been a turning point, at least in the western world. The rise of the feminist movement at that time, particularly in the United States (and paralleled and emulated elsewhere), was central to this change, as attempts were increasingly made to bring issues of violence against women into public discussion and debate. (It is worth noting that the term 'sexual harassment' stems from this period: it emerged from a 'Speak Out against Sexual Harassment' conference organized at Cornell University in May 1975 and investigations by that university's Human Affairs Program, and through reporting in *The New York Times* a few months later.)[13] A major intervention was the passionate volume about rape first published by Susan Brownmiller in 1975 (reprinted many times since and translated into more than a dozen languages), *Against Our Will*.[14] Brownmiller's underlying thesis, that rape essentially 'is nothing more or less than a conscious process of intimidation by which all men keep *all women* in a state of fear' (emphasis in the original),[15] has been both influential and controversial. *Against Our Will* was written during a time when the number of rapes reported in the United States was increasing rapidly, but during which the subject had not really been given much attention by historians. That was soon to change, however, as the focus of academic activism shifted from the political revolts of the late 1960s to a campaign that had violence against women at the centre of its concerns.

Looking back at the genesis of her book, Brownmiller has observed: '*Against Our Will* was published in the middle of a feminist decade of theory and action when women overturned many hidebound assumptions about our ordained place in that order. [...] In the 1970s, unprecedented strategies against rape – speak outs, crisis centres, 24-hour hotlines, state-by-state campaigns to amend unfair criminal codes – erupted across the country and spread through the western world.'[16] She went on to stress the importance of a change in perspective about sexual violence that occurred at that time: 'The absolute brilliance and *sine qua non* of the American anti-rape movement was its focus on the victim's perspective – a fresh idea in its day, unbelievable as that may sound.' This reflects both the influence of the feminist movement and a general shift in how violence, sexual or other, has come to be discussed: to a 'focus on the victim's perspective'. It was to be the victim's perceptions that framed the understanding of the violent act. Brownmiller also put her finger on another important point: that it may now sound 'unbelievable' not to approach such violence from the victim's perspective. Empathy with the victim has become central to an understanding of sexual violence.

The feminist campaign against rape, which grew in the 1970s and did so much to put the issue onto the public agenda, emerged from the protest and civil-rights movements of the 1960s. Many of the feminist activists of the 1970s had been involved in the American non-violent civil-rights and anti-war movements of the previous decade. Brownmiller herself had been a civil-rights activist and a volunteer on the 1964 'Freedom Summer' organized by SNCC and the Congress of Racial Equality (CORE). Then came 1968: 'I was marching against the war in Vietnam, when the Women's Liberation Movement erupted.'[17] That eruption led to important change during the following decade, both the enactment of legislation against sex discrimination in employment and education, and action against violence directed against women. New York Radical Feminists held their first conference on rape (organized by Brownmiller) in 1971; the battered women's movement was founded; and women's shelters and crisis centres were established across the United States.[18] The issue of violence against women had been placed squarely on the public agenda.

These developments were not unique to the United States. In other western countries, attitudes with regard to violence against women also changed from the 1970s onwards, and since the beginning of the 1980s there has been a worldwide trend towards reforming legal codes so as to expand the definition of what is considered to be rape (with regard both to who can be considered a victim and to what constitutes rape, i.e. the definition of rape no longer being restricted to non-consensual vaginal intercourse).[19] That is to say, over the past four decades or so, the scope of rape laws has expanded to 'cover many more actors and many more acts'.[20] During a time when cultural taboos about public discussion of sexual behaviour were dissolving, violent sexual behaviour could be debated more openly. Forceful campaigns by feminists thus had a growing impact on popular attitudes and then on legislation. As the authors of a 1987 study by the Bavarian Bureau of Criminal Investigation on 'violence of men against women' put it: 'It is not the extent of "violence against women" that is new, what is new is that this violence no longer is accepted but instead is problematized, attacked, assessed anew and rejected.'[21] This has been a driving force behind changes in legal frameworks, in law-enforcement practice, in media reporting with regard to intimate, sexual violence, to violence in spheres which for a long time essentially had been regarded as private matters and not really of public concern. No longer were beatings and sexual assaults to be tolerated just because they occurred behind closed doors.

The recent evolution in attitudes towards violence against women has affected not only how people in the West regard behaviour in their own societies and cultures. It has also been reflected in the ways they view other societies and the dismay at the treatment of women and children and the tolerance of intimate violence elsewhere. Concern about the position of women in Afghanistan is a prominent recent example. Despite the passage in 2009 of a law on the 'Elimination of Violence Against Women',[22] violence – sexual and other – against women remains common in Afghanistan, is generally not prosecuted in the courts, and has been a subject for frequent condemnation in western media. Voices are raised against 'the shameful violence against women in Afghanistan'; rousing calls are published for ending the 'discrimination of women and violence against them [that] has been anchored in the Afghan society for centuries';[23] outrage is expressed about a 'new Afghanistan law to silence victims of violence against women' (i.e. to ban relatives of a person accused of such violence to testify against them, in a country where 'most violence against women [...] is within the family').[24] This may say as much about contemporary western attitudes towards the subject as it does about what has occurred in that war-torn country.

The same may be said about reactions to the practice of 'honour' killings, which sadly have been a frequent occurrence in South Asia and have spilled over into immigrant communities in western countries (including the United Kingdom, Germany, Sweden, Norway, the United States and Canada),[25] and which have been condemned by the Human Rights Committee of the United Nations.[26] The message seems clear: we in the West have moved on to enlightened values whereby violence against women, domestic and intimate violence, have finally received the censure they deserve, and people elsewhere have some catching up to do.

Nevertheless, there should be little cause for complacency in the western world. Although considerable public attention is now given to domestic and intimate violence, although the statistics employed to buttress arguments about such violence are never likely to be precise, and although we probably will remain unable to draw completely reliable conclusions about whether it has been increasing or decreasing over time, domestic violence has been and remains widespread across all societies. Violence is a recurrent feature of family life, life that often is far removed from the idyllic picture of the happy household. Parents batter children, husbands batter wives and (although less frequently reported) wives batter husbands, and when sexual violence takes place it occurs more often than not between people who live under the same roof. Indeed, such intimate violence is probably the most common and widespread type of violence worldwide.

For many years, violence against women and children within the family was regarded as something normal or at least tolerable, and not meriting censure or legal penalty (even if, as Robert Calvert has observed for the US, 'one can only speculate as to whether the husband ever had an unrestricted right to beat his wife or whether certain activities of the husband were sanctioned by the courts and the general public').[27] However, this no longer necessarily is the case.[28] In recent decades, such assumptions have been called into question and, no less significant, are no longer reflected in legal codes. The change did not occur overnight. The shift in attitudes, and the relationship of the law and legal sanctions to domestic violence, has a longer history. The recognition that violence within the household and in the marriage bed was not necessarily legitimate did not materialize suddenly in the second half of the twentieth century. In the United States, for example, the common-law principle that a husband was legally entitled to 'physically chastise an errant wife' had already been overruled by courts in the 1870s (although one may question how much this actually affected behaviour behind closed doors during the late nineteenth century).[29] In England, the presumed legal right of a husband to inflict moderate corporal punishment on his wife in order to keep her 'within the bounds of duty' was removed in 1891.[30] Nevertheless, it was not really until the last quarter of the twentieth century that a fundamental revision was made in legal frameworks with regard to the most difficult area of domestic violence – the rape by a husband of a wife.

The recent change in perceptions and in the legal position of rape within marriage – which may be the most prevalent category of rape – provides one of the clearest indications of the heightened sensitivity towards violence that has characterized the social and cultural history of the western world since roughly the middle of the twentieth century. Introducing an article on 'The Family Context of Marital Rape', published in 1986 in what was then the new *Journal of Family Violence*, Lee Bidwell and Priscilla White asserted with their first sentence that 'sexual violence against females in our society is a growing problem'.[31] Leaving aside the question of how one might measure whether the problem in fact was 'growing' or not, it certainly was *seen* to be growing by the academic community and the public at large. At the time – in the mid-1980s – Bidwell and White predicted, rather pessimistically, that 'it probably will be a long time before every state [in the US] has a comprehensive marital rape law'.[32] In fact, only seven years later, in 1993, marital rape laws were on the books in every state in America. How did this come about?

Until quite recently, forcing sex on one's wife was not legally considered to be rape. The wishes of the woman at the time were not considered paramount since she was regarded to have consented to sex by the contract of marriage. At a time when (in England) a woman lost her own civil identity by marrying and a wife consequently was considered to be in effect a man's property rather than an individual in her own right,[33] there was no legal space within which to define forcible sexual intercourse within marriage as rape. 'Rape was considered a crime against another man's property rather than a violation against a woman's body and personal integrity. As a result, common law dictated that it was impossible for husbands to steal (i.e., rape) their own property (i.e., wives); thus marital rape was considered a legal impossibility.'[34] A similar situation existed in the United States, where rape had commonly been defined as 'sexual intercourse with a female not his wife without her consent'.[35] By exempting husbands thus from prosecution for raping their wives, this effectively provided them with what has been described as a 'licence to rape'.[36] Even where wife-beating was increasingly frowned upon – even where (according to Lawrence Stone, writing about eighteenth-century England), there had been a 'transformation of values' that involved a 'greater sensitivity to cruelty and violence',[37] and where overt physical cruelty became largely illegal by the end of the nineteenth century[38] – sexual violence that occurred within marriage was not yet a focus of substantial public concern or subject to legal sanction. The forward march of the 'civilizing process' had not reached the bedroom, which remained a private space.[39]

Indeed, the advance of civility and politeness, in making it more difficult for intimate violence to be discussed in the open, may have made it more difficult for sanctions to be applied against it. As Margaret Hunt has pointed out, 'it is very difficult to intervene in the unspeakable'.[40] Whether bourgeois women in fact were completely defenceless before violent husbands is a matter of debate. Elizabeth Foyster asserts that 'over the course of the eighteenth and nineteenth centuries, the middle classes sought to distance themselves from physically violent behaviour', and 'marital violence formed part of the public discourse'.[41] Nevertheless, it would take two centuries before marital violence in private was regarded with the same opprobrium in public and marital rape became subject to legal sanction.

The first state to abolish the distinction between rape outside marriage and rape within marriage was Soviet Russia, which took this revolutionary step in 1922;[42] from 1932 in Czechoslovakia a man could be prosecuted for raping his wife;[43] and in 1965 Sweden criminalized marital rape.[44] Whether these pioneering legal steps had much practical effect seems doubtful, and when the Swedish law was assessed in 1976, it was found that there had been only four reports of marital or cohabitation rape and no convictions. In any event, it was not really until the 1970s that the major shift in public attitudes towards domestic violence and in the responses of state institutions occurred, most importantly in the United States.

In December 1978, in Oregon, John Rideout became the first man in American history to be prosecuted for allegedly raping his wife.[45] The year before, the Oregon legislature had removed the common-law exemption that husbands could not be prosecuted for rape within marriage. At that time, only three American states – Delaware and Iowa, as well as Oregon – had ceased to recognize 'marital privilege' as a defence against the charge of rape; elsewhere in the United States, the definition of rape remained framed in common-law terms as 'the forcible penetration of the body of a woman not the wife of the perpe-trator'. In the event, John Rideout was acquitted. However, the trial received extensive media coverage and attracted wide public attention (not least when John Rideout and his wife Greta appeared on nationwide television, on *Good Morning America*),[46] and was followed by the abolition of marital exemptions to the charge of rape in many other states. By July 1980, nine American states had made rape in marriage a criminal offence, and in 1989 the number had grown to forty-two;[47] and on 5 July 1993 mari-tal rape became a crime in all states in the US.[48]

In the United Kingdom, the marital rape exemption was abol-ished as a result of a decision of the Appellate Committee of the House of Lords in October 1991.[49] This effectively overturned more than two centuries of English legal practice, based upon the proposition, articulated by English Chief Justice Sir Matthew Hale during the seventeenth century and published in 1736, that 'the husband cannot be guilty of a rape committed by him-self upon his lawful wife, for by their mutual matrimonial consent and contract the wife hath given herself up in this kind unto her husband which she cannot retract'.[50] (This 'was a licence also recognized in Scotland by Baron [David] Hume's treatise on Scottish Criminal Law (1797), which in effect main-tained that a husband could not be charged with raping his wife, because a wife had given her implied consent to sexual intercourse with her husband as a normal occurrence within marriage.')[51] This was not to say that a husband had an absolute right to commit violence against his wife. He could be prose-cuted for assault and battery; he could be charged with sodomy; and he was not allowed to murder. But forced vaginal inter-course was not subject to legal sanction. As Joanna Bourke has observed, 'a husband may not have absolute rights over his wife's entire body, but her vagina was legally assumed to be at his beck and call'.[52] Hale's proposition was widely, but not universally, accepted, and from the middle of the nineteenth century voices were raised in objection to the legal position of a wife that allowed her husband (in the words of John Stuart Mill) to 'claim from her and enforce the lowest degradation of a human being, that of being made an instrument of an animal function contrary to her inclinations'.[53]

It would not be until the last decade of the twentieth century that Hale's proposition was finally jettisoned. In their 1991 judgement, the Law Lords reasoned:

Hale's proposition reflected the state of affairs in these respects at the time it was enunciated. Since then the status of women, and particularly of married women, has changed out of all recognition in various ways which are very familiar and upon which it is unnecessary to go into detail. Apart from property matters and the availability of matrimonial remedies, one of the most important changes is that marriage is in modern times regarded as a partnership of equals, and no longer one in which the wife must be the subservient chattel of the husband. Hale's proposition involves that by marriage a wife gives her irrevocable consent to sexual intercourse with her husband under all circumstances and irrespective of the state of her health or how she happens to be feeling at the time. In modern times any reasonable person must regard that conception as quite unacceptable.[54]

The Law Lords proceeded from 'the belief that the marital exemption for rape ought to be abolished because the principle of implied consent on which it is grounded is anachronistic – no longer an accurate representation of the position of wives'.[55] In fact, their ruling was quite overdue, and the Hale proposition was already being circumvented by courts that began devising exceptions to the rule (although as late as in 1991 there still were cases where judges did not prove quite so enlightened).[56] In contemporary Britain, where a woman is regarded as an individual and not as an entity submerged in a marriage, the supposed marital exemption in rape had become 'quite unacceptable'. There had been a profound shift in public understanding of the acceptability of intimate violence against women.

Other countries took similar steps at roughly the same time. In France, attitudes similar to those enunciated by Sir Matthew Hale for England had been expressed well into the twentieth century. In a debate in the French *Sénat* as late as June 1978, Louis Virapoullé, a centre-right politician from Réunion (Outre-mer), declared baldly: 'There is no possibility of rape within a lawful union, because what then would become of conjugal duties?'[57] French law was revised in 1980, whereby rape was defined as 'any act of sexual penetration, whatever nature it may be, committed on another person by violence, coercion or surprise', a definition that did not rule out the idea of rape within marriage (or, for that matter, rape by someone of the same sex); however, the matter of marital rape itself was deliberately ignored at the time.[58] In the years that followed, the *Cour de cassation* (Supreme Court of Appeal) gradually moved towards admitting the existence of rape within marriage, and with an appeal decision in June 1992 the court made it clear that forcible sexual intercourse between spouses could be judged as rape. In 1994 the French *Code pénal* was revised further and violence committed by a spouse or cohabitee was recognized as aggravating circumstances, strengthening the custodial penalties for rape.[59]

Germany followed suit a few years later. There, the legal assumptions dating at least from the previous century had also been similar to those articulated by Sir Matthew Hale for England. In the nineteenth century the influential jurist (and president of the Frankfurt *Vorparlament* in 1848) Karl Joseph Anton Mittermaier declared: 'Whoever like the husband has a complete right to sexual intercourse [*Beischlaf*], does not make himself guilty of rape [*Notzucht*] by forcing the same.'[60] It was not until the late twentieth century that the legal position changed. As elsewhere, in West Germany campaigning by the women's movement during the 1970s and 1980s had brought the issue of violence against women into the public arena. Women's refuges were opened, and by the mid-1980s even leading Christian Democratic politicians (notably the Christian Democrat government ministers Heiner Geißler and Rita Süssmuth) had expressed their support for changes in the law on rape. In 1987, Rita Süssmuth, then 'Women's Minister' (i.e. Minister for Family Affairs, Senior Citizens, Women and Youth), stated flatly that 'this gap in the penal law will be closed'.[61] However, it was not until 1997, a quarter of a century after the first attempt by Social Democrats to reform the penal code with regard to sexual crime, that the law regarding rape was subject to a major reform.[62] The legal distinction between 'Vergewaltigung' (rape) and 'sexuelle Nötigung' (indecent assault) was lifted and the offence was defined as one committed against 'another person' – a change that for the first time extended the scope of the law to male victims of rape as well as to rape within marriage.[63] (Germany was not the first country to drop gender references from rape legislation; South Africa stripped gender from its rape laws in 1988.)[64] In 2004, German law was taken a step further, so that rape was no longer to be prosecuted only when charges were levelled by the alleged victim; instead it became an 'Offizialdelikt', i.e. an offence that the state has a responsibility to prosecute.

What began with a North American and European understanding of intimate violence has achieved global resonance. In the last twenty years or so, rape within marriage has been recognized as such and become grounds for legal prosecution in numerous countries, and marital rape was referred to specifically in the 'Declaration on the Elimination of Violence against Women', proclaimed by the United Nations General Assembly on 20 December 1993.[65] As of 2014, marital rape is considered a criminal offence in thirty-nine countries around the globe, including, in addition to most European states, countries in Africa (Zimbabwe, South Africa), Latin America (Argentina, Ecuador), and Asia (Hong Kong, Taiwan).[66]

Of course, changes in law do not necessarily lead to changes in the bedroom. Married women continue to be subjected to sexual violence by spouses, and it can be very difficult to mount an effective prosecution where 'it's his word against hers' and there is no corroboration by a third party. Nevertheless, changes in public perceptions and the fact that sexual violence within marriage is no longer legitimate (even if it continues to be widespread) reflect a shift in attitudes towards violence. The result has been a growing willingness to acknowledge, report and prosecute rape, including rapes committed by spouses, cohabitees or acquaintances of the victim. Against the background of a steep rise in the number of rapes recorded in the United States (from 21,400 in 1964, 55,400 in 1974, 84,230 in 1984 to 109,590 in 1992),[67] the director of the National Clearinghouse on Marital and Date Rape in Berkeley, California, could report with satisfaction in 1991: 'Prosecutors have historically been more comfortable pursuing stranger rape, but that is changing by leaps and bounds. Very serious criminal charges are now routinely filed in cases involving acquaintance rape. The whole atmosphere has changed, as more people come to understand that "no" means "no".'[68]

From the 1970s, domestic violence, in the way we have come to understand the term, has become a major topic for discussion in the media and an increasingly important concern for those employed in social services, medical care and the criminal-justice system.[69] In Britain, the reporting of sex crime, most of which appeared in the sensationalist, popular press in the 1950s and 1960s, surfaced increasingly on the pages of 'quality' newspapers during the 1970s and 1980s.[70] In the United States, the sociologist Nancy Berns observed in 1999:

Today not only is there a domestic violence vocabulary and a host of social science theories, but domestic violence is represented in talk shows, movies, and popular magazines. Social scientists have generated a vast literature on domestic violence, some of which has entered the popular media and the consciousness of its consumers.[71]

Until the late 1970s, the media used the term 'domestic violence' to refer to riots and terrorism. However, with the rise of the battered women's movement, terms such as 'battered women' and 'battered woman syndrome' were coined and began appearing in the media.[72]

At the same time as domestic violence was attracting attention from the criminal-justice system and from social scientists and the media, western countries saw the creation and remarkable proliferation of shelters for battered women. This, too, was a consequence of raised public awareness of domestic violence against women, and was also driven in large measure by feminist activists. The first modern women's shelter was the Chiswick Women's Aid that was opened by Erin Pizzey in Chiswick, in west London, in 1971, and by 1980 roughly 150 women's shelters were operating in England. In the United States, the first such shelter was established by a feminist legal-aid collective in St Paul, Minnesota, in 1973, and by the mid-1980s there were over a thousand shelters across the US, offering a range of services for battered women.[73] Increasingly, these shelters received public funding, from state and local government – a measure of changes in public attitudes and increasingly broad acceptance of the problem and the need to do something about it.

Elsewhere there were similar developments. In Germany, the first modern shelter for women (*Frauenhaus*) opened in West Berlin in 1976.[74] Shelters opened soon thereafter in Switzerland and Austria. In Sweden, the first shelters were established in

1979, first in Gothenburg and then in Stockholm; in 1984 a 'National Organization of Shelters for Battered Women in Sweden' was created; and by the mid-1990s the number of shelters in Sweden was nearly ninety (all of which received state funding).[75] And after the Communist dictatorship in the German Democratic Republic collapsed in 1989, within months dozens of women's centres and shelters for battered women were set up in eastern Germany.[76] By that point the need to establish such shelters seemed obvious – another sign that public attitudes towards domestic violence had changed profoundly.

At the same time, violence against women and the plight of battered women increasingly became a matter for intervention by the courts. In the United States, the battered women's movement looked to the criminal-justice system to address its concerns. The aim was to raise public consciousness about domestic violence and its impact both on the victims themselves and on their families and society more generally.[77] They succeeded. Fundamental changes occurred in how the police and the legal system dealt with accusations of violence against women. Thus police were required, as a result of mandatory arrest laws, to take suspects into custody where there was probable cause to believe that an assault had taken place. Once charges were brought, the case had to go to court even if the alleged victim (who may have been subjected to pressure from her abuser) wished to drop charges; restraining orders, protection and financial support were provided in order to facilitate filing charges and leaving an abusive relationship.[78]

Like the establishment of shelters for battered women, the provision of restraining orders against those considered likely to display violent behaviour signified a shift not only in the role of the state but also in public attitudes towards intimate violence, and not only in the US. In the United Kingdom as well, the police began to devote greater attention to domestic violence. In 1986, described as a 'watershed year in the area of domestic violence, as it began to be recognized and treated as a serious social problem', the Home Office offered guidance to police, emphasizing the 'overriding concern to reduce the risk of further violence [...] after the departure of the police from the scene'.[79] While the actual effectiveness of police intervention in cases of domestic violence may be debated, there was clearly a growing expectation that the criminal-justice system should take it seriously.

Not only violence against women but also violence against children has attracted growing concern in recent decades. A major issue has been corporal punishment: should smacking children be regarded as a private matter, to be tolerated or even commended as an effective way to impart discipline, or should it be viewed as a public concern, to be curbed or even prosecuted? The concern is not new. In April 1860, in Eastbourne on the south coast of England, the fifteen-year-old schoolboy Reginald Cancellor was killed accidentally by his schoolmaster, Thomas Hopley. Hopley had been granted permission by Reginald's father to inflict 'severe corporal punishment' on the adolescent, who by all accounts was an obstinate pupil. He died as a result of the beating he received. Hopley was indicted for manslaughter, and the resulting trial was given sensationalist treatment in the press, sparking demands for 'the abolition of all corporal punishment in the schools of England' (the *Brighton Advertiser*, 11 May 1860) and 'the total abolition of corporal punishment' (the *Brighton Examiner*, 31 July 1860).[80]

Although inflicting 'moderate and reasonable corporal punishment' was not considered to be against the law of England, and although Hopley maintained that 'he acted for good, in an age which accepted his actions were not abnormal',[81] he was judged to have used 'excessive chastisement' and was therefore convicted of manslaughter and sentenced to four years' imprisonment. It was not until the late twentieth century that the demand of the *Brighton Advertiser* would be satisfied (while that of the *Brighton Examiner* remains unrealized). The Prevention of Cruelty to Children Act of 1904 endorsed the 'right of any parent, teacher or other person having the lawful charge of a child or young person to administer reasonable punishment to him';[82] and Britain was the last country in western Europe to end corporal punishment in schools: corporal punishment was not abolished in state schools in England until 1987, and in private schools not until 1999. The 'total abolition of corporal punishment' in England, however, has not yet been achieved.

In the United States, the application of corporal punishment was also debated in the nineteenth century. There, the great educational reformer Horace Mann, after his appointment as secretary of the Massachusetts Board of Education in 1837, provoked a heated public dispute with thirty-one Boston schoolmasters when he criticized the practice of indiscriminate corporal punishment in the city's schools (drawing unfavourable comparisons with Prussian schools, which he had visited and claimed functioned well without resorting to physical coercion).[83] It was, however, some time before his fellow Americans followed Mann's lead. While the state of New Jersey brought an end to corporal punishment in schools in 1867, it took more than a century before another state – Massachusetts in 1972 – followed suit.[84] By the end of the twentieth century just over half of American states had banned the practice.

In the twentieth century it was the Swedes who were pioneers in efforts to do away entirely with corporal punishment (followed in short order by the other Nordic countries). Whereas the corporal punishment of children had been widespread in Sweden until the early twentieth century – there even were books written about how one could beat children most effectively[85] – over the course of the twentieth century a series of changes in law did away with corporal punishment step by step. (Corporal punishment was abolished in *Gymnasien* in Sweden already in 1928.) Then, in 1979, Sweden became the first country worldwide in which corporal punishment was prohibited completely. In the debate about the ban in the Swedish parliament – where the bill was passed by 259 votes against only six in opposition – one (conservative) deputy asserted that 'in a free democracy like ours we use words as arguments not blows. We talk to people not beat them.'[86] From 1979, according to the Swedish Parenthood and Guardianship Code, 'a child should not be subjected to corporal punishment or other humiliating treatment'. The aim of the code was not to imprison parents for smacking their children, but to achieve a change in public attitudes towards corporal punishment and thus eventually its disappearance. In this the reform met with considerable success. A rather remarkable transformation in Swedish popular opinion occurred during the last third of the twentieth century: whereas in 1965 more than half (53 per cent) of Swedes approved of corporal punishment, in 1971 the comparable figure was 35 per cent and by 1994 it had fallen to a mere 11 per cent.[87] One may question the degree to which changes in legislation altered popular opinion or to which changes in popular opinion led to legislative reform – and, of course, married women continue to be raped and children continue to be beaten. Nevertheless, the fact that such behaviour no longer is accepted generally suggests that a significant shift in popular opinion with regard to violence occurred during the last three decades of the twentieth century.

This shift was paralleled in other countries. While child welfare attracted increasing concern from the late nineteenth and early twentieth centuries onwards, it took some time before domestic violence against children, including physical 'chastisement' by parents, really came to be challenged. In the United Kingdom, the landmark 1908 Children Act (a part of the wave of social legislation passed by the Liberal Party after its landslide victory of 1906) created a separate juvenile justice system, reflecting the growing belief that children were different from adults and therefore needed special treatment and protection from detrimental influences, and extending legal protection for child and youth welfare (introducing, among other things, juvenile courts and the registration of foster parents). Yet it left the right of parents to punish their children, to apply corporal punishment in their homes and against their children, essentially untouched: 'Nothing in the Part of this Act shall be construed to take away or affect the right of any parent, teacher, or other person having the lawful control or charge of a child or young person to administer punishment to such child or young person.'[88]

At times, parents actively were encouraged to use corporal punishment to discipline their children. In Ireland (all of which had been part of the UK when the 1908 Children Act was passed), recommendations came from the bench, for example, to a father that 'what this boy needs is a good thrashing' (the advice of a district justice in 1930 in the Roscommon District Court to the father of two boys charged with housebreaking) and to a mother that her son's school attendance might improve if she beat him occasionally; in 1957 a district justice in the Dublin Children's Court 'advised a mother that "a few whacks of a stick"' would bring her delinquent son '"to his senses"'.[89] Although the law formally protected children from assault, it also gave parents the right to discipline their children, and thus the courts were not inclined to interfere with the use of corporal punishment in the home.

Attitudes changed during the second half of the twentieth century. Harry Hendrick has noted for the UK that 'by the end of the 1960s, a new problem had arrived: child abuse', and that 'sexual abuse was *the* child protection issue from about 1984'.[90] In the United States at the same time there was 'an almost unbelievable increase in public awareness' of child abuse: whereas in 1976 polling evidence revealed that only about 10 per cent of Americans viewed child abuse as a serious problem, in a 1982 poll 90 per cent of those surveyed regarded it as such.[91]

While there were differing opinions about the cause of the problem – whether it be the character of the abusing parent or social inequality and poverty – there was agreement that domestic violence against children was a public concern and not just a private affair. Public interest in child abuse and violence against children was amplified by notorious cases, given prominence in the press. In the United Kingdom, the battering to death by her stepfather of seven-year-old Maria Colwell, whose killing in Brighton in January 1973 led to the first of thirty-four inquiries into the deaths of children known to social services departments of local authorities over the next fourteen years,[92] has not been forgotten more than four decades later. Public concern about child protection and calls for state intervention grew, and by the end of the twentieth century public attitudes in the UK about the supposed 'right' of parents to hit their children had altered significantly. While the UK has not (yet) followed Sweden's example and prohibited parents from hitting their children – indeed, in 1994 the High Court upheld the right of a childminder to smack children in her care, with the permission of their parents[93] – corporal punishment in schools is no longer permitted and the National Society for the Prevention of Cruelty to Children has been active in calling for extending the ban to the home and for the right of children to be free of all forms of physical punishment.[94]

In Germany, changes have gone further than in Britain, reflecting the diminishing acceptance of violence generally in German society. In July 2000, the German Civil Code, which previously had affirmed the right of the father to use appropriate means of discipline against his child, was amended to prohibit corporal punishment in the home, asserting that children had 'a right to a non-violent upbringing'. Consequently 'corporal punishment, psychological injuries and other humiliating measures' were prohibited. German child-care law went further, and was amended so as to place a duty on the authorities to 'promote ways in which families can resolve conflict without resort to force'.[95] This was a culmination of public discussion about corporal punishment that had been underway almost since the end of the Second World War and that formed part of the general liberalization of West German society that occurred in the wake of war and National Socialism.[96] While heated debate about corporal punishment in schools had taken place in the 1950s, when the courts allowed moderate corporal punishment to be employed, and although the great majority of West Germans continued to approve of the corporal punishment of children well into the 1970s,[97] the tide was turning. Dirk Schumann has observed that 'at the end of the 1940s almost all the *Länder* of the Federal Republic granted teachers the right to carry out corporal punishment; in the early 1970s almost all of them revoked it';[98] and in 1976 the German Supreme Court ruled that corporal punishment in schools had no legal basis.[99]

The shift in attitudes that culminated in the banning of corporal punishment of children in Germany had its roots not only in the anti-authoritarian movements of the 1960s and 1970s, but also in the development of new, 'democratic' conceptions of fatherhood in post-war West Germany. Post-war criticism of authoritarian, patriarchal models of fatherhood – at a time when millions of fathers were missing as a result of wartime losses – was not least a criticism of 'fathers who raised their children with "authoritarian [...] and violent methods"' and who allegedly 'had been the midwives of the Nazi dictatorship'.[100] The 'new models of domestic masculinity, so central to the early West German quest for democracy', meant, in Till van Rahden's formulation, substituting 'gentle fatherhood instead of militarized masculinity'.[101] Violence was out; the 'playful father' was in. 'Democratic fatherhood' was non-violent fatherhood, and was to help ensure that Germany would not revert to its authoritarian, militaristic and violent past. Even so, a recent (2012) study based on interviews with German parents found (not

191

altogether surprisingly) that corporal punishment in the home had not disappeared: four out of ten parents admitted to smacking their children on the bottom, and one in ten on the face (although they reported immediately regretting what they had done).[102] Nevertheless, opinion research in Germany has indicated that over the past couple of decades the proportion of parents regarding non-violent education as the ideal has grown – by 2005 it stood at 90 per cent.[103]

In France, the story has been rather more ambiguous. There, the 'right of correction' that teachers enjoyed from the early nineteenth century (and confirmed in a Supreme Court ruling in 1908, allowing them to apply corporal punishment) has been modified but not completely abolished; court decisions in 2000 and 2002 ruled out habitual and 'non-educational' corporal punishment and acts such as pulling hair, kicking behinds or slapping faces.[104] Corporal punishment in the home has remained lawful, however, under the customary 'right of correction'. Recently there have been calls for reform in France, and in 2010 a bill aimed at prohibiting all corporal punishment in childrearing was filed in the National Assembly, but it failed to be debated. According to a study carried out in 2007, 82.5 per cent of parents questioned agreed that 'non-violent child-rearing is the ideal'; however, 61 per cent of grandparents and 53 per cent of parents questioned in another study said that they opposed a ban on the corporal punishment of children.[105]

Over the past three decades, the right of children to be free of violence has been recognized – if not necessarily practised or enforced – in a growing number of countries. Children are seen to have a right to a non-violent environment. In November 1989, the United Nations General Assembly adopted the 'United Nations Convention on the Rights of the Child', according to which states were required to 'take all appropriate legislative, social and educational measures to protect the child from all forms of physical and mental violence, injury or abuse, neglect or negligent treatment, maltreatment or exploitation, including sexual abuse, while in the care of parent(s), legal guardian(s) or any other person who has the care of the child' (Article 19.1).[106] The convention since has been ratified by 193 states, leaving only Somalia, South Sudan and the United States. (Somalia and the USA have signed the convention but not ratified it.)

While the UN convention does not mention corporal punishment explicitly, in recent years numerous countries have followed the Swedish lead and banned it. By the end of the twentieth century, the corporal punishment of children had been prohibited both in school and in the home in all the Scandinavian countries save Iceland, as well as in Austria, Cyprus, Latvia and Croatia, and by 2010 it had been prohibited in a further twenty-six countries (including Bulgaria, Israel, Germany, Iceland, Ukraine, Hungary, Greece, the Netherlands, New Zealand, Uruguay, Spain, Costa Rica, Poland and Albania). Huge numbers of children certainly continue to be neglected, beaten, injured and abused, but there now is international agreement that such behaviour is illegitimate.

Domestic violence, whether against children or adults, is now considered widely to be an evil for which no excuses can be made. It is never out of the news, and is constantly in the public consciousness. Everyone, it seems, wants to express opposition to it. Campaigns have been launched by local-government authorities for 'Zero Tolerance of Violence against Women' (e.g. in Edinburgh in 1992); police forces have sponsored media campaigns with messages such as 'Family Violence is a Crime' (e.g. in New Zealand in 1997); charities have mounted advertising campaigns against the abuse of children (e.g. Barnardo's in the UK in 2001); corporations have supported campaigns against violence against women (e.g. Liz Claiborne and Philip Morris in the 1990s).[107] Children are encouraged to ring confidential telephone lines (e.g. ChildLine in the UK, established in 1986 by the television presenter Esther Rantzen and part of the NSPCC since

2006); numerous telephone helplines have been set up in order to facilitate the reporting of domestic violence (e.g. the National Domestic Violence Hotline in the United States); adults are admonished to be on the lookout for signs of domestic violence. In the United States, even beauticians have been encouraged to participate, by 'CUT IT OUT: Salons Against Domestic Abuse' (first established in Birmingham Alabama in 2002), and to be trained 'on how to recognize the signs of abuse and safely refer victims to help'.[108]

Ideas and ideals about protecting women and children from violence, articulated in the nineteenth century, have not only been widely accepted within numerous countries but have also become the subject of international codes and a basis for legal obligation and state action. Since the early 1990s, international law has come to recognize violence against women and domestic violence as a violation of human rights, notably with the United Nations General Assembly Declaration on the Elimination of Violence against Women of 1993.[109] More recently, the UN has identified violence against women and domestic violence as a form of torture, and the Council of Europe Task Force to Combat Violence against Women, including Domestic Violence, has called for a legally binding convention encompassing domestic violence. In 2011, the Council of Europe Convention on Preventing and Combating Violence against Women and Domestic Abuse included an obligation on the signatories to 'take the necessary legislative or other measures to set up statewide round-the-clock (24/7) telephone helplines free of charge to provide advice to callers, confidentially or with due regard to their anonymity, in relation to all forms of violence covered by the scope of this Convention'.[110] Such initiatives may not necessarily prevent violence, but they place it within a new legal, political and social context. Bonita Meyersfeld observes, introducing her analysis of *Domestic Violence and International Law*:

State institutions cannot stay the blow of a violent fist. However, once charged with the knowledge of such violence, they can provide an effective response, a haven for recuperation, facilities for rehabilitation, and an expression of remorse and condemnation of such violence. Such measures would radically change the experience of the victim, limiting her pain to the period of the violence and not a moment beyond.[111]

As Meyersfeld writes, domestic violence has been identified as 'a global human rights concern', and 'there is evidence in international law of a *developing* norm that domestic violence against women is a human rights violation and that this norm is in the process of maturing into a universally binding principle of international law'.[112] Increasingly, people are seen to have a *right* not to be subjected to violence, in private as well as in public.

How might the increased sensitivity about intimate and domestic violence be explained? The growth of feminist movements from the late 1960s and 1970s has certainly been a major contributory factor, but this is only part of the story and may be as much a symptom of underlying change as its cause. More generally, the change may reflect an embrace of 'individualized models of society' in the western world since the Second World War, whereby the concerns, sensibilities and rights of the individual occupy centre stage. Of course, the focus on the individual did not begin in 1945; it had been embedded in the Declaration of the Rights of Man of 1789. Nevertheless, the Second World War 'marked a watershed [that] spurred the long-term trend toward individualization, ushering western-born models of individualized societies onto an increasingly globalized stage'; following the Second World War 'many countries reclassified sex crimes from offences against morality, the family, good customs, honour, or chastity – prioritizing the corporate order – to offences against liberty, self-determination, or physical integrity – emphasizing individual freedom'.[113]

With the spread of liberal democracy and the language of universal human rights, alongside the development of modern means of birth control, the understanding of the purpose of sex changed: in the context of 'post-war individualization', whereby men and women are understood to be free and equal individual entities, 'increasingly, sex was conceived through an individualized prism' and, consequently, 'consent emerged as the cardinal rule of sexual relations'.[114] Thus violence and coercion, whether in public or in private, could not be justified or condoned, and social, cultural and legal codes increasingly came to reflect that.[115] It is the individual, the victim, who has become the focus of concern.

Yet not all individuals are viewed equally, for violence tends to be perceived as more of a 'male' trait – an assumption that lies behind many of the changes discussed above. The growing concern about domestic violence has – perhaps understandably – focused on women, who more often than not (even if not necessarily in all cases) are on the receiving end. The impetus for taking domestic violence seriously, for providing refuge for its victims and for ensuring that the criminal-justice system deal with it firmly has come in large measure from a feminist movement that grew phenomenally in strength and influence across the western world and beyond since the 1960s. The increased sensitivity with regard to domestic violence is in large measure an increased sensitivity towards male violence against women, and it is aimed against the idea that masculinity needs to be equated with violence. The 'new models of domestic masculinity' are those that should allow for gentleness, and the changes outlined in this chapter suggest that this perception has been making headway.

Domestic and intimate violence has come to attract attention and opprobrium in the western world to an extent that is truly remarkable. Accusations of such behaviour can now destroy public careers. One recent example is that of Carlos Henriquez, who had been a member of the Massachusetts House of Representatives representing Dorchester, in Boston. On 6 February 2014, the Massachusetts House of Representatives expelled Henriquez, who was removed after he had been convicted of domestic violence, having been charged with assaulting his girlfriend.[116] This marked the first time in nearly a century that a member had been expelled from the chamber. (The last previous expulsion had taken place in 1916, when Representative Harry Foster was expelled after he was found to have 'collected money from people interested in legislation now pending'.)

The vote in the Massachusetts legislature was overwhelming: 146–5, after a mere two hours of debate. A few days previously, before sentencing Henriquez to serve six months in prison with a further two years suspended, and requiring him to complete a 'batterers' programme', the presiding Judge Michele Hogan stated: 'There's much too much domestic violence in this country, in this community. A woman and her word are to be respected. When a woman tells you she does not want to have sex, that means: "I do not want to have sex." And after she says that you don't hit her, you don't punch her, you don't take her on a ride she doesn't want to go on.'[117]

Michele Hogan's unequivocal statement is a sign of our times – a clear declaration of how intimate violence has come to be regarded and of how attitudes have evolved. The battering of women, the rape of wives, the beating of children, and the murder of women in so-called 'honour killings' are not new phenomena. Today, however, they are subjects of increased public awareness and condemnation. These crimes are recognized as crimes; and cultures of tolerance towards domestic and intimate violence are being dismantled, at least in western countries. The legal and, increasingly, social and cultural equality of women, the increased visibility of women in the public sphere, and the growing importance of the individual with the development of western individualized societies have changed the boundaries between public violence and intimate violence and its acceptability. The fate of Ana Orantes sadly is not unique. However, the fact that we know her name is an indication that something has changed, that we have witnessed a cultural shift of huge proportions.

VII

Control

Today there is general agreement that violence can and should be controlled. A civilized society is one in which violence is kept in check; a well-functioning state is one that can prevent violence and protect its citizens from violence; well-adjusted, civilized individuals are those who can and do keep violent urges under control. These assumptions are so widely held that they may seem hardly to require elucidation. Yet while a modern, well-ordered society rests upon the effective control of violence, that control involves a fundamental paradox, articulated by the German sociologist Heinrich Popitz: 'Social order is a necessary condition for containing violence – violence is a necessary condition for maintaining social order.'[1] Thus there may be no escaping violence, even when one succeeds in controlling it. An effective criminal-justice system must be able to apply force if it is to suppress and prevent violence, and sanctions against violent behaviour are necessary if people are to adhere to codes of behaviour that inhibit violence.

This, in essence, frames the two 'fundamentally opposite' models of an order that controls violence: 'on the one hand, forced, repressive pacification by a state wielding superior power; and on the other hand, the self-regulation of social relations by mechanisms of socialization, social control and market forces'.[2] The two models – essentially that posited by Thomas Hobbes (that the state is tasked with repressive pacification) on the one hand and that posited by Adam Smith (that self-regulation exerts control) on the other – may be 'opposite' when it comes to controlling violence, but they also are interrelated. The existence of a state apparatus that effectively maintains law and order frames popular expectations about what is and is not acceptable behaviour; and the existence of social and cultural norms that inhibit violent behaviour make it easier for the state to maintain the peace and to keep violence under control. In both respects, people expect that violence should be controlled effectively, either by an effective state apparatus (and in particular its law-enforcement organizations) or by social and cultural norms that are taken to be signs of civilized behaviour. Whether the police actually function in this way, or whether social norms actually do inhibit violence is another matter. The point is that they are expected to do so.

Introducing their recent collection on the control of violence, Andrea Kirschner and Stefan Malthaner observe that 'one of the core challenges faced by societies in all cultures and ages is that of limiting, and if possible preventing, destructive violence':[3]

The modern world, with all its faith in technical progress, long believed that social processes were completely controllable. This belief was supported and reiterated in theories of modernization and civilization. Against the background of growing prosperity, these theories held that modern societies had been pacified through an increasingly successful combination of control by the state and emotional self-restraint by the individual. [...] But the twentieth century's record on violence is not unambiguous. Considering the unparalleled number of casualties caused by wars, civil strife, genocide, and totalitarian and dictatorial regimes in the twentieth century, there are good reasons to doubt the assumption that social development and the consolidation of governmental control mechanisms result in a general decrease in violence.[4]

There may be trust that in the modern, developed world violence can be controlled, but there also is fear that we may be skating on rather thin ice – not only because of the explosions of violence in our recent past but also because the institutions on which we rely to suppress violence sometimes themselves behave violently and possess a tremendous potential for violence. A strong state today is capable both of suppressing violence and of exercising force to a degree unimaginable a century or two ago.

The suppression of violence and the capability to exercise violence are thus bound up with one another, for the control of violence by the state requires that, if necessary, it can apply force effectively. Indeed, among the defining characteristics of modern, developed societies are the effort made and resources expended to secure and maintain control over violence, in order to protect not only the state but also the population as a whole. A well-functioning state is capable of ensuring 'community safety',[5] of maintaining the peace and enabling the citizenry to enjoy a life free of violent threat.

The 1960s and, particularly, the 1970s, appear to have constituted a pivotal moment in the evolution of the control of violence by the state. Well-publicized rises in recorded violent crime (after a period of relatively low crime rates) and an expansion of the size and reach of government, alongside a mushrooming of academic research (much of it funded by agencies with an interest in social policy)[6] into various aspects of violence and the growing influence of feminist perspectives, led to heightened concern that violence, private as well as public, be kept in check. Efforts to do this may or may not have succeeded, but a broad consensus formed that violence across the board – from premeditated murder to the physical and verbal abuse of women and children – is something deviant,[7] that it must be brought under control, and that a main task of the forces at the disposal of the state is to do just that. Ideally, this is to be accomplished with a minimum of overt violence: police brutality is routinely condemned, even if in practice it has occurred all too frequently and is often difficult to prosecute.[8] The proper task of the police has been to prevent violence, not to provoke it. Whereas at one time (Peter King notes for early-modern England), 'physical violence was regarded as an acceptable instrument of social policy [and] accepted as the primary means by which the state punished offenders',[9] by the second half of the twentieth century the state was expected to prevent violence, not to apply it (at least not internally).

It has been some time since physical violence was 'accepted as the primary means by which the state punished offenders'. Of course, violence continued to be employed by police during the twentieth century, although increasingly it has attracted censure. This can be seen in the reactions to one of the worst instances of police violence in Europe since the Second World War, the massacre by police of at least forty and perhaps as many as 200 Algerians demonstrating in Paris on 17 October 1961. This outrage was largely ignored for decades, but recently it has received appropriate acknowledgement.[10] Although violence on so large a scale has been the exception in the West, police have employed excessive force on occasion when confronting crowds: French police responded violently to student demonstrations in Paris in 1968, as did the Metropolitan Police to the demonstrations against the 'Poll Tax' in London in March 1990 and Italian police to demonstrators protesting against the meeting of the G8 in Genoa in July 2001. When rioting erupted in numerous cities across the United States during the 1960s, police (and National Guard) tactics often exacerbated already tense situations and sparked violence.

More recently, the rioting in Los Angeles in April 1992 cast a revealing light on the role of the police in provoking violence and on the expectation that they should control it. In the unrest in Los Angeles, which followed the acquittal of four (white) police officers involved in the brutal beating of an African-American man, Rodney King, in March 1991 after a high-speed car chase, fifty-three people died and over 2,000 were injured, more than 13,000 people were arrested and estimates of the resulting property damage were as high as $900 million. Popular anger at the police behaviour led to efforts to introduce legislation at both California state and US federal level to prohibit conduct by police officers that deprived individuals of their civil rights.[11] After King died, in June 2012, the Reverend Al Sharpton was quoted as saying that 'history will record that it was Rodney King's beating and his actions that made America deal with the excessive misconduct of law enforcement'.[12] This may have been something of an overstatement, but the beating of Rodney King certainly drew renewed attention to police violence and to the role of the police in maintaining (or endangering) law and order.

The problem of police behaviour *vis-à-vis* disadvantaged minority communities has not been exclusive to the United States. According to one analysis of twenty-four riots between 1990 and 1995 in the *banlieues*, the poor suburbs of French cities that are home to recent immigrants and their children, at least ten resulted from the direct or indirect involvement of police or private security guards in the deaths of minority ethnic youths.[13] In 2005, Nicolas Sarkozy, French Interior Minister at the time, may have aided his future campaign for the presidency of the Republic when he called for a tough response against those he publicly labelled '*racaille*' ('riff-raff' or 'rabble') and held responsible for the explosion of violence (largely, it must be said, against property) that occurred in October and November of that year. Whether that helped to bring the violence under control is another matter.

Concern about urban unrest led to critical thinking about police tactics. If the police were to control such violence effectively, they needed to establish better relations with the communities in which the violence occurred. Researchers who had investigated the police role in inner-city rioting in San Francisco and Boston during the late 1960s concluded: 'Police–community relations are critical to controlling collective violence and if we wish to reduce the likelihood of future rioting, police and city leaders must be ever vigilant in monitoring and ameliorating law enforcement abuses that might damage relationships between the authorities and those whom they serve and protect.'[14] The mission to 'serve and protect' involves controlling potentially violent behaviour among the police themselves as well as among the public. That, it seems, requires a closer relationship between the police and those that they are expected to 'serve and protect'.

Consequently, considerable attention has been devoted to what was termed 'community policing', an approach that was the subject of a great deal of public discussion during the late 1980s and the 1990s (and that was lauded by President Bill Clinton in his State of the Union address of January 1994). As an American academic observer noted in 2001, 'community policing is the order of the day'.[15] In 1994, The New York Times, described the 'community policing' model being promoted by New York City Police Commissioner William Bratton (better-known as the chief advocate of a 'zero tolerance' model of policing) as 'the most promising trend in urban law enforcement', that 'aims to involve police departments in crime prevention, not just crime reaction'. It went on to say:

Community policing is not about brawny police officers being tied down delivering social work sermons. It involves quite a different role for the alert and caring police officer. It asks the officer to use the information gathered on the beat to notify relevant city agencies to problems like substance abuse, domestic violence, child neglect, gangs and sexual exploitation before they lead to serious crimes.[16]

That is to say, police were to be proactive, to involve members of the community in crime-fighting, and to prevent violence from arising rather than just responding to it after it had occurred. This model proved attractive not only in the Anglo-Saxon world but also beyond, from France (where the model of the *police de proximité* was introduced in 1998), to Singapore (otherwise noted for its tough approach to crime, and where the Japanese Koban – neighbourhood police post – system was introduced in 1983)[17] and to Chile (where national policy favoured a community-based approach to policing, and where there is greater trust in the police than elsewhere in Latin America).[18] The idea of community policing often harked back to a supposedly simpler time, with police patrolling on bicycles and creating a less intimidating impression.[19] In Britain, the idea of 'community policing' conjured up images of a peaceful, orderly countryside policed by the 'village bobby' – 'the idea of the police bringing the apparent order of the countryside to the chaos of the city'.[20] Regardless of whether it was accurate, it could offer an imagined picture of a harmonious and essentially non-violent relationship between the police and the community for which they were responsible.

While there has been considerable discussion about what police strategies and tactics might be most effective for maintaining social order, there is general agreement that the control of violence and the provision of security – understood as an absence of violence and of the threat of violence – is a central task of the state. Accordingly, modern police forces, whose task is to protect not just the rulers but also the general public, have grown enormously in size and scope during the twentieth century. The criminal-justice system in the wider sense has been tasked not just with apprehending those who commit violent crime but also with providing 'structured programmes for adolescents and adults who have shown repeated aggression or been convicted of personal violence'. That is to say, the therapeutic state is charged both with suppressing violence and with changing the behaviour of those regarded as prone to committing violence.[21] Behaviour that may previously have been regarded as a private affair or as broadly socially acceptable (or at least tolerable), and that may have been regulated informally within the community, has become increasingly subject to state control. Citizens in prosperous, developed societies have come to expect protection by state organizations whose job it is to control and prevent outbreaks of violence. The state is expected to provide security not just for itself but also for its citizens.

This is relatively new. Roger Lane (whose academic research has focused on the study of violence in nineteenth-century urban America) offers a revealing description of conditions in Massachusetts in 1835:

> Neither fits of violence nor bouts of drunkenness disrupted any vital patterns. Individual problems, sins or even crimes, were not generally cause for wider social concern. Under these circumstances, the Commonwealth [of Massachusetts] could afford a fairly high degree of lawlessness. No city in the state boasted a professional police, and the machinery of justice was not equipped to handle many cases. Many of the more common forms of violence or crime were simply not reported to the agents of the law, as those affected either shrugged off their injuries or struck back directly.[22]

From the perspective of the late twentieth century (when the passage above was written), conditions in the still largely rural Massachusetts of the 1830s seemed far away indeed. It was not really until the late nineteenth century that things began to change, but even after the introduction of uniformed constables to cities in the US, police in urban America were singularly ineffective in combating crime. The most perceptive historian of American policing, Eric Monkkonen, noted that 'the idea that people have a right to be free of crime in their daily lives and that the government has an obligation to provide this security was new to nineteenth-century America' (and, it may be said, new to Europe as well); yet at that time 'the police spent the most useful of their long hours on duty reporting open sewers, shooting stray dogs, and arresting drunks'. They did not make much of an impact on violent crime.[23] Such a state of affairs would probably have been regarded as a public scandal a hundred years later – even if, as two American observers put it in 1988, 'most of the time, cops passively patrol and provide emergency services'.[24] To Americans during the late twentieth century (and not just to them), it had become almost unimaginable that violent crime might not have been a matter of 'wider social concern', that in most cases the agents of state were not present to intervene, and that those on the receiving end of violent acts 'either shrugged off their injuries or struck back directly'.

The expectation that the police are obliged to protect the public and the assumption that the state possesses the ability comprehensively to control interpersonal violence are rather recent phenomena. In the United States, until the late nineteenth century, the police acted less as an organ of crime control and more as a general social service – as 'civil servants of general resort', who performed tasks ranging from inspecting weights and measures to running soup kitchens, housing the homeless and recovering lost children. According to Monkkonen, the

American police shed their wider social service functions and narrowed their focus to crime, 'to respond more directly to crimes of violence', a transformation that he sees as having occurred in the mid-1890s.[25]

In Europe, the shift in the perceived responsibility of state and police with regard to interpersonal violence occurred in a different context. In much of Europe, unlike in the United States or Britain (though not Ireland), armed, militarized police institutions developed during the nineteenth century. The model originated in France with the *Gendarmerie nationale* that developed out of the *Maréchaussée* during the eighteenth century and was exported by Napoleon. This shaped police formations across Europe, including the *Carabinieri* in Italy and the *Guardia Civil* in Spain, and even had its parallel in the United Kingdom with the Royal Irish Constabulary.[26] The tasks of these gendarme formations included suppressing crime and maintaining public order, and effectively introducing and representing the state in the countryside (among other things, by suppressing brigands, enforcing conscription, and assisting with the collection of taxes). They were therefore important agents of state-building, representing and enforcing the authority of government in the nation states of the nineteenth century. Only more recently has the control of interpersonal violence *per se* (including domestic violence) become a core responsibility of the state and of the police. As Lawrence Sherman has put it, we keep 'our hands clean by assigning our primitive responses to violence to the police, leaving them to suffer with the paradox of causing harm to prevent harm'.[27] This is the paradox identified by Heinrich Popitz, which lies at the core of policing in contemporary developed societies. The control of overt, open violence has in effect been contracted out to the state, to the police, who may have to apply violence in order to control it.

Given that the growth of modern police forces in the late nineteenth and early twentieth centuries coincided with the growth of industrial societies in Europe and North America, it is hardly surprising that interventions by police in labour disputes formed a major aspect of their ostensible attempts to control violence. Labour unrest posed a significant challenge to public order, with strikes and lock outs threatening and leading to serious violence on numerous occasions both before and after the First World War. Although police (and, on occasion, the army) were often accused of being called upon to intervene in effect on the side of employers, at least in England (where from 1875 peaceful picketing by trade-union members was legally permitted) their task was formally to prevent 'disturbances of the peace'.[28] Although individual police officers often sympathized with strikers, and although their primary task was to preserve order, police (and, on occasion, army) intervention could provoke violence as much as control it – as the history of British miners' strikes from the 1890s to the 1920s through to the 1980s illustrates.[29] Protecting the peaceful, non-violent 'British Way of Life' was often interpreted as suppressing strikes, as for example during the General Strike of 1926. Similar conclusions could be drawn for the United States, where police, who were employees of local governments, both sympathized with strikers on occasion and could intervene violently in effect on the side of employers (as, for example, in the Chicago 'Memorial Day Massacre' of 30 May 1937, during the 'Little Steel Strike', when police fired into a crowd of unarmed strikers in front of Republic Steel's South Chicago factory and killed ten of them).[30]

In Imperial Germany too, while interventions by the police were regarded as being in the general (if undefined) interest of 'the maintenance of public peace, order and security',[31] their presence also could and did lead to violence rather than controlling it.[32] After the First World War, in the conflict-ridden context of the Weimar Republic, German police were pulled sharply between, on the one hand, an aspiration to be a professional force whose purpose was to protect the public and, on the other, tactics befitting a quasi-militarized armed force capable of unleashing considerable violence.[33] More recently, the role of the police in conflicts such as the British miners' strike of 1984–5, the troubles in Northern Ireland, the anti-'Poll Tax' demonstration in London in March 1990, the attacks on foreigners in Rostock-Lichtenhagen in Germany in August 1992,[34] and the rioting that erupted in the *banlieues* of Paris and of other French cities in October and November 2005, in London in August 2011 and in Stockholm in May 2013, show that the police remain in a complicated and ambivalent position: responsible for keeping the peace, sometimes succeeding and sometimes unable to maintain or restore order, sometimes being the targets of violence and sometimes being the source of violence themselves.

The contemporary focus of the police on fighting crime, controlling private violence and suppressing public disorder can be seen as a narrowing of the role of the police compared with their nineteenth-century predecessors. However, in another sense, more expansive definitions of violence and security have led to a broadening of what may be considered the tasks of police in recent decades. Perhaps the clearest evidence of this is the policing of intimate, domestic violence (discussed in Chapter VI). This represents a contrast not only between practice in recent decades and that of a century or more ago, but also between the West and the rest: policing in ordered, developed countries has become something different from, and is perceived to be different from, policing in less stable and less developed countries, where the state is not necessarily expected to intervene in domestic violence. At the turn of the millennium, Hispanic immigrants in the United States were interviewed about domestic violence and the police. One interviewee, a woman from El Salvador living in Phoenix, Arizona, 'laughed when asked if she ever thought of calling the police back home in the case of domestic violence', and said:

The police? Who would think of calling the police back there [in El Salvador]? If you called them they'd think it's a prank and they won't even bother coming! No one does that. Everyone will laugh if a woman calls for help if her husband is beating her.

Another Salvadorian woman, living in San Francisco, responded similarly but then went on to observe that 'as a woman, one has rights in this country [i.e. in the USA]'. A man from Guatemala echoed these perceptions: 'No, there's no way the police [in Guatemala] will come if a woman calls them. That [calling the police] wouldn't happen anyway, but I've heard it's different here.'[35] Of course, actual police responses may not have met these expectations. However, expectations are important, not only in that they allow people to feel more secure and to become more willing to report domestic violence to the authorities. They also reveal differences between perceptions of police behaviour and police functions in the countries of their birth and in their adopted homes. The physical journey to the United States paralleled the journey across time within western countries, in that people came to expect the state to provide for 'community safety' and to intervene in cases of violence, even when it occurs in private.

Nevertheless, in most instances where violence occurs, in domestic settings and behind closed doors, the state does not get involved. Those on the receiving end usually do not report the incident or press charges, and the police generally do not intervene. Of course, it is impossible to know precisely what proportion of domestic violence is not reported, but the vast majority of incidents probably fall into this category. According to one American study, based on data collected nationally during 1995–6 and made available in the National Violence against Women Survey, 'only about one out of four incidents are reported'.[36] Violence was less likely to be reported where the victim knew the offender, and there were a number of reasons for a reluctance to report – including fear of reprisal, concern that the police would not take the matter seriously, economic dependence, embarrassment – but the most frequent reason has been the belief that the incident was 'too minor'. But what constitutes the threshold of what is considered to be 'too minor'? This appears to be something that has altered over time; in the United States, for example, there has been an 'increase in the reporting of all types of assault' in recent decades.[37] Victims of violence have become more willing to look to the state to get the violence to stop. Indeed, in 1977 the New York Police Department was sued by a group of women because the police had failed to arrest husbands who had beaten them repeatedly.[38]

The increased willingness to report assault reflected a changing political, social and cultural milieu in which growing publicity was given to the issue of domestic violence. It also followed from the lowering of legal barriers to the arrest of offenders and the introduction of mandatory arrest laws for domestic violence (although in some cases this in fact may have served to inhibit reporting of domestic violence, due to a reluctance to see a close acquaintance arrested).[39] Overall, the threshold of what should be reported and prosecuted appears to have fallen, and the expectation that the state, in the shape of the criminal-justice system, can and should intervene to control such violence, has risen – at times to a disproportionate degree. In January 2014 in China, a small town in central Maine, police were called to a house after a neighbour raised the alarm. According to the local newspaper, the *Kennebec Journal*:

> A Hanson Road woman called police Jan. 27 after hearing what she believed to be a fight coming from a home separated by woods just a short distance away. The caller feared she had overheard domestic violence at the home.

'The caller reported she heard screaming,' according to an activity log provided by Maine State Police.

Trooper Thomas Bureau, accompanied by three other troopers, went to the house. Bureau spoke to the neighbour, who raises pigs.

'The homeowner stated her male pig was screaming because he was in a pen with five other female pigs in heat,' according to the police report.

Police determined there was no assault and no disturbance, 'other than the screaming male pig.'[40]

One may laugh at the neighbour's mistake, but her decision to report the 'screaming' to the police was a revealing response to what she believed to have been domestic violence. Would counterparts of this neighbour have referred a matter like this to the police a hundred years ago? Probably not.

During the 1970s, police in the US came in for sharp criticism for failing to intervene sufficiently in cases of domestic violence. According to one study of 'violence against wives' published in 1979, police officers were *very unlikely* [emphasis in the original] to make an arrest when the offender has used violence against his wife', whereas 'in other violent situations, officers typically arrest the attacker regardless of the characteristics of the victim and offender or the circumstances surrounding the crime'.[41] Shortly thereafter, the authors of an article published in the *Law & Society Review* thundered: 'The message behind the criticisms of police practice in domestic disturbances is clear: police are not doing their job.'[42] While the authors went on to admit that 'it is not entirely clear what that job is or should be', they expected more energetic intervention and 'a more liberal use of the arrest option' in cases of domestic violence.[43]

More broadly, in its statement on the 'Standards of the Urban Police Function' approved initially in 1979, the American Bar Association included among the 'major current responsibilities of the police' – in addition to identifying and apprehending criminal offenders, preserving civil order, and reducing the opportunities for committing crime (e.g. through police patrols) – the following: to 'aid individuals who are in danger of physical harm', to 'resolve conflict', and 'to create a feeling of security in the community'.[44] These responsibilities for controlling violence arise not only from the responsibility to enforce the criminal law but also from 'community pressures on the police'. While the responsibility for apprehending criminals and preserving civil order clearly would have been recognized by police forces in the late nineteenth and early twentieth centuries, the responsibility of protecting people at *risk* of physical harm and resolving domestic conflict is new. The state is expected to shoulder a responsibility for creating a 'feeling of security' from violence in private as well as in public.

From the mid-1970s, police forces in the United States were increasingly pressured to intercede in cases of domestic violence, through civil lawsuits and legislation as well as policy initiatives.[45] In the years that followed, the expectation that the state would intervene in instances of domestic violence became steadily more explicit. In 1984, in the middle of Ronald Reagan's presidency, the 'Final Report' of the US Attorney General's Task Force on Family Violence made this clear in recommendations that included the following: 'Family Violence should be recognized and responded to as a criminal activity [...] Law enforcement officials, prosecutors, and judges should develop a coordinated response to family violence' and 'Consistent with state law, the chief executive of every law enforcement agency should establish arrest as the preferred response in cases of family violence'.[46] By 1986, six states had passed mandatory arrest laws 'when probable cause exists and the offender is on the scene' and 'forty-seven large city police departments had adopted a policy of mandatory or presumptive arrests for family fights'.[47] 'Family fights' now constituted violent behaviour that

214

the state was expected to bring under control. And in 1996 the US Congress passed the Violence Against Women Act. By providing funding for the investigation and prosecution of crimes of violence against women and establishing an 'Office on Violence Against Women' within the US Department of Justice, the act 'transformed the nation's response to domestic violence and sexual assault'.[48] This constituted an unambiguous statement that it was the job of the state to intervene in cases of domestic violence, and one that met with agreement among leading police officers.[49] By the end of the last millennium, domestic violence had come to be regarded not as a private concern to be tolerated but as a public matter to be brought under control.

The reduction in tolerance for domestic violence was paralleled by a growing participation of women in policing. Although there had been isolated instances of women working for urban police departments (dealing with cases involving women and children) during the nineteenth century, the employment of women in police forces has been essentially a twentieth-century phenomenon. In Britain, women were used by the police to monitor the behaviour of women near army camps or working in munitions factories during the First World War, and after appointing fifty women in 1919 the Metropolitan Police in London continued regularly to employ a small number of female officers (increasing to 155 in 1939).[50] In Germany (where, as in Britain, a number of German cities had employed 'female police assistants' and 'welfare women' to assist with social-welfare tasks before the First World War), the first proper policewomen were employed in Cologne in 1923, and in 1926–7, Baden, Saxony, Hamburg and Prussia had chosen to establish women's police formations.[51]

More women found their way into police forces during the Second World War, but not really until the 1970s were women integrated into the police on the same terms as men (in the UK this followed from the gender equality legislation of the early 1970s),[52] and not really until the 1980s did women begin to assume leadership positions in the police.[53] Thus the achievement of women's participation in policing on roughly equal terms occurred at about the same time as violence regarded as meriting police intervention extended to areas traditionally viewed as spheres appropriate for intervention by women, i.e. child abuse and domestic violence. What had been regarded as 'soft' policing (i.e. associated with social and welfare work),[54] alongside the development of juvenile courts, – the 'policing of families' – became accepted as part of the public campaign to control violence.

The involvement of women in policing is but one part of the growth of police forces that has taken place across the developed world during the nineteenth and, particularly, the twentieth centuries. In Germany, for example, the numerical strength of the police increased enormously following unification in 1871 and reached a total of roughly 100,000 by 1913; it then climbed to 150,000 during the Weimar Republic and, following the extraordinary period of National Socialist dictatorship and military occupation following German defeat, resumed its upward trend after the Second World War: the number of police in the Federal Republic (i.e. West Germany) alone increased from 112,000 in 1950 to nearly 150,000 in 1955 and to more than 200,000 by the beginning of the 1980s.[55] At the end of the twentieth century (i.e. in 1999), the number of police officers in Germany peaked at 252,230 (after which time the number declined slightly).[56]

In the United States, where the development of internal security was not interrupted by war and dictatorship, the numbers of police also soared over the twentieth century, not just in absolute terms but also relative to the population. In 1900, Los Angeles had fewer than 100 police officers in a city with a population of 102,479 inhabitants; in 1988 it had 7,733 police officers (and another 2,470 civilian employees of the police) in a city that had grown to over 3.4 million inhabitants – making the ratio of police employees to inhabitants roughly three times what it had been at the turn of the century. Chicago saw a similar development, with the ratio of police to population moving from 1:630 in 1900 to 1:275 in 1988.[57] Between 1970 and 1990 the number of full-time police in the United States increased by 70.7 per cent (while the number of recorded violent crimes rose by 147 per cent);[58] and since the end of the twentieth century that trend has continued, with the number of police continuing to increase, from 637,551 in 1999 to 706,886 in 2009.[59]

While increases in police numbers have been fuelled by increases in recorded crime – according to David Bayley, 'detailed analysis has shown that communities hire more police when they see crime rates rising'[60] – this has not necessarily resulted in a straightforward growth in the number of officers employed directly to combat and control violence. Some of the growth resulted from the increasing bureaucratization of policing, with paperwork drawing members of the force away from walking the beat (or driving around in patrol cars); and an increasing proportion of police time over the course of the twentieth century has been devoted to tasks that have little to do with the control of violence, in particular controlling motor-vehicle traffic.[61] However, the increase in the size and strength of police forces in the West (as opposed to the socialist states of post-war eastern Europe, or in the developing world) was also a response to popular pressure, from voters receptive to pledges to increase police numbers in order to combat violent crime. Of all the tasks assigned to police forces, it is combating violent crime that the public tends to value the most. For example, in a random-sample survey of 698 residents conducted in Prince George, British Columbia, in 2001, when interviewees were asked to rate the relative importance of various aspects of the job of the Royal Canadian Mounted Police, the most important functions were seen to be 'protecting people' and 'investigating and apprehending criminals', while 'traffic and highway enforcement' was regarded as the least important.[62]

The concern to control violence – to be 'protecting people' and 'apprehending criminals' – has been a major engine of the growth of the state over the twentieth century. It also is a measure of the success of a state: whether it is able to secure and maintain an effective monopoly of violence within its territory. A strong state is a state that can control and suppress violence internally; a weak state leaves it to members of the public to deal with violent behaviour on their own, often by employing violence themselves. The breakdown of a state's ability to meet the expectations of its population to live secure lives largely free of the threat of violence (in public and, increasingly, in private), has contributed decisively to the collapse of the legitimacy of states and political systems. This occurred in Germany in the wake of the First World War, when the new democratic state not only had to cope with the consequences of military defeat and hyperinflation, but also faced violent political unrest and a crime wave that undermined personal security.[63] The inability to control violence, to meet what its citizens had come to regard as a basic responsibility of a modern state, proved deeply damaging to the legitimacy of the Weimar Republic. Nevertheless, Weimar Germany was not what today we would describe as a 'failed state'; it maintained a functioning bureaucracy and police (which were expanded and used to terrible effect first at home and then across the European continent during the 1930s and 1940s). The recent history of Somalia, which after 1991 no longer possessed a functioning government and whose capacity to protect the civilian population from violence evaporated, offers a most extreme case: without the ability to control violence or to provide even rudimentary security within its territory, it was no longer really a state at all.

Within a more restricted frame, the failure of government organizations to control violent crime has contributed significantly to the recent decline and bankruptcy of some American cities, most notably of Detroit (where the population declined from 1,849,568 inhabitants in 1950 to 713,777 in 2010, by which time it had topped the list of 'America's Most Dangerous Cities').[64] Here was a 'failed state' at municipal level. Few cities in the western world have faced greater challenges in recent decades than has Detroit, where poverty, unemployment and collapsing infrastructure formed a milieu in which violent crime, in particular youth violence, became endemic, threatening the future of the city. In a plan drafted in 2012 to confront the problem of youth (and gang) violence, the 'top priority' of the city administration was defined as 'public safety'.[65] It was admitted that 'more enforcement and more young men in prison will not solve our challenges around violence'. Instead, the goal was to have 'a city where youth and education are valued, it is safe to walk the streets, conflicts are resolved non-violently, and young men and women have real job and career opportunities'. The path to non-violent Detroit was viewed in cultural terms, in 'changing culture to embrace non-violent conflict resolution':

> Too many youth are taught, from a very early age, that violence is a legitimate strategy to solve everyday problems. And, more violence emerges from a seemingly endless cycle of revenge. That must change. We are using restorative practices; conflict resolution methods that help build positive relationships and restore a sense of community.

Consequently, 'prevention strategies are our first choice'. To some extent, this choice was forced on the municipal government, not just by the scale of the problem but also by the difficulties involved in pursuing a policy of suppressing violence when the police force had been shrinking for years due to the city's cata-strophic financial problems.[66] However, underlying this initiative is the assumption that a government that cannot control vio-lence is failing its citizens.

Police protection from violent crime – effective intervention to control violence – has come to be regarded as something to which all citizens are entitled. Its absence is regarded as a viola-tion of citizens' rights. To take another contemporary example from the United States: recently the city administration of Harvey, Illinois, described as 'an often lawless suburb twenty miles south of downtown Chicago' with a population of roughly 25,000 overwhelmingly African-American and Hispanic resi-dents, has faced scathing criticism for a failure to provide adequate protection against violent crime. Established in 1891 as a temperance settlement intended to be a model of Christian virtue, Harvey has been down on its luck in recent decades. Its population has been in decline for the past forty years and its level of unemployment stands well above the average for the state and the country; its crime rate has been over three times the United States average (having the fifth highest number of robberies per 10,000 inhabitants among American cities in 2006, and being among the top fifty for murders per 10,000 inhabi-tants) while its ratio of police to residents was lower than the Illinois average.[67] It had become, so the *Chicago Tribune* editori-alized, 'a city where residents are victimized three times – by criminals, by dysfunctional policing and finally by outsiders turning a blind eye'.[68] According to Cook County Sheriff Tom Dart:

> There are a lot of really good families that live out there. The notion that because of where they live, they get less police protection, substandard police protection, no police protec-tion – that's appalling. Nobody in our county, frankly no one in our state, should accept that as being OK.[69]

The first duty of government, it seems, is to control violence; no one should be without the state's protection against violent crime.

In recent decades, concern about crime, and especially violent crime, has fuelled not only increases in police forces but also harsher custodial sentencing ('three strikes and you're out') and a phenomenal growth in prison populations and incarceration rates, at least in the United States. It seems almost unbelievable today, but during the 1930s incarceration rates in the US were roughly comparable or lower than those in many European countries, and in the 1960s the United States still 'was in the mainstream' (i.e. with the death penalty 'withering away' and the incarceration rate dropping). By the end of the twentieth century, however, the proportion of the population behind bars in the US was six to twelve times that of other western countries.[70] After roughly half a century during which incarceration rates had remained relatively stable,[71] from the beginning of the 1970s there was an explosion in the number of prisons and of prisoners in the United States.[72] The year 1973 appears to have been a turning point. After 1973, most American states passed mandatory sentencing laws, and the chances of a prison sentence following arrest rose for all types of offences (whether covered by mandatory sentencing or not) as more people were convicted and a greater proportion of those convicted were given prison sentences. Consequently, between 1973 and 1989 the prison population of the United States trebled, and by the end of 1989 roughly 610,000 people were incarcerated in state prisons alone in the United States.[73] (State prisons held 92 per cent of the American prison population at that time.) Twenty years later, even that extraordinary figure had more than doubled. According to the US Department of Justice, as of the end of 2009 there were 1,613,740 prisoners altogether under the jurisdiction of federal (208,118 prisoners) or state (1,405,622 prisoners) correctional authorities in the United States, of whom

1,500,278 were male; the majority of prisoners in state institutions (but only a small minority in federal institutions) had been incarcerated for violent offences (murder, manslaughter, rape, other sexual assault, robbery, assault, etc.), in part a consequence of the fact that they received longer sentences than did those convicted of non-violent offences.[74]

Is this extraordinary growth in custodial sentencing a sign of 'American exceptionalism', of the idea that the United States is qualitatively different from other nation states? Certainly the US had higher rates of recorded violent crime (particularly gun crime) than did many other western countries. Public opinion favoured tough sentencing, and politicians used the issue of crime to get elected. The phenomenal increase in incarceration was a political response to the perceived problem of crime and the control of violence, in a political system remarkably open to the pressure of public opinion. The criminologist and academic campaigner against excessive incarceration in the United States Michael Tonry, has asserted: 'American imprisonment rates did not rise because crime rates rose. They rose because American politicians wanted them to rise.'[75] They reflected changes not so much in crime rates as in public attitudes (often fuelled by reporting in the media) about the need to control violence, and a determination to accomplish this by locking up more people.

While the enormous numbers of people imprisoned in the United States exceeded – both absolutely and relative to population – those of most other countries, the US has not been alone in seeing an increase in the prison population in recent decades. In the United Kingdom, there has been a continual rise in the prison population since the end of the Second World War (when the total stood at only around 15,000), with a significantly higher rate of increase from the mid-1990s (due in large measure to a rise in the proportion of custodial sentences being handed out to convicted offenders).[76] The growth in the number of prisoners in Britain, particularly during the last third of the twentieth century, resulted from political interventions that both reflected and affected popular attitudes towards crime and punishment. This paralleled to some extent developments in the United States, although the consequences were not so extreme. In 1970, the issue of crime and the need to deal with problems of public order surfaced in the Conservative Party election manifesto;[77] in October 1993 the Home Secretary Michael Howard famously proclaimed at the Conservative Party Conference that 'prison works' – an assertion which was followed by a steep rise in the UK prison population. Howard justified his policy by claiming that prison 'ensures that we are protected from murderers, muggers and rapists', although the majority of offenders have been convicted not for crimes of violence but for property offences.[78] The spectre of violence was, and remains, an important factor in mobilizing support for policies that have led to the prison population in England and Wales (including those held in immigration removal centres) rising to a record high of 88,179 prisoners in December 2011.[79]

Trends elsewhere have been less clear. In Germany, after an initial increase during the early 1990s, following unification, the number of prisoners has remained fairly steady over the past couple of decades, with 71,303 in 1995, 80,201 in 2005, and 72,295 in 2009.[80] As in the United States, in Germany there was, as opinion surveys identified, a desire for greater police powers and tougher sentencing,[81] yet the incarceration rate did not skyrocket as it had in the US. In France, where there has been a greater tendency to use fines rather than custodial sentences, the number of prison inmates rose steeply during the 1970s and 1980s, from 34,083 in 1974 to 52,658 in 1993, and thereafter increased slowly: it stood at just over 50,000 in 2000, just over 55,000 in 2003, and rose to a little over 60,000 in 2007.[82] In Belgium, there has been a moderate increase in recent years, from 8,176 in 1998 to 9,950 in 2007, while in Spain the prison population rose by roughly 50 per cent (from 44,747 to 67,100) whereas in Portugal the prison population fell by roughly a fifth (from 14,330 to 11,587) during the same period.[83] This somewhat mixed picture suggests that one needs to be careful about drawing general conclusions. However, it does appear that the political system of the United States, and to a somewhat lesser extent that of the United Kingdom, have been particularly vulnerable to public pressure for tougher sentencing.

Whether increased police presence and harsher sentencing have actually succeeded in controlling violence is another matter, and is probably impossible to determine. These developments may be evidence more of *concern* to control violence than of actual success in doing so. In his excellent study of 'American Homicide', Randolph Roth concluded: 'Neither the drop in homicide during the Great Depression and the Cold War nor the rise in homicide in the 1960s and 1970s makes sense if we try to ascribe them to changes in law enforcement, the recent performance of the economy, or other time-honoured explanations.'[84] Larger police forces, harsher sentencing and bigger prisons may not actually control violence, but they do reflect public concerns about the threat of violence and personal security.

'Security' indeed has become a major preoccupation of our age. Governments promise security, and have grown huge organizations devoted to it. The frequency with which the term 'security' has been employed since the Second World War is remarkable, and was particularly conspicuous in the former socialist states of eastern Europe. There, the German Democratic Republic built up its infamous massive secret-police organization, the Ministry of State Security (*Staatssicherheit*, or 'Stasi'), and its 'People's Police' (*Volkspolizei*), 'the entire activity' of which as well as that of 'the other organs of the Ministry of the Interior' was aimed to ensure 'that impeccable public order and security, a lofty legal order and legal security as well as the strict maintenance of socialist legality' be maintained in order to underpin the 'political stability, internal solidity and dynamic development of the GDR'.[85] The former Czechoslovak Socialist Republic had its State Security; the Romanian Communist regime had its *Securitate*, the name popularly given to the government's Department of State Security; and the Soviet Union had its Committee for State Security, the KGB (the title of the USSR's main security agency from 1954 to 1991), and the Russian Federation has its FSB – its Federal Security Service.

Of course, the preoccupation with security was by no means exclusive to the former socialist regimes. Until 1966, the French National Police went under the name *Sûreté nationale*; the Belgian government has its State Security Service; and since the terrorist attacks of September 2001 the United States has seen the establishment in 2002 and massive growth of its Department of Homeland Security, whose mission includes 'preventing terrorism and enhancing security',[86] to become the third largest cabinet department of the US Federal Government, with over 240,000 employees as of the beginning of 2014.[87] However, there is a difference. While the main purpose of the security organizations in the former Communist regimes in eastern Europe was to suppress internal dissent and thus protect the regime from its citizens, the main purpose of government security organizations in the West has been to protect the population from the threat of violence. The focus here has not been on the security of the state so much as it has been on the security of the individual citizen. By the end of the twentieth century, the concept of 'security' had expanded such that the perceived threat to internal security encompassed 'not only the threat to the state order but at the same time to the life and limb of the individual'.[88]

The growth of governmental organizations tasked with security has been paralleled by a mushrooming in the number and size of private security firms. Security has become one of the great growth industries of the last half-century. In the United

States, which has been in the vanguard of this development, by the mid-1990s the number of people employed in security was more than double what it had been a quarter of a century earlier. According to an account published in 1994:

> In a society characterized as ever more fearful of rising crime and violence, public and private security occupations now account for at least 1.6 per cent of all working Americans. This is twice the percentage for 1970 and few other occupations are growing as rapidly according to the Department of Labour.[89]

In Europe, the private business of security grew rapidly as well. For example, by the late 1980s, the number of private security guards in France exceeded the number of gendarmes;[90] between 1981 and 1995 the number of private security firms in France more than quadrupled (from 606 to 2,568), and the number of private security personnel increased between 1983 and 1998 from 11,500 to 94,000 (and stood at perhaps 130,000 six years later).[91] In Germany in 1991, the number of private security personnel at roughly 190,000 was not that much smaller than the total personnel of the police at 245,000, and its financial turnover had doubled over the previous five years (against a background of what was described as 'growing criminality').[92] By the beginning of the 1990s, there were twice as many people employed by private security firms in Britain and Canada as there were by the public police.[93] According to one study of 'the future of policing', published in 1996: 'It is hardly an accident that the expansion of private security as well as the development of community policing coincided with rising crime rates throughout the developed world.'[94] Fear of violence and the obsession with bringing it under control nurtured a huge private industry.

In more recent years the growth of the 'security' industry has continued unabated. The remarkable rise of G4S (a result of the 2004 merger of Group 4 Falck and Securicor, and with over 650,000 employees operating in 125 different countries) to become the largest employer listed on the London Stock Exchange and the largest security company on earth, is conspicuous testimony to the growth of the private security industry.[95] Its core activities include guarding property, protecting private individuals, operating prisons and detention centres on behalf of governments, as well as transporting cash (e.g. to bank cash machines). While a substantial proportion of its activities are carried out in developing countries, over two thirds of the revenue of G4S comes from Europe and North America – the regions that over the past half-century have become most acutely sensitive about violence.

Yet another sign of the enhanced concern to control violence against the individual has been the spread of the concept of 'human security', as something that is supposed to guide politicians and policy makers. The term has been advanced by western governments, in particular those of Canada and Norway, and has gained traction in academic publications and universities.[96] The concept was introduced in the 1994 'Human Development Report', an annual publication of the United Nations Development Programme (UNDP); according to the UNDP, it 'equates security with people rather than territories, with development rather than arms'.[97] It has since become the most widely cited and 'most authoritative' statement of what 'human security' is taken to consist of.[98] According to the UNDP Report: 'The concept of security has for too long been interpreted narrowly: as security of territory from external aggression, or as protection of national interests in foreign policy or as global security from the threat of nuclear holocaust. [...] Forgotten were the legitimate concerns of ordinary people who sought security in their daily lives.' The idea was to apply the assumed 'peace dividend' that was supposed to follow the end of the Cold War not only to provide 'safety from such chronic threats as hunger, disease and repression', but also 'protection from sudden and hurtful disruptions in the patterns of daily life – whether in homes, in jobs or in communities'.[99] Among the seven key elements of human security identified in the report was personal security, which encompassed security from acts of violence, including war, torture, crime, domestic violence, and even traffic accidents. 'Human security' was defined so broadly that it could cover almost anything, and therefore as an analytical tool it may leave something to be desired. Nevertheless, the very lack of limits to what constitutes personal security is indicative of how understandings of violence and the need to control it have broadened.

Discussion about the control of violence has understandably focused largely on institutional efforts to prevent, suppress or combat violent behaviour, in the first instance by the state. However, the control of violence involves not only external constraints and restraints. It also involves internal and internalized checks on behaviour, the cultural norms that bring about self-control, the normative constraints that are often regarded as characteristic of 'civilization'. This thesis is associated with great German-Jewish sociologist Norbert Elias, who argued that central to the 'process of civilization' was the acceptance of self-control, self-restraint and civility (first by the elite of the absolutist state of the seventeenth and eighteenth centuries and later among broader sections of the population). Consequently and over time, self-control with respect to emotions – and thus to violence – became internalized, in effect something natural.[100] Heated, emotional responses to disputes gave way, so the argument went, to a willingness to settle disputes peacefully, by recourse to law rather than to overt, immediate individual violence. According to Elias, 'during the past five hundred years we have moved from a formidable violence – which we can imagine only with great difficulty – to a lessening of violence and a greater self-control with regard to aggression'.[101]

Leaving aside how one might actually measure increases or decreases in violence over the centuries (something that Elias did not do), there is much to be said for the suggestion that social and cultural taboos have served to control violence – that emotional identification and empathy among members of (European) society grew as social interaction became increasingly complex and as powerful centralized states were able to exert greater control over the exercise of violence and thus to provide new levels of personal security alongside high degrees of social interdependence. Control of emotions and identification with and empathy for others thus buttressed self-restraint and 'civilized' behaviour. Instead of resting simply upon external threats and sanctions, the control of violence became internalized.

Although they offer insight into the control of violence in the western world, Elias's conclusions about the development of self-restraint and civility were at odds with the explosions of violence in Europe during the first half of the twentieth century. (His *Über den Prozeß der Zivilisation – The Civilizing Process –* was completed in 1936 and first published in 1939, on the eve of the Second World War; two years later Elias's mother met her death, he assumed at Auschwitz. He dedicated the post-war edition of the two-volume study to the memory of his parents.) Elias recognized that the collapse of civilized behaviour and return to barbarity and violence unleashed by his native Germany raised disturbing questions, and he prefaced his reflections on the violence that he had witnessed in inter-war Germany by stating: 'The civilization of which I speak is never completed and always endangered.'[102] The thesis of the 'process of civilization' also could be challenged for its apparently Eurocentric nature (although Elias rejected this objection), and is something conspicuous by its absence in the 'extremely violent societies' recently described by Christian Gerlach.[103] Elias's central point, however, was that not just European but 'all societies

229

have to socialize their members into shared understandings about the importance of observing constraints on violence'.[104] Some have, and some have not. It may be that the effectiveness of modern states, the unprecedented prosperity enjoyed by hundreds of millions of people since the middle of the twentieth century, and the complexity of human interaction within a relatively stable and peaceful environment have combined to facilitate the spread of self-restraint with regard to violence.

Therefore to the paradox with which this chapter began – that 'social order is a necessary condition for containing violence' while at the same time 'violence is a necessary condition for maintaining social order' – perhaps another should be added: while social order may be a necessary condition for containing violence, the existence of a culture of restraint and self-control with regard to violence may be a necessary condition for maintaining social order. Nevertheless, as the blood-soaked history of the twentieth century demonstrated, the dream of a society free of violence has remained precisely that: a dream. That dream has been a powerful cultural and political force during the second half of the twentieth century. We seem to be committed to the control of violence as never before – whether through international organizations such as the United Nations, through well-resourced police forces and expanding prison systems, or through the promotion of cultures of non-violence and 'using restorative practices; conflict resolution methods that help build positive relationships and restore a sense of community'. This may (as Steven Pinker asserts) or may not have led to actual reductions in the violence that people inflict on one another. However, it has resulted in far-reaching changes in the ways in which people have understood and regarded violence and what can and should be done about it.

VIII

Memories

In the early 1990s, an acrimonious public debate erupted in Germany over plans to turn the interior of the neoclassical *Neue Wache* (New Guard House) on Berlin's Unter den Linden into a national memorial site. The *Neue Wache* had already gone through many incarnations since it was designed by Karl Friedrich Schinkel and built between 1816 and 1818. Originally intended for the guard of the *Kronprinzenpalais* across the boulevard, it remained such until the collapse of the monarchy in 1918. After the First World War, and after considerable debate, the *Neue Wache* was renovated to become Germany's central 'Memorial Site for the Fallen of the World War', which was dedicated in 1931.[1] After Hitler came to power it was renovated again, to become the 'Place of Honour of those Killed During the World War', and remained so until the end of the Second World War, by which time it had been severely damaged. Between 1957 and 1960 the war-damaged building was renovated yet again, this time to become the German Democratic Republic's 'Memorial to the Victims of Fascism and Militarism', and in 1969 an 'eternal flame' was placed within a large glass block in the centre of the structure. The 'eternal flame' burned for barely two decades, until German re-unification, when it was extinguished. On 14 November 1993, on Germany's 'people's day of mourning', the newly re-renovated *Neue Wache* was opened once more, this time as the 'Central Place of Memory of the Federal Republic of Germany for the Victims of War and Tyranny'. The newest reincarnation of the *Neue Wache* was dedicated to 'the victims of war and the rule of violence' (*Opfer von Krieg und Gewaltherrschaft*), with an enlarged bronze replica of Käthe Kollwitz's *Pietà* (*Mutter mit totem Sohn* – 'mother with dead son'), four times as high as the original that Kollwitz had sculpted in 1937, placed where the 'eternal flame' of socialist East Germany once had burned.[2]

This latest dedication provoked heated controversy and upset. The focus of anger was the lumping together of all victims of war and violence:

The peoples who have suffered through war [...] their citizens, who were persecuted and lost their lives ... the fallen of the world wars ... the innocent, who died in war and through the consequences of war, in the homeland, in captivity, and during the expulsions ... the millions of murdered Jews ... the murdered Sinti and Roma ... all those who were killed because of their descent, their homosexuality, or because of illness and weakness ... all the murdered, whose right to life was denied them ... the people who had to die because of their religious or political convictions ... the women and men who sacrificed their lives in resisting the tyranny ... the women and men who were persecuted and murdered because they resisted totalitarian dictatorship after 1945.[3]

In deciding to restore the *Neue Wache* and to turn it into a memorial site dedicated to the victims of violence generally, Chancellor Helmut Kohl hoped to signal Germany's transition to being a normal country once again – with a monument where foreign dignitaries could lay their wreaths when making official visits to its capital. Who, after all, could object to a memorial dedicated to victims of violence? However – and this was the fundamental criticism – the memorial in effect was dedicated simultaneously to the memory of *Wehrmacht* soldiers who had died while serving and fighting for the National Socialist regime and to the memory of Jews, of Sinti and Roma, and of countless other civilians who had been murdered by that same regime.[4] Far from deflecting controversy, the blurring of the distinctions between soldiers who fell in battle, civilians who died during the wartime bombing or fleeing from their homes in what had been East Germany, and millions of people killed in campaigns of genocide proved well suited to arousing cultural sensitivities and political division. Not only did this put the soldier and the concentration-camp prisoner on the same level, but using the term 'victim' (as the historian Reinhart Koselleck argued at the time) removed a sense of agency, implying 'that all Germans were in some ways victims of a hegemonic amorphous regime', failing to 'introduce the question of perpetrators', and inducing 'an institutionalized forgetfulness'.[5]

The point of referring to the *Neue Wache* controversy is not to take sides retrospectively in the dispute that surrounded its resurrection as a site of official memory of violence in a united Germany. Instead, it is to observe that the attempt to find a common denominator that might be acceptable to all interested parties, and to seek 'the reinvention of Germany as a normal nation',[6] involved identification with 'the victims of violence' (whoever they might be). Although this formula did not succeed in preventing discord in 1990s Germany, it was both an obvious choice and a revealing expression of how violence has come to be remembered in the western world. Violence is remembered through memorials to its victims, a category that has become increasingly expansive and inclusive. This focus owes much to the First World War and its aftermath, to the impressive attempts, particularly by the French and the British, to commemorate the unprecedented numbers of people who had been killed in that conflict. Rather than glorifying war and violence, the tone of the memorials tended to be sombre, mournful, and in some cases openly hostile towards the violence of the Great War. These were monuments to the victims of violence.

British and French reactions to the slaughter of the 1914–1918 war, a war that for both countries caused more deaths than any other in their histories, were in the vanguard of a transition from the glorification of war and towards the rejection of war and violence. In both countries, as Alex King has noted in his fine study of British war memorials of the Great War, 'both popular and official thought stressed the ideal of averting future wars'.[7] War was 'horror'. In 1921, the anonymous *Times Literary Supplement* reviewer of Wilfred Owen's first book of poems (while criticizing Owen's 'moral revolt' as 'largely misplaced') praised the poet who 'opens up and exposes us to a great range of realities, realities which, because of the horror and anguish associated with them, men do conspire to gloss over and hush up. War, in a word, involves savagery; it demands of men such cruel outrage against their human instincts that as a moral experience it is essentially unbearable.'[8] Philip Gibbs, who had been an officially accredited British war correspondent during the First World War and was deeply affected by what he had witnessed, wrote that war memorials 'should be not only reminders of the great death that killed the flower of our race but warning of what war means in slaughter and ruin, in broken hearts and agony'.[9] In France, the nine-year-old schoolgirl who, after being taken to see anti-war films in the summer of 1937, wrote that 'war is a horror', was both representative of the society and culture in which she had been raised and a harbinger of things to come.[10] The sombre atmosphere of the ossuary at Douaumont above Verdun (with its interior walls bearing inscriptions from the survivors of military units to the memory of their fallen comrades), the empty tomb of the Cenotaph in Whitehall and the gigantic memorial designed by Edwin Lutyens at Thiepval for 'The Missing of the Somme', reflect the sentiments of 'the thousands of veterans who fervently commemorated war in order not to inflict it on their children'.[11]

Among the most remarkable anti-war war memorials of the inter-war period is the monument to the dead of the First World War at Gentioux, a small village in the Limousin region of central France. The monument consists of a column with the names of fifty-eight dead from the village, in front of which stands a bronze statue of a young boy – a war orphan – with an outstretched clenched fist before the inscription *maudite soit la guerre* ('cursed be war').[12] The Gentioux monument is perhaps the most famous example of war memorials with pacifist motifs (grieving widows and orphaned children, rather than resolute or heroic soldiers) constructed in various places across France, and its subsequent history tells us a great deal about how war and violent death were commemorated over the course of the twentieth century. Built in 1922, at the initiative of the village's socialist mayor (a war veteran, Jules Coutaud), the monument aroused controversy from the outset. The prefecture refused to be represented at the unveiling, and consequently the monument was not officially dedicated. It became (and has remained) a traditional site for anti-war protests and pacifist demonstrations on 11 November; soldiers from the nearby army camp were ordered to turn their heads away when walking past the monument, which was officially inaugurated only in 1985 (and then only by chance when officers attended a wreath-laying ceremony at the monument).[13] In 1990, it was entered onto the inventory of French historic monuments, and the plaque on which *maudite soit la guerre* is inscribed was declared irremovable. It is the acceptance in the late twentieth century of even the most extreme representations of a condemnation of war that illustrates the extent to which attitudes towards war and violence changed. What began as an angry, partisan condemnation of the violence of war had become by the last decades of the twentieth century an iconic and uncontroversial representation of uncompromising opposition and hostility to war.

In Germany, the development of public memories of violence was rather different than that in France and Britain. While the First World War, and the enormous casualties that arose from it, provided a massive shock – Germany lost almost as many soldiers as did France and Britain combined – and led some to condemn violence, pacifism was far from the dominant response during the inter-war years when looking back on the 1914–1918 conflict. In a memorable phrase, Wolfram Wette has described pacifists as being among 'the best-hated people' in Germany during the final years of the Weimar Republic.[14] That is not to say that the rejection of war and violence had no resonance during the post-war years, but responses in Germany to the losses of the First World War were divided. On the one hand, as in France and Britain, millions of soldiers returned from the front in 1918 and 1919 determined to put the violence of war behind them; many, like my grandfather who served as an officer on the Western Front and returned after the war to his village in south-western Germany, married and started a small business, returned to (re)establish a peaceful civilian existence. On the other hand, aggressive, war-affirming narratives and memorials were more common in Germany than they were in France or Britain. Few war memorials carrying an anti-war or pacifist message were unveiled in Weimar Germany, and representations of the war that sought to present a pacifist message often were hotly contested.[15] Although one should not exaggerate the differences between France and Germany,[16] cultures of defeat were not the same as cultures of victory (however sombre they may have been in inter-war France).

It was not really until after 1945 that in Germany the balance changed fundamentally, as opinion came more to resemble the sorts of popular attitudes that had been prevalent in France and Britain during the inter-war period. After the Second World War, the human losses and material destruction left behind by the conflict, a war which devastated the country and left behind more than twice as many German dead as had the First World War, came to provide the public focus for how Germans framed their war memories. Violence was now condemned, unequivocally, and in the early years of the Federal Republic, the Second World War was remembered publicly in terms of violence and victimhood.[17] On 18 February 1951, the German *Bundestag* observed an hour of commemoration not just for fallen German soldiers but for all victims of war, including those who had died in the bombings, in the expulsions and in the concentration camps. Instead of the '*Heldengedenktag*' ('Heroes' Remembrance Day') instituted by the Nazis in 1934 (and held in the spring), in 1952 the practice of the '*Volkstrauertag*' ('People's Day of Mourning'), instituted initially in 1919, was resuscitated and shifted back to November, the traditional month of mourning. Memorials to the civilian victims of war were erected across the country, usually employing religious imagery (mourning angels, crosses, pietàs) and usually erected in churchyards or other secluded places. And during the early 1950s, POW memorials were created, in part as a call for the repatriation of those still in captivity.[18] The common inscription on the memorials – 'For the victims of war and violence' – was echoed in the memorial (re)constructed in the *Neue Wache* a half a century later. In a deliberately vague manner, all victims of violence could be remembered.

In terms of the public genuflections towards the victims of violence, Germany seems to have joined the new western European cultural mainstream after defeat in the Second World War. Cultural integration paralleled political integration. There was an extraordinary transformation in how violence was remembered in Germany over the course of the twentieth century, as the terrible experiences of violence during two world wars and the National Socialist dictatorship were followed by a remarkable transition to a democratic and non-violent civic culture.[19] German civil society became notably peaceful and opposed to violence. In this regard, Germany became normal, perhaps even hyper-normal.[20] This transformation is encapsulated neatly by the inscription now to be found on the *Siegestor* (Victory Gate) in Munich, the triumphal arch completed in 1852 to honour the Bavarian army and to mark the northern end of the city's grand avenue, the Ludwigstraße, near the university.[21] During the Second World War, the *Siegestor* was damaged by bombing which destroyed its top section and the quadriga that had stood there, and it was rebuilt in 1958 (the year of Munich's 800th anniversary). However, the rebuilding was not a restoration, and the effects of the war were not hidden. Where the gate had been damaged, a sheer surface was created for a new inscription. On the southern face of the arch, facing the *Feldherrenhalle* (where the National Socialists had staged memorial ceremonies in honour of their martyrs killed in the 1923 putsch attempt), it reads: *Dem Sieg geweiht, vom Krieg zerstört, zum Frieden mahnend* (Dedicated to Victory, Destroyed by War, Admonishing for Peace). On a monument originally dedicated to the Bavarian army, there now is a pointed reminder of the consequences of war and a call for peace. The memory of violence and war was evoked in order to prevent such things from happening again.

The ways in which Germans reflected publicly on their violent past demonstrates the importance of political context and the political uses of commemoration. The ways in which violence, particularly the violence of war, is remembered publicly, are never neutral, whatever those who are involved in planning memorials and public ceremonies may believe. Government offices and publicly sponsored research institutions have both extended our knowledge of the violent histories of the twentieth century and played a major role in setting agendas for how these histories are understood and represented. Examples abound. Among the more prominent has been the huge research project of the former West Germany's Federal Ministry for Expellees, Refugees and War-Disabled during the 1950s, involving the collection of eyewitness and victims' accounts of the expulsion of Germans from regions east of the post-war Oder-Neiße border and the publication of an extensive multi-volume 'documentation' on the subject between 1954 and 1960.[22] Another is the Imperial War Museum in London, which was established in 1917 and which has devoted substantial effort in recent decades to collecting documentary, pictorial and oral testimony about and by those who experienced modern warfare. In Péronne in northern France (which had been the German headquarters during the Battle of the Somme in 1916), the *Historial de la Grande Guerre* (Museum of the Great War) opened in 1992 – a museum, documentation centre and international research institution devoted to investigating and representing the experiences of German, French and British participants in the First World War on the Western Front. And in Washington, the United States Holocaust Memorial Museum, which opened in 1993, includes not only a museum that has become one of the major destinations for visitors to the American capital but also a well-funded centre that supports path-breaking research on genocide.

All of these institutions reflect the cultural, ideological and political contexts in which they were established and in which they operate. In post-war West Germany, the memories of the expulsion of millions of Germans from their homes at the end of the Second World War constituted an important element of a new identity as victims. In the United Kingdom, memories of war as reflected in the Imperial War Museum changed from honouring the achievements of soldiers at war to stressing the pity and horror of war. In France, the *Historial de la Grande Guerre* strives to impart a realistic understanding of the experiences of those who had to fight in the trenches of northern France. And the United States' Holocaust Museum is a grand attempt to allow visitors to identify with the victims of the worst violence of the twentieth century. In each case, memories of violence are organized around the experiences of the victims, by public institutions that seek thus to distance themselves from violence.

Not only has the commemoration of violence generally come to evoke condemnation and mourning, but over the twentieth century it has increasingly been *individual* victims who are remembered, even if there were no identifiable remains. In the Holocaust Museum in Washington, and in the exhibition space underneath the Memorial to the Murdered Jews of Europe in the centre of Berlin, the fate of individuals is given prominence. War memorials now commonly list the names of all the dead, not just celebrate the officers, a practice already seen in Britain after the Boer War and employed widely in the wake of the First World War (when, in Britain, reference to the rank of the dead was frequently omitted).[23] On the French anti-war war memorial at Gentioux, on the pillar behind the bronze statue of the orphan boy, one finds a list of the dead, 'particularly long for such a small village'.[24] Throughout France, local monuments recorded the names of the dead of the Great War.[25] 'In the absence of bodies, names served both to trigger memory and to construct it as a responsibility, and a right, of the local community.'[26] The memory of the dead of the war was determined by the fate they had suffered and the community from which they had come, not by the rank they had attained. In Germany, too, company and communal war memorials from the First World War featured lists of the dead (including that of my great-uncle on a memorial plaque in the village of Bonfeld, in south-western Germany).[27]

In the United Kingdom, lists of the war dead may be found on plaques in railway stations, parks, schools and colleges. The largest British battlefield memorial, the Memorial of the Missing of the Somme designed by Edwin Lutyens and built between 1928 and 1932 at Thiepval near the town of Albert in northern France, is a magnificent monument to the missing, who are remembered individually: a 46-metre-high agglomeration of brick arches, resting on sixteen piers faced with Portland stone with fifty-six wall panels on which are carved the names of over 73,357 soldiers lost during the battles at the Somme between 1916 and 1918 and who had no known grave.[28] A similar approach was taken in the 'Hall of Memory' of the Menin Gate Memorial (the first of the Imperial War Graves Commission's 'Memorials to the Missing'), designed by the more conservative architect Reginald Blomfield and opened in July 1927 at the eastern side of Ypres (Ieper) in Belgium. There, the names of nearly 55,000 Commonwealth soldiers who had been killed in the Ypres salient and whose bodies never were found or identified are carved onto stone panels.[29] Although the Menin Gate Memorial was attacked bitterly at the time by the poet Siegfried Sassoon as a 'sepulchre of crime',[30] it became a focus of grief for relatives of the dead. It was described in travel books during the early 1930s as 'one of the most hallowed spots in Europe', a place of 'brooding sorrow' and of 'hollow victory',[31] and it has remained a site of pilgrimage on the First World War tourist trail.

Nevertheless, the forms of memorialization chosen at Thiepval and Ypres, or even at Gentioux, did not represent a universally accepted response to the challenge of remembering the war dead after 1918. The memories of many disappeared with the dead, particularly in eastern Europe, where revolutionary upheaval and extreme economic dislocation not merely shook social and political structures but destroyed them. As Bruce Scates and Rebecca Wheately have pointed out, there 'some soldiers simply stood outside the ambit of commemoration. In 1917, the newly formed Bolshevik government renounced involvement in imperialist war and with it the memory of over a million war dead.'[32] It was the successor to that government which, after the Second World War, constructed massive, heroic monuments to the dead of the Soviet Union's 'Great Patriotic War', monuments that glorify their wartime deeds but that seem strangely out of place in today's Europe.

Yet there is a sense in which Soviet war memorials such as the gigantic statues at the Mamayev Kurgan overlooking Volgograd (formerly Stalingrad) and in the Treptower Park in Berlin reflect a change in how the violence of war tended to be commemorated after the Second World War as opposed to the First. Whereas after the First World War, at least in western Europe, the emphasis was on a cult of the dead, on the dead themselves, after the Second World War the focus was provided more by the sites of the violence and destruction.[33] The focus of the latter is on the places where victims and soldiers died – on where the violence occurred – rather than on the communities from which the soldiers came. Thus memorials have been constructed at the sites of massacres (such as at Oradour-sur-Glane in France and at Lidice in the Czech Republic), of concentration and extermination camps, of battles and of bombing (for example, with the preservation of the ruins of bombed-out churches). Nevertheless, the emphasis remains on the violence done to individuals – as in the stated aim of the memorial at Lidice ('to take care of the permanent preservation of the town of Lidice and of its residents who in [sic] 10.6.1942 became the victims of Nazi violence'),[34] or in the placing of plaques in the preserved ruins of Oradour listing the names and professions of the individuals who had lived there before the massacre of 10 June 1944.[35]

Over the twentieth century, listing the names of individual dead became an accepted artistic form for war memorials around the world. Probably the best-known is the Vietnam Veterans Memorial, designed by Maya Lin (who was then a 21-year-old architecture student at Yale University and who had been inspired by Lutyens's Memorial to the Missing of the Somme at Thiepval)[36] and built in 1982 on the Mall in Washington DC: a wall on which are engraved on polished, reflective black stone the names of the over 58,000 Americans who died in that war. It is a motif that was also adopted both for the '*Monumento a los Caídos en Malvinas*' ('Monument for the Fallen in the Malvinas' [Falklands]) in the Plaza General San Martín in Buenos Aires and for the Falklands War Memorial at Stanley on the islands themselves. These monuments do not celebrate heroism in war but reflect (and, in the case of the Vietnam Veterans Memorial by Maya Lin, reflect quite literally) loss. They embody a condemnation of violence, not a celebration.

Listing the names of the dead is a form of commemoration not just of soldiers, but also of civilians who have lost their lives in acts of violence. This, too, has its precedents in the first half of the twentieth century. One early example, commemorating an outrage largely forgotten today, is the memorial at Bath, Michigan, where the worst massacre of schoolchildren in American history occurred in 1927. (On 18 May 1927, a local farmer and school-board member, embittered about tax increases levied to pay for the new school, laid explosives in the Bath Consolidated School and timed explosions that claimed the lives of thirty-eight schoolchildren and five adults.)[37] The site contains no representation of the victims, no statues of children. Instead, there is a simple metal plaque on a large boulder, 'In memory of those who perished in the Bath School Disaster, May 18, 1927', with the names of those who died, a sign outlining what occurred, and the cupola of the school building (since demolished) that was subsequently built on the site of the Bath Consolidated School. However, as so often happens, there also was something of a human memorial: a community of victims. Tom Holton, whose mother and uncle were in the half of the school that was not blown up on that day in 1927, reported in 1999 that 'for more than seventy years the survivors of the disaster have met in the spring of each year to continue their survival bonding with each other'.[38]

And so it continues. Framing the memory of violent incidents are the victims, the individual people with whom we identify. Names without bodies frame the memory of bodies without names.[39] When the memorial to commemorate the victims of the attacks of 11 September 2001 at the New York World Trade Center was designed, the form chosen was both sensitive to painful memories of that act of violence and predictable in its form: it included the names of all the victims – two pools of water filling the footprints of the original twin towers, around the rims of which are bronze strips bearing the names of the 2,983 people who died there in the terrorist attacks, most of whose remains could not be found or identified.

Remembering violence has become remembering the victims of violence, and central to the commemoration of acts of violence is a sense of empathy – a term introduced into the English language by the British psychologist Edward Titchener in 1909[40] – of identification with the victims. This can be seen clearly in the ways in which the most notorious massacre in Canada in recent times has been remembered. In the late afternoon of 6 December 1989, Marc Lépine (born Gamil Gharbi) entered the *École Polytechnique de Montréal* armed with a semi-automatic rifle and a hunting knife. In a self-styled campaign against 'feminists', Lépine proceeded to kill fourteen women engineering students and injured another ten women and four men before shooting himself. The murders deeply shocked the Canadian public, led to the passage of stricter gun-control legislation, have been commemorated in memorial sites in various places across Canada, and continue to be a reference point for Canadians campaigning against violence against women. Two years after the massacre, the Canadian government designated 6 December as a National Day of Remembrance and Action on Violence Against Women, and since that time events across

Canada to remember women victimized by violence have been held on the day. In one such gathering, in Brant, Ontario (a municipality of about 35,000 people roughly 100 kilometres south-east from Toronto) in 2012, a group of fifty people came together at a local cultural centre to remember women victims of violence. One of those who took part explained: 'I came out to remember everyone that has been taken from us through violence. I have lost friends and family through violence, too. It gives them rest to remember them.' Another, a second-year student at Laurier University's nearby Brantford campus, declared: 'I came out to remember the women who lost their lives in the Montreal Massacre. It is about being thankful for the opportunities I have. It really is about not forgetting that horrible things like that have happened.'[41]

This is how acts of violence have come to be situated in public memory: in an unambiguous manner we remember the victims. After the shooting on 14 December 2012 at the Sandy Hook Elementary School in Newtown, Connecticut, during which twenty children and six members of the school staff were murdered by twenty-year-old Adam Lanza, President Barack Obama led the public mourning. He began his speech at an Interfaith Prayer Vigil at Newtown High School two days after the shooting by saying, 'We gather here together in memory of twenty beautiful children and six remarkable adults.'[42] It was an eloquent speech, and revealing of how violence is remembered, for Adam Lanza had killed not twenty-six but twenty-seven people before turning the gun on himself. It was the innocent children and the teachers who died while trying to shield their pupils who were remembered, not the mother Nancy Lanza, whose Bushmaster rifle Adam Lanza had used to carry out the massacre.

A decade earlier, also after a school massacre, the president of Germany Johannes Rau had struck a somewhat different note. Rau addressed a huge public memorial event in Erfurt a week after the shooting of 26 April 2002, when nineteen-year-old Robert Steinhäuser killed thirteen teachers, two students and a police officer at the city's *Gutenberg Gymnasium* before killing himself. Rau, who was known for his Christian piety, pointedly included the families of *all* the dead and their families in his thoughts when he delivered his funeral speech to the crowd assembled in the city's Cathedral Square: 'My thoughts also go out to the family of the perpetrator. No one can fathom their pain, their grief and indeed their shame. I want to say to you: Whatever a human being has done; he remains a human being.'[43] These were remarkable, courageous words – words that fully addressed the void left by the killings. They were remarkable because statements by leading public figures after such violent outrages usually limit their identification to the innocent victims, and do not extend it to perpetrators. Usually there is little room for a public recognition of the complexities that often surround acts of violence. The categories of 'victim' and 'perpetrator' are complex, but it is rare that the complexities are addressed openly.

Memories of violence are not only public affairs; they do not coalesce just around public monuments and public acts of commemoration. A new focus was provided by photography, not least by photography of war and of the victims of war. With new technology and cheaper cameras, during the First World War for the first time soldiers themselves were able to take snapshots. Consequently, photographs of the war were provided not just by governments and the armed forces but also by soldiers themselves.[44] Despite censorship, an enormous amount of photographic material emerged from the war, including photographs of the dead and wounded. Collections of war photos were published in the years that followed the fighting, offering what Ernst Jünger described, in the introduction to the collection *Das Antlitz des Weltkrieges* (*The Face of the World War*) published in 1930, as 'a singular view of horror and of the desolation of the landscape that will in all probability never be repeated'.[45] As we know, however, it was repeated. War photography became a staple of journalism throughout the twentieth century. Thus it became possible not just to imagine acts of wartime violence but also to have a photographic record of the results of that violence – of the ruins of buildings, of devastated landscapes, of the injuries of the wounded, of corpses. Although it gives a less accurate sense of war than is often imagined, photographic evidence both exuded an air of authenticity and framed the ways in which war, and the violence of war, were remembered (and continue to be remembered to this day). The acts of violence may have been ephemeral, but the photographic record is not.

Sometimes images remain embedded into memory even where there are no photographs, no tangible record of the event. For many people who have been confronted directly by the horrors and violence of war, it was the actual encounter with corpses that made an indelible impression. Sixty years after the end of the Second World War, the German-Jewish violinist Michael Wieck wrote of his experiences as a sixteen-year-old in Königsberg in East Prussia after the city had been occupied by the Soviet Army:

> The city still was littered with unburied dead. They buried soldiers, but the troops did not regard themselves responsible for civilians. So it now was our task to search houses and cellars, courtyards and gardens for corpses, in order to 'dispose' of them. One could not really describe it as burying. I have to bring myself to describe what we did. The first removal was of a partly naked young woman with dried streams of blood around the vagina and the mouth, lying on the ground floor of a half-burnt-out house. She had a delicate, tender face. We carried her with gloves – which they gave us – by the arms and legs out to the street; we had to throw her into the nearest bomb crater. Others brought a man who had been shot. They

threw him on top of the woman. The corpses were about a week old, and had already begun to decompose. [...] I can still remember almost all of these poor murdered women and men; I see not just their faces but also their various positions and sometimes the objects that surrounded them. Children as well as old people; most of them shot, some stabbed or strangled.[46]

Images such as these – memories of the corpses of people who died violent deaths – are difficult to remember and probably impossible to forget. Friedrich Nietzsche famously wrote: 'If something is to stay in the memory, it must be burned in: only that which never ceases to *hurt* stays in the memory.'[47] These are images that are burned into memory, and they never cease to hurt; but (in the west) they are held by people living in societies and cultures where such scenes are almost incomprehensible.

Another account, this one written by a US Army sergeant describing what he saw at Dachau on 3 May 1945, shortly after the camp was liberated:

The air [...] was filled with the smell of lime and the unfor- gettable smell of the dead. Facing us was a big grey building with a grey wall, about 10 feet high, all around it. To the left of this building and wall were fifty rail cars. [...] In at least forty of the cars including the four open ones, there were dead, starved, emaciated bodies lying in every conceivable posi- tion. They wore striped suits (prisoner's uniform), parts of which seem to have been torn from their bodies in their death throes, thus revealing the wax-like skin of the dead. In a lot of grass, opposite the train, were three dead SS guards, evidently beaten to death, because there were terrific bruises all over their bodies. They were dressed in civilian clothes which were partly ripped from their bodies. One of the bodies had part of its skull ripped open but in general they looked very well fed compared to the starved dead bodies of their victims opposite them on the train. [...]

We walked into a fenced-in portion of ground which housed the crematorium.

The rooms where the bodies were kept were about 10 feet high and 17 feet square filled with layer upon layer of human bodies. They were piled as you would pile cord wood ready for burning. The stench was horrible.[48]

This description was part of a report deposited in the US National Archives and that lay there for decades. The author was my father. He never talked about this with his children as we were growing up, although we knew that he had been among the troops that liberated the concentration camp at the end of the war. He described it, in a sparse, almost monosyllabic account when, a few years before he died, I asked him about his experiences at Dachau in 1945.

While such scenes were burned into the memories of those who saw corpses, for millions of the dead there were no remains, no images, no graves. Memories of war and violence during the twentieth century have been framed not just by the presence of visual evidence but also by absence – by the fact that millions of people effectively vanished. In the First World War, during which the great majority of casualties on the Western Front resulted from artillery fire, soldiers were literally blown to pieces: there was nothing left, providing the *raison d'être* for monuments to the missing such as at Thiepval and making all the more fitting the choice of a cenotaph, an empty tomb, as a central war memorial in London and in many other cities around the English-speaking world.[49]

This also provided the basis for creating what has become an internationally accepted focus for memories of wartime losses: the tomb of the unknown soldier. After the First World War, an unknown soldier was first buried in France after a ceremony at the *Arc de Triomphe* on 11 November 1920 (the second anniversary of the Armistice), and on the same day a British 'unknown warrior' was interned in Westminster Abbey – a practice copied subsequently in numerous countries around the world, from Australia to Poland, Russia and Ukraine, from Belgium to Canada and Chile. A single, unknown victim of the war would represent all those who met violent death in combat.

While the two countries – France and Britain – that had begun the practice of interning a single unknown soldier both suffered far greater losses during the First World War than in the Second, the reverse was the case for other combatant nations. In many respects, the challenge of remembering the disappeared was even greater after 1945. During the Second World War, tens of thousands of people who were killed in bombing campaigns were literally incinerated, as the bombing left behind mutilated bodies, body parts and burnt and shredded human remains. Disposal of unidentified and unidentifiable remains became an increasingly difficult problem, and in the most extreme cases was accomplished simply by burning the bodies *en masse* – as in February 1945 in Dresden, where in order to avoid outbreaks of disease thousands of corpses were stacked on a metal grate in the *Altmarkt* in the old city, doused with petrol and set alight, and the resulting ashes were buried in a communal grave.[50] The bodies may have disappeared – although in Dresden more than 1,800 skeletons were unearthed as the city was rebuilt after the war[51] – but the ruins of bombed cities provided reminders of the violence of war for years. (But there, too, often it was absence – for example, an empty space where once had stood a house destroyed by bombing or fighting on the ground – that evoked memories of the war.)

The bombing of Dresden has become one of the best-known (if often inaccurately remembered) chapters in the chronicle of violence and death during the last months of the Second World

War, but it is only one part of the awful story. The last months of
the Second World War were the most bloody, and when the
Second World War ended, millions of people were missing.
Bombing, flight, expulsion, arrest and incarceration, as well as
the fighting, claimed huge numbers of lives, leaving survivors
often without knowledge as to whether their relatives were alive
or dead. In Germany – where in the last months of the war military casualties were the highest of the entire conflict (and the
Wehrmacht lost 450,000 dead in January 1945 alone) and where
the reporting of German casualties largely broke down, where
bombing had made millions homeless, where millions of
soldiers had been taken prisoner (hundreds of thousands of
whom later died in captivity),[52] and where over eleven million
Germans had fled westwards ahead of the advancing Soviet
Army or subsequently were expelled from their erstwhile
homes in eastern Europe (of whom roughly 500,000 died)[53] –
the fate of millions remained unknown. Those who died in air
raids could usually be buried in marked graves, as could many
of those killed in the fighting inside Germany. But what of the
missing? Neil Gregor has written sensitively about post-war
Nuremberg, where cemeteries 'contain not only epitaphs
mourning those killed in air raids, or those killed in action near
the city and thus buried in marked graves, but numerous
examples of gravestones erected in memory of those who had
not been officially recorded as dead but who were missing in
action – many contain epitaphs such as "Fritz H., missing in
East Prussia, Jan. 1945", or "Heinz B., lost in the East, 1944".'[54]
After the Second World War, German society, like many societies
across Europe and Asia, was haunted for years by the missing
victims of war and violence.

Most extreme were the challenges posed by complete erasure
of victims of campaigns of genocide. Millions of people who
met their deaths in the killing fields of the Second World War, in
the extermination camps, in the Gulag, were either dumped in

unmarked mass graves or turned to ash. For many of these people, no one was left to mourn, and there was no grave of a missing child, a lover or a parent. In recent decades, attempts have increasingly been made to preserve and honour the memory of the victims of genocide in the absence of proper burial sites. But how does one remember the violence committed against Jews murdered in the camp at Betżec in south-eastern Poland, into which as far as we know more than 400,000 entered between March 1942 and June 1943 and only two emerged alive?[55] Or at Treblinka, where by the end of 1942 more than 700,000 people had been murdered but where (as at Betżec) in 1943 the camp was liquidated, the buildings removed and the grounds planted over, leaving no trace of what had been perpetrated there?[56] One can only mark the sites where the victims died and disappeared.

Elsewhere, where murder had been carried out by shooting rather than by gas, there were mass graves. On the north-eastern outskirts of Riga lies the Bikernieki Forest, the largest Second World War killing site in Latvia. Between 30,000 and 35,000 people (including my grandparents) met their deaths there – German Jews deported from the *Reich* in late 1941, as well as Latvian Jews, Soviet POWs and political prisoners. Today a substantial memorial stands in the forest. Dedicated in 2001 (sixty years after the deportation of German Jews to their deaths in Latvia), it consists of a central site with a black granite altar in the middle of roughly 5,000 exposed ragged granite stones, arranged in sections to represent the cities from which the Jews had been deported. From this, central memorial paths lead into the forest, where fifty-five mass graves are delineated with low concrete borders and where concrete pillars are embossed with, variously, the Star of David, the crown of thorns and the cross (symbolizing Jewish, political and Christian victims respectively). The memorial is reached by footpath from a main road that cuts the large forest in two, and is signalled by engraved stone markers along the road with inscriptions in Latvian, Hebrew, German, Russian and English. There have been periodic ceremonies held at the site, and delegations visit from Germany, but on most days few people visit the memorial, just perhaps the occasional foreign traveller who has come to see where family members had been killed. Local residents do come to the forest, sometimes walking their dogs through the pine trees. It is not really their site of memory. What happened there cannot be remembered, only imagined.

Nevertheless, some were left to tell their stories after 1945. In the early post-war years, after the initial shock that accompanied the liberation of Dachau, Bergen-Belsen and Buchenwald in 1945, accounts of what had happened in the camps were largely the work of former prisoners. It was their memories of violence that informed the first studies of the camps immediately after the war.[57] Not really until the 1960s and 1970s did the historical profession catch up and focus serious attention on the history of the concentration and extermination camps of German-occupied Europe during the Second World War. This has not meant that memories of what occurred were relegated to a lesser role, however. In recent decades they have been collected, catalogued and preserved with almost obsessive energy by the staffs of research centres, libraries and community education centres in Israel, Europe and North America. The evidence thus preserved presents a valuable and difficult resource: a combination of recollections – some mistaken and confused, and some devastatingly accurate – and of emotions ranging from eagerness to be understood and to bear witness, to anger and hatred and to grief and guilt, and offered to an often uncomprehending younger audience who can hardly conceive such violence. The rabbi and broadcaster Hugo Gryn, who had survived the camps but had lost much of his family, and who died in 1996, reflected on the purpose and the difficulties of relating such memories:

This was my thought: that one day these people who made murder a virtue and the death of innocents a cause for celebration, that they be exposed and made accountable and brought before some bars of civilized practice. Yes – and be punished for it!

There is also a sadness that will not go away. I keep seeing my brother and grandparents in the selection line in Auschwitz, and so many aunts and uncles and cousins and friends and neighbours – indeed most of the Jewish community of my hometown – slowly, unknowingly walking to their deaths. I think of all the love and laughter and learning that was extinguished with their lives – and often wonder how it was that I survived. Perhaps to give just this kind of testimony. [...] There is a bit in me that would like to be anaesthetized and have all the memory of Auschwitz wiped out. But that cannot be, because so much of what I am was forged there and so much that could have been perished there.[58]

Memories of such things are difficult to admit and to express, for bystanders as well as for victims. They can be ambivalent, half-hidden, and as time passes one's relationship to the memories changes. In 1998, the Israeli author Aharon Appelfeld wrote in the *New Yorker* about returning (with a film crew) to his native village in Poland after more than half a century:

What does a child of eight and a half remember? Almost nothing. But, miraculously, that 'almost nothing' has nourished me for years. Not a day passes when I'm not at home. That 'almost nothing' is the well from which I draw and draw, and it seems that there is no end to its waters.

However, his memory of the village of his childhood was far from idyllic:

Who would imagine that in this village, on a Saturday, our Sabbath, sixty-two souls, most of them women and children, would fall prey to pitchforks and kitchen knives, and I, because I was in a back room, would manage to escape to the cornfields and hide?

Upon his return Appelfeld spoke with villagers, and asked them where the Jews killed during the war had been buried, but no one seemed to be able to answer – until 'a tall peasant came up, and, as if in an old ceremony, the village people explained to him what I wanted to know. He raised his arm and pointed: it was over there, on a hill.' Appelfeld went on:

It turned out that what the people of the village had tried to conceal from me was well known, even to the children. I asked several little children, who were standing near the fence and looking at us, where the Jews' graves were. Right away, they raised their hands and pointed.

After they went to the hill, and 'finally one of them said, "Here is the grave." He pointed at an uncultivated field. "Are you sure?" I asked. "I buried them," the peasant replied. He added, "I was sixteen."'[59] There are memories of violence and murder that everyone knows and no one admits to knowing without being prodded, 'memories' known to children born half a century after the violence occurred.

Let us hear one further voice – that of the Israeli historian Otto Dov Kulka, who as an adolescent survived Theresienstadt, Auschwitz and the death marches of early 1945, and who has given us one of the most remarkable, searching testimonies of that most horrible chapter of our history. At one point he looks back on his recorded memories of the 'landscapes of the Metropolis of Death':

The pervasive, all-governing element in them is the immut-
able law, utterly impersonal, of the Great Death. In contrast
there are the more personal games of the 'small death'. Almost
absent – in truth, completely absent – is another element, so
well known from the memoirs and testimonies about daily life
in the concentration camps. I mean the violence, the cruelty,
the torture, the individual killings, which, as far as I can make
out – though I generally avoid reading such texts – are portrayed as the everyday routine of that world of the camps. I
am obliged to ask myself whether anything of that violence
and cruelty remains in my memory. [...] What's puzzling is
that I possess almost no such memories; I have to think hard
and scan the images that remain engraved in one form or
another – as experiences, as colours, as impressions – in order
to isolate in them something of a type that I could describe as
violence.[60]

Violence may be the great obsession of our time and place. We
may seek to preserve our memories of it, to reflect on it in memoirs and in memorials devoted to the victims of the great
explosions of violence that have marked the history of the twentieth century. Yet there are experiences that can transcend, or
that can smother, memories of violence.

It is not only the victims of violence who are left with the
challenge of memory. Perpetrators have to deal with memories
of violence as well, memories that can be even more difficult
since they do not lend themselves to accepted ideas about violence as victim narratives often do. Millions of soldiers returned
from war with memories that they somehow had to deal with
after their return to civilian life. Some felt that they had to suppress their memories, which had no place in a peaceful civil
society; some felt guilt or shame at what they had witnessed or
had done; and the memories often remained with them to the
end of their lives. In 1960, a French soldier of the First World

War recalled a night-time encounter in September 1914, when he shot and killed two Germans, men he did not see: 'The two cries, so alike, that I still hear them after more than forty years.'[61] Memories of killing are often bound up with feelings of guilt, and leave the killer with the task somehow of justifying violent actions that in civil society cannot easily be justified. The recollections of another French soldier of the First World War provide a revealing example:

As we reached the top, five or six wretched soldiers, stupefied by the pounding fire, emerged out of their hole in front of me. In the confusion of action I could not see that they were unarmed and were putting their hands up. I was startled despite everything, for I was alone and separated from my companions, and in an uncontrollable reflex my finger pressed the trigger and shot one of the poor wretches full in the chest. He was unarmed, and was surrendering. Ignoring his companions, who scurried down the slopes to save their lives, I bent over him as if to seek forgiveness. I do not know whether there was reproach in his gaze. I did not dare look into his dying eyes. With his hand clenched over the hole in his chest he tried to stop the blood spurting out. He was still sufficiently conscious to get his wallet out of his inside pocket of his tunic, and hold it out to me. I opened it quickly and found photographs. A very young wife, two young children. I understood his gesture and the wish it expressed. I made him understand that the photos would be sent back to his family. His eyes thanked me. I could already see the shadow of death across his face. I held my water bottle to his lips, and with a final twitch he died in my arms.

I have often seen the ghost of this dead man since then. I reject the responsibility for my deeds, I hand it over to others, for as an eighteen-year-old soldier I should have had other examples to follow. Alas, it is only human beings, whoever they may be, who can make war with a spirit of humanity.[62]

Shortly after the Second World War, the British psychoanalyst Edward Glover claimed that 'it is impossible for man to break the tabu [sic] on killing [...] without sooner or later suffering from unconscious guilt'.[63] Memories of violence are often bound up with memories of fear and of hatred, emotions that can be difficult to express in a cultural context where violence and hatred are regarded as unacceptable. According to the Hungarian-born Jewish psychoanalyst Therese Benedek, who emigrated to the United States in 1936, former combatants were averse to talking about their experiences because they wanted to avoid dredging up unwelcome, 'humiliating' memories: 'With the killing he has to remember the fear he experienced and the threatening depth of his own emotions, so different from what he had been taught all his life.'[64] War memoirs may express this, but most ex-soldiers do not write memoirs. One who did was Eugene Sledge, who described his experiences as a young American marine in the South Pacific during the Second World War in one of the finest accounts of war ever published. More than three decades after the end of the war, Sledge wrote in the preface to his book:

> My Pacific war experiences have haunted me, and it has been a burden to retain this story. But time heals, and the nightmares no longer wake me in a cold sweat with pounding heart and racing pulse. Now I can write this story, painful though it is to do so. In writing it I'm fulfilling an obligation I have long felt to my comrades in the 1st Marine Division, all of whom suffered so much for our country. None came out unscathed. Many gave their lives, many their health, and some their sanity. All who survived will long remember the horror they would rather forget.[65]

Fear, hatred, shame and guilt, alongside pride at having served his country, emerge from the descriptions (in a prose all the more powerful for being straightforward and unembellished) of his experiences. In his description of one encounter, of the taking of a Japanese pillbox on Peleliu in 1944, all these emotions surface together:

> [...] even before the dust settled, I saw a Japanese soldier appear at the blasted opening. He was grim determination personified as he drew back his arm to throw a grenade at us.
>
> My carbine was already up. When he appeared, I lined up my sights on his chest and began squeezing off shots. As the first bullet hit him, his face contorted in agony. His knees buckled. The grenade slipped from his grasp. All the men near me [...] had seen him and began firing. The soldier collapsed in the fusillade, and the grenade went off at his feet.
>
> Even in the midst of these fast-moving events, I looked down at my carbine with sober reflection. I had just killed a man at close range. That I had seen clearly the pain on his face when my bullets hit him came as a jolt. It suddenly made the war a very personal affair. The expression on that man's face filled me with shame and then disgust for the war and all the misery it was causing.
>
> My combat experience thus far made me realize that such sentiments for an enemy soldier were the maudlin meditations of a fool. Look at me, a member of the 5th Marine Regiment [...] feeling ashamed because I had shot a damned foe before he could throw a grenade at me! I felt like a fool and was thankful my buddies couldn't read my thoughts.[66]

Not all soldiers were able to handle such horrible experiences and maintain their mental balance. One former marine who had served in Vietnam related the following while being treated in

1987 by the Veterans Administration for Post-Traumatic Stress Disorder:

> Our squad was cut off. NVA [North Vietnamese Army] was close enough to lob grenades into our position. Perimeter fire kept them back, but when we stopped firing, they lobbed grenades in. The grunt [marine] next to me was on the ground, curled into a ball and crying. Whenever I attended to him, more grenades were lobbed in. I returned to firing, and the guy jumped up and ran away from our position. I shot him in the back. For years I felt justified. Now I feel guilty. He was only eighteen. It was his first fire fight, and he couldn't handle it.[67]

Another Vietnam combat veteran, also being treated in 1987, found it impossible to leave behind his feelings of anger:

> I have no problem keeping anger alive. [...] During my second tour, I was in an assault on a large village. It was ringed around two-thirds by dug-in army. Our helicopter landed outside the village. I was leaning against it. Smoking, when firing begins: a Cobra [helicopter gunship] slants down and pours high-volume fire into the village. You can't see anything because of the smoke – awful smell – all kinds of shit burning. We entered the village, and there were bodies all over the place. Near me, there was a dead old woman and a young girl – but the girl was alive. She'd lost one leg and was going around in a circle on the ground, crying out but not making any sound. The marine next to me takes out a gun and shoots her in the head. I was completely pissed by the whole fucking thing, all of it. All I wanted to do was trash people and that's what I did. I didn't care who they were, and I'd just as well have killed US. Back in the helicopter, I could hardly control myself from killing

the pilot. I just pissed out the door and emptied my M16 into a pig. Now I hate everyone. I don't have a special target for my anger.[68]

Unlike Sledge, and unlike the men who subsequently related their wartime experiences in Vietnam in group-therapy sessions, many hundreds of thousands, perhaps millions of soldiers would never describe their experiences and emotions so openly. Doris Lessing wrote in a short biographical essay that her father – who had volunteered in 1914, lost his leg (cut off at mid-thigh after being shattered by shrapnel) and afterwards suffered from depression – told her:

> You should always remember that sometimes people are all seething underneath. You don't know what terrible things people have to fight against. [...] When I was like that, after I lost my leg, I went to a nice doctor man and said I was going mad, but he said, don't worry, everyone locks up things like that. You don't know – horrible, horrible, awful things. I was afraid of myself, of what I used to dream. I wasn't myself at all.[69]

Lessing wrote of her father: 'I think that the best of my father died in that war, that his spirit was crippled by it.' Describing how her father talked about his war experiences (beyond the 'stereotyped phrases'), she went on to write: 'There was an undercurrent of memories, dreams, emotions much deeper, more personal. This dark region in him, fate-ruled, where nothing was true but horror, was expressed inarticulately, in brief, bitter exclamations or phrases of rage, incredulity, betrayal.'[70]

The anxieties and emotional damage that memories of wartime violence may bring have been the subject of mounting concern and voluminous research about the psychological consequences of combat. While many British servicemen who fought in the Boer War (1899–1902) were discharged with what was diagnosed at the time as a 'disordered action of the heart', and 'while every major war in the last century involving western nations has seen combatants diagnosed with a form of post-combat disorder',[71] it is with Britain's experience of the Great War that the modern history of this phenomenon really developed. During and after the First World War, attention was devoted to what was labelled 'shell shock' – a term coined by the British psychiatrist Charles Myers in *The Lancet* in 1915 to describe a set of disabling injuries suffered by men at the front, and thought to be caused by injury to the nerves during combat due in particular to artillery fire. It was 'a condition in which the link between an individual's memory and his identity is severed', and that (subsumed under different rubrics at different times) has 'come to symbolize traumatic injury and traumatic memory throughout the twentieth century'.[72] In German the term was *Kriegsneurose* ('war neurosis') or *Kriegshysterie* ('war hysteria'), labels suggesting that men had succumbed to a condition (hysteria) associated with women; by 1918 at least 5 per cent of hospital beds in military bases in Germany were reserved for cases of 'war hysteria'.[73] Although most combat veterans did not appear to have suffered from 'shell shock' or its equivalents, and although most of those who did were able to live with it in one way or another, the condition presented military medical facilities with a substantial problem. There certainly were many men who could admit 'the joys associated with combat' and for whom 'satisfaction and excitement outweighed distressing experiences',[74] yet for many others their memories of violence not only haunted them for years afterwards but also undermined their sense of identity, their understanding of who they were.

Although the Second World War was in large measure a war of movement, unlike the stationary warfare on the Western Front of 1914–1918 that had given rise to 'shell shock', the underlying problem remained. Memories of violence again shattered the mental health of combat veterans and again the medical and psychiatric professions were mobilized to deal with the problem. This time round the discussion was of 'war neurosis', 'combat fatigue' or 'battle exhaustion', with which the American and Canadian armed forces saw that they had to contend. Decades afterwards, 'combat fatigue' among veterans of the Second World War continued to be regarded as a problem, and in 1965 it was reported in the United States that 'the sweaty hands, jumpiness and nightmares of combat fatigue still plague many veterans of World War II. Although twenty years have passed since they came home, combat fatigue victims still suffer from the combat symptoms they experienced during the traumatizing events of war.'[75]

However, it was with America's Vietnam War that memories of violence and psychological trauma really entered public discussion, and not just with regard to the effects of the war. During the second half of the twentieth century, the psychological problems arising from combat not only received greater attention but were also seen as a way to understand the 'traumatic memory' of violence generally, and in a way that underscored the status of the soldier as victim. The attention focused on what now was labelled Post-Traumatic Stress Disorder (PTSD), a term coined in the 1970s (and formally recognized as a medical diagnostic classification in 1980) for symptoms that result from experiencing 'an event that is outside the range of usual human experience and that would be markedly distressing to almost anyone',[76] an event that usually has involved violence. It is, Allan Young has written, 'a disease of time [...] The disorder's distinctive pathology is that it permits the past (memory) to relive itself in the present.'[77] PTSD has been defined generally as a 'mental health problem that can occur after someone goes through a traumatic event like war, assault or disaster'.[78] In the United States, PTSD was associated with veterans of the

Vietnam War, and early proponents of the diagnosis were linked with the anti-war movement of the time. Derek Summerfield has written in the *British Medical Journal*:

> The new diagnosis was meant to shift the focus of attention from the details of a soldier's background and psyche to the fundamentally traumatogenic nature of war. [...] Vietnam veterans were to be seen not as perpetrators or offenders but as people traumatized by roles thrust on them by the US military. Post-traumatic stress disorder legitimized their 'victimhood', gave them moral exculpation, and guaranteed them a disability pension because the diagnosis could be attested to by a doctor.[79]

This triggered a huge amount of psychiatric research on combat-related reactions to trauma from the late 1960s and the early 1970s onwards, and by September 1999 the National Center for Post-Traumatic Stress Disorder in the United States had indexed over 16,000 English-language publications on the subject.[80] During the 1980s, a massive National Vietnam Veterans' Readjustment Study was conducted (with the resulting 3,000-page report published in 1988), and it found that while the majority of soldiers experienced few symptoms of psychological disorders after returning, a sizeable minority did. Since that time, and with the succession of wars fought by western forces in the Middle East (as well as UK deployments in Northern Ireland), attention has been given to the possible occurrence of PTSD among returning soldiers of America's allies as well, e.g. those of Germany and the United Kingdom.[81] It even became recognized in a country where previously such ideas were quite foreign and where endurance and stoicism, not trauma and victimhood, have been emphasized: in Russia in the wake of the USSR's war in Afghanistan. Catherine Merridale notes that the Soviet Union's Afghan war 'did not fade away for many of those who fought it. Afghan veterans had seen fear, injury and death on a scale and in a setting which marked them for life.'[82] Contact with western, especially American, psychotherapy did the rest, and a new expression was introduced into the Russian language: *post-travmaticheskii stress*.

PTSD has become an accepted framework for understanding memories of war and violence, in civil societies in which violent behaviour is generally regarded as undesirable and even deviant. It offers a way of attempting to comprehend what perhaps is essentially incomprehensible. Martha Ramos, an American who described herself as 'the wife of a Vietnam veteran who is suffering from PTSD', married for over thirty years, wrote a poem entitled 'The Effects of War':

War is a terrible thing.
The after-effects are unimaginable.
People killed, injured, and lives changed.
Anger. Illness, depression, and so much more.
Families affected by not knowing what is wrong. Why is he
*   always angry?*
Nothing makes him happy. Will this upset him if I tell him?
I've been told be patient. I tell my children he is getting help.
But is it really helping? We don't see it.
Even after forty years the effects of war are unimaginable.[83]

Traumatic memories of war are seen to be embedded in those who experienced violence and continue to live with it 'even after forty years'. In 1965, Herbert Archibald, then chief of the mental hygiene clinic at the Veterans Administration Hospital in Oakland, California, and Read Tuddenham, a professor of psychology at the University of California at Berkeley, claimed on the basis of a study of 157 combat veterans that 'the combat fatigue syndrome, which was expected to vanish with the passage of time, has proved to be chronic, if not irreversible in certain of its victims'.[84] More recently, the director of a Veterans Administration Medical Center in Vermont noted: 'We still see veterans from as long ago as World War II who report suddenly having memories or dreams from combat after more than six decades. This is common and a normal response for most people. Like any difficult event, memories do come back from time to time.'[85] It may be that the widespread public discussion of PTSD made it easier for sufferers and possible sufferers to identify their symptoms, to speak about them with a vocabulary not available to people a century or more ago, and to bring them to the attention of medical practitioners (in institutions created to deal with the problem), and both patients and medical practitioners are probably more attentive to symptoms that are related to contemporary health concerns.[86] But there is no denying that the problems of PTSD and how to deal with traumatic memories of wartime violence loom large in public perceptions.

Post-Traumatic Stress Disorder has been linked not only with soldiers who saw combat. In recent decades it has come to be regarded as an anxiety disorder that affects individuals in many different environments and ensues after a variety of traumatic events, events characterized often (but not always) by violence. The diagnosis has, according to Derek Summerfield, 'become almost totemic', and the use of it has spread globally, not just by military medical services but also by humanitarian programmes.[87] Andrew Pomerantz, a psychiatrist and the chief of mental health services for the VA Medical Center in White River Junction, Vermont, has observed:

The 1980s represented a real shift in opinion away from this [PTSD] being just a specific combat syndrome to one that could occur to anybody under the right conditions. The original diagnostic criteria for PTSD were all about traumatic experience outside the realm of normal human experience.

The sad fact is that as time [went] on, we found [that] more and more awful things happen to people that are within the realm of normal human experience, so that part of the diagnosis, the criteria, has evolved and was changed in the 1990s to refer to a stressful experience and described in the manner of how it's experienced by the person going through it. And so certainly [it includes] rape, domestic violence, assault, hurricanes, floods, earthquakes, natural disasters of all kinds, things that nature does to us and things that we do to each other.[88]

Post-Traumatic Stress Disorder has become a framework for understanding memories of violence across the board. People from all walks of life are now considered to be at risk of developing PTSD – victims of violent crime; members of the armed forces and police; victims of war, terrorism and torture; survivors of accidents and disasters; women who have had a difficult experience of childbirth as well as people diagnosed with life-threatening illnesses. Women are believed to be more at risk than men.[89] It thus has become almost synonymous with memories of violence that are understood as traumatic – where violent events are believed to cause psychological wounds, trauma, that do not heal and cannot really be forgotten. Thus the epidemic of PTSD diagnosed not only among soldiers from western countries who had been in combat but increasingly also among the population at large, and the 'veritable trauma industry comprising experts, lawyers, claimants, and other interested parties'[90] perhaps reveals as much about contemporary attitudes towards violence as about the conditions of those who claim to have experienced it.

It has been argued throughout this book that contemporary attitudes reflect heightened sensitivity towards violence, fear of violence and the consequences of violence. Memories of violence as they came to be expressed during the second half of the

twentieth century both exerted a broad fascination and simultaneously were increasingly out of step with cultural values that
rejected and condemned violence. Increasing attention was paid
to memories of violence, in societies and cultures that increasingly rejected violence. This has framed the ways in which
violence – whether the violence of war, the violence of street
crime or the violence of the bedroom – has been remembered
and understood. Today, we remember violence more, if only to
reject it.

In 1927, the Austrian writer Robert Musil remarked that 'there
is nothing in the world as invisible as monuments'.[91] The events
and concerns that led to their construction tend to be forgotten
over time, and the monuments become parts of the landscape
that are hardly noticed any longer. Thus it is their fate to become
invisible.[92] Similarly, it may be the fate of memories of violence to
fade. As Amélie Lebraud, a survivor of the Oradour massacre as
a fifteen-year-old at the time, asked after the funeral of another,
older survivor in 1988: 'After us, who will remember?'[93]
Memories of pain and fear, like grief and mourning, inevitably
have a limited shelf life. New experiences push the old into the
background; older generations pass away, and with them their
memories of violence and their trauma pass away; younger generations take the stage for whom the stories of violence past are
not their concern. Yet at the same time there always are new concerns, new fears, new anxieties about violence that take the place
of the old. Old memories of violence inevitably fade, and new
ones inevitably take their place. Millions of people may (or may
not) experience a diminution of actual violence in their everyday
lives, and in the West few have had to face the sorts of horror that
confronted their grandparents and great-grandparents. But that
has not prevented us from devoting huge efforts to memorialize,
commemorate and remember acts of violence. That, indeed, is a
characteristic of our age.

IX

Conclusion

How do we view violence? It has been argued in this book that attitudes towards violence underwent a significant change in the western world during the course of the twentieth century, particularly during its second half. The discussion has been inevitably and necessarily impressionistic, and of course there have been exceptions to the general trend. The acceptance and indeed the glorification of violence clearly have not been expunged from society and politics in the western world, nor are they ubiquitous or unchallenged elsewhere. However, concern about violence seems generally to have become an obsession in the western world. Violence, it seems, is never out of the spotlight, and has come to be regarded as a fundamental enemy of our supposedly civilized society.

Violence has been the object of countless research projects and the subject of countless publications; libraries are filled with studies of violence and how to diminish or cure it; academic institutes, government agencies and civil-society organizations devote huge efforts and resources to the study of violence and its prevention. Violence has been regarded as deviant behaviour that can be treated and modified, provided that one recognizes its causes and takes the necessary steps to deal with them – whether that be through advancing the 'civilizing process', through achieving political emancipation, through the establishment of a more egalitarian social and economic order, through sympathetic personal relations, or through psychoanalysis.[1] The concern about the ease with which people overcome social and normative constraints and engage in shocking violence – about how 'ordinary men' can become murderers[2] – reflects both a belief (and a hope) that violence is abnormal and a fear that anyone can become a perpetrator of violence and that therefore we need to understand and if possible cure such behaviour. It may be, as Jörg Baberowski has written, 'a pious wish [that] violence can be exorcized and we ourselves could live for ever in peace and security'.[3] Nevertheless, this has not prevented us from continuing to wish and, in many cases, to believe that it is possible to banish violence from our lives – to hope 'that the dark sides of life remain able to be controlled, that the excesses that advance towards us as news from far-away countries remain where they are: far from our civilized world, in which that which elsewhere is an everyday experience cannot occur'.[4] Whether as a fear that it can erupt at any time or as a hope that we can master it and get it under control, violence has become an obsession for our times.

How might this be explained? The answer no doubt lies in part in the extraordinarily bloody history of the first half of the twentieth century: the colossal eruptions of violence during the two world wars and the civil wars that followed them, the monstrous campaigns of forced removal and genocide, the unprecedented bombing campaigns, the unspeakable violence committed by governments on their own people, the rise of paramilitarism and political extremism that eroded normative constraints developed during the course of the nineteenth century and that constituted a frontal assault on civilized enlightenment values. In short, this produced what can be described as a shock of violence.[5] Although human behaviour did not change fundamentally and although terrible eruptions of violence certainly did not cease to occur after 1945, the shock at the horrors of the first half of the century reverberated in calls of 'no more war' and 'never again' during the second.

It seems hardly coincidental that areas of the world that have experienced the worst explosions of deadly violence in recent decades had been left largely untouched during the first half of the twentieth century by the world wars and the campaigns of 'ethnic cleansing' and genocide that had accompanied them. Recent sites of genocide – one thinks of Rwanda, where some 800,000 people were slaughtered in a campaign of ethnic violence in little over three months, or the Congo, where millions have died in probably the bloodiest conflict on earth over the past decade in what has been described as 'the world's deadliest place'[6] – have been far from the locations where mass killing took place during the first half of the twentieth century (which were in Europe and east Asia). In one sense it is a long way from Auschwitz to Kigali; in another it is not very far at all.

It also seems hardly coincidental that many of the worst excesses of violence during the twentieth century occurred beyond the reach of coherent state structures and outside places of urban settlement.[7] This is true not just of the genocides in Rwanda and Cambodia, the mass slaughter in Indonesia in the mid-1960s, the conflict in the Congo and the crimes committed against the civilian population that accompanied America's Vietnam War; the fact that what Christian Gerlach has described as 'extremely violent societies' tend to be found in less-developed regions of the world.[8] It also describes many of the worst violent excesses in Europe during the first half of the twentieth century. The great slaughterhouses of that era were situated in the 'bloodlands' of eastern Europe, far from the comfortable bourgeois civilization that had developed in the more urbanized and developed west of the continent.[9] Of course one cannot

271

draw a precise line of demarcation between a supposedly civilized west and a supposedly uncivilized east, but the territories where people suffered the worst of the violence – e.g. Belarus, which lost a quarter of its entire population during the Second World War, or the Polish-Ukrainian borderlands, where purges, deportations, German racial policies and wartime slaughter destroyed a multi-ethnic society between the 1920s and the 1950s[10] – were in largely rural eastern Europe. Industrialized killing often occurred in non-industrialized environments.

While the unprecedented violence during the first half of the twentieth century was not necessarily a product of modernity, the contemporary sensitivity to violence may well be. A number of developments made this possible.

The first, already referred to above, is the *shock of the eruptions of violence during the first half of the twentieth century*. George Kennan famously referred to the First World War as the 'seminal catastrophe' of the twentieth century. It not only brought the industrial war and mass slaughter of the Western Front but, perhaps even more importantly, in the east it led not only to the deaths of millions of soldiers but also to mass forced removal of civilians, pogroms, the destruction of communities and the disintegration of governing structures, rampant paramilitarism and civil war. The genie was let well and truly out of the bottle, and many people were horrified by what they then saw. Confidence that had grown over the course of the nineteenth century that violence could be tamed, that warfare could be governed by rules, that religious difference need not be resolved through killing, was shattered by the First World War and its aftermath. Instead of being the 'war to end all wars', the First World War was followed by a second, even more destructive, world war that left even more dead, injured, homeless and uprooted in its wake. Instead of a triumph of popular sovereignty that would guarantee the peaceful coexistence of different nationalities and ethnic groups, one saw the most terrible campaigns of genocide that the world had ever seen. Instead of the triumph of democratic government, there was the fall of an 'iron curtain' across the European continent, behind which dictatorial 'people's democracies' were imposed. Looking back over the rubble in the late 1940s, it was understandable that many people felt shock and were determined to rein in violence. Surely, after Auschwitz, Dresden and Hiroshima, there was an urgent need to contain the frightening human potential for violence.

The second is the *unprecedented economic boom that the West enjoyed after the Second World War*. Good intentions about the need to control violence may not have had much resonance had it not been for the economic boom of the decades after the Second World War, bringing a prosperity that gave people much more to lose from violence and less to gain. After the economic insecurity and instability that had characterized the first half of the twentieth century, people in western Europe and North America benefited from the greatest economic expansion that the world had seen. Living standards improved substantially during the 1950s and 1960s, and the fruits of economic growth were widely, if not universally, shared. As Prime Minister Harold Macmillan famously declared during the 1957 British general election campaign, 'most of our people have never had it so good'. For the majority of the populations of these countries this meant that the desperate economic insecurities that previously had fuelled violence (e.g. the upsurge in political violence during the inter-war years) diminished. Where young men are able to secure steady employment, establish a household and take on family responsibilities, the social space available for violence in the public sphere is reduced. At the same time, the spread of economic well-being meant that violence could be perceived more readily as a threat. Economic improvement gave millions of people an enhanced interest in maintaining a peaceful environment, and could underpin expectations that others would behave in a more peaceable manner as well. Where the threat of economic hardship receded, the balance between the attractions and the disadvantages of violence shifted towards the better.

Third, *state structures became more stable, and more capable of maintaining civil peace.* The control of violence became easier to accomplish and state organizations could be relied upon to secure what Norbert Elias referred to as the internal pacification of society. State and political structures themselves became more secure and, able to apply new technologies and to enjoy greater legitimacy in the eyes of the population, state apparatuses became increasingly capable of intervening where and when violence surfaced or threatened. Political stability also underpinned the stability of legal codes, so that the law could be relied upon for controlling violence. The apparent stability of states in the developed world after 1945 no doubt had a lot to do with the Cold War, which in effect froze political developments in Europe for roughly four decades. This was true not only on the western side of the Cold-War divide, but also on the eastern side (where, for example, a suffocating but remarkably non-violent stability descended on the former German Democratic Republic following the suppression of the June 1953 uprising and the construction of the Berlin Wall in August 1961). The stability of state structures in turn permitted and heightened expectations that the state could and should intervene in ever-broader areas of social life in order to control violent behaviour, not just on the streets but also in the home. When people become convinced that the state can intervene to control violence, there is less incentive to take the law into one's own hands. As the state became more capable of intervening, the expectation grew that it should.

Fourth, *changes in life expectancy, demographic structures and the vast improvements in public hygiene and medical provision over the past century* have meant that death is no longer so much a part of life. This parallels observations made by Norbert Elias in *The Loneliness of the Dying*, in which he posited that as more people die in institutions they pass away in emotional isolation from the rest of society. This not only affects the dying themselves; it also reflects and affects social attitudes in general, in that it pushes death further from people's consciousness.[11] This in turn affects attitudes towards violence, for if there is a 'relatively high degree of protection against violence from other people enjoyed by members of more developed societies' and if the normal picture of dying is first and foremost that 'of a peaceful death in bed resulting from illness and the infirmity of age', then 'violent death at the hands of another person, appears exceptional and criminal'.[12] In societies where infant mortality has been reduced dramatically, where death in childbirth is exceptional rather than commonplace, where family size has fallen and where life expectancy has increased and most people die at a relatively advanced age, life is perceived as more precious. Therefore, life-threatening violence becomes all the greater a threat. As life in developed societies has become more predictable and the likelihood of a sudden and violent death has diminished, the threat posed by (deadly) violence may seem more frightening as it becomes exceptional. If we expect to live long and healthy lives, and to have painless deaths due to advances in palliative care, the spectre of lethal or wounding violence may seem more menacing, threatening to steal from us what increasingly we have come to regard as a birthright.

Fifth, the *transformation in the position of women in society and the increased presence of women in the public sphere* has contributed to changes in the ways in which violence is viewed. The greater prominence of women in public life, where they are fully fledged citizens and occupy prominent positions of responsibility, has provided the context for growing public concern about and sensitivity towards domestic and sexual violence, to violence against women, in particular. Public consciousness about such violence, and about the need for the criminal-justice system to devote attention to it, was raised in particular by women's groups. More generally, the increased visibility of women in public life may have tempered the public acceptability of supposedly masculine values of aggression and toughness – cultural values that underpinned tolerance or approval of violence.

Sixth, *civil society in the West has become more distanced from war and from the military.* However it may be dressed up, the purpose of armed forces remains, if necessary, to apply force. Their core purpose is violence. Yet the relationship of armed forces to the societies that provide the soldiers and which they are supposed to defend, and how they have fought wars, have undergone significant change since the Second World War. The era of mass, conscripted armies came to an end, and civilian populations in the West came to expect that wars were conducted far away, with relatively few 'boots on the ground', with few casualties, and that few if any sacrifices would be demanded of the civilian populations back home. Even during America's Vietnam War, living standards within the United States were hardly affected by the demands of war; government and public expected that they could have both guns and butter. Since the Second World War neither the United States, nor Canada, nor Australia, nor the United Kingdom, nor any western European country has experienced war on its own territory. They have jettisoned conscription and their armed forces are but a fraction of the size that they were when the Second World War ended. For example, the German armed forces, which grew to a strength of nearly half a million troops during the Cold War, were reduced to 370,000 after German unification and by February 2014 had fallen to 184,000.[13] The British Army, which abandoned conscription at the end of the 1950s, numbered 364,100 in 1950, had shrunk to 152,800 in 1990 and employed a mere 108,900 regular soldiers in 2010.[14] And even the United

States, the greatest military power that the world has ever seen, has not been immune to the trend: the US Army, which numbered 1.6 million in 1968 at its peak during the Vietnam War, had fallen in size to roughly half a million by the new millennium.[15] This means that a steadily smaller proportion of the population have experienced life in the military. Whereas in the 1950s and 1960s a substantial proportion of the adult male population of most western countries had known life in uniform and war, once the post-war generations came of age this no longer was the case. No longer is the army, as it once was regarded in Imperial Germany, the 'school of the nation'.

Seventh, the *reporting of violence in the media gained a new quality* with the use of communications technology and the dissemination of visual evidence to the public. The development of photo-journalism and of the film, television and video recording of war and other scenes of violence brought a second-hand awareness of the ghastly consequences of violence to many more people, and made it at once more difficult to accept heroic myths that may have glorified or excused violence and easier to empathize with the victims of violence. The reporting of the Vietnam War, and the critical photo-journalism that accompanied it, present the best-known example of how the reporting of war in the television age made civilians aware of wartime violence in a new way. They could see the images, but did not feel the pain.

Media coverage of acts of violence – whether these be in wars far away or physical attacks, murders and rapes nearby – has contributed to another important source of public sensitivity with regard to violence: fear. Incessant, often sensational and often misleading reporting of acts of violence is well suited to fanning fears, whereby life is perceived as dangerous and one easily can imagine becoming a victim. The fear of becoming a victim of violent crime in western societies, of rape or of murder, is quite out of proportion with the actual risk. In the United

States, for example, according to a survey in the late 1970s, over half of women expressed fear of being raped, a proportion that Joanna Bourke notes was '900 times higher than the percentage raped' (presumably in a given year); and the discrepancy between fear of being murdered and actually being murdered was far greater still.[16] The media have fanned fears of violent crime, even though crime rates generally have been falling in the western world in recent years, and while sensationalism and lurid crime reporting were neither new nor exclusive to the late twentieth century, they fed concerns about violence and strengthened demands to take measures to control it.

None of these developments was sufficient on its own to bring about the shift in attitudes described in this book. Rather it was the combination of them that enabled that shift to occur. The obsessively critical attitudes towards violence that had such a resonance after the Second World War were not new. In many respects they represented a realization of ideas and concerns that had been circulating since the late eighteenth century. However, it was the remarkable political, social, economic and cultural context of the western world during the second half of the twentieth century that allowed them to resonate so power-fully. In this context, hopes that seemed to have been blasted in the explosions of violence that had engulfed much of the world during the first half of the twentieth century gained new strength during the second.

After the Second World War people were determined to put the violence of their immediate past behind them, to forget their violent recent histories and to build 'normal' peaceful lives.[17] Europe's post-war recovery, Tony Judt has argued, was made possible by and rested for a quarter of a century upon 'a com-forting amnesia' (a phrase that Judt borrowed from Hans Magnus Enzensberger).[18] That amnesia allowed Europeans to focus on the violence done to them while conveniently forgetting much of the violence that they had done to others – a process that was particularly striking in Germany after the war.[19] People thus were able to substitute heroic and/or victim narratives for difficult and often unpalatable episodes of their recent past, and consequently to progress unencumbered by heavy mental baggage towards what appeared a peaceful, non-violent post-war world.

It is this desire to leave violence and the memories of violence behind that helped to give the 1950s and the early 1960s their peculiar quality. This may help to explain, for example, the strange public silence in Germany about the mass rapes that occurred in the country when the Soviet Army arrived in the spring of 1945, something that only really became a subject of wide public discussion from the 1980s onwards. It also may help to explain the relative absence of public (but not private) engagement with the dimensions of the murder of the Jews of Europe until the last quarter of the twentieth century, when research into the subject mushroomed and countless memorial sites were created. With the coming of age of post-war generations – who had not experienced the terrible violence of the 1940s – also came a heightened sensitivity towards, indeed an obsession with, violence in western societies. The rise of the feminist movement, which played a central role in focusing attention on domestic violence and violence against women, was an important part of this process. The 'memory boom' of recent decades – a 'memory boom' that focused in particular on experiences of the First World War (as those who fought in it were passing away) and on the genocide of European Jews – also may be understood in this context. The sensitivity towards violence posited in this book can be approached not least in generational terms – an observation which suggests perhaps that it too may be a passing phase.

The remarkable amplification of concern about violence thus appears to be the product of a particular time and place. Therefore the trend outlined here – the broadening of public sensitivity towards violence and of a conviction that violence needs to be combated in all walks of life – is not necessarily evidence of the achievement of an irreversible consensus favouring non-violence and sweet reason. This is not necessarily a story of progress, of an irreversible process of the triumph of enlightenment values led by the West into peaceful uplands where the rest of the world someday may follow. The explosions of violence across Europe during the first half of the twentieth century, and the atrocities committed during the civil wars in Yugoslavia more recently, have demonstrated that the protective shell that 'civilization' provides is less solid than many would like to think. We may live in a largely peaceful society, in which violence is almost universally condemned, but we can never be sure that it will not erupt again close to home. Jörg Baberowski, whose work on the violence of the Stalinist USSR has not inclined him towards optimism, admonishes: 'Whoever speaks of the success of the process of civilization closes his eyes to violence.'[20] Yet Norbert Elias was not naïve when he examined the 'process of civilization'. Elias looked back in horror at what had happened in his native Germany during the 1930s and 1940s, at the violence and barbarity that reversed that process and that claimed the life of his mother, and warned that the civilization of which he spoke 'is never completed and always endangered'.[21] He was right.

Acknowledgements

The seeds of this book were planted a decade ago when I co-taught a 'Comparative Special Subject' on 'Violence' with my colleague at the University of York, Stuart Carroll, with whom I learned a great deal. It also reflects my previous research, which for more than three decades has concentrated on the (extremely violent) history of Germany during the first half of the twentieth century. Along the way, I have been helped by many friends and colleagues, who no doubt will be able to find fruits of our conversations here. I hope that they will not be disappointed.

Completing this book also would not have been possible without institutional support, for which I am very grateful. I therefore want to express my appreciation to the *Institut für Zeitgeschichte* in Munich, to its former director Horst Möller, who invited me to the institute, and to its present director Andreas Wirsching, who hosted me during my time there as a *'Gastwissenschaftler'* in the spring of 2011. My greatest institutional debt is to the Freiburg Institute for Advanced Studies, where I was a Fellow at the School of History during 2012. I would like to express my thanks to the then directors of the FRIAS School of History – Ulrich Herbert, Jörn Leonhard and Wolfgang Eßbach – and to my fellow Fellows, whose friendship and contributions to a thriving intellectual environment helped me enormously – in particular Martin Geyer, Thomas Lindenberger, Hans Joas, John Horne, and Jörg Baberowski. I also am grateful to the History Department at the University of York, for a period of research leave in 2013–2014 that allowed me to complete the manuscript. The demands of university teaching in the UK have become so great in recent years that without periods of research leave and the hospitality of institutes where one is free to read and to write, it would have been impossible to complete this book. I am not alone in my debt to institutions such as FRIAS, where scholarship has been valued. Without them we would be much the poorer.

Notes

Introduction

1 Michael Geyer, 'Some Hesitant Observations Concerning "Political Violence"', *Kritika: Explorations in Russian and Eurasian History*, vol. 4, no. 3 (New Series), p. 695.

2 Etienne G. Krug, Linda L. Dahlberg, James A. Mercy, Anthony B. Zwi and Rafael Lozano (eds.), *World Report on Violence and Health* (Geneva, 2002), p. ix. Accessed: http://whqlibdoc.who.int/publications/2002/9241545615_eng.pdf.

3 Christian Gerlach, 'Extremely Violent Societies: An Alternative to the Concept of Genocide', *Journal of Genocide Research*, vol. 8, no. 4, December 2006, pp. 455–71; Christian Gerlach, *Extremely Violent Societies: Mass Violence in the Twentieth-Century World* (Cambridge, 2010).

4 Charles Tilly, 'Violence, Terror, and Politics as Usual', *Boston Review*, Summer 2002. Accessed: http://new.bostonreview.net/BR27.3/tilly.html.

5 See Henry R. Luce, 'The American Century', *Life*, 17 February 1941, pp. 61–5. In that article, Luce wrote: 'So far, this century of ours has been a profound and tragic disappointment. No other century has been so big with progress for human progress and happiness. And in no one century have so many men and women and children suffered such pain and anguish and bitter death.' (p. 64.)

6 David G. Winter, 'Power, Sex, and Violence: A Psychological Reconstruction of the 20th Century and an Intellectual Agenda for Political Psychology', *Political Psychology*, vol. 21, no. 2, p. 384.

7 Till Bastian, *Das Jahrhundert des Todes: Zur Psychologie von Gewaltbereitschaft und Massenmord im 20. Jahrhundert* (Göttingen, 2000), p. 7.

8 Niall Ferguson, *The War of the World: History's Age of Hatred* (London, 2006), pp. xxxiv–xxxv. Ferguson goes on to discuss the issue of comparative levels of war-related violence at some length in a thoughtful appendix (pp. 647–54). In it he notes, I think correctly, that:

the interesting question is not really, 'Why was the twentieth century more violent than the eighteenth or nineteenth?', but, 'Why did extreme violence happen in Poland, Serbia and Cambodia more than England, Ghana and Costa Rica?'; and 'Why did so much more extreme violence happen between 1936 and 1945 than between 1976 and 1985?' (p. 649.)

9 Ibid., pp. 646, 654.
10 For a penetrating critique of Ferguson's book, see Benjamin Ziemann, 'Anekdoten statt Analysen', *Die Zeit*, 12 December 2006.
11 See Ferguson, *The War of the World*, pp. 653–4, where he asserts that the twentieth century:

was undeniably unique in two respects. The first was that it witnessed a transformation in the kind of war waged by developed western societies against one another. [...] The second feature that makes the twentieth century beyond question unique – and which remains the paradox at its heart – is the way that leaders of apparently civilized societies were able to unleash the most primitive murderous instincts of their fellow citizens. The Germans were not Amazonian Indians.

12 For example, reflecting on the leader of a political movement and ideology that both glorified violence and applied it on a horrific scale, in his biography of Hitler Ian Kershaw refers to the 'Nazi assault on the roots of civilization' and 'the most profound collapse of civilization in modern times'. See Ian Kershaw, *Hitler 1889–1936: Hubris* (Harmondsworth, 1998), p. xxx; Ian Kershaw, *Hitler 1936–1945: Nemesis* (Harmondsworth, 2000), p. 841.
13 Norbert Elias, *Über den Prozeß der Zivilisation: Soziogenetische und psychogenetische Untersuchungen* (Frankfurt am Main, 1976). For a critical view, see Ian Burkitt, 'Civilization and Ambivalence', *The British Journal of Sociology*, vol. 47, no. 1 (1996), pp. 135–50.
14 Dan Diner, 'Perspektivenwahl und Geschichtserfahrung. Bedarf es einer besonderen Historik des Nationalsozialismus?', in Walter H. Pehle (ed.), *Der historische Ort des Nationalsozialismus. Annäherungen* (Frankfurt am Main, 1990), pp. 94–113.
15 See especially Zygmunt Bauman, *Modernity and the Holocaust* (Cambridge, 1989). For an interesting critique of Bauman's discussion of modernity and genocide, see Michael Freeman, 'Genocide, Civilization

and Modernity', *The British Journal of Sociology*, vol. 46, no. 2 (1995), pp. 207–23.

16 Deutsches Historisches Institut Warschau, *Jahresbericht 2009* (Warsaw, 2010), p. 22.

17 See Peter H. Wilson, *Europe's Tragedy: A New History of the Thirty Years War* (London, 2009), pp. 779–851; Alan Forrest, Karen Hagemann and Jane Rendall (eds.), *Soldiers, Citizens and Civilians: Experiences and Perceptions of the Revolutionary and Napoleonic Wars, 1790–1820* (Basingstoke, 2008).

18 Mark Mazower, 'Violence and the State in the Twentieth Century', *The American Historical Review*, vol. 107, no. 4, p. 1158.

19 This is true not only for the First World War, but also for the Second. See Richard Bessel, 'Death and Survival in the Second World War', in Michael Geyer and Adam Tooze (eds.), *Cambridge History of the Second World War, Total War – Economy, Society and Culture at War* (forthcoming, Cambridge University Press).

20 Steven Pinker, 'A History of Violence', *New Republic*, 19 March 2007. Accessed: http://pinker.wjh.harvard.edu/articles/media/2007_03_19_New%20Republic.pdf.

21 Steven Pinker, *The Better Angels of our Nature: The Decline of Violence in History and its Causes* (London and New York, 2011), p. xxi.

22 Pinker, 'A History of Violence', op. cit.

23 Habbo Knoch, 'Einleitung: Vier Paradigmen des Gewaltdiskurses', in Uffa Jensen, Habbo Knoch, Daniel Morat and Miriam Rürup (eds.), *Gewalt und Gesellschaft: Klassiker modernen Denkens neu gelesen* (Göttingen, 2011), p. 14.

24 http://www.colorado.edu/cspv/.

25 Patrick H. Tolan, 'Understanding Violence', in Daniel J. Flannery, Alexander T. Vazsonyi and Irwin D. Waldman (eds.) *Cambridge Handbook of Violent Behavior and Aggression* (New York, 2007), p. 9.

26 According to the *Oxford Dictionary of English*, edited by Angus Stevenson (3rd edition, 2010) 'violence' is defined as follows:

noun [mass noun]
1. behaviour involving physical force intended to hurt, damage, or kill someone or something: *violence erupted in protest marches | domestic **violence against** women | the fear of physical violence. screen violence. (Law)* the unlawful exercise of physical force or intimidation by the exhibition of such force.
2. strength of emotion or of a destructive natural force: *the violence of her own feelings*

27 Felicity Kaganas, 'Domestic Violence', in Peter Cane and Joanne Conaghan (eds.), *The New Oxford Companion to Law*. Accessed: http://www.oxford reference.com/views/ENTRY.html?subview=Main&entry=t287.e679.

28 Krug et al., *World Report on Violence and Health*, p. 5.

29 Ibid.

30 Quoted in Christine Chinkin, 'Violence against Women: The International Legal Response', *Gender and Development*, vol. 3, no. 2, June 1995, p. 26.

31 Sally Engle Merry, 'Rights, Religion, and Community: Approaches to Violence against Women in the Context of Globalization', *Law & Society Review*, vol. 35, no. 1 (2001), p. 39.

32 Thomas Sheridan, *A complete dictionary of the English language, both with regard to sound and meaning. One main object of which is, to establish a plain and permanent standard of pronunciation. To which is prefixed a prosodial grammar* (London, 1789), p. 598.

33 N. Bailey, *An Universal Etymological English Dictionary* (Edinburgh, 1800), p. 879.

34 *Webster's Revised Unabridged Dictionary,* p. 1611. Accessed: http://machaut. uchicago.edu/?resource=Webster%27s&word=violence&use1913=on&use1828=on.

35 Rafael Moses, 'Empathy and Dis-Empathy in Political Conflict', *Political Psychology*, vol. 6, no. 1 (1985), p. 136.

36 Omer Bartov, 'Genocide and the Holocaust: What Are We Arguing About?', in Uffa Jensen et al. (eds.), *Gewalt und Gesellschaft*, p. 393.

37 Most notably in the widely acclaimed work of Saul Friedländer, who is both a prominent historian and a Shoah survivor: *Nazi Germany and the Jews: The Years of Persecution 1933–1939* (London, 1997), and *Nazi Germany and the Jews: The Years of Extermination, 1939–1945* (London, 2007). See also Christian Wiese and Paul Betts (eds.), *Years of Persecution, Years of Extermination: Saul Friedländer and the Future of Holocaust Studies* (London and New York, 2010).

38 For example, Linda Gordon, *Heroes of Their Own Lives: The Politics and History of Family Violence, Boston 1880–1960* (New York, 1988); Elizabeth Foyster, *Marital Violence: An English Family History, 1660–1857* (Cambridge, 2005); Molly Warrington, '"I Must Get Out": The Geographies of Domestic Violence', *Transactions of the Institute of British Geographers*, vol. 26, no. 3 (2001), pp. 365–82.

39 Ute Volmerg, 'Gewalt im Alltag oder die Ghettoisierung des Bösen', in Hessische Stiftung Friedens- und Konfliktforschung (ed.), *Faszination der Gewalt: Politische Strategie und Alltagserfahrung* (Frankfurt am Main, 1983), pp. 16–17.

40 For perceptive comments along these lines, see Stuart Carroll, 'Introduction', in Stuart Carroll (ed.), *Cultures of Violence: Interpersonal Violence in Historical Perspective* (Basingstoke, 2007), pp. 3–13. For an overview of research, see Dirk Schumann, 'Gewalt als Grenzüberschreitung: Überlegungen zur Sozialgeschichte der Gewalt im 19. und 20. Jahrhundert', *Archiv für Sozialgeschichte*, no. 37 (1997), pp. 366–86.

41 See, for example, the encyclopedic *Cambridge Handbook of Violent Behavior*

and Aggression edited by Daniel J. Flannery et al. (New York, 2007). This handbook claims to represent 'the most current and up-to-date research from leading experts around the world', yet here the 'world' seems to consist largely of the United States, with some contributors working in Canada, the UK, the Netherlands and Poland as well.

I. Spectacle

1   Robert L. Teague, 'Griffith is Victor', *The New York Times*, 25 March 1962, p. 201, Section 5.
2   Stephen Hunter, '"Ring of Fire" Connects With True Story of A Fatal Blow', *Washington Post*, 20 April 2005, p. C01. Accessed: http://www.washingtonpost.com/wp-dyn/articles/A3109-2005Apr19.html.
3   'The Manly Art', *The New York Times*, 27 March 1962, p. 30.
4   Letter to the editor by Abbie L. Gottlieb, New York, March 28, 1962, *The New York Times*, 31 March 1962, p. 24.
5   Deane McGowan, 'Clamor Grows Here and Abroad for End to Professional Boxing', *The New York Times*, 5 April 1962, p. 52.
6   'Doyle Dies of Injuries Suffered in Cleveland Bout with Robinson', *The New York Times*, 26 June 1947, p. 28.
7   Julius R. Ruff, *Violence in Early Modern Europe 1500–1800* (Cambridge, 2001), p. 171. Ruff observes that 'indeed, an English champion boxer drew up the first modern boxing rules in 1743 after his blows killed an opponent'.
8   See Donald Kyle, *Spectacles of Death in Ancient Rome* (London, 1998); David Potter and David Mattingly, *Life, Death, and Entertainment in Roman Society* (Ann Arbor, MI, 1999); Alison Futrell, *Blood in the Arena: The Spectacle of Roman Power* (Austin, 1997); Andrew W. Lintott, *Violence in Republican Rome* (Oxford, 1968).
9   Richard van Dülmen, *Theater des Schreckens: Gerichtspraxis und Strafrituale in der frühen Neuzeit* (Munich, 1985); Richard J. Evans, *Rituals of Retribution: Capital Punishment in Germany, 1600–1987* (London, 1997), pp. 27–64.
10 Thus the account by John Taylor, who witnessed a public execution by breaking at the wheel in Hamburg in August 1616. Quoted Evans, *Rituals of Retribution*, pp. 27–8.
11 See van Dülmen, *Theater des Schreckens*, pp. 7–8; Maria R. Boes, 'Public Appearance and Criminal Judicial Practices in Early Modern Germany', *Social Science History*, vol. 20, no. 2 (Summer, 1996), pp. 270–1; Louis P. Masur, *Rites of Execution: Capital Punishment and the Transformation of American Culture, 1776–1865* (New York, 1989), pp. 26–7.
12 Masur, *Rites of Execution*, p. 26.
13 van Dülmen, *Theater des Schreckens*, p. 10.
14 Michel Bée, 'Le spectacle de l'exécution dans la France d'Ancien Régime', *Annales: Histoire, Sciences Sociales*, vol. 38, no. 4 (1983), p. 849.

15   William D. Barry, 'Exposure, Mutilation, and Riot Violence at the *Scalae Gemoniae* in Early Imperial Rome', *Greece & Rome*, vol. 55, no. 2 (October 2008), p. 239. See also Michel Foucault, *Discipline and Punish: The Birth of the Prison* (New York, 1977), pp. 59–65; Natalie Zemon Davis, 'The Rites of Violence: Religious Riot in Sixteenth Century France', *Past & Present* 59 (1973), pp. 51–91, esp. pp. 55–65; Peter Linebaugh, 'The Tyburn Riot against the Surgeons', in Douglas Hay et al. (eds.), *Albion's Fatal Tree: Crime and Society in Eighteenth-century England* (New York, 1975), pp. 65–117, esp. pp. 79–102; Douglas Hay, 'Crime and Justice in Eighteenth- and Nineteenth-century England', *Crime and Justice*, vol. 2 (1980), pp. 54–5 ('processions to gallows in London were ended because of frequent riots'); Barbara Diefendorf, 'Prologue to a Massacre: Popular Unrest in Paris: 1557–1572', *The American Historical Review*, vol. 90, no. 5 (1985), pp. 1067–91, esp. pp. 1073, 1085–7; Evans, *Rituals of Retribution*, pp. 193–201, emphasizing in particular the interruption of execution ritual as a cause of riot, beginning in the early nineteenth century. V. A. C. Gatrell, *The Hanging Tree: Execution and the English People, 1770–1868* (Oxford, 1994), pp. 90–105 suggests a more deferential English crowd.

16   Annulla Linders, 'The Execution Spectacle and State Legitimacy: The Changing Nature of the American Execution Audience, 1833–1937', *Law & Society Review*, vol. 36, no. 3 (2002), p. 607.

17   Pieter Spierenburg, *The Spectacle of Suffering: Executions and the Evolution of Repression; from a Preindustrial Metropolis to the European Experience* (Cambridge, 1984), p. 183.

18   Spierenburg, *The Spectacle of Suffering*, p. 183.

19   *Morning Herald*, 17 January 1834; *Morning Herald*, 1 June 1832. Quoted in J. S. Cockburn, 'Punishment and Brutalization in the English Enlightenment', *Law and History Review*, vol. 12, no. 1 (Spring, 1994), p. 155.

20   *Liverpool Mercury*, 28 December 1847.

21   Randall McGowen, 'Civilizing Punishment: The End of the Public Execution in England', *The Journal of British Studies*, vol. 33, no. 3 (July 1994), p. 257.

22   House of Commons Debate, *Hansard*, 6 March 1866, vol. 181, col. 1621. Accessed: http://hansard.millbanksystems.com/commons/1866/mar/06/leave-first-reading-1#S3V0181P0_18660306_HOC_68.

23   Mr Edward Knatchbull-Hugessen, House of Commons Debate, *Hansard*, 5 March 1868, vol. 190, col. 1135. Accessed: http://hansard.millbanksystems.com/commons/1868/mar/05/second-reading#column_1135. See also Gatrell, *The Hanging Tree*, p. 592.

24   Mr William Gregory, House of Commons Debate, *Hansard*, 21 April 1868, vol. 191, col. 1045. Accessed: http://hansard.millbanksystems.com/commons/1868/apr/21/committee#S3V0191P0_18680421_HOC_31.

25   Michael H. Reggio, 'History of the Death Penalty', accessed: http://www.pbs.org/wgbh/pages/frontline/shows/execution/readings/history.html;

Pieter Spierenburg, 'From Amsterdam to Auburn: An Explanation for the Rise of the Prison in Seventeenth-Century Holland and Nineteenth-Century America', *Journal of Social History*, vol. 20, no. 3 (Spring, 1987), p. 455. See Hugo Adam Bedau, *The Death Penalty in America* (New York, Oxford, 1982), p. 7.

26 See Jim Rice, '"This Province, so Meanly and Thinly Inhabited': Punishing Maryland's Criminals, 1681–1850', *Journal of the Early Republic*, vol. 19, no. 1 (1999), pp. 15-42; Masur, *Rites of Execution*.

27 Linders, 'The Execution Spectacle and State Legitimacy', op. cit., pp. 607–8.

28 Spierenburg, *The Spectacle of Suffering*, pp. 198–9.

29 See Gordon Wright, *Between the Guillotine and Liberty: Two Centuries of the Crime Problem in France* (Oxford, 1983), pp. 167–73. Cited in Gatrell, *The Hanging Tree*, pp. 596–7.

30 See, for example, the photograph of German soldiers hanged publicly in Kiev in 1946 after they had been convicted of war crimes, in Tony Judt, *Postwar: A History of Europe since 1945* (London, 2005).

31 Catherine Epstein, *Model Nazi: Arthur Greiser and the Occupation of Western Poland* (Oxford, 2010), pp. 1, 331, 334–5.

32 Andrzej Gass, 'Auschwitz Commandant Rudolf Hoess on the Gallows', *Focus Historia*, vol. 1 (2007). Excerpted in www.en.auschwitz.org/m/index.php?option=com_content&task=view&id=481&Itemid=8.

33 J. William Harris, 'Etiquette, Lynching, and Racial Boundaries in Southern History: A Mississippi Example', *The American Historical Review*, vol. 100, no. 2 (1995), p. 393. For a discussion of the ritualistic aspects of some lynchings, see W. Fitzhugh Brundage, *Lynching in the New South: Georgia and Virginia, 1880–1930* (Urbana, IL, 1993), pp. 36–45.

34 Quotations from Todd E. Lewis, 'Mob Justice in the "American Congo": "Judge Lynch" in Arkansas during the Decade after World War I', *The Arkansas Historical Quarterly*, vol. 52, no. 2 (1993), pp. 157–8.

35 See www.memphispressscimitar.com/THE_HISTORY.html.

36 Richard Maxwell Brown, *Strain of Violence: Historical Studies of American Violence and Vigilantism* (New York, 1975), pp. 217–8.

37 Stewart E. Tolnay and E. M. Beck, *A Festival of Violence: An Analysis of Southern Lynchings, 1882–1930* (Urbana, IL, and Chicago, 1992), pp. 20–54. Brown, *Strain of Violence*, p. 215. See also Michael J. Pfeifer, *Rough Justice: Lynching and American Society, 1874–1947* (Urbana, IL, 2004).

38 Statistics provided by the archives at Tuskegee Institute. Accessed: http://www.law.umkc.edu/faculty/projects/ftrials/shipp/lynchingyear.html.

39 See *The New York Times*, 9 July 1922: 'Political Effect of the Dyer Bill'; William B. Hixson Jr., 'Moorfield Storey and the Defense of the Dyer Anti-Lynching Bill', *The New England Quarterly*, vol. 42, no. 1 (1969), p. 66.

40 Walter T. Howard, 'Vigilante Justice and National Reaction: The 1937 Tallahassee Double Lynching', *The Florida Historical Quarterly*, vol. 67, no. 1 (1988), p. 45.

41 'Two Negro Youths Lynched in Florida', *The New York Times*, 21 July 1937, p. 7.

42 Lewis, 'Mob Justice in the "American Congo"', op. cit., pp. 180–3.

43 For example, in rural Michigan, where the KKK was very strong in the mid-1920s. See Craig Fox, *Everyday Klansfolk: White Protestant Life and the KKK in 1920s Michigan* (East Lansing, MI, 2011).

44 'Lynch Negro in Florida as Girl's Slayer', *Chicago Daily Tribune*, 27 October 1934, p. 1. See also James R. McGovern, *Anatomy of a Lynching: The Killing of Claude Neal* (Baton Rouge, LA, 1982).

45 Howard Smead, *The Lynching of Mack Charles Parker* (Oxford and New York, 1986), p. x–xi.

46 Kari Frederickson, '"The Slowest State" and "Most Backward Community": Racial Violence in South Carolina and Federal Civil-Rights Legislation, 1946–1948, *The South Carolina Historical Magazine*, vol. 98, no. 2 (1997), p. 179.

47 For example: 'Lynching Hit in London', *The New York Times*, 19 August 1946, p. 4: 'The *London Sunday Pictorial* today carried a double-paged spread on the recent lynchings at Monroe, Ga., and observed editorially that "America has nerve" to attack British action in India and Palestine.'

48 Quoted in Frederickson, '"The Slowest State" and "Most Backward Community"', op. cit., p. 177. See also Harvard Sitkoff, 'Harry Truman and the Election of 1948: The Coming of Age of Civil Rights in American Politics,' *Journal of Southern History*, vol. 37 (1971), p. 611.

49 Quoted in Frederickson, '"The Slowest State" and "Most Backward Community"', op. cit., p. 189.

50 'The Text of President Truman's Message on Civil Rights', *The New York Times*, 3 February 1948, p. 22.

51 Frank Orme, 'The Television Code', *The Quarterly of Film, Radio and Television*, vol. 6, no. 4 (1952), p. 408.

52 Richard J. Gelles and Murray A. Straus, *Intimate Violence: The Causes and Consequences of Abuse in the American Family* (New York, 1988), p. 197.

53 B. J. Bushman and L. R. Huemann, 'Effects of Televised Violence on Aggression', in D. G. Singer and J. L. Singer (eds.), *Handbook of Children and the Media* (Thousand Oaks, CA, 2001), p. 227. Quoted in Cynthia Carter and C. Kay Weaver, *Violence and the Media* (Buckingham and Philadelphia, 2003), p. 72.

54 Richard B. Felson, 'Mass Media Effects on Violent Behaviour', *Annual Review of Sociology*, vol. 22 (1996), p. 103.

55 Simon J. Bronner, 'Contesting Tradition: The Deep Play and Protest of Pigeon Shoots', *Journal of American Folklore*, vol. 118, no. 270 (2005), pp. 409, 425.

56 http://www.bbc.co.uk/news/world-europe-10798210; http://www.
thefirstpost.co.uk/66466,news-comment,news-politics,catalonia-votes-
to-ban-barcelonas-bullfights-hemingway.

57 Quoted in Stanley Brandes, 'Torophiles and Torophobes: The Politics of
Bulls and Bullfights in Contemporary Spain', *Anthropological Quarterly*,
vol. 82, no. 3 (2009), pp. 789–90.

58 'Lynda Robb Johnson Interview: November 22, 1963 and the Transition'.
Accessed: www.transition.lbjlibrary.org/items/show/67632.

59 See Carter and Weaver, *Violence and the Media*, pp. 52–70.

60 Jason Burke, 'Diary', *London Review of Books*, vol. 23, no. 6, pp. 38–9.
Accessed: http://www.lrb.co.uk/v23/n06/jason-burke/diary.

61 Spierenburg, *The Spectacle of Suffering*, p. 83.

62 Until the end of the eighteenth century in England, for example, whip-
pings – of both men and women – were carried out in public. See J. S.
Cockburn, *Law and History Review*, vol. 12, no. 1 (Spring, 1994), p. 160.
According to Cockburn: 'Women, like men, were stripped to the waist
and scourged through the streets "at the cart's arse" (as it was pungently
described) until the blood flowed.'

63 Spierenburg, *The Spectacle of Suffering*, p. vii.

II. Religion

1 Peter L. Berger, The Desecularization of the World: A Global Overview',
in Peter L. Berger (ed.), *The Desecularization of the World: Resurgent
Religion and World Politics* (Washington, DC, 1999), pp. 2–3; Astrid Reuter
and Hans G. Kippenberg, 'Einleitung', in Astrid Reuter and Hans G.
Kippenberg (eds.), *Religionskonflikte im Verfassungsstaat* (Göttingen, 2010),
p. 11. See also Martin Riesebrodt, *Die Rückkehr der Religionen: Fundamentalismus und der 'Kampf der Kulturen'* (2nd edn., Munich, 2001). For the
secularization thesis, see Steve Bruce, *Religion in the Modern World: From
Cathedrals to Cults* (Oxford, 1996).

2 Grace Davie, 'Europe: The Exception That Proves the Rule?', in Berger
(ed.), *The Desecularization of the World*, p. 65.

3 Madawi Al-Rasheed and Marat Shterin, 'Introduction – Between Death
of Faith and Dying for Faith: Reflections on Religion, Politics, Society and
Violence', in Madawi Al-Rasheed and Marat Shterin (eds.), *Dying for
Faith: Religiously Motivated Violence in the Contemporary World* (London
and New York, 2009), p. xvii.

4 For example, discussing 'religious civil wars' during the last sixty years
of the twentieth century, Monica Duffy Toft asserts: 'First, religious civil
wars made up one third of all civil wars fought from 1940 to 2000, and
there is little sign that this proportion will decline any time soon. Second,
among the world's major religions, Islam was involved in just over 80
per cent of these civil wars.' See Monica Duffy Toft, 'Religion, Rationality,

and Violence', in Jack Snyder (ed.), *Religion and International Relations Theory* (New York, 2011), p. 125.

5 Text of the sermon in *The Times*, 27 July 1982, p. 12: 'Runcie praises courage in the Falklands and remembers Ulster and Argentina'.

6 Cahal B. Daly, 'Violence or Non-Violence?', *The Furrow*, vol. 23, no. 2 (1972), p. 103.

7 'Homily of His Holiness John Paul II', Drogheda, 29 September 1979. Accessed: http://www.vatican.va/holy_father/john_paul_ii/homilies/1979/documents/hf_jp-ii_hom_19790929_irlanda-dublino-drogeda_en.html. On the role of Cahal Daly, see *The New York Times*, 1 January 2010, p. B6: 'Cardinal Cahal Daly Dies at 92; Led Irish Church'.

8 House of Lords debate on 'Christians in the Middle East', *Hansard*, 9 December 2011, vol. 733, col. 957.

9 'Address of His Holiness Benedict XVI at the Meeting for Peace in Assisi', 27 October 2011. Accessed: http://www.vatican.va/holy_father/benedict_xvi/speeches/2011/october/documents/hf_ben-xvi_spe_20111027_assisi_en.html.

10 Peter Steinfels, 'Beliefs', *The New York Times*, 29 September 2001, p. D4.

11 Quoted in Hans G. Kippenberg, *Gewalt als Gottesdienst: Religionskriege im Zeitalter der Globalisierung* (Munich, 2008), p. 11.

12 James K. Wellman, Jr., 'Is War Normal for American Evangelical Religion?', in James K. Wellman, Jr. (ed.), *Belief and Bloodshed: Religion and Violence across Time and Tradition* (Lanham, MD, 2007), pp. 205–7.

13 'Defensive Action Statement', accessed: www.armyofgod.com/defense.html. See also Mark Juergensmeyer, 'Christian Violence in America', *Annals of the American Academy of Political and Social Science*, vol. 558, 'Americans and Religions in the Twenty-First Century' (1998), pp. 88–100.

14 Thus the announcement of the Saddleback Church for a 'Domestic Violence Prevention Planning Meeting' on 30 November 2011. Accessed: https://www.saddleback.com/corona/events/eventdetails.aspx?id=43466.

15 See Ehud Sprinzak, *The Ascendance of Israel's Political Right* (New York, 1991); Ehud Sprinzak, 'Extremism and Violence in Israel: The Crisis of Messianic Politics', *Annals of the American Academy of Political and Social Science*, vol. 555 (1998), pp. 114–26; Ehud Sprinzak, *Brother against Brother: Violence and Extremism in Israeli Politics from the Altelena to the Rabin Assassination* (New York, 1999), chapter 7; Robert Eisen, *The Peace and Violence of Judaism: From the Bible to Modern Zionism* (Oxford, 2011), pp. 145–61; Simon Dein, 'Jewish Millennialism and Violence', in Al-Rasheed and Shterin (eds.), *Dying for Faith*, pp. 153–63.

16 See McCandlish Phillips, 'Jewish Militants Step Up Activity', *The New York Times*, 25 June 1969, p. 25. Kahane, who emigrated to Israel in 1971

and founded the radical right-wing (and subsequently banned) Kach movement, preached a radical and violent religious Zionism and managed to win a seat in the Knesset in 1984. He was shot and killed in New York in 1990. Baruch Goldstein was a disciple of Kahane and a member of Kach.

17 'Defense League Scored by Rabbi', *The New York Times*, 18 May 1969, p. 81.

18 Richard Drake, 'Julius Evola, Radical Fascism, and the Lateran Accords', *The Catholic Historical Review*, vol. 74, no. 3 (1988), p. 403.

19 Richard J. Wolff, 'Catholicism, Fascism and Italian Education from the Riforma Gentile to the Carta Della Scuola 1922–1939', *History of Education Quarterly*, vol. 20, no. 1 (1980), p. 9.

20 Quoted in 'Senate Approves Vatican Accords', *The New York Times*, 26 May 1929, p. 26. See also Wolff, 'Catholicism, Fascism and Italian Education', op. cit., pp. 11–13.

21 Adrian Lyttelton, *The Seizure of Power: Fascism in Italy 1919–1929* (3rd edn., Abingdon, 2004), p. 349; R. J. B. Bosworth, *Mussolini* (London, 2002), pp. 237–9.

22 Quoted in Bosworth, *Mussolini*, p. 258.

23 Richard Bessel, *Political Violence and the Rise of Nazism: The Storm Troopers in Eastern Germany 1925–1934* (New Haven and London, 1984), pp. 97–112.

24 '*MIT BRENNENDER SORGE*. Encyclical of Pope Puis XI on the Church and the German Reich to the Venerable Brethren the Archbishops and Bishops of Germany and Other Ordinaries in Peace and Communion with the Apostolic See', 14 March 1937. Accessed: http://www.vati can.va/holy_father/pius_xi/encyclicals/documents/hf_p-xi_enc_ 14031937_mit-brennender-sorge_en.html. See also William M. Harrigan, 'Nazi Germany and the Holy See, 1933–1936: The Historical Background of Mit brennender Sorge', *The Catholic Historical Review*, vol. 47, no. 2 (1961), pp. 164–98.

25 See Paul E. Sigmund, 'Revolution, Counter-revolution, and the Catholic Church in Chile', *Annals of the American Academy of Political and Social Science*, vol. 483 (1986), pp. 25–35.

26 See, for example, the discussion of developments in Columbia by Daniel H. Levine and Alexander W. Wilde, 'The Catholic Church, "Politics" and Violence: The Columbian Case', *The Review of Politics*, vol. 39, no. 2 (1977), pp. 220–49.

27 Quoted in Levine and Wilde, 'The Catholic Church, "Politics" and Violence', op. cit., pp. 237–8. The authors of this article went on to note: 'In theological terms, the bishops follow the gospels and Pope Paul VI's continual injunctions to avoid violence. Given Columbia's recent history, their analysis has a strong practical appeal, as political involvement and violence are associated in Columbia with intense conflict, massive destruction, and grave threats to the very existence of the church'

(p. 239).

28 'An Introduction to the World Council of Churches', accessed: http://www.oikoumene.org/fileadmin/files/wcc-main/2010pdfs/WCCintro_ENG.pdf.

29 'Promoting Just Peace', accessed: http://www.oikoumene.org/en/programmes/public-witness-addressing-power-affirming-peace/promoting-just-peace.html

30 'Mid-term of the Ecumenical Decade to Overcome Violence 2001–2010: Churches Seeking Reconciliation and Peace', p. 2, accessed: http://www.oikoumene.org/en/folder/documents-pdf/pb-17-dov-midterm.pdf

31 See www.rk-world.org/wcrp.aspx. Pope John Paul II addressed the Sixth World Assembly of the World Conference on Religion and Peace in November 1994, and declared: 'Violence in any form is opposed not only to the respect which we owe to every fellow human being; it is opposed also to the true essence of religion.' See www.vatican.va/holy_father/john_paul_ii/speeches/1994/november/documents/hf_jp-ii_spe_1994 1103_religioni-pace_en.html.

32 Appleby, *The Ambivalence of the Sacred*, p. 6.

33 See paragraphs 138 and 139 of the Outcome Document of the High-level Plenary Meeting of the [United Nations] General Assembly in September 2005: www.responsibilitytoprotect.org/index.php/component/article/35-r2pcs-topics/398-generalasserublyr2p.excvpt-from-outcome-document (1).pdf. See also the account of the discussion in January 2012 in the *Religionspolitischer Atelier* of the Humboldt University in Berlin in March 2012: www2.evangelisch.de/themen/politik/discussion-gibt-es-einen-gerechten-Krieg56827.

34 Benedict XV, 'The Pope's Appeal for Peace', *Advocate of Peace (1894–1920)*, vol. 77, no. 11 (1915), p. 262.

35 On Pius XII's anti-communism as a prime motivation for his policies, see Peter C. Kent, *The Lonely Cold War of Pope Pius XII* (Montréal, 2002). See also the new biography by Robert A. Ventresca, *Soldier of Christ: The Life of Pope Pius XII* (Cambridge, MA, 2013).

36 For example, 'Text of Pope Pius' Appeal for Peace', *The New York Times*, 2 September 1943, p. 4.

37 *Washington Post and Times-Herald*, 9 October 1958, p. D2. See also 'Pope Pius XII: Crusader for Peace', *Chicago Daily Tribune*, 9 October 1958, p. A2.

38 Lawrence S. Wittner, *The Struggle Against the Bomb, Volume II: Resisting the Bomb – A History of the World Nuclear Disarmament Movement, 1954–1970* (Stanford, 1997), p. 185.

39 Lawrence S. Wittner, 'The Forgotten Years of the World Nuclear Disarmament Movement, 1975–78', *Journal of Peace Research*, vol. 40, no. 4 (2003), p. 437.

40 'Gerechtigkeit schafft Frieden: Wort der Deutschen Bischofskonferenz zum Frieden 18 April 1983', in *Hirtenworte zu Krieg und Frieden: Die Texte*

der katholischen Bischöfe der Bundesrepublik Deutschland, der Deutschen Demokratischen Republik, der Niederlande, Österreichs, der Schweiz, Ungarns und der Vereinigten Staaten von Amerika (Cologne, 1983), p. 63.

41 See Mary Fulbrook, 'Popular Discontent and Political Activism in the GDR', *Contemporary European History*, vol. 2, no. 3 (1993), pp. 278–9; Mary Fulbrook, *Anatomy of a Dictatorship: Inside the GDR 1949–1989* (Oxford, 1995), pp. 202–25.

42 Quoted in B. Welling Hall, 'The Church and the Independent Peace Movement in Eastern Europe', *Journal of Peace Research*, vol. 23, no. 2 (1986), p. 198.

43 James F. Findlay, 'Religion and Politics in the Sixties: The Churches and the Civil Rights Act of 1964', *The Journal of American History*, vol. 77, no. 1 (1990), p. 67.

44 'Violence in Electronic Media and Film: A Policy Statement Approved by the General Board of the National Council of the Churches of Christ in the USA, November 11, 1993', accessed: http://nationalcouncilofchurches-us/common-witness/1993/media-violence.php

45 Marie M. Fortune and Frances Wood, 'The Center for the Prevention of Sexual and Domestic Violence: A Study in Applied Feminist Theology and Ethics', *Journal of Feminist Studies in Religion*, vol. 4, no. 1 (Spring, 1988), pp. 116.

46 Hans Joas, 'Der Traum von der gewaltfreien Moderne', in Hans Joas, *Kriege und Werte: Studien zur Gewaltgeschichte des 20. Jahrhunderts* (Göttingen, 2000), p. 51.

47 See, for example, Kirk Willis, '"God and the Atom": British Churchmen and the Challenge of Nuclear Power 1945–1950', *Albion: A Quarterly Journal Concerned with British Studies*, vol. 29, no. 3 (1997), pp. 422–57. Willis writes:

In the aftermath of Hiroshima and Nagasaki, that is, British churchmen claimed for themselves not a, but the leading role in determining the future of British society. 'If mankind will turn to God the Creator and seek his help to find his will, which is peace, there is hope,' claimed the Dean of Salisbury in a statement echoed in churches and chapels across Britain. 'If not, despair. The choice is inescapable.' (p. 424.)

48 Ibid., p. 428.

49 A. W. Harrison, 'Renunciation of War', *Methodist Recorder*, 13 September 1945, p. 11. Quoted in Kirk Willis, '"God and the Atom": British Churchmen and the Challenge of Nuclear Power 1945–1950', op. cit., p. 435.

50 Joachim Köhler and Damian van Melis, 'Einleitung der Herausgeber', in Joachim Köhler and Damian van Melis (eds.), *Siegerin in Trümmern: Die Rolle der katholischen Kirche in der deutschen Nachkriegsgesellschaft* (Stuttgart, 1998), p. 11.

51 Anselm Doering-Manteuffel, 'Die "Frommen" und die "Linken" vor der Wiederherstellung des bürgerlichen Staats: Integrationsprobleme und Interkonfessionalismus in der frühen CDU', in Jochen-Christoph Kaiser and Anselm Doering-Manteuffel (eds.), *Christentum und politische Verantwortung: Kirchen in Nachkriegsdeutschland* (Stuttgart, 1990), p. 90; Martin Greschat, 'Zwischen Aufbruch und Beharrung: Die evangelische Kirche nach dem Zweiten Weltkrieg', in Victor Conzenius, Martin Greschat and Hermann Kochen (eds.), *Die Zeit nach 1945 als Thema der kirchlichen Zeitgeschichte* (Göttingen, 1988), pp. 112–4; Martin Greschat, *Die evangelische Christenheit und die deutsche Geschichte nach 1945: Weichenstellungen in der Nachkriegszeit* (Stuttgart, 2002), pp, 310–4; Damian van Melis, '"Strengthened and Purified through Ordeal by Fire": Ecclesiastical Triumphalism in the Ruins of Europe', in Richard Bessel and Dirk Schumann (eds.), *Life after Death: Approaches to a Cultural and Social History of Europe during the 1940s and 1950s* (Cambridge, 2003), pp. 231–41.

52 Quoted in Martin Greschat, '"Rechristianisierung" und "Säkularisierung": Anmerkungen zu einem europäischen konfessionellen Interpretationsmodell', in Kaiser and Doering-Manteuffel (eds.), *Christentum und politische Verantwortung*, p. 6.

53 'Die Stuttgarter Schuldbekenntnis', printed in Martin Greschat (ed.), *Im Zeichen der Schuld: 40 Jahre Stuttgarter Schuldbekenntnis, Eine Dokumentation* (Neukirchen-Vluyn, 1985), pp. 45–6.

54 Robert Wuthnow, *The Restructuring of American Religion: Society and Faith since World War II* (Princeton, 1988), pp. 35–45.

55 Dianne Kirby, 'The Cold War, the Hegemony of the United States and the Golden Age of Christian Democracy', in Hugh McLeod (ed.), *The Cambridge History of Christianity, Volume 9: World Christianities c. 1914– c. 2000* (Cambridge, 2006), pp. 297–9.

56 John C. Bennett, *Christian Ethics and Social Policy* (New York, 1946), p. 90. Quoted in Wuthnow, *The Restructuring of American Religion*, p. 39.

57 Callum G. Brown, *The Death of Christian Britain: Understanding Secularisation, 1800–2000* (London, 2001), p. 170.

58 Hans Joas, 'Der Traum von der gewaltfreien Moderne', op. cit., p. 51.

59 Eisen, *The Peace and Violence of Judaism*, p. 3.

60 For example, the anthropologist (and self-confessed 'secular humanist') Hector Avalos, *Fighting Words: The Origins of Religious Violence* (Amherst, NY, 2005), p. 18, notes that 'while it does not always cause violence, religion is inherently prone to violence'. Avalos proceeds from the premise that 'most violence is due to scarce resources, real or perceived', that 'when religion causes violence, it often does so because it has created new scarce resources', and that 'religious conflict relies solely on resources whose scarcity is wholly manufactured by, or reliant on, unverifiable premises' (p. 18). Avalos believes accordingly that 'secular humanist hegemony [...] holds the best prospect for a non-violent global

society' (p. 29). See also Regina M. Schwartz, *The Curse of Cain: The Violent Legacy of Monotheism* (Chicago and London, 1997), who argues that monotheism is inherently violent, since monotheistic religions recognize only one deity and consequently regard the worship of anything else as a transgression. Among the most strident, and articulate, exponents of the view that religion is by nature violent, irrational and intolerant is Christopher Hitchens, *God is Not Great: How Religion Poisons Everything* (New York, 2007).

61   Arthur Schopenhauer, *Religion: A Dialogue and Other Essays* (New York, 2007), p. 37.

62   William T. Cavanaugh, *The Myth of Religious Violence: Secular Ideology and the Roots of Modern Conflict* (Oxford, 2009), p. 4.

63   Ibid., pp. 3–5. For Cavanaugh, who teaches at the University of St Thomas in St Paul, Minnesota, 'there is no transhistorical and transcultural essence of religion that essentialist attempts to separate religious violence from secular violence are incoherent'. Cavanaugh argues further that: 'in what are called "Western" societies, the attempt to create a transhistorical and transcultural concept of religion that is essentially prone to violence is one of the foundational legitimating myths of the liberal nation-state'. He sees this in very instrumentalist terms:

My hypothesis is that religion-and-violence arguments serve a particular need for their consumers in the West. These arguments are part of a broader Enlightenment narrative that has invented a dichotomy between the religious and the secular and constructed the former as an irrational and dangerous impulse that must give way in public to rational, secular forms of power. In the West, revulsion toward killing and dying in the name of one's religion is one of the principal means by which we become convinced that killing and dying in the name of the nation-state is laudable and proper.

64   See, for example, Wellman, Jr (ed.), *Belief and Bloodshed*.

65   Philip Benedict, *Rouen during the Wars of Religion* (Cambridge, 1981), p. 240.

66   See Stuart Carroll, *Blood and Violence in Early Modern France* (Oxford, 2006), pp. 264–84 ; James B. Wood, *The King's Army: Warfare, Soldiers and Society during the French Wars of Religion, 1562–76* (Cambridge, 1996), pp. 6–7, 10, 29.

67   See, for example, the illuminating account of the violence between the Muslim and Hindu communities in pre-Partition Bengal by Patricia A. Gossman, *Riots and Victims: Violence and the Construction of Communal Identity among Bengali Muslims, 1905–1947* (Boulder, CO, 1999).

68   See, for example, the description by Martha Nussbaum of violence that erupted in Gujarat, in western India, in March 2002, *The Clash Within: Democracy, Religious Violence, and India's Future* (Cambridge,

MA, 2007), p. 2.

69 Denis Crouzet, *Les Guerriers de Dieu: La violence au temps des troubles de religion vers 1525–vers 1610*, vol. 1 (Seyssel, 1990), pp. 233–317; Caroline Ford, 'Violence and the Sacred in Nineteenth-Century France', *French Historical Studies*, vol. 21, no. 1 (Winter, 1998), p. 105.

70 Hugh McLeod, *The Religious Crisis of the 1960s* (Oxford, 2007), p. 20.

71 I am indebted to Wolfgang Eßbach for these suggestions for a typology of religion since the early-modern period. Wolfgang Eßbach, 'Zur Typologie europäischer Religionen zwischen Christentum und religiöser Indifferenz in der Moderne' (FRIAS Vortrag, Freiburg, 26 October 2012).

72 See Mark Levene, 'Frontiers of Genocide: Jews in the Eastern War Zones, 1914–1920 and 1941', in Panikos Panayi (ed.), *Minorities in Wartime: National and Racial Groupings in Europe, North America and Australia during the Two World Wars* (Oxford and Providence, 1993), pp. 83–117. Levene notes: 'By the end of the civil war [in 1920] possibly as many as 120,000 Jews in hundreds of pogroms all over southern Russia and the Ukraine had met violent deaths, while possibly double that number were to die from the pogroms' indirect results, traumatization, disease, starvation and neglect' (p. 105).

73 Jan Gross, *Neighbors: The Destruction of the Jewish Community of Jedwabne* (Princeton and Oxford, 2001).

74 For an overview, see David Vital, *A People Apart: The Jews in Europe 1789–1939* (Oxford, 1999), pp. 283–90, 569–75, 581–2.

75 Jan Gross, *Fear: Anti-Semitism in Poland after Auschwitz – An Essay in Historical Interpretation* (Princeton, 2006), pp. 81–166. For contemporary accounts in the western press, see 'Poles Kill 26 Jews in Kielce Pogrom', *The New York Times*, 5 July 1946, pp. 1, 5; 'Kielce Progrom: First Full Account of the Outrage', *Manchester Guardian*, 13 July 1946, p. 5. *The New York Times* reported: 'It is a sad and tragic fact when all shades of Warsaw political opinion are agreed that, despite the fraction of the pre-war Jewish population at present in Poland, there is more anti-Semitism in Poland now than in the history of this traditionally anti-Jewish country.'

76 Henry Morgenthau Sr., Report of the Mission of the United States to Poland, Paris, 3 October 1919, accessed: http://en.wikisource.org/wiki/Mission_of_The_United_States_to_Poland:_Henry_Morgenthau,_Sr._report; William W. Hagen, 'Murder in the East: German-Jewish Liberal Reactions to Anti-Jewish Violence in Poland and Other East European Lands, 1918–1920', *Central European History*, vol. 34, no. 1 (2001), p. 12.

77 Gross, *Neighbors*, pp. 147–51.

78 Natalie Zemon Davis, 'The Rites of Violence: Religious Riot in Sixteenth-Century France', *Past & Present*, no. 59 (1973), pp. 51–91.

79 *EKD-Ratsvorsitzender*, Präses Manfred Kock, 'Aufruf zur Ökumenischen Dekade "Gewalt überwinden" im Rahmen des 28: Deutschen Evangelischen Kirchentages in Stuttgart', Hannover, 18 June 1999, accessed: http://www.ekd.de/presse/631.html. See also 'Kock ruft Kirchen

zur Beteiligung an ökumenischer Dekade gegen Gewalt auf, "Menschen müssen lernen, nicht mehr wegzusehen"', Stuttgart, 18 June 1999, accessed: http://www.ekd.de/presse/630.html. Manfred Kock was the Chairman of the EKD from 1997 until 2003. See also Joachim J. Savelsberg, 'Religion, Historical Contingencies, and Institutional Conditions of Criminal Punishment: The German Case and Beyond', *Law and Social Inquiry*, vol. 29, no. 2 (2004), pp. 394–5.

80 Davie, 'Europe: The Exception?', op. cit., pp. 74–5.
81 See Hugh McLeod, *Religion and the People of Western Europe 1789–1989* (2nd edn., Oxford, 1997), pp. 132–54.
82 See Michael O. Emerson and David Hartman, 'The Rise of Religious Fundamentalism', *Annual Review of Sociology*, vol. 32 (2006), pp. 127–44. Emerson and Hartman note that: 'secularization theory failed to anticipate something: that the demystification of the world provided within it the seeds both for the remystification of the world and resistance to the demystification' (p. 128). See also Bruce B. Lawrence, *Defenders of God: The Fundamentalist Revolt Against the Modern Age* (London, 1990); Peter L. Berger, *A Far Glory: The Quest for Faith in an Age of Credulity* (New York, 1992); Berger (ed.), *The Desecularization of the World*.

III. Revolution

1 Daniel Roche, 'La violence vue d'en bas: Réflexions sur les moyens de la politique en période révolutionnaire', *Annales: Histoire, Sciences Sociales*, vol. 44, no. 1 (1989), pp. 47–65. See also the introductory remarks in Serif A. Mardin, 'Ideology and Religion in the Turkish Revolution', *International Journal of Middle East Studies*, vol. 2, no. 3 (1971), p. 197.
2 George L. Mosse, 'Fascism and the French Revolution', *Journal of Contemporary History*, vol. 24, no. 1 (1989), p. 7.
3 Arno Mayer, *The Furies: Violence and Terror in the French and Russian Revolutions* (Princeton, 2001), p. 4.
4 Said Amir Arjomand, 'Iran's Islamic Revolution in Comparative Perspective', *World Politics*, vol. 38, no. 3 (1986), p. 387. Arjomand takes particular aim at the generalizations by Theda Skocpol, *States and Social Revolutions: A Comparative Analysis of France, Russia and China* (Cambridge, 1979), and observes of the Iranian Revolution of 1979: 'If the Shah's regime collapsed despite the fact that his army was intact, despite the fact that there was no defeat in war, and despite the fact that the state faced no financial crisis and no peasant insurrections, where does all this leave the usual generalizations about revolutions? Mostly in the pits.'
5 Mayer, *The Furies*, p. 3. For Hannah Arendt's judgements, see her *On Revolution* (New York, 1965), p. 13. Arendt's book, first published in 1963 (and thus well before the events that ended Communist rule in eastern Europe) focused on the American and French Revolutions.

6   Robert Gildea has observed of the 'events' in France that 'May 1968 was a carnivalesque inversion of all rules and norms imposed by society'. See Robert Gildea, *France since 1945* (Oxford, 1996), p. 152.

7   Michelle Zancarini-Fournel, 'Genre et politique: Les années 1968', *Vingtième Siècle: Revue d'histoire*, no. 75, p. 134.

8   Interview from 24 May 2007, quoted in Robert Gildea, Gudni Jóhannesson, Chris Reynolds and Polymeris Voglis, 'Violence', in Robert Gildea, James Mark and Anette Warring (eds.), *Europe's 1968: Voices of Revolt* (Oxford, 2013), p. 260.

9   *Der Spiegel*, 1968, no. 20, 13 May 1968, pp. 115–6. See also Ingrid Gilcher-Holtey, 'Mai 68 in Frankreich', in Ingrid Gilcher-Holtey (ed.), *1968: Vom Ereignis zum Gegenstand der Geschichtswissenschaft* (Göttingen, 1998), pp. 20–1.

10 See the introductory remarks in Simon Prince, 'The Global Revolt of 1968 and Northern Ireland', *The Historical Journal*, vol. 49, no. 3 (2006), pp. 851–2.

11 Ingrid Gilcher-Holtey, 'May 1968 in France: The Rise and Fall of a New Social Movement', in Carole Fink, Philipp Gassert and Detlef Junker (eds.), *1968: The World Transformed* (New York, 1998), p. 253.

12 Describing the violent night of 10–11 May 1968 in Paris, Marc Rohan wrote: 'The battle lasted for four hours and the violence was the worst that metropolitan France had known since the war. There were hundreds of wounded on both sides [i.e. students and police], although miraculously no deaths.' See Marc Rohan, *Paris '68: Graffiti, Posters, Newspapers, and Poems of the Events of May 1968* (London, 1988), p. 34. Given that over a hundred people were killed in the Paris police massacre of 17 October 1961, it was myopic but also revealing that the violence of May 1968 could be termed 'the worst that metropolitan France had known since the war'.

13 Simon Schama, *Citizens: A Chronicle of the French Revolution* (London, 1989), p. xv.

14 Alexis de Tocqueville, *L'Ancien Régime* (trans. M. W. Patterson) (Oxford, 1962), p. 15. See also Eli Sagan, *Citizens and Cannibals: The French Revolution and the Origins of Ideological Terror* (Lanham, MD, and Oxford, 2001), pp. 367–71.

15 Caroline Ford, 'Violence and the Sacred in Nineteenth-Century France', *French Historical Studies*, vol. 21, no. 1 (1998), p. 105.

16 See Colin Lucas, 'Revolutionary Violence, the People, and the Terror', in *The Terror*, vol. 4 of Keith Michael Baker (ed.), *The French Revolution and the Creation of Modern Political Culture* (Oxford, 1994), pp. 57–79.

17 Patrice Gueniffey, on the Terror, quoted in D. M. G. Sutherland, *The French Revolution and Empire: The Quest for a Civic Order* (Oxford, 2003), p. 176. See also D. M. G. Sutherland, *Murder in Aubagne: Lynching, Law, and Justice during the French Revolution* (Cambridge, 2009).

18 Mark Levene, *Genocide in the Age of the Nation State, Volume 2: The Rise of*

the West and the Coming of Genocide (London and New York, 2005), p. 104.

19 Quoted in Levene, *Genocide in the Age of the Nation State, Volume 2*, p. 104.

20 Quoted in Reynald Secher and Jean Meyer, *Le génocide franco-français: la Vendée-Vengé* (Paris, 2006), p. 32.

21 Sutherland, *The French Revolution and Empire*, p. 222.

22 Quoted in Secher and Meyer, *Le génocide franco-français*, p. 33.

23 The Law of 22 Prairial Year II (10 June 1794), in John Hall Stewart, *A Documentary Survey of the French Revolution* (New York, 1963), pp. 528–31.

24 Schama, *Citizens*, p. 837.

25 Jonathan Sperber, *The European Revolutions, 1848–1851* (Cambridge, 1994), pp. 77, 192–3, 198–9.

26 Quoted in Robert Tombs, 'Paris and the Rural Hordes: An Exploration of Myth and Reality in the French Civil War of 1871', *The Historical Journal*, vol. 29, no. 4, December 1986, p. 795.

27 Robert Tombs, *The Paris Commune 1871* (London, 1999), p. 214.

28 Leon Trotsky, preface to Charles Talès, *La Commune de 1871* (Paris, 1924), quoted in Tombs, *The Paris Commune 1871*, p. 201.

29 Orlando Figes, *A People's Tragedy: The Russian Revolution 1891–1924* (London, 1996), p. 357.

30 Leon Trotsky, *The History of the Russian Revolution* (London, 1934), p. 228.

31 See James Ryan, '"Revolution is War": The Development of the Thought of V. I. Lenin on Violence, 1899–1907', *Slavonic and East European Review*, vol. 89, no. 2 (2011), pp. 248–73.

32 David Shub, 'New Light on Lenin', *The Russian Review*, vol. 11, no. 3, July 1952, p. 136.

33 V. I. Lenin, 'Comrade Workers, Forward to the Last, Decisive Flight!', in V. I. Lenin, *Collected Works, Volume 28: July 1918–March 1919* (Moscow, 1965), pp. 56–7.

34 Figes, *A People's Tragedy*, pp. 510–11.

35 *Pravda*, 25 December 1918. Quoted in J. N. Westwood, *Endurance and Endeavour: Russian History 1812–1992* (4th edn., Oxford, 1993), p. 256.

36 Peter Holquist, *Making War, Forging Revolution: Russia's Continuum of Crisis 1914–1921* (London, 2002), p. 169.

37 Quoted in Figes, *A People's Tragedy*, p. 641.

38 Peter Holquist, '"Conduct Merciless Mass Terror": Decossackization on the Don, 1919', *Cahiers du Monde Russe*, vol. 38, no.1/2 (1997), p. 132. See also Holquist, *Making War, Forging Revolution*, pp. 166–205; Shane O'Rourke, *The Cossacks* (Manchester, 2007), pp. 244–51. O'Rourke speaks of 'the genocide of the Cossacks'.

39 Quoted in Holquist, '"Conduct Merciless Mass Terror"', op. cit., p. 134. Also Holquist, *Making War, Forging Revolution*, pp. 180–1; O'Rourke, *The Cossacks*, p. 247.

40 On this theme, see especially Peter Gatrell, *A Whole Empire Walking: Refugees in Russia during World War I* (Bloomington, IN, 1999).

Violence

41 Holquist, *Making War, Forging Revolution*, p. 204.

42 Holquist, '"Conduct Merciless Mass Terror"', op. cit., p. 133.

43 Graeme J. Gill, *Peasants and Government in the Russian Revolution* (London, 1979), pp. 141–9 (quotation from p. 145).

44 Figes, *A People's Tragedy*, p. 525.

45 Quoted in Viktor G. Bortnevski, 'White Administration and White Terror (The Denikin Period)', *The Russian Review*, vol. 52, no. 3 (1993), p. 356.

46 Quoted in Bortnevski, 'White Administration and White Terror', op. cit., p. 357.

47 Ibid., p. 357

48 Anton Ivanovich Denikin, *Ocherki russkoi smuti* (Paris, 1922), vol. 2, p. 206. Quoted in Bortnevski, 'White Administration and White Terror', op. cit., p. 365.

49 Richard Pipes, *Russia under the Bolshevik Regime 1919–1924* (London, 1995), pp. 99–114.

50 See Robert Gerwarth and John Horne, 'Vectors of Violence: Paramilitarism in Europe after the Great War, 1917–1923', *The Journal of Modern History*, vol. 83, no. 3 (2011), pp. 489–512; Robert Gerwarth and John Horne (eds.), *War in Peace: Paramilitary Violence in Europe after the Great War* (Oxford, 2012).

51 Peter A. Toma, 'The Slovak Soviet Republic of 1919', *American Slavic and East European Review*, vol. 17, no. 2 (1958), p. 211.

52 The classic account of this is Emil Julius Gumbel, *Vier Jahre politischer Mord* (Berlin-Fichtenau, 1922).

53 See Heinrich August Winkler, *Von der Revolution zur Stabilisierung: Arbeiter und Arbeiterbewegung in der Weimarer Republik 1918 bis 1924* (Berlin and Bonn, 1984), pp. 515–8. Béla Kun was among the ultra-left Communists who went to Berlin at this time to urge comrades to action.

54 James Krapfl, 'Civic Forum, Public against Violence, and the Struggle for Slovakia', (Spring 2009), p. 3. Accessed: http://iseees.berkeley.edu/bps/publications/2009-08-Krapfl.pdf.

55 See Clare Thomson, *The Singing Revolution: A Political Journey through the Baltic States* (London, 1992); Warren Waren, 'Theories of the Singing Revolution: An Historical Analysis of the Role of Music in the Estonian Independence Movement', *International Review of the Aesthetics and Sociology of Music*, vol. 43, no. 2 (2012), pp. 439–51; Henri Vogt, *Between Utopia and Disillusionment: A Narrative of the Political Transformation of Eastern Europe* (New York and Oxford, 2005), pp. 20–36.

56 James Krapfl, 'Civic Forum, Public against Violence, and the Struggle for Slovakia', (Spring 2009), p. 10. Accessed: http://iseees.berkeley.edu/bps/publications/2009-08-Krapfl.pdf.

57 Quoted in Guntis Šmidchens, 'National Heroic Narratives in the Baltics as a Source for Non-violent Political Action', *Slavic Review*, vol. 66, no. 3 (2007), p. 484.

58 Fulbrook, *Anatomy of a Dictatorship*, p. 254.

59 Michael Richter, *Die Friedliche Revolution: Aufbruch zur Demokratie in*

Notes

Sachsen 1989/90, vol. 1 (Göttingen, 2009), p. 274.

60 'Information des 1. Sekretärs der SED-Bezirksleitunf Potsdam, Genossen Günther Jahn, am 13.10.1989 vor leitenden Kadern des Bezirks über die am 12.10.1989 stattgefundene Beratung des Politbüros der ZK der SED mit dem 1. Sekretären der SED-Bezirksleitung (Aufzeichungsnotizen)', Potsdam, 13 October 1989. Printed in Reinhard Meinel and Thomas Wernicke (eds.), *Mit tschekistischem Gruß: Berichte der Bezirksverwaltung für Staatssicherheit Potsdam 1989* (Potsdam, 1990), p. 160.

61 Fulbrook, *Anatomy of a Dictatorship*, p. 255.

62 Quoted in Richter, *Die Friedliche Revolution*, p. 449.

63 See '"Chinesische Lösung". Wollten Stasi-Leute ein Blutbad unter Demonstranten provozieren?', *Der Spiegel*, 18 December 1989, pp. 42–4.

64 Reinhart Schönsee and Gerda Lederer, 'The Gentle Revolution', *Political Psychology*, vol. 12, no. 2 (1991), p. 324.

65 '"Die Karre steckte tief im Dreck": Egon Krenz über das Honecker Buch "Der Sturz"', in *Der Spiegel*, 4 February 1991, p. 59.

66 Eckhard Bahr, *Sieben Tage im Oktober: Aufbruch in Dresden* (Leipzig, 1990), p. 135: Detlev K, Tonbandprotokoll, Frühjahr 1990.

67 Vogt, *Between Utopia and Disillusionment*, p. 24.

68 Quoted in Vogt, *Between Utopia and Disillusionment*, p. 23.

69 Elizabeth Pond, 'A Wall Destroyed: The Dynamics of German Unification in the GDR', *International Security*, vol. 15, no. 2 (1990), p. 50.

70 Quoted in Vogt, *Between Utopia and Disillusionment*, p. 54.

71 For example, in Latvia, where the protest movement for independence honoured King in its literature. See Mara Lazda, 'Reconsidering Nationalism: The Baltic Case of Latvia in 1989', *International Journal of Politics, Culture and Society*, vol. 22, no. 4 (2009), pp. 528–9.

72 Timothy Garton Ash, 'At stake in Ukraine's drama is the future of Putin, Russia and Europe', *The Guardian*, 21 February 2014. Accessed: www.theguardian.com/commentisfree/2014/feb/21/ukraine-putin-russia-europe-independence-disintegration

73 For example, see the official description of the German Democratic Republic published in the lavish illustrated volume celebrating forty years of the GDR shortly before its demise – Klaus Ullrich, Peter Seifert, Brigitte Müller and Horst Sauer (eds.), *Deutsche Demokratische Republik* (Leipzig, 1989) – in which it was asserted (p. 23) that the GDR aimed 'right from the beginning to help to create a permanent peaceful order in Europe'.

74 Mayer, *The Furies*, p. 4.

75 Ibid., p. 8.

76 Quoted in Pipes, *Russia under the Bolshevik Regime*, p. 343.

77 Ibid., p. 351.

78 See Arjomand, 'Iran's Islamic Revolution in Comparative Perspective', op. cit.

79 Holquist, *Making War, Forging Revolution*, p. 204.

80 Mayer, *The Furies*, p. 4.

81   Ibid., p. 24.

IV. Politics

1   Richard Bessel, 'The Potempa Murder', *Central European History*, vol. 10 (1977), pp. 241–54.
2   Ian Kershaw, *The 'Hitler Myth': Image and Reality in the Third Reich* (Oxford, 1987), pp. 53–4.
3   Manuel Álvarez Tardío, 'The Impact of Political Violence during the Spanish Election of 1936', *Journal of Contemporary History*, vol. 48, no. 3 (2013), p. 465.
4   Donald Richter, 'The Role of Mob Riot in Victorian Elections, 1865–1885', *Victorian Studies*, vol. 15, no. 1 (1971), pp. 20–1; Clive Emsley, *Hard Men: The English and Violence since 1750* (London, 2005), p. 124.
5   Ernst Jünger, *Der Kampf als inneres Erlebnis* (Berlin, 1928), pp. 70–1.
6   Carl von Clausewitz, *On War*, Chapter One, 'What is War', paragraph 24: 'We see, therefore, that War is not merely a political act, but also a real political instrument, a continuation of political commerce, a carrying out of the same by other means.' Accessed: http://oll.libertyfund.org/index.php?option=com_content&task=view&id=1123&Itemid=290.
7   On the violent legacy of the First World War in Europe, see Robert Gerwarth, 'The Continuum of Violence', in Jay Winter (ed.), *The Cambridge History of the First World War, Volume II: The State* (Cambridge, 2014), pp. 638–62.
8   See especially the collection by Gerwarth and Horne (eds.), *War in Peace*, and Robert Gerwarth, 'The Central European Counter-Revolution: Paramilitary Violence in Germany, Austria and Hungary after the Great War', *Past & Present*, no. 200 (2008), pp. 175–209.
9   For this argument, see George L. Mosse, *Fallen Soldiers: Reshaping the Memory of the World Wars* (New York, 1990).
10   See Julia Eichenberg and John Paul Newman, 'Introduction: Aftershocks: Violence in the Dissolving Empires after the First World War', *Contemporary European History*, vol. 19, no. 3, pp. 183–94.
11   Jens Petersen, 'Violence in Italian Fascism, 1919–1925', in Wolfgang J. Mommsen and Gerhard Hirschfeld (eds.), *Social Protest, Violence and Terror in Nineteenth- and Twentieth-Century Europe* (London, 1982), p. 275. Petersen quotes L. Salvatorelli and G. Mira, *Storia d'Italia nel periodo fascista* (Turin, 1957), p. 168.
12   Quoted in Petersen, 'Violence in Italian Fascism', op. cit., p. 276.
13   On the violence that was endemic particularly in rural Italy before the First World War, see Paul Corner, 'The Road to Fascism: An Italian Sonderweg?', *Contemporary European History*, vol. 11, no. 2 (2002), pp. 273–95.
14   Paul Corner, *Fascism in Ferrara 1915–1925* (Oxford, 1975), p. 139. See also Andreas Wirsching, 'Political Violence in France and Italy after 1918',

Journal of Modern European History, vol. 1, no. 1 (2003), pp. 67–8.

15 *Giornale d'Italia*, 23 January 1921. Quoted in Corner, *Fascism in Ferrara*, p. 139.

16 Paul Corner, 'Italian Fascism: Whatever Happened to Dictatorship?', *The Journal of Modern History*, vol. 74, no. 2 (2002), p. 331.

17 Roberta Suzzi Valli, 'The Myth of Squadrismo in the Fascist Regime', *Journal of Contemporary History*, vol. 35, no. 2, April 2000, p. 132. See also Michael Ebner, *Ordinary Violence in Mussolini's Italy* (Cambridge, 2011).

18 Ebner, *Ordinary Violence in Mussolini's Italy*, p. 3. See also Adrian Lyttelton, 'Fascism and Violence in Post-war Italy: Political Strategy and Social Conflict', in Mommsen and Hirschfeld (eds.), *Social Protest, Violence and Terror in Nineteenth- and Twentieth-Century Europe*, pp. 257–74; Petersen, 'Violence in Italian Fascism', op. cit., pp. 275–99.

19 See Ebner, *Ordinary Violence in Mussolini's Italy*, pp. 8–9. Emilio Gentile observes, taking Fascist rhetoric perhaps a bit too much at face value:

Fascists considered themselves to be the prophets, apostles and soldiers of a new 'patriotic religion', which had arisen in the purifying violence of the war, and which had been consecrated with the blood of the heroes and martyrs who had sacrificed themselves finally to achieve the 'Italian revolution'.

See Emilio Gentile, 'Fascism as Political Religion', *Journal of Contemporary History*, vol. 25, no. 2/3 (1990), p. 234.

20 Ebner, *Ordinary Violence in Mussolini's Italy*, p. 14.

21 Dick Geary, *European Labour Protest 1848–1939* (London, 1981), p. 118; Franz-Josef Brüggemeier, *Leben vor Ort: Ruhrbergleute und Ruhrbergbau 1889–1919* (Munich, 1983), pp. 230–2.

22 A. J. Ryder, *The German Revolution of 1918: A Study of German Socialism in War and Revolt* (Cambridge, 1967), pp. 214–5; Martin H. Geyer, *Verkehrte Welt: Revolution, Inflation und Moderne, München 1914–1924* (Göttingen, 1998), p. 88; Gavriel D. Rosenfeld, 'Monuments and the Politics of Memory: Commemorating Kurt Eisner and the Bavarian Revolutions of 1918–1919 in Post-war Munich', *Central European History*, vol. 30, no. 2 (1997), pp. 227–8; Hans Mommsen, *The Rise and Fall of Weimar Democracy* (Chapel Hill and London, 1996), pp. 46–8.

23 The classic text on this subject is Gumbel, *Vier Jahre politischer Mord*. According to Gumbel's calculations, twenty-two people were murdered by perpetrators from the left and 332 were murdered by perpetrators from the right.

24 Martin Schuster, 'Die SA in der nationalsozialistischen "Machtergreifung" in Berlin and Brandenburg 1926–1934' (Phil. Diss., Technische Universität Berlin, 2005), p. 215.

25 Joseph Goebbels, *Kampf um Berlin* (9th printing, Berlin, 1936), p. 30.

26 Bessel, *Political Violence and the Rise of Nazism*, p. 75.

27 See Eve Rosenhaft, *Beating the Fascists? The German Communists and Political Violence* (Cambridge, 1983); Eve Rosenhaft, 'Organizing the Lumpenproletariat: Cliques and Communists in Berlin during the Weimar Republic', in R. J. Evans (ed.), *The German Working Class, 1888–1933: The Politics of Everyday Life* (London, 1981), pp. 174–219; Eve Rosenhaft, 'Working-class Life and Working-class Politics: Communists, Nazis and the State in the Battle for the Streets, Berlin, 1928–1932', in Richard Bessel and E. J. Feuchtwanger (eds.), *Social Change and Political Development in Weimar Germany* (London, 1981), pp. 214–7.

28 Quoted in Thomas Kurz, *'Blutmai': Sozialdemokraten und Kommunisten im Brennpunkt der Berliner Ereignisse von 1929* (Berlin, 1988), p. 20.

29 Richard Bessel, 'Policing, Professionalism and Politics in Weimar Germany', in Clive Emsley and Barbara Weinberger (eds.), *Policing Western Europe: Politics, Professionalism and Public Order, 1850–1940* (Westport, CT, 1991), pp. 201–2.

30 Chris Bowlby, 'Blutmai 1929: Police, Parties and Proletarians in a Berlin Confrontation', *The Historical Journal*, vol. 29, no. 1 (Mar., 1986), pp. 137–58; Kurz, *'Blutmai'*.

31 Rosenhaft, *Beating the Fascists?*, p. 113.

32 Geheimes Staatsarchiv preußischer Kulturbesitz Berlin, Hauptabteilung I, Rep. 77, Tit. 4043, Nr. 126.

33 See Sven Reichardt, *Faschistische Kampfbünde: Gewalt und Gemeinschaft im italienischen Faschismus und in der deutschen SA* (Cologne, Weimar and Vienna, 2002).

34 This is discussed by Ebner, *Ordinary Violence in Mussolini's Italy*, p. 32. For Germany, see Bessel, *Political Violence and the Rise of Nazism*, pp. 75–96. For discussion of the 'SA-sub-culture', see also Peter Longerich, *Die braunen Bataillone: Die Geschichte der SA* (Munich, 1989), pp. 115–79.

35 Robert Gerwarth and John Horne, 'Vectors of Violence: Paramilitarism in Europe after the Great War, 1917–1923', *The Journal of Modern History*, vol. 83, no. 3 (2011), p. 509.

36 Piotr Wróbel, 'The Seeds of Violence: The Brutalization of an East European Region, 1917–1921', *Journal of Modern European History*, vol. 1, no. 1 (2003), p. 136.

37 Jerzy Holzer, 'The Political Right in Poland, 1918–39', *Journal of Contemporary History*, vol. 12, no. 3 (1977), p. 405.

38 Tardío, 'The Impact of Political Violence', op. cit., p. 466.

39 See Julián Casanova, 'Terror and Violence: The Dark Face of Spanish Anarchism', *International Labor and Working-Class History*, no. 67 (2005), pp. 81–4.

40 Stanley G. Payne, 'Political Violence during the Spanish Second Republic', *Journal of Contemporary History*, vol. 25, no. 2/3 (1990), p. 270.

41 Tardío, 'The Impact of Political Violence', op. cit., p. 468.

42 See Payne, 'Political Violence during the Spanish Second Republic', op. cit.; Tardío, 'The Impact of Political Violence', op. cit., pp. 469–70; Stanley

G. Payne, *Spain's First Democracy: The Second Republic, 1931–1936* (Madison, WI, 1993), pp. 359–64. According to data collected by Edward Malefakis, there were 269 deaths in political conflicts in Spain between 3 February and 17 July 1936. See Juan J. Linz, 'From Great Hopes to Civil War: The Breakdown of Democracy in Spain', in Juan J. Linz and Alfred Stepan (eds.), *The Breakdown of Democratic Regimes: Europe* (Baltimore, 1978), p. 188.

43 'Discurso de José Antonio Primo de Rivera exponiendo los puntos fundamentales de Falange española, pronunciado en el Teatro de la Comedia de Madrid, el día 29 de octubre de 1933.' Accessed: http://www.segundarepublica.com/index.php?id=78opcion=b.

44 Quoted in Payne, 'Political Violence during the Spanish Second Republic', op. cit., p. 277.

45 Tardío, 'The Impact of Political Violence', op. cit., pp. 484–5.

46 Andreas Wirsching, 'Political Violence in France and Italy after 1918', *Journal of Modern European History*, vol. 1, no. 1 (2003), p. 66.

47 According to La Roque, writing in 1934: 'Rejecting violence is not the same as fearing it. Opposing its use does not mean excluding the possibility of using it.' In a speech at Bordeaux in 1937 he asserted that while 'we are horrified by violence ... we are not afraid of violence. We are organized to counter violence and if the men of violence think they can rise up, I, La Roque, in the name of all of you, tell them: they will be crushed.' Quoted in William D. Irvine, 'Fascism in France and the Strange Case of the Croix de Feu', *The Journal of Modern History*, vol. 63, no. 2 (1991), p. 276.

48 Kevin Passmore, 'Boy Scouting for Grown-ups? Paramilitarism in the Croix de Feu and the Parti Social Français', *French Historical Studies*, vol. 19, no. 2 (1995), pp. 532, 549.

49 Wirsching, 'Political Violence in France and Italy', op. cit., p. 74.

50 Passmore, 'Boy Scouting for Grown-ups?', op. cit., p. 529.

51 Wirsching, 'Political Violence in France and Italy', op. cit., p. 75.

52 Adrian Gregory, 'Peculiarities of the English? War, Violence and Politics: 1900–1939', *Journal of Modern European History*, vol. 1, no. 1 (2003), p. 47.

53 Eric J. Leed, *No Man's Land: Combat and Identity in World War I* (Cambridge, 1979), pp. 202–3.

54 Gregory, 'Peculiarities of the English?', op. cit., p. 53.

55 Ibid., p. 54.

56 Martin Pugh, 'The British Union of Fascists and the Olympia Debate', *The Historical Journal*, vol. 41, no. 2 (1998), p. 529.

57 Thus the characterization by Robert Skidelsky in his classic account, *Politicians and the Slump: The Labour Government of 1929–1931* (London, 1967), p. 386.

58 Stephen M. Cullen, 'Political Violence: The Case of the British Union of Fascists', *Journal of Contemporary History*, vol. 28, no. 2 (1993), pp. 245–67.

59 Quoted in Cullen, 'Political Violence', op. cit., p. 258.

60 Martin Pugh notes, however, that the Rothermere press did not abandon Mosley immediately, and quotes the *Sunday Dispatch* on 17 June 1934, ten days after the rally at Olympia: 'When the necessity is forced upon them, the Blackshirts are able and willing to meet violence with violence.' See Pugh, 'The British Union of Fascists and the Olympia Debate', op. cit., p. 536.

61 Public Order Act 1936. Accessed: www.legislation.gov.uk/ukpga/Edw8and1Geo6/1/6.

62 Jean Fourastié, *Les trente glorieuses, ou la révolution invisible de 1946 à 1975* (Paris, 1979).

63 BBC, 'Clashes and boycott mar Bangladesh election', 5 January 2014. Accessed: www.bbc.co.uk/news/world-asia-25602436. 'At least 11 people were killed during Sunday's polling. Dozens have died in the run-up to the election. Scores of polling stations have been torched.'

64 Karla Zabludovsky, 'Mexico's Election Violence Said to Be Worst in Years', *The New York Times*, 5 July 2013. Accessed: www.nytimes.com/2013/07/07/world/americas/mexicos-election-violence-is-said-to-be-worst-in-years.html.

65 'Nigeria Political Violence Increasing Before Election', 29 January 2003, posted in *Africa Action Africa Policy E-Journal*, 3 February 2003, University of Pennsylvania African Studies Center. Accessed: www.africa.upenn.edu/Urgent_Action/apic-020303.html. For details of the serious and widespread political violence in Nigeria at the time, see the extensive report published by Human Rights Watch, 'Testing Democracy: Political Violence in Nigeria' (www.refworld.org/docid/45d2f6992.html). As this report demonstrates, the political violence in Nigeria was magnified by the ethnic and religious fault lines that have characterized the country.

66 When Moro was kidnapped his five bodyguards were killed. There remains considerable scepticism in Italy as to whether the Red Brigades were solely responsible for the death of Aldo Moro, and conspiracy theories have abounded. See Richard Drake, 'Why the Moro Trials Have Not Settled the Moro Murder Case: A Problem in Political and Intellectual History', *The Journal of Modern History*, vol. 73, no. 2 (2001), pp. 359–78.

67 Alberto Ronchey, 'Guns and Gray Matter: Terrorism in Italy', *Foreign Affairs*, vol. 57, no. 4 (1979), p. 931.

68 Drake, 'Why the Moro Trials Have Not Settled the Moro Murder Case', op. cit., pp. 369–70.

69 Ronchey, 'Guns and Gray Matter', op. cit. p. 933.

70 Payne, 'Political Violence during the Spanish Second Republic', op. cit., p. 285.

71 BBC, 'Basque Eta ex-inmates recognize "damage" from violence', 4 January 2014. Accessed: www.bbc.co.uk/news/world-europe-25605457.

72 See Michael Richards, *A Time of Silence: Civil War and the Culture of Repression in Franco's Spain, 1936–1945* (Cambridge, 1998); Paul Preston, *The Spanish Holocaust: Inquisition and Extermination in Twentieth-Century*

Spain (London, 2013).

73 For this argument, see Richard Bessel, 'The War to End All Wars: The Shock of Violence in 1945 and its Aftermath in Germany', in Alf Lüdtke (ed.), *The No Man's Land of Violence: Extreme Wars in the 20th Century* (Göttingen, 2006), pp. 71–99.

74 Karen Rasler, 'War Accommodation, and Violence in the United States, 1890–1970', *The American Political Science Review*, vol. 80, no. 3 (1986), pp. 933, 936.

75 Paul Ortiz, *Emancipation Betrayed: The Hidden History of Black Organizing and White Violence in Florida from Reconstruction to the Bloody Election of 1920* (Berkeley, Los Angeles and London, 2005), pp. 205–28.

76 Kenneth Jackson, *The Ku Klux Klan in the City, 1915–1930* (New York, 1967); Fox, *Everyday Klansfolk*. During the 1920s the KKK extended even to the Canadian prairies. See Julian Sher, *White Hoods: Canada's Ku Klux Klan* (Vancouver, 1983).

77 This is catalogued, incident by incident, in Christopher Hewitt, *Political Violence and Terrorism in Modern America: A Chronology* (Westport, CT, and London, 2005).

78 Joseph E. Luders, 'Civil Rights Success and the Politics of Racial Violence', *Polity*, vol. 37, no. 1 (2005), p. 110.

79 E.g. in Atlanta. See Luders, 'Civil Rights Success and the Politics of Racial Violence', op. cit., pp. 116–8. Similarly in Arkansas: see Brent Riffel, 'In the Storm: William Hansen and the Student Non-violent Coordinating Committee in Arkansas, 1962–1967', *Arkansas History Quarterly*, vol. 63, no. 4 (2004), p. 407.

80 Hannah Arendt assessed the prospects of non-violent politics similarly, if more pessimistically: 'If Gandhi's enormously powerful and successful strategy of non-violent resistance had met with a different enemy – Stalin's Russia, Hitler's Germany, even pre-war Japan, instead of England – the outcome would not have been decolonialization, but massacre and submission.' See Hannah Arendt, *On Violence* (Orlando and London, 1970), p. 53.

81 Riffel, 'In the Storm', op. cit., p. 406.

82 See Clayborne Carson, *In Struggle: SNCC and the Black Awakening of the 1960s* (Cambridge, MA., 1995).

83 Student Non-violent Coordinating Committee, 'Statement of Purpose 1960', as revised 29 April 1962. Accessed: www.nationalhumantiescen ter.org/pds/maai3/protest/text2/snccstatementofpurpose.pdf.

84 Riffel, 'In the Storm', op. cit., pp. 416–7.

85 See *The New York Times*, 28 July 1967, p. 14: 'S.N.C.C Head Advises Negroes in Washington to Get Guns'.

86 Announcing the name change, Brown said: 'If the situation demands that you retaliate violently, you would no longer be hindered or hampered by "non-violent" in the organization's name.' See *The New York Times*, 23 July 1969, p. 25: '"Non-Violent" out of S.N.C.C.'s Name'.

87 William Hansen, writing in 2004, quoted in Riffel, 'In the Storm', op. cit., p. 418.

88 Quoted in John Herbers, 'Summer's Urban Violence Stirs Fears of Terrorism', *The New York Times*, 21 September 1971, p. 1. Lloyd Cutler subsequently served as a White House counsel to Presidents Carter and Clinton.

89 In March 2001, the US Supreme Court ruled that the Klan was allowed to participate in a Missouri 'Adopt-A-Highway' programme. The KKK had applied in 1994 to adopt a half-mile section of Interstate Highway 55; Missouri rejected the application, after which the KKK sued and got a ruling in their favour; then the State of Missouri appealed to the US Supreme Court. The Klan was represented in the case by the American Civil Liberties Union. See 'Supreme Court Rules KKK Can "Adopt a Highway"', accessed: usgovinfo.about.com/library/weekly/aa030501a.htm.

90 Mark Potok, senior fellow at the Southern Poverty Law Center, quoted in an Associated Press report, 'UPDATE: Georgia Rejects KKK's "Adopt-A-Highway" Application'. Accessed: newsone.com/2020221/kkk-georgia-adopt-a-highway-program/.

91 Quoted in Daniel W. Drezner, 'The Rarity of American Political Violence', *Foreign Policy*, 11 January 2011. Accessed: www.foreignpolicy.com/posts/2011/01/11/the_rarest_event_in_the_american_polity.

92 Roberta Senechal de la Roche, 'Collective Violence as Social Control', *Sociological Forum*, vol. 11, no. 1, March 1996, p. 98.

93 T. Robert Gurr, 'The History of Protest, Rebellion, and Reform in America: An Overview', in Ted Robert Gurr (ed.), *Violence in America, Volume 2: Protest, Rebellion, Reform* (Newbury Park, CA, 1989), p. 13. Quoted in de la Roche, 'Collective Violence as Social Control', op. cit., p. 98.

94 George Monbiot, 'Violence is Our Enemy', *The Guardian*, 1 May 2001, p. 17.

95 Charles Tilly, *The Politics of Collective Violence* (Cambridge and New York, 2003), p. 44.

96 Arendt, *On Violence*, p. 56.

97 Ibid., p. 52.

98 A revealing graphic representation of this is the recent mapping of 'Major Episodes of Political Violence 1946–2012' compiled by Monty G. Marshall, the director of the Center for Systemic Peace near Washington, in Vienna, Virginia. Accessed: http://www.systemicpeace.org/warlist. htm. The CSP is concerned with 'the problem of political violence within the structural context of the dynamic global system'.

V. War

1 Calley was convicted of murder, the only soldier to be convicted for his

role in the massacre, and given a life sentence. He served three and a half years under house arrest at Fort Benning, Georgia, before being pardoned by President Richard Nixon. See George Esper, '"It's Something You've Got to Live With": My Lai Memories Haunt Soldiers', Associated Press, 13 March 1988. Accessed: www.articles.latimes.com/1988-03-13/news/mn-1573_1_front-lines.

2 Transcript of the interview by Mike Wallace of Paul Meadlo, *The New York Times*, 25 November 1969, p. 16.

3 David K. Shipler, 'Mike Wallace: The Question That Changed America', *The Shipler Report: A Journal of Fact and Opinion*, 10 April 2012. Accessed: shiplerreport.blogspot.co.uk/2012/04/mike-wallace-question-that-changed.html.

4 '1968, Forty Years Later: My Lai Massacre Remembered by Survivors, Victims' Families and US War Vets', 17 March 1968, transcript of interview with Seymour Hersh. Accessed: www.democracynow.org/2008/3/17/1968_forty_years_later_my_lai.

5 'The Massacre at Mylai', in *Life*, vol. 67, no. 23, 5 December 1969, pp. 36–45.

6 Survey results of telephone surveys conducted on 1 April and 5–6 April 1971 for President Nixon. Accessed: www.law2.umkc.edu/faculty/projects/ftrials/mylai/surveyresults.html.

7 Niall Ferguson, *The Pity of War* (London, 1998), pp. 357–63 (quotations on pp. 357, 363). See also Joanna Bourke, *An Intimate History of Killing: Face-to-Face Killing in Twentieth-Century Warfare* (London, 1999); Edgar Jones, 'The Psychology of Killing: The Combat Experience of British Soldiers during the First World War', *Journal of Contemporary History*, vol. 41, no. 2 (2006). Suggestions along similar lines for the French army during the First World War may be found in Stéphane Audoin-Rouzeau and Annette Becker, *1914–1918: Understanding the Great War* (London, 2002), pp. 39–42. Theodore Nadelson, who was a psychiatrist at the Boston Veterans Administration Hospital, reached similar conclusions about American ex-soldiers who had served in Vietnam and who he treated. See Theodore Nadelson, *Trained to Kill: Soldiers at War* (Baltimore, 2005).

8 'Discours de notre camarade Brana, directeur d'école à Bayonne, à l'occasion de la remise de la rosette qui lui était faite', *Cahiers de l'Union fédérale*, 15 August 1936, cited by Antoine Prost, *Histoire sociale de la France au XXe siècle* (Paris, 1971/3), pp. 205–6. Quoted in Audoin-Rouzeau and Becker, *1914–1918*, p. 42.

9 Bourke, *An Intimate History of Killing*, p. 1.

10 J. Glenn Gray, *The Warriors: Reflections on Men in Battle* (New York, 1970), pp. 28, 29, 52, 135. Cited in Jones, 'The Psychology of Killing', op. cit., pp. 229–230.

11 Carl von Clausewitz, *On War* (trans. J. J. Graham) (London, 1977), p. 88.

12 See Alexander Watson, *Enduring the Great War: Combat, Morale and Collapse in the German and British Armies, 1914–1918* (Cambridge, 2008),

p. 6; Stéphane Audoin-Rouzeau, 'Combat and Tactics', in Winter (ed.), *The Cambridge History of the First World War, Volume II*, pp. 155–8.

13 Jones, 'The Psychology of Killing', op. cit., p. 237.

14 Benjamin Ziemann, 'Soldiers', in Gerhard Hirschfeld, Gerd Krumeich and Irina Renz (eds.), *Brill's Encyclopedia of the First World War, Volume I* (Leiden, 2012), p. 119. For percentages of French dead and wounded, see also Jean-Jacques Becker and Gerd Krumeich, *Der Grosse Krieg: Deutschland und Frankreich im Ersten Weltkrieg 1914–1918* (Essen, 2010), pp. 166–7.

15 Benjamin Ziemann, 'Soldiers', op. cit., p. 120.

16 This was the case for both the French and the German armies, and the British Army suffered its highest losses not in 1916 (the time of the Battle of the Somme) but when the Germans launched their spring offensive in March and April 1918. See Michael S. Neiberg, 'World War I', in Roger Chickering, Dennis Showalter and Hans van den Ven (eds.), *The Cambridge History of War, Volume IV: War and the Modern World* (Cambridge, 2012), pp. 192–3.

17 For this argument, see Richard Bessel, 'Violence and Victimhood: Looking Back at the World Wars in Europe', in Jörg Echternkamp and Stefan Martens (eds.), *Experience and Memory: The Second World War in Europe* (New York and Oxford, 2010).

18 Charles Tilly, 'Violence, Terror, and Politics as Usual', accessed: http://www.newbostonreview.net/BR27.3/tilly.html, originally published in the Summer 2002 issue of *Boston Review*.

19 Simon Chesterman, 'Introduction: Global Norms, Local Contexts', in Simon Chesterman (ed.), *Civilians in War* (Boulder CO, 2001), p. 2. Chesterman's source for this is Geraldine van Bueren, 'The International Legal Protection of Children in Armed Conflicts', *International and Comparative Law Quarterly*, vol. 43 (1994), pp. 809–10.

20 Wilson, *Europe's Tragedy*, pp. 786–95 (quotations from pp. 790, 791).

21 Charles J. Esdaile, *The Wars of Napoleon* (London, 1995), p. 299.

22 See the table in Wilson, *Europe's Tragedy*, p. 787.

23 John Mueller, *The Remnants of War* (Ithaca, NY, and London, 2004), p. 40; Ian Kershaw, 'War and Political Violence in Twentieth-Century Europe', *Contemporary European History*, vol. 14, no. 1 (2005), p. 109. Kershaw bases his conclusion on the tables in Norman Davies, *Europe: A History* (Oxford and New York, 1996), p. 1328.

24 Within Europe at least 7.7 million people were displaced during the First World War; and while all sides engaged in the practice, it was in the East, particularly with the Russian 'Great Retreat' from April to October 1915, that the greatest numbers were forcibly uprooted: at least 300,000 Lithuanians, 250,000 Latvians, at least half a million Jews and between 750,000 and perhaps 1 million Poles were deported to the Russian interior. The tally of human displacement in the Russian Empire was staggering: over 3.3 million refugees by the end of 1915, and more than 6 million – roughly 5 per cent of the Empire's total population – by the

beginning of 1917. See Nick Baron and Peter Gatrell, 'Population Displacement, State-Building and Social Identity in the Lands of the Former Russian Empire, 1917–1923', *Kritika: Explorations in Russian and Eurasian History*, vol. 4, no. 1 (2003); Peter Gatrell, 'Introduction: World Wars and Population Displacement in Europe in the Twentieth Century', *Contemporary European History*, vol. 16, Special Issue 04 (2007), p. 418; Alan Kramer, *Dynamic of Destruction: Culture and Mass Killing in the First World War* (Oxford, 2007), p. 151; Alan Kramer, 'Deportationen', in Gerhard Hirschfeld, Gerd Krumeich and Irina Renz (eds.), *Enzyklopädie Erster Weltkrieg*, pp. 434–5; Joshua A. Sanborn, 'Unsettling the Empire: Violent Migrations and Social Disaster in Russia during World War I', *The Journal of Modern History*, vol. 77, no. 2 (2005), p. 310; Gatrell, *A Whole Empire Walking*, p. 3.

25 Mueller, *The Remnants of War*, pp. 32–4.

26 The texts of the Hague Conventions may be found at the website of the Avalon Peace Project of the Yale Law School: www.avalon.law.yale.edu/subject_menus/lawwar.asp.

27 Quoted in the 'Foreword' to Chesterman (ed.), *Civilians in War*, p. x.

28 Mueller, *The Remnants of War*, p. 43.

29 Omer Bartov, 'Industrial Killing: World War I, the Holocaust, and Representation' (paper presented at the 17th Annual Holocaust Conference at Millersville University of Pennsylvania, 14 April 1997). Accessed: www.millersville.edu/holocon/files/INDUSTRIAL KILLING.pdf. The book in question is Omer Bartov, *Murder in Our Midst: The Holocaust, Industrial Killing, and Representation* (New York and Oxford, 1996).

30 Kenneth O. Morgan, 'England, Britain and the Audit of War: The Prothero Lecture', *Transactions of the Royal Historical Society*, Sixth Series, vol. 7 (1997), pp. 131–2.

31 See Holger Afflerbach, *Falkenhayn: Politisches Denken und Handeln im Kaiserreich* (Munich, 1994); Holger Afflerbach, 'Die militärische Planung des Deutschen Reichs', in Wolfgang Michalka (ed.), *Der Erste Weltkrieg: Wirkung, Wahrnehmung, Analyse* (Munich, 1994), S. 279–318; Robert Foley, *German Strategy and the Path to Verdun: Erich von Falkenhayn and the Development of Attrition, 1870–1916* (Cambridge, 2005); Ian Ousby, *The Road to Verdun: World War I's Most Momentous Battle and the Folly of Nationalism* (London, 2002); Alastair Horne, *The Price of Glory: Verdun 1916* (Harmondsworth, 2007); Alain Denizot, *Douaumont: 1914–1918: vérité et légende* (Paris, 1998).

32 Andree Lambers, 'Die Schlacht von Verdun in der militärgeschichtlichen Rezeption, 1919–1945' (Phil. Diss. Univ. Osnabrück, 2007), p. 1.

33 Ibid., pp. 4, 15.

34 Robin Prior and Trevor Wilson, 'Gallipoli', in Hirschfeld, Krumeich and Renz (eds.), *Brill's Encyclopedia of the First World War, Volume I*, p. 556; Robert Rhodes James, *Gallipoli* (London, 1965), p. 348; Trevor Wilson, *The Myriad Faces of War: Britain and the Great War, 1914–1918* (Cambridge,

1986), pp. 130–40.

35 Quoted in Jenny Macleod, *Reconsidering Gallipoli* (Manchester, 2004), p. 12.

36 Mustafa Aksakal has observed: 'While European scholars have been writing from a Europe that has laid down its weapons, emphasizing the tragic – and, increasingly, the unnecessary – nature of the war, in the Middle East the war's memory is entangled with fundamental stories of independence struggles and national liberation.' Mustafa Aksakal, 'The Ottoman Empire', in Jay Winter (ed.), *The Cambridge History of the First World War, Volume I: Global War* (Cambridge, 2014), p 461.

37 Peter H. Hoffenberg, 'Landscape, Memory and the Australian War Experience, 1915–18', *Journal of Contemporary History*, vol. 36, no. 1 (2001), pp. 111, 114.

38 J. M. Winter, *Sites of Memory, Sites of Mourning: The Great War in European Cultural History* (Cambridge, 1995).

39 Eugen Weber, *The Hollow Years: France in the 1930s* (London, 1996), p. 21.

40 Wolfram Wette, 'Ideologien, Propaganda und Innenpolitik als Voraussetzungen der Kriegspolitik des Dritten Reiches', in Wilhelm Deist, Manfred Messerschmidt, Hans-Erich Volkmann and Wolfram Wette, *Das Deutsche Reich und der Zweite Weltkrieg, Volume 1: Ursachen und Voraussetzungen der deutschen Kriegspolitik* (Stuttgart, 1979), pp. 85–8. For a discussion of the pacifist movements in Weimar Germany, see Reinhold Lütgemeier-Davin, 'Basismobilisierung gegen den Krieg: Die Nie-wieder-Krieg Bewegung in der Weimarer Republik', in Karl Holl and Wolfram Wette (eds.), *Pazifismus in der Weimarer Republik: Beiträge zur historischen Friedensforschung* (Paderborn, 1981).

41 Robert Weldon Whalen, *Bitter Wounds: German Victims of the Great War, 1914–1939* (Ithaca, NY, and London, 1984), pp. 121–9, 150; Richard Bessel, *Germany after the First World War* (Oxford, 1993), pp. 258–9.

42 *Deutschland-Berichte der Sozialdemokratischen Partei Deutschlands (Sopade) 1934–1940, Zweiter Jahrgang 1935* (Frankfurt am Main, 1980), pp. 276–82, 412.

43 Ernst Friedrich, *Krieg dem Kriege!; guerre à la guerre!; War against War; oorlog an den oorlog!* (Berlin, 1924). See also Dora Apel, 'Cultural Battlegrounds: Weimar Photographic Narratives of War', *New German Critique*, no. 76 (Winter, 1999), pp. 49–84 (here p. 49).

44 Apel, 'Cultural Battlegrounds', op. cit., pp. 53–4.

45 Ibid., pp. 49–50.

46 Karma Nabulsi, 'Evolving Conceptions of Civilians and Belligerents: One Hundred Years After the Hague Peace Conferences', in Chesterman (ed.), *Civilians in War*, p. 18.

47 Heinrich Schwendemann, 'Strategie der Selbstvernichtung: Die Wehrmachtführung im "Endkampf" um das "Dritte Reich"', in Rolf-Dieter Müller and Hans-Erich Volkmann (eds.), *Die Wehrmacht: Mythos und Realität* (Munich, 1999), p. 233.

48 BA-MA, RW4, Nr. 709, f. 160: 'Notiz für Gen. Lt. Winter!', 'Betr. Schutz-

zonen für die Zivilbevölkerung in Berlin', dated in pencil '16/4'. Keitel's comments added in pencil.

49   Schwendemann, 'Strategie der Selbstvernichtung', op. cit., pp. 224–44; Bernd Wegner, 'Hitler, der Zweite Weltkrieg und die Choreographie des Untergangs', *Geschichte und Gesellschaft*, vol. 26, no. 3 (2000), pp. 492–518. Generally, see Richard Bessel, *Germany 1945: From War to Peace* (London and New York, 2009), pp. 93–147.

50   Quoted in John R. Smith, *The War in the Pacific: Cartwheel – The Reduction of Rabaul* (Washington DC, 1959), p. 294.

51   Richard Overy, *The Bombing War: Europe 1939–1945* (London, 2013), pp. 556–82.

52   John Dower, *War without Mercy: Race and Power in the Pacific War* (London and Boston, 1986), pp. 40–1.

53   Quoted in Dower, *War without Mercy*, p. 41.

54   Quoted in Tami Davis Biddle, 'Bombing by the Square Yard: Sir Arthur Harris at War, 1942–1945', *The International History Review*, vol. 21, no. 3 (1999), pp. 641–2. On Harris's conviction that killing the German people was the purpose of Bomber Command, see also Overy, *The Bombing War*, p. 287.

55   Quoted in Richard Overy, 'Allied Bombing and the Destruction of German Cities', in Roger Chickering, Stig Förster and Bernd Greiner (eds.), *A World at Total War: Global Conflict and the Politics of Destruction, 1937–1945* (Cambridge, 2005), p. 290.

56   Overy, *The Bombing War*, p. 14.

57   Giovanni Rebora, *Culture of the Fork: A Brief History of Food in Europe* (New York, 2001), p. 166.

58   Overy, *The Bombing War*, pp. 29–32.

59   *The New York Times*, 20 March 2003, p. A20: 'Bush's Speech on the Start of War'. On 10 April 2003, while the invasion of Iraq was underway, George W. Bush and Tony Blair broadcast an 'Address to the Peoples of Iraq', in which Bush asserted that 'We are taking unprecedented measures to spare the lives of innocent Iraqi citizens', and Blair stated that 'We will continue to do all we can to avoid civilian casualties'. See the transcripts of the taped statements of Bush and Blair in *The New York Times*, 11 April 2003, p. B8: 'Bush's Words to Iraqis: "We Will Help You Build"'. Also George W. Bush and Tony Blair, 'Address to the Peoples of Iraq', www.american rhetoric.com/speeches/wariniraq/gwbushiraq41003.htm.

60   Michael Knights, 'Sparing Civilians', *World Today*, vol. 59, no. 4 (2003), p. 6.

61   Overy, *The Bombing War*, p. 17.

62   For the transcript of the film, *The Fog of War: Eleven Lessons from the Life of Robert S. McNamara*, which was released in 2003, see http://www.errol morris.com/film/fow_transcript.html.

63   Benjamin Ziemann, '"Vergesellschaftung der Gewalt" als Thema der Kriegsgeschichte seit 1914: Perspektiven und Desiderate eines Kon z-

eptes', in Bruno Thoß and Hans-Erich Volkmann (ed.), *Erster Weltkrieg Zweiter Weltkrieg: Ein Vergleich: Krieg, Kriegserlebnis, Kriegserfahrung in Deutschland* (Paderborn, Munich, Vienna and Zürich, 2002), p. 735.

64 See John Ramsden, *Don't Mention the War: The British and the Germans since 1890* (London, 2006), pp. 212–53.

65 Michael Geyer, 'Cold War Angst: The Case of West-German Opposition to Rearmament and Nuclear Weapons', in Hanna Schissler (ed.), *The Miracle Years: A Cultural History of West Germany* (Princeton and Oxford, 2001), p. 387.

66 Holger Afflerbach, 'Das Militär in der deutschen Gesellschaft nach 1945', in Holger Afflerbach and Christoph Cornelißen (eds.), *Sieger und Besiegte: Materielle und ideele Neuorientierungen nach 1945* (Tübingen and Basel, 1997), p. 263; Bundeswehr, 'Anzahl der gestellten Anträge auf Anerkennung als Kriegsdienstverweigerer pro Jahr. Stand 28. Februar 2009'. Accessed:www.zivildienst.de/lang_de/Navigation/DasBAZ/ Presse/Statistikangebot/Statistikangebot_node.html_nnm=true.

67 Ute Frevert, *Die Kasernierte Nation: Militärdienst und Zivilgesellschaft in Deutschland* (Munich, 2001), p. 346.

68 See the issue of the *Mitteilungsblatt des Instituts für soziale Bewegungen* no. 32 (2004), edited by Benjamin Ziemann, on 'Peace Movement in Western Europe, Japan and the USA since 1945'.

69 See Charles Chatfield, 'Peace as a Reform Movement', *OAH Magazine of History*, vol. 8, no. 3 (1994), pp. 10–14.

70 Jay Winter, *Dreams of Peace and Freedom: Utopian Moments in the Twentieth Century* (New Haven and London, 2006), pp. 48–74.

71 Benjamin Ziemann, 'Peace Movements in Western Europe, Japan and the USA since 1945: Introduction', op. cit., p. 6.

72 Quoted in William M. Donnelly, '"The Best Army that Can Be Put in the Field in the Circumstances": The US Army, July 1951–July 1953', *The Journal of Military History*, vol. 71, no. 3 (2007), p. 844.

73 Quoted in Harry G. Summers, Jr., 'Lessons: A Soldier's View', *The Wilson Quarterly*, vol. 7, no. 3 (Summer, 1983), p. 133.

74 Edgar Jones, 'Historical Approaches to Post-Combat Disorders', *Philosophical Transactions: Biological Sciences*, vol. 361, no. 1468, 29 April 2006, p. 541. The study cited is E. Jones et. al., 'Post-Combat Syndromes from the Boer War to the Gulf: a Cluster Analysis of their Nature and Attribution', *British Medical Journal* (2002), pp. 321–4.

75 Robert J. Graham, 'Vietnam: An Infantryman's View of Our Failure', *Military Affairs*, vol. 48, no. 3 (1984), p. 134.

76 See Ian Brown, 'Logistics', in Winter (ed.), *The Cambridge History of the First World War, Volume II*, pp. 218–9.

77 Joseph Paul Vasquez III, 'Shouldering the Soldiering: Democracy, Conscription, and Military Casualties', *The Journal of Conflict Resolution*, vol. 49, no. 6 (2005), p. 849.

78 These figures come from Deborah White, 'Iraq War Facts, Results &

Statistics at January 31, 2012'. Accessed: www.usliberals.about.com/od/homelandsecurit1/a/IraqNumbers.htm.

79 www.icasualties.org.

80 www.history-of-american-wars.com/vietnam-war-casualties.html.

81 Using figures from Bessel, *Germany after the First World War*, p. 6.

82 Vasquez, op. cit., 'Shouldering the Soldiering', p. 850.

83 William A. Boettcher III and Michael D. Cobb, 'Echoes of Vietnam? Casualty Framing and Public Perceptions of Success and Failure in Iraq', *The Journal of Conflict Resolution*, vol. 50, no. 6 (2006), pp. 834–5.

84 Edward N. Luttwak, 'Where Are the Great Powers? At Home with the Kids', *Foreign Affairs*, July/August 1994, p. 23ff.

85 Timothy Garden, 'Iraq: The Military Campaign', *International Affairs*, vol. 79, no. 4 (2003), p. 702.

86 Williamson Murray, 'Conventional War, 1945–1950', in Chickering, Showalter and van den Ven (eds.), *The Cambridge History of War, Volume IV*, p. 499.

87 Michael Hickey, 'The Korean War: An Overview' (2011). Accessed: www.bbc.co.uk/history/worldwars/coldwar/korea_hickey_01.shtml#four. Jon Halliday and Bruce Cumings, *Korea: The Unknown War* (London, 1988), pp. 200–1. Halliday and Cumings estimate that 'some 1 million Chinese soldiers probably died', as well as 'about 500,000 North Korean soldiers'.

88 Quoted in George C. Herring, 'America and Vietnam: The Unending War', *Foreign Affairs*, vol. 70, no. 5 (1991), p. 114.

89 Patrick Wintour, 'Multicultural Britain rejecting foreign conflict, MoD admits', *The Guardian*, 23 January 2014. Accessed: www.theguardian.com/uk-news/2014/jan/22/multicultural-britain-foreign-conflict-mod.

90 This comes from an article by Robert Kagan, 'Power and Weakness', *Policy Review* , no. 113 (2002), where Kagan argues that the 'essential truth' in this regard is that 'the United States and Europe are fundamentally different today [...] on major strategic and international questions today, Americans are from Mars and Europeans are from Venus'. The phrase is repeated on the first page of Robert Kagan, *Paradise and Power: America and Europe in the New World Order* (London, 2003), p. 3.

91 Kagan, *Paradise and Power*, p. 3.

92 According to the German Marshall Fund Transatlantic Trends Survey for 2012, 'pluralities in the United States (49 per cent) and the EU (48 per cent) said that intervention [in Libya] had been the right thing to do. German Marshall Fund, 'Transatlantic Trends: Key Findings 2012', p. 8. Accessed: www.trends.gmfus.org/files/2012/09/TT-2012-Key-Findings-Report.pdf.

93 www.dailykos.com/story/2014/02/26/128077/-Elizabeth-Warren-Gives-Speech-at-Georgetown-University-Focusing-on-Civilian-Casualties#.

94 Isabel V. Hull, *Absolute Destruction: Military Culture and the Practices of*

War in Imperial Germany (Ithaca, NY and London, 2005), quotation from p. 262.

VI. Women and Children

1 Inmaculada Montalbán Huertas, 'La lacra de la violencia de género', *El País*, 16 December 2007. Accessed: Http://elpais.com/diario/2007/12/16/andalucia/1197760924_850215.html.

2 Michele C. Black, Kathleen C. Basile, Matthew J. Breiding, Sharon G. Smith, Mikel L. Walters, Melissa T. Merrick, Jieru Chen, and Mark R. Stevens, 'National Intimate Partner and Sexual Violence Survey: 2010 Summary Report' (Atlanta, 2011), pp. 1–2. Accessed: http://www.cdc.gov/violenceprevention/pdf/nisvs_executive_summary-a.pdf.

3 Diana E. H. Russell, *Rape in Marriage* (revised edn., Bloomington and Indianapolis, 1990), p. 57.

4 Raquel Kennedy Bergen and Elizabeth Barnhill, 'Marital Rape: New Research and Directions'. Accessed: www.vawnet.org/applied-research-papers/print-document.php?doc_id=248.

5 Tamar Lewin, 'Tougher Laws Mean More Cases Are Called Rape', *The New York Times*, 27 May 1991, p. 8.

6 Kate Painter, 'Wife Rape in the United Kingdom', paper presented at the American Society of Criminology 50th Anniversary Meeting, 20–23 November 1991, San Francisco, pp. 12, 32. Accessed: www.crim.cam.ac.uk/people/academic_research/kate_painter/wiferape.pdf.

7 Ibid., p. 15.

8 Bergen and Barnhill, 'Marital Rape: New Research and Directions', op. cit. Russell, *Rape in Marriage*, pp. 87–101. In Painter's study, '70 per cent of wives raped had been hit by their husbands', and 'a third of the entire sample of women surveyed reported being hit or threatened by their husbands but the majority of these assaults/threats were not sex related'. See Kate Painter, 'Wife Rape in the United Kingdom', op. cit., p. 22.

9 Foyster, *Marital Violence*, pp. ix–x.

10 Most prominently, Russell, *Rape in Marriage*. See also Diana E. H. Russell, *The Politics of Rape: The Victim's Perspective* (Lincoln, Nebraska, 2003) (originally, New York, 1984); Judge Peter Gibson, The Law Commission, HMSO, *Rape within Marriage* (London, 1990); Gail Savage, '"The Instrument of an Animal Function": Marital Rape and Sexual Cruelty in the Divorce Court, 1858–1908', in Lucy Delap, Ben Griffin and Abigail Wills (eds.), *The Politics of Domestic Authority in Britain since 1800* (Basingstoke, 2009). In 1986 the *Journal of Family Violence* began publication.

11 Kersti Yllo, 'Wife Rape: A Social Problem for the 21st Century', *Violence against Women*, vol. 5, no. 9 (1999), p. 1059. Yllo lamented, however, that

as of the time of her writing 'academics and activists (with a few notable exceptions) have said little and done less about marital rape'.

12 European Commission, Special Eurobarometer 344, *Domestic Violence against Women Report* (Brussels, 2010), pp. 10–11.

13 Enid Nemy, 'Women Begin to Speak Out Against Sexual Harassment at Work', *The New York Times*, 19 August 1975, p. 38; R. Amy Elman, *Sexual Subordination and State Intervention: Comparing Sweden and the United States* (Providence and Oxford, 1996), p. 38; Carrie N. Baker, *The Women's Movement against Sexual Harassment* (New York, 2008), p. 1.

14 Susan Brownmiller, *Against Our Will: Men, Women, and Rape* (New York, 1975).

15 Ibid., p. 15.

16 This is from the preface to a recent e-book edition, and may be found on the internet at www.barnesandnoble.com/sample/read/9780449908204.

17 http://www.susanbrownmiller.com/susanbrownmiller/html/bio.html.

18 Baker, *The Women's Movement against Sexual Harassment*, p. 14.

19 This striking development can be seen in graphic form on the table in David John Frank, Tara Hardinge and Kassia Wosick-Correa, 'The Global Dimensions of Rape-Law Reform: A Cross-National Study and Policy Outcomes', *American Sociological Review*, vol. 74, no. 2 (2009), p. 273.

20 Ibid., p. 274.

21 Wiebke Steffen u.a., *Gewalt von Männern gegenüber von Frauen* (Bayer, Landeskriminalamt, Munich, 1987), p. 3. Quoted in Erich Elsner and Wiebke Steffen, *Vergewaltigung und sexuelle Nötigung in Bayern* (Munich, 2005), p. 11.

22 This law criminalized domestic violence, child and forced marriages and forced self-immolation, and was approved by decree by President Hamid Karzai; however, its passage by parliament was stalled as calls were made that its provisions were 'un-Islamic'. See Alissa J. Rubin, 'Afghan Effort to Get Justice for Women Seems to Stall', *The New York Times*, 8 December 2013. Accessed: www.nytimes.com/2013/12/08/world/asia/justice-for-abused-afghan-women-still-elusive-un-report-says.html

23 Mohammed Musa Mahmodi, 'Die Schändliche Gewalt gegen Frauen in Afghanistan', *Die Welt*, 25 January 2012. Accessed: www.welt.de/debatte/die-welt-in-worten/article13833106/Die-schaendliche-Gewalt-gegen-Frauen-in-Afghanistan.htm. The author of this article, published in a major German national newspaper, is the director of the Independent Human Rights Commission for Afghanistan.

24 Emma Graham-Harrison, 'New Afghanistan law to silence victims of violence against women', *The Guardian*, 4 Feb. 2014. (Accessed: www.theguardian.com/world/2014/feb/04/afghanistan-law-victims-violence-women.)

25 See Amnesty International, 'Document: Pakistan Honour Killings of Women and Girls' (1999). Accessed: www.amnesty.org/en/library/asset/ASA33/018/1999/en/952457dd-e0f1-11dd-be39-2d4003be4450/

asa330181999en.html; Amin A. Muhammad, 'Preliminary Examination of so-called "Honour Killings" in Canada' (2013) (presented to the Family and Youth Section, Department of Justice Canada, June 2010). Accessed: www.justice.gc.ca/eng/rp-pr/cj-jp/fv-vf/hk-ch/hk_eng.pdf.

26 In 2000, the UN Human Rights Committee commented on article 3 of the International Covenant on Civil and Political Rights, that 'The commission of so-called "honour crimes", which remain unpunished constitutes a serious violation of the Covenant'. Quoted in Muhammad, 'Preliminary Examination of so-called "Honour Killings" in Canada', op. cit., p. 6.

27 Robert Calvert, 'Criminal and Civil Liability in Husband-Wife Assaults', in Suzanne K. Steinmetz and Murray A. Straus (eds.), *Violence in the Family* (New York, 1974), p. 89.

28 Yves Michaud, *La violence* (Paris, 1986), p. 4.

29 In a judgement in North Carolina in 1874, it was declared:

We may assume that the old doctrine that a husband had a right to whip his wife, provided he used a switch no bigger than his thumb, is not the law in North Carolina. Indeed, the courts have advanced from that barbarism until they have reached the position that the husband has no right to chastise his wife under any circumstances. (State v. Oliver, 70 N.C.60, 1874)

Nevertheless, the court went on to say:

If no permanent injury has been inflected, nor malice, cruelty nor dangerous violence shown by the husband, it is better to draw the curtain, shut out the public gaze, and leave the parties to forget and forgive. (State v. Oliver, 70 N.C.60, 1874)

Quoted in Calvert, 'Criminal and Civil Liability in Husband-Wife Assaults', op. cit., p. 89.

30 See *Encyclopaedia Britannica*, Eleventh Edition, vol. vii (New York, 1910), p. 189; R. v Jackson (1891) 1 Q.B. 671] Accessed: www.studylight.org/enc/bri/view.cgi?n=7888.

31 Lee Bidwell and Priscilla White, 'The Family Context of Marital Rape', *Journal of Family Violence*, vol. 1, no. 3, (1986), p. 277.

32 Ibid., p. 278.

33 According to William Blackstone, *Commentaries on the Laws of England*, Book 1, Chapter 15 ('Of Husband and Wife'), accessed www.ebooks.adelaide.edu.au/b/blackstone/william/comment/book1.15.html:

By marriage, the husband and wife are one person in law: that is, the very being or legal existence of the woman is suspended during the marriage, or at least is incorporated and consolidated into that of the husband: under whose wing, protection, and cover, she performs everything.

34 Jennifer A. Bennice and Patricia A. Resick, 'Marital Rape: History, Research, and Practice', *Trauma Violence Abuse*, vol. 4, no. 3 (2003), p. 229.

35 Victoria R. Garnier Barshis, 'The Question of Marital Rape', *Women's Studies International Forum*, no. 6 (1983), p. 383; Raquel Kennedy Bergen, 'Marital Rape' (1999), accessed: 'Publication: In Brief, Violence Against Women Online Resources', http://www.taasa.org/library/pdfs/TAASA Library104.pdf), p. 2.

36 Bergen and Barnhill, 'Marital Rape: New Research and Directions', op. cit.

37 Lawrence Stone, 'The History of Violence in England: Some Observations: A Rejoinder', *Past & Present*, no. 108 (1985), pp. 219, 220.

38 Garnier Barshis, 'The Question of Marital Rape', op. cit., p. 383.

39 Elizabeth Foyster, 'Creating a Wall of Silence? Politeness and Marital Violence in the English Household', *Transactions of the Royal Historical Society*, Sixth Series, vol. 12 (2001), p. 410; Norbert Elias, *The Civilizing Process: The History of Manners* (Oxford, 1978), esp. p. 190.

40 Margaret Hunt, 'Wife Beating, Domesticity and Women's Independence in Eighteenth-Century London', *Gender and History*, vol. 4, no. 1 (1992), p. 23.

41 Elizabeth Foyster has argued that 'codes of politeness [...] did not leave middle-class women vulnerable and helpless in the face of abusive husbands' and that in England during the eighteenth and nineteenth centuries there was no 'conspiracy of silence about the subject of marital violence'. See Foyster, 'Creating a Wall of Silence?', op. cit., pp. 398–402.

42 Dorothy McBride Stetson, 'Law and Policy: Women's Human Rights in Russia', in Wilma Rule and Norma C. Noonan (eds.), *Russian Women in Politics and Society* (Westport, CT, and London, 1996), p. 160.

43 Russell, *Rape in Marriage*, p. 334.

44 Elman, *Sexual Subordination and State Intervention*, p. 90.

45 See Russell, *Rape in Marriage*, pp. 18–26; http://law.jrank.org/pages/13228/Oregon-v-Rideout.html; Lisa M. Cuklanz, *Rape on Trial: How the Mass Media Construct Legal Reform and Social Change* (Philadelphia, 1996).

46 Cuklanz, *Rape on Trial*, p. 9.

47 Russell, *Rape in Marriage*, p. xviii.

48 Bergen, 'Marital Rape' op. cit., p. 2.

49 www.bailii.org/uk/cases/UKHL/1991/12.html: (23 October 1991). See also Vanessa Laird, 'Reflections on R v R', *The Modern Law Review*, vol. 55, no. 3 (1992), pp. 386–92; The *Guardian*, 30 October 1991, p. 23: 'Rape of a Wife is Unlawful'. In 1994 the definition of rape was expanded to include non-consensual penile-anal intercourse. See Philip N. S. Rumney, 'The Review of Sex Offences and Rape Law Reform: Another False Dawn', *The*

Modern Law Review, vol. 64, no. 6 (2001), p. 891.

50 Quoted in Russell, *Rape in Marriage*, p. 17; also in R v R [1991] UKHL 12 (23 October 1991), op. cit. See also Joanna Bourke, *Rape: A History from 1860 to the Present* (London, 2008), pp. 307–8.

51 Painter, 'Wife Rape in the United Kingdom', op. cit., p. 3.

52 Bourke, *Rape*, p. 308.

53 John Stuart Mill, *The Subjection of Women* (London, 2001), p. 47 (first published in London, 1869). See also Bourke, *Rape*, p. 308.

54 R v R [1991] UKHL 12 (23 October 1991), op. cit.

55 Vanessa Laird, 'Reflections on R v R', *The Modern Law Review*, vol. 55, no. 3 (1992), p. 386.

56 Painter, 'Wife Rape in the United Kingdom', op. cit., p. 4.

57 L. Virapoullé, *Journal officiel*, Sénat, séance du 28 juin 1978, p. 1843. Quoted in L. Georges Vigarello, *Histoire du viol* (Paris, 1998), p. 266.

58 Vigarello, *Histoire du viol* (Paris, 1998), p. 266.

59 'Dossier de presse: Campagne contre le viol conjugal', p. 3. Accessed: www.west-info.eu/to-love-the-beast-france-sexual-violence-women-domestic-violence/vio-conjugal/.

60 Quoted in *Der Spiegel*, vol. 41, no. 27, 20 June 1987, p. 31.

61 '"Vergewaltigung ist nie ein Kavaliersdelikt": Frauenministerin Rita Süssmuth über die geplante Änderung des Sexualstrafrechts', *Der Spiegel*, vol. 41, no. 27 (20 June 1987), p. 34.

62 The delay was due in part to concern that recognition of rape within marriage would open the door to abortion, which was permitted in the case of rape. See Margrit Gerste, 'Endlich: Vergewaltigung in der Ehe gilt künftig als Verbrechen', *Die Zeit*, 16 May 1997. Accessed: www.zeit.de/1997/21/ehe.txt.19970516.xml.

63 *Strafgesetzbuch*, § 177 Sexuelle Nötigung; Vergewaltigung, in: http://www.gesetze-im-internet.de/stgb/__177.html. See also Elsner and Steffen, *Vergewaltigung und sexuelle Nötigung in Bayern*, p. 12.

64 David John Frank, Tara Hardinge and Kassia Wosick-Correa, 'The Global Dimensions of Rape-Law Reform: A Cross-National Study and Policy Outcomes', *American Sociological Review*, vol. 74, no. 2 (2009), p. 273.

65 'Declaration on the Elimination of Violence against Women', Article 2a. Accessed: http://www.un-documents.net/a48r104.htm.

66 Sheri and Bob Stritof, 'Is Marital Rape a Crime?'. Accessed: www.marriage.about.com/cs/maritalrape/f/maritalrape10.htm. They base their list on Country Reports on Human Rights Practices released by the US State Department, Bureau of Democracy, Human Rights and Labor.

67 However, subsequently the numbers declined, to 90,178 in 2000 and 84,376 in 2012. See 'United States Crime Rates 1960–2012', accessed: www.disastercenter.com/crime/uscrime.htm. It is not the absolute numbers, but rather the trends that are important here, for as Joanna Bourke writes: 'Only a small proportion of women report their rape. Fear of not

being believed, concerns about re-victimization, anxiety about being judged in turn and the discomfort of the interrogation and the medical examination are some of the factors responsible for the failure to complain. Victims also admit that they are often uncertain whether a crime has actually been committed. Reprisals, especially if the offender is a partner or ex-partner, are common.' See Bourke, *Rape*, p. 394.

68 Quoted in Tamar Lewin, 'Tougher Laws Mean More Cases Are Called Rape', *The New York Times*, 27 May 1991, p. 8.

69 This was the case not only in the Anglo-Saxon world. See, for example, Ingrid Kaiser, *Gewalt in häuslichen Beziehungen. Sozialwissenschaftliche und evolutionsbiologische Positionen im Diskurs* (Wiesbaden, 2012), pp. 11–12.

70 Carter and Weaver, *Violence and the Media*, p. 36.

71 Nancy Berns, '"My Problem and How I Solved It": Domestic Violence in Women's Magazines', *The Sociological Quarterly*, vol. 40, no. 1 (1999), p. 85.

72 Ibid., p. 86.

73 Elman, *Sexual Subordination and State Intervention*, pp. 35–6; Kathleen J. Tierney, 'The Creation of the Wife Beating Problem', *Social Problems*, vol. 29, no. 3 (1982), p. 207.

74 Sibylle Kappel and Erika Leuteritz, 'German Women Create Shelters', *Off Our Backs*, vol. 11, no. 6 (1981), p. 22.

75 Elman, *Sexual Subordination and State Intervention*, pp. 39–41.

76 Myra Marx Ferree, '"The Time of Chaos Was the Best": Feminist Mobilization and Demobilization in East Germany', *Gender and Society*, vol. 8, no. 4 (1994), p. 605.

77 Rekha Mirchandani, 'What's so Special about Specialized Courts? The State and Social Change in Salt Lake City's Domestic Violence Court', *Law & Society Review*, vol. 39, no. 2 (2005), p. 386. See also Richard J. Gelles, 'Power, Sex and Violence: The Case of Marital Rape', *The Family Coordinator*, Jg. 26, Nr. 4 (1977), pp. 339–47; Susan Maidment, 'The Law's Response to Marital Violence in England and the USA', *International and Comparative Law Quarterly*, vol. 26 (1977), pp. 403–44.

78 Mirchandani, 'What's so Special about Specialized Courts?', op. cit., pp. 386–7.

79 Sam Wright, 'The Role of the Police in Combatting Domestic Violence', in R. Emerson Dobash, Russell P. Dobash and Lesley Noaks (eds.), *Gender and Crime* (Cardiff, 1995), p. 412.

80 Hiroaki Terasaki, 'Newspapers and Educational Journals on School Corporal Punishment in Nineteenth Century England: Regina v. Hopley of 1860 reconsidered, Part II'. Accessed: www.repository.dl.itc.u-tokyo .ac.jp/dsace/bitstream/2261/848/1/KJ00002401025.pdf. The schoolmaster, Thomas Hopley, was found guilty of manslaughter and sentenced to four years in prison. See Jacob Middleton, 'Thomas Hopley and Mid-Victorian Attitudes to Corporal Punishment', *History of Education*, vol. 34, no. 6 (2005), pp. 599–615; Marie Parker-Jenkins, *Sparing the Rod: Schools, Discipline and Children's Rights* (Stoke on Trent, 1999),

pp. 5, 12–13.

81 Quoted in Parker-Jenkins, *Sparing the Rod*, p. 5.

82 Ibid., pp. 14–15.

83 James P. Jewett, 'The Fight against Corporal Punishment in American Schools', *History of Education Journal*, vol. 4, no. 1 (1952), p. 6. The Principals Association of Boston countered that 'the fear of physical pain [...] will have its place' in maintaining school discipline. Mann himself was not totally opposed to corporal punishment, and believed that 'in the present state of society, and with our present inexperienced and untrained corps of teachers, punishment, and even corporal punishment, cannot be dispensed with'. He also wrote: 'When an angry man chastises a child, it is not punishment; it is downright fighting, and so much more the criminal and disgraceful, as the person assailed is a child, and not a man.' (In the next sentence he stipulated that 'blows should never be inflicted on the head'.) Yet he went on to state: 'Corporal punishment should be with a rod, rather than with a ferrule, and below the loins or upon the legs, rather than upon the body or hand. In regard to the severity of punishment, it is obvious that it must be a reality, and not a sham. If the lightning never struck, nobody would be afraid of the thunder. [...] In all schools that are rightly governed, it is the mortification of being punished, quite as much as the bodily smart or tingling, which causes it to be deprecated, and gives it efficacy.' See Horace Mann, 'Lecture VII: On School Punishments', *Lectures and Annual Reports on Education* (Cambridge, MA, 1867), pp. 352, 354, 367.

84 Parker-Jenkins, *Sparing the Rod*, p. 111.

85 Tor Sverne, 'Children's Rights in Scandinavia in a Legal and Historical Perspective', *Family and Conciliation Courts Review*, vol. 31, no. 3 (1993), pp 299–300.

86 Quoted in Sverne, 'Children's Rights in Scandinavia', op. cit., p. 301. See also Parker-Jenkins, *Sparing the Rod*, p. 104.

87 Joan E. Durrant, 'Evaluating the Success of Sweden's Corporal Punishment Ban', *Child Abuse & Neglect*, vol. 23, no. 5 (1999), table on p. 438.

88 Quoted in Moira J. Maguire and Séamus Ó. Cinnéide, '"A Good Beating Never Hurt Anyone": The Punishment and Abuse of Children in Twentieth Century Ireland', *Journal of Social History*, vol. 38, no. 3 (Spring, 2005), p. 636. For discussion of the 1908 Children Act, see Harry Hendrick, *Child Welfare: England 1872–1989* (London and New York, 1994), pp. 121–6.

89 Maguire and Cinnéide, '"A Good Beating Never Hurt Anyone"', op. cit., pp. 636–7.

90 Harry Hendrick (ed.), *Child Welfare and Social Policy: An Essential Reader* (Bristol, 2005), pp. 46, 48.

91 Richard J. Gelles, *Family Violence* (Newbury Park, 1987), p. 86.

92 Hendrick, *Child Welfare*, pp. 246–9, 253–4; Hendrick (ed.), *Child Welfare and Social Policy*, p. 47.

93   Harry Hendrick, *Children, Childhood and Society, 1880–1990* (Cambridge, 1997), p. 99. See also Harry Hendrick, *Child Welfare: Historical Dimensions, Contemporary Debate* (revised edn., Bristol, 2003).

94   Hendrick, *Children, Childhood and Society*, p. 98.

95   See the 'Germany – Country Report' of the Global Initiative to End All Corporal Punishment of Children, October 2013. Accessed: www.end corporalpunishment.org/pages/pdfs/states-reports/Germany.pdf.

96   On this theme, see above all Ulrich Herbert, 'Liberalisierung als Lernprozeß: Die Bundesrepublik in der deutschen Geschichte – eine Skizze', in Ulrich Herbert (ed.), *Wandlungsprozesse in Westdeutschland: Belastung, Integration, Liberalisierung 1945–1980* (Göttingen, 2002), pp. 7–49.

97   In 1977 it was reported that, according to a poll taken by the Institut für Demoskopie Allensbach, 70 per cent of West Germans approved of corporal punishment. See 'Hirn statt Hosenboden', *Der Spiegel*, 3/1977, 10 January 1977, p. 50.

98   Dirk Schumann, 'Legislation and Liberalization: The Debate About Corporal Punishment in Schools in Post-war West Germany, 1945–1975', *German History*, vol. 25, no. 2 (2007), p. 193.

99   Dirk Schumann, 'Authority in the "Blackboard Jungle": Parents and Teachers, Experts and the State, and the Modernization of West Germany in the 1950s', in *GHI Bulletin*, no. 33 (Fall 2003), p. 76.

100 Till van Rahden, 'Paternity, Rechristianization, and the Quest for Democracy in Post-war West Germany, in Germany', *Forschungsberichte aus dem Duitsland Instituut Amsterdam*, Nr. 4 (2008), p. 60. See also Till van Rahden, 'Wie Vati die Demokratie lernte: Zur Frage der Autorität in der politischen Kultur der frühen Bundesrepublik', *WestEnd: Neue Zeitschrift für Sozialforschung*, vol. 4, no. 1 (2007), pp. 113–26.

101 Rahden, 'Paternity, Rechristianization, and the Quest for Democracy', op. cit., p. 65.

102 See the 'Germany – Country Report' of the Global Initiative to End All Corporal Punishment of Children, October 2013, op. cit.

103 K.D. Bussmann, 'Report über die Auswirkungen des Gesetzes zur Ächtung der Gewalt in der Erziehung: Vergleich der Studien von 2001/2002 und 2005 – Eltern, Jugend- und Expertenbefragung – Zusammenfassung für die Homepage des BMJ', p. 8. Accessed: www.bussmann2.jura-uni-halle.de/FamG/Bussmann_OnlineReport.pdf.

104 See the 'France – Country Report' of the Global Initiative to End All Corporal Punishment of Children, October 2013. Accessed: www.end corporalpunishment.org/pages/pdfs/states-reports/france.pdf.

105 K. D. Bussmann, *The Effect of Banning Corporal Punishment in Europe: A Five-Nation Comparison* (Martin-Luther-Universität Halle-Wittenberg, 2009), and Union of Families in Europe, *POUR ou CONTRE les fessées* (Tassin, 2009). Cited in the 'France – Country Report' of the Global Initiative to End All Corporal Punishment of Children, October 2013, op.

cit.

106 'Convention on the Rights of the Child', Article 19.1. Accessed: www.ohchr.org/EN/ProfessionalInterest/Pages/CRC.aspx.

107 Carter and Weaver, *Violence and the Media*, pp. 130–4.

108 See www.probeauty.org/cutitout/. Also: Denise Lavoie, 'Mass. Beauticians Taught to Spot Domestic Violence', 2 February 2014, WBUR website. Accessed: www.wbur.org/2014/02/02/mass-beauticians-spot-domestic-violence.

109 Bonita C. Meyersfeld, 'Introductory Note to the Council of Europe Convention on Preventing and Combating Violence Against Women and Domestic Violence', *International Legal Materials*, vol. 51, no. 1 (2012), p. 106. For the UN Declaration: G.A. Res. 48/104, U.N. Doc A/RES/48/104, 20 December 1993.

110 See the text of the Convention in Meyersfeld, 'Introductory Note to the Council of Europe Convention', op. cit., p. 118 (for 'Article 24 – Telephone helplines').

111 Bonita Meyersfeld, *Domestic Violence and International Law* (Oxford, 2010), p. xxxv.

112 Ibid., pp. 1, 3.

113 See David John Frank, Bayliss J. Camp and Steven A. Boutcher, 'Worldwide Trends in the Regulation of Sex, 1945 to 2005', *American Sociological Review*, vol. 75, no. 6 (2010), p. 870–1.

114 Ibid., pp. 870–1. See also David John Frank and Elizabeth M. McEneaney, 'The Individualization of Society and the Liberalization of State Policies on Same-Sex Sexual Relations, 1984–1995', *Social Forces*, vol. 77, no. 3 (1999), pp. 911–43.

115 This has been reflected in recent alterations in legal codes. For example, rape has been reclassified in Poland from a Crime of Lasciviousness to an Offence against Liberty, and in the Philippines from a Crime against Chastity to a Crime against Modesty and Sexual Liberty. See David John Frank, Tara Hardinge and Kassia Wosick-Correa, 'The Global Dimensions of Rape-Law Reform: A Cross-National Study and Policy Outcomes', *American Sociological Review*, vol. 74, no. 2 (2009), p. 276.

116 Steve LeBlanc and Bob Salsberg, 'Mass. House Votes To Expel Jailed Rep. Henriquez', 6 February 2014. Accessed: www.wbur.org/2014/02/06/carlos-henriquez-expulsion-vote.

117 Andy Metzger, 'Dorchester Rep. Henriquez Gets Jail Time After Assault Conviction', 15 January 2014. Accessed: www.wbur.org/2014/01/15/carlos-henriquez-convicted. In a statement after his arrest in July 2012, Henriquez had asserted that he had 'worked tirelessly with multiple agencies and organizations who champion against the issue of domestic violence. It is a mission I am committed to in my personal and public life.'

VII. Control

1 Quoted in Andrea Kirschner and Stefan Malthaner, 'Control of Violence – An Analytical Framework', in Wilhelm Heitmeyer, Heinz-Gerhard Haupt, Andrea Kirschner and Stefan Malthaner (eds.), *Control of Violence: Historical and International Perspectives on Violence in Modern Societies* (New York and London, 2011), p. 3. Heinrich Popitz was the son of the Prussian Finance Minister Johannes Popitz, who was hanged in 1944 as a consequence of his involvement in the bomb plot against Hitler.

2 Kirschner and Malthaner, 'Control of Violence – An Analytical Framework', op. cit., p. 7.

3 Ibid., p. 3.

4 Ibid., p. 4.

5 David Weisburd and John E. Eck, 'What Can Police Do to Reduce Crime, Disorder, and Fear?', *Annals of the American Academy of Political and Social Science*, vol. 593 (May, 2004), p. 43.

6 Mary R. Jackman, 'Violence in Social Life', *Annual Review of Sociology*, vol. 28 (2002), p. 392.

7 Ibid., pp. 387–8.

8 For the United States at the end of the twentieth century, see Marshall Miller, 'Police Brutality', *Yale Law & Policy Review*, vol. 17, no. 1 (1998), pp. 149–200.

9 Peter King, 'Punishing Assault: The Transformation of Attitudes in the English Courts', *The Journal of Interdisciplinary History*, vol. 27, no. 1 (1996), p. 43.

10 See Jim House and Neil MacMaster, *Paris 1961: Algerians, State Terror, and Memory* (Oxford, 2006).

11 Marshall Miller, 'Police Brutality', op. cit., p. 163. For a short account of the role of the media in the resulting trial, see Carter and Weaver, *Violence and the Media*, pp. 30–2.

12 'Rodney King Dies at 47; Police Beating Victim Who Asked "Can We All Get Along?"', *The New York Times*, 17 June 2012. Accessed: www.nytmes.com/2012/06/18/us/rodney-king-whose-beating-led-to-la-riots-dead-at-47.html?pagewanted=all&_r=0.

13 Dilip Subramanian, 'Riots and the Immigrant Community', *Economic and Political Weekly*, vol. 40, no. 49 (2005), p. 5157.

14 Anthony Daniel Perez, Kimberly M. Berg and Daniel J. Myers, 'Police and Riots, 1967–1969', *Journal of Black Studies*, vol. 34, no. 2 (2002), p. 176.

15 David Thacher, 'Conflicting Values in Community Policing', *Law & Society Review*, vol. 35, no. 4 (2001), p. 765.

16 'Community Policing, Bratton Style', *The New York Times*, 31 January 1994, p. A16.

17 Jarmal Singh, 'Community Policing in the Context of Singapore'. Accessed: www.unafei.or.jp/english/pdf/PDF-rms/no56/56-11.pdf

18 See Lucia Dammert and Mary Fran T. Malone, 'Does It Take a Village? Policing Strategies and Fear of Crime in Latin America', *Latin American Politics and Society*, vol. 48, no. 4 (2006), pp. 28, 37–40, 42–3.

19 Gwendolyn Ng, 'Cops on bikes are making a comeback', *AsiaOne*, 21 May 2012. This includes a photograph of 'Corporal Alan Tan, togged out in casual attire' and 'who will cycle around the neighbourhood to build a closer bond with residents'. Accessed: www.news.asiaone.com/News/Latest+News/Singapore/Story/A1Story20120521-347096.html.

20 Ian Loader, 'Policing and the Social: Questions of Symbolic Power', *The British Journal of Sociology*, vol. 48, no. 1 (1997), Note 4, pp. 16–17.

21 James McGuire, 'A Review of Effective Interventions for Reducing Aggression and Violence', *Philosophical Transactions: Biological Sciences*, vol. 363, no. 1503, 12 August 2008, p. 2577.

22 Roger Lane, 'Urbanization and Criminal Violence in the Nineteenth Century: Massachusetts as a Test Case', in Lawrence M. Friedman and Harry N. Scheiber (eds.), *American Law and the Constitutional Order* (2nd edn., Cambridge, MA, 1988), p. 196.

23 Eric H. Monkkonen, *Police in Urban America, 1860–1920* (Cambridge, 1981). Quotations from pp. 1, 151.

24 Jerome H. Skolnick and David H. Bayley, 'Theme and Variation in Community Policing', *Crime and Justice*, vol. 10 (1988), p. 3.

25 Eric H. Monkkonen, 'History of Urban Police', *Crime and Justice*, vol. 15 (1992) (quotation from p. 556). Monkkonen went on to write: 'By the end of World War I, police were in the business of crime control. Other city- or state-run agencies had taken over their former noncrime control activities.' (p. 557) Other writers date the transformation posited by Monkkonen at various points during the first half of the twentieth century.

26 See Clive Emsley, *Gendarmes and the State in Nineteenth-Century Europe* (Oxford, 1999).

27 Lawrence W. Sherman, 'Perspectives on Police and Violence', *Annals of the American Academy of Political and Social Science*, vol. 452 (1980), p. 2.

28 Clive Emsley, 'Polizei und Arbeitskonflikte – England und die USA im Vergleich (1890-1939)', in Alf Lüdtke (ed.), *'Sicherheit' und 'Wohlfahrt': Polizei, Gesellschaft und Herrschaft im 19. und 20. Jahrhundert* (Frankfurt am Main, 1992), pp. 190–1.

29 On the miners' strikes in Yorkshire in 1893 and in South Wales in 1925, see Emsley, 'Polizei und Arbeitskonflikte', op. cit., pp. 192, 200–1. See also Jane Morgan, *Conflict and Order: The Police and Labour Disputes in England and Wales 1900–1939* (Oxford, 1987); Roger Geary, *Policing Industrial Disputes, 1893–1985* (Cambridge, 1985).

30 Emsley, 'Polizei und Arbeitskonflikte', op. cit., p. 206; Illinois Labor History Society 'Memorial Day Massacre' (no date, accessed: www.illinoislaborhistory.org/memorial-day-massacre.html). Taking the side of the police and the employers against the strikers (a 'mob' that 'had been inflamed by the speeches of C.I.O. organizers'), the *Chicago Daily Tribune* reported that the members of the 'mob' were 'armed with an assortment of weapons including *firearms, clubs, chunks of steel, and pepper* [emphasis

in the original] to throw into the eyes of the police', and that the police behaved 'with scrupulous correctness': 'It was their duty under the laws of Illinois to protect the lives of more than a thousand workmen in the mill. It was the duty of the police, also, to protect the property of the company. [...] Fortunately the police were able to control the situation with relatively little loss of life.' See 'Murder in South Chicago', *Chicago Daily Tribune*, 1 June 1937, p. 12. See also *Life*, 14 June 1937, pp. 30–1.

31   R. Lemke, *Die Preußische Exekutiv-Polizei: Wie sie war, wie sie ist und wie sie sein müßte* (Osnabrück, 1904), p. 196. Quoted in Herbert Reinke, '"... hat sich ein politischer und wirtschaftlicher Polizeistaat entwickelt": Polizei und Großstadt im Rheinland vom Vorabend des Ersten Weltkrieges bis zum Beginn der zwanziger Jahre', in Lüdtke (ed.), *'Sicherheit' und 'Wohlfahrt'*, p. 224.

32   For example, in Bochum in March 1912. See David Crew, *Town in the Ruhr: A Social History of Bochum, 1860–1914* (New York, 1979), pp. 159–60.

33   See Richard Bessel, 'Militarisierung und Modernisierung: Polizeiliches Handeln in der Weimarer Republik', in Lüdtke (ed.), *'Sicherheit' und 'Wohlfahrt'*, pp. 323–43.

34   For an account of the violence in Rostock-Lichtenhagen in 1992, see Panikos Panayi, 'Racial Violence in the New Germany 1990–93', *Contemporary European History*, vol. 3, no. 3 (1994), pp. 270–2.

35   Cecilia Menjívar and Olivia Salcido, 'Immigrant Women and Domestic Violence: Common Experiences in Different Countries', *Gender and Society*, vol. 16, no. 6 (2002), pp. 910–11.

36   Richard B. Felson and Paul-Philippe Paré, 'The Reporting of Domestic Violence and Sexual Assault by Nonstrangers to the Police', *Journal of Marriage and Family*, vol. 67, no. 3 (2005), p. 601.

37   Ibid., p. 609.

38   James Q. Wilson, 'What Can the Police Do About Violence?', *Annals of the American Academy of Political and Social Science*, vol. 152 (1980), p. 18. Wilson cites: Bruno v. Codd, reported in *New York Law Journal*, 6 July 1977.

39   Wilson, 'What Can the Police Do About Violence?', op. cit., p. 18; Felson and Paré, 'The Reporting of Domestic Violence and Sexual Assault', op. cit., pp. 7–8.

40   Craig Crosby, 'Screaming male pig concerns neighbor in China', *Kennebec Journal*, 3 Feb. 2014. Accessed: www.kjonline.com/news/Screaming_male_pig_concerns_neighbor_in_China_.html?searchterm=pig.

41   Rebecca Emerson Dobash and Russell Dobash, *Violence Against Wives: A Case Against Patriarchy* (New York, 1979), p. 207.

42   Sarah Fenstermaker Berk and Donileen R. Loseke, '"Handling" Family Violence: Situational Determinants of Police Arrest in Domestic Disturbances', *Law & Society Review*, vol. 15, no. 2 (1980–1981), p. 319. Berk and Loseke also note: 'As front-line agents of social control in domestic disturbances, police are the proximate representatives of state

policy' (p. 318). See also Sam White, 'The Role of the Police in Combating Domestic Violence', in Rebecca Emerson Dobash (ed.), *Gender and Crime* (Cardiff, 1995), pp. 410–28.

43 Berk and Loseke, '"Handling" Family Violence', op. cit., p. 343.

44 American Bar Association, 'Standards on Urban Police Function'. Accessed: http://www.americanbar.org/publications/criminal_jus tice_section_archive/crimjust_standards_urbanpolice.htm.

45 Kathleen J. Ferraro, 'Policing Woman Battering', *Social Problems*, vol. 36, no. 1 (1989), p. 61.

46 *Attorney General's Task Force on Family Violence Final Report September 1984* (Washington, 1984), pp. 10, 17. See also Ferraro, 'Policing Woman Battering', op. cit., p. 61.

47 Ferraro, 'Policing Woman Battering', op. cit., p. 61.

48 Thus the verdict of the Obama White House, which also asserted that 'since the passage of the act, the annual incidence of domestic violence has dropped by more than 50 per cent'. See http://www.whitehouse. gov/blog/2011/11/30/reauthorizing-violence-against-women-act. The act was drafted by then Senator Joe Biden, who regarded it as the most important piece of legislation that he had introduced in the Senate.

49 Carolyn Schleuter and Vinita Jethwani, 'Integrity, Action, Justice: Leadership Committed to Ending Violence Against Women', *The Police Chief*, vol. 71, no. 11 (November 2004). Accessed: http://www.policechief magazine.org/magazine/index.cfm?fuseaction=display&article_id=443 &issue_id=11200.

50 Louise A. Jackson, 'Care or Control? The Metropolitan Women Police and Child Welfare, 1919–1969', *Historical Journal*, vol. 46, no. 3, pp. 623–48; Clive Emsley, *Crime and Society in Twentieth-Century England* (London, 2011), p. 164.

51 Ursula Nienhaus, 'Einsatz für die "Sittlichkeit": Die Anfänge der weib-lichen Polizei im Wilhelminischen Kaiserreich und in der Weimarer Republik', in Lüdtke (ed.), *'Sicherheit' und 'Wohlfahrt'*, pp. 243, 250–1.

52 See Emsley, *Crime and Society in Twentieth-Century England*, p. 164; International Centre for the History of Crime, Policing and Justice, 'The Women Police'. Accessed: http://www.open.ac.uk/Arts/history-from-police-archives/Met6Kt/WomenPolice/wpAttRec.html.

53 The first woman to be named chief of police in a major American city was Penny Harrington, in Portland Oregon, in 1985. See National Center for Women & Policing, 'A History of Women in Policing'. Accessed: http://womenandpolicing.com/history/historytext.htm.

54 Jackson, 'Care or Control?', op. cit., p. 624.

55 See Richard Bessel, 'Policing, Professionalization and Politics in Weimar Germany', in Emsley and Weinberger (eds.), *Policing Western Europe*, p. 190; Hans Lisken and Erhard Denninger, *Handbuch des Polizeirechts* (3rd edn., Munich, 2001), A 55, 79, 87.

56 European Commission, Eurostat, 'Statistiken zur Kriminalität'. Accessed:

www.epp.eurostat.ec.europa.eu/statistics_explained/index.php/Crime
_statistics/de.

57 Albert J. Reiss, Jr., 'Police Organization in the Twentieth Century', *Crime and Justice*, vol. 15 (1992), pp. 56–7. On the sharp increase in the number of policemen in America's big cities during the inter-war period, see, Robert M. Fogelson, *Big-City Police* (Cambridge, MA, 1977), p. 124.

58 David H. Bayley, *Police for the Future* (New York and Oxford, 1994), p. 4.

59 European Commision, Eurostat, 'Statistiken zur Kriminalität' .

60 Bayley, *Police for the Future*, p. 4.

61 For Britain, see Clive Emsley, '"Mother, What Did Policemen Do When There Weren't Any Motors?" The Law, the Police and the Regulation of Motor Traffic in England, 1900–1939', *The Historical Journal*, vol. 36, no. 2 (1993), pp. 357–81. For post-war West Germany, see Gerhard Fürmetz, '"Kampf um den Straßenfrieden": Polizei und Verkehrsdisziplin in Bayern zwischen Kriegsende und beginnender Massenmotorisierung', in Gerhard Fürmetz, Herbert Reinke and Klaus Weinhauer (eds.), *Nachkriegspolizei: Sicherheit und Ordnung in Ost- und Westdeutschland 1945–1960* (Hamburg, 2001), pp. 199–228. For Toronto, see Helen Boritch and John Hagan, 'Crime and the Changing Forms of Class Control: Policing Public Order in "Toronto the Good", 1858–1955', *Social Forces*, vol. 66, no. 2 (1987), p. 321. For an idea of what the policing of traffic meant for the police in mid-twentieth-century urban America, see C. G. Regan, 'Reorganization of the Chicago Police Department Traffic Bureau', *The Journal of Criminal Law and Criminology*, vol. 39, no. 6 (1949), pp. 790–801.

62 Alex C. Michalos, 'Policing Services and the Quality of Life', *Social Indicators Research*, vol. 61, no. 1 (2003), p. 9.

63 See Bessel, *Germany after the First World War*; Geyer, *Verkehrte Welt*; Dirk Schumann, *Political Violence in the Weimar Republic, 1918–1933: Fight for the Streets and Fear of Civil War* (New York and Oxford, 2009).

64 Nathan Bomey and John Gallagher, 'How Detroit Went Broke', *Detroit Free Press*, 15 September 2013, accessed: www.freep.com/interactive/article/20130915/NEWS01/130801004/Detroit-Bankruptcy-history-1950-dent-pension-revenue; 'Detroit Tops The 2012 List Of America's Most Dangerous Cities', *Forbes*, 18 October 2012, accessed: www.forbes.com/sites/danielfisher/2012/10/18/detroit-tops-the-2012-list-of-americas-most-dangerous-cities/. For a statistical analysis of the relationship between crime and urban population decline in the United States, see Julie Berry Cullen and Steven D. Levitt, 'Crime Urban Flight, and the Consequences for Cities', *The Review of Economics and Statistics*, vol. 81, no. 2 (1999), pp. 159–69.

65 'Preventing Youth Violence: Detroiters Working Together to Help Youth Succeed', March 2011, p. 2. Accessed: www.detroitmi.gov/Portals/0/docs/mayor/Initiatives/Detroit YVP Plan (Mar 2011).pdf.

66 In the ten years to 2011, the Detroit police force saw its numerical

strength reduced by one third. See 'Preventing Youth Violence', op. cit., p. 13.

67 Data taken from www.city-data.com/city/Harvey-Illinois.html.

68 Quoted in 'Harvey, Ill.: A city abused and ignored', *Chicago Tribune*, 13 February 2014. Accessed: www.chicagotribune.com/news/opinion/edi torials/ct-scandals-in-harvey-illinois-edit-20140213,0,1433521.story.

69 'Harvey, Ill.: A city abused and ignored', op. cit.

70 Michael Tonry, 'Why Are US Incarceration Rates So High?', *Crime and Delinquency*, vol. 45, no. 4, pp. 419–20.

71 Alfred Blumstein, 'Prison Populations: A System out of Control?', *Crime and Justice*, vol. 10 (1988), p. 237.

72 Deborah Che, 'Constructing a Prison in the Forest: Conflicts over Nature, Paradise, and Identity', *Annals of the Association of American Geographers*, vol. 95, no. 4 (2005), p. 810. Michael Tonry observes that 'the number of people locked up has increased by five times in the past quarter century, from about 300,000 in 1972 to 1,802,496 in mid-1998'. See Tonry, 'Why Are US Incarceration Rates So High?', op. cit., p. 421.

73 Patrick A. Langan, 'America's Soaring Prison Population', *Science*, New Series, vol. 251, no. 5001 (1991), pp. 1568–9. See also Thomas B. Marvell, 'Sentencing Guidelines and Prison Population Growth', *The Journal of Criminal Law and Criminology*, vol. 85, no. 3 (1995), pp. 696–709. In 1970, there were only 196,429 prisoners in state and federal prisons; by the end of December 1986, the comparable figure had reached 546,659 prisoners, and in mid-1986, there were an additional 274,444 prisoners in local jails. See Blumstein, 'Prison Populations: A System out of Control?', op. cit., p. 232.

74 Heather C. West, William J. Sabol, and Sarah J. Greenman, 'Bureau of Justice Statistics: Prisoners in 2009', revised 27 October 2011. Accessed: http://bjs.ojp.usdoj.gov/content/pub/pdf/p09.pdf.

75 Tonry, 'Why Are US Incarceration Rates So High?', op. cit., p. 422.

76 Nick Flynn, *Introduction to Prisons and Imprisonment* (Winchester, 1998), pp. 18–19.

77 Emsley, *Hard Men*, p. 170.

78 Flynn, *Introduction to Prisons and Imprisonment*, pp. 14, 43.

79 Gavin Berman, 'Prison Population Statistics', House of Commons Library (last updated 23 February 2012), pp. 1–2. In November 2011, the Scottish prison population reached a record high of 8,301.

80 Statitisches Bundesamt, *Justiz auf einen Blick, Ausgabe 2011* (Wiesbaden, 2011), p. 29.

81 See 'Wo lernt man das denn?', *Der Spiegel*, vol. 49, no. 3, 17 January 1994, pp. 70–4; 'Projekt Deutschland 2000: Sehnsucht nach Law and Order', *Der Spiegel*, vol. 53, no. 33, 10 August 1998, pp. 40–5.

82 Jacques de Maillard and Sebastian Roché, 'Crime and Justice in France: Time Trends, Policies and Political Debate', *European Journal of Criminology*, vol. 1, no. 1 (2004), pp. 122–3. See also: http://epp.euro

stat.ec.europa.eu/portal/page/portal/crime/documents/prison.pdf.

83   http://epp.eurostat.ec.europa.eu/portal/page/portal/crime/docu
     ments/prison.pdf.

84   Randolph Roth, *American Homicide* (Cambridge, MA, and London, 2009),
     p. 473.

85   Ministerium des Innern: Kommission zur Erforschung und Ausarbeit-
     ung der Geschichte der Deutschen Volkspolizei (ed.), *Geschichte der
     Deutschen Volkspolizei, Band 2 1961–1985* (Berlin, 1987), p. 371.

86   www.dhs.gov/mission.

87   www.dhs.gov/about.

88   Theresa Furrer, *Bedrohte Sicherheit: Untersuchungen zu einem fragmentierten
     Begriff* (Zürich, 2008), p. 22.

89   Nigel South, 'Privatizing Policing in the European Market: Some Issues
     for Theory, Policy, and Research', *European Sociological Review*, vol. 10, no.
     3 (1994), p. 222.

90   Ibid., p. 221.

91   de Maillard and Roché, 'Crime and Justice in France', op. cit.,
     pp. 1229–30,

92   '"Die Polizei kommt nicht hinterher": Private Sicherheitsdienste: Boom
     durch wachsende Kriminalität', *Der Spiegel*, vol. 46, no. 42, 14 October
     1991, p. 34.

93   Bayley, *Police for the Future*, p. 11.

94   David H. Bayley and Clifford D. Shearing, 'The Future of Policing', *Law
     & Society Review*, vol. 30, no. 3 (1996), p. 598.

95   'G4S A company profile', Corporate Watch. Accessed: http://www.cor
     poratewatch.org/?lid=337.

96   Roland Paris, 'Human Security, Paradigm Shift or Hot Air?', *International
     Security*, vol. 26, no. 2 (2001), p. 87.

97   http://hdr.undp.org/en/reports/global/hdr1994/.

98   Paris, 'Human Security', op. cit., p. 90. Paris's source for the quotation is:
     John G. Cockell, 'Conceptualizing Peacebuilding: Human Security and
     Sustainable Peace', in Michael Pugh (ed.), *Regeneration of War-Torn
     Societies* (London, 2000), p. 21.

99   Paris, 'Human Security', op. cit., p. 90.

100 Elias, *Über den Prozeß der Zivilisation*.

101 This is from an interview with Elias published in Stanislas Fontaine,
     'The Civilizing Process Revisited: Interview with Norbert Elias', *Theory
     and Society*, vol. 5, no. 2 (1978), p. 248.

102 Norbert Elias, 'Zivilisation und Gewalt: Über das Staatsmonopol der
     körperlichen Gewalt und seine Durchbrechungen', in Norbert Elias,
     *Studien über die Deutschen: Machtkämpfe und Habitusentwicklung im 19.
     und 20. Jahrhundert* (Frankfurt am Main, 1994), p. 225.

103 Gerlach, *Extremely Violent Societies*.

104 Andrew Linklater, 'Norbert Elias, The "Civilizing Process" and the
     Sociology of International Relations', *International Politics*, vol. 41, no. 1

(2004), p. 6).

VIII. Memories

1   See Sean A. Forner, 'War Commemoration and the Republic in Crisis: Weimar Germany and the Neue Wache', *Central European History*, vol. 35, no. 4 (2002), pp. 513–49; Siobhan Kattago, *Ambiguous Memory: The Nazi Past and German National Identity* (Westport, CT, and London, 2001), pp. 130–4; Rudy Koshar, *From Monuments to Traces: Artifacts of German Memory, 1870–1990* (Berkeley, CA, and London, 2000), pp. 107–9.

2   See Kattago, *Ambiguous Memory*, pp. 129–41; Siobhan Kattago, 'Representating German Victimhood and Guilt: The Neue Wache and Unified German Memory', *German Politics and Society*, vol. 16 (1998), no. 3, pp. 86–104; Brian Ladd, *The Ghosts of Berlin: Confronting German History in the Urban Landscape* (Chicago, 1997), p. 217–24; Wolfgang Kruse, 'Schinkels Neue Wache in Berlin: Zur Geschichte des modernen politischen Totenkultes in Deutschland', *Zeitschrift für Geschichtswissenschaft*, vol. 50 (2002), pp. 419–35; Michael Jeismann (ed.), *Mahnmal Mitte: Eine Kontroverse* (Cologne, 1999).

3   See Omer Bartov, 'Defining Enemies, Making Victims: Germans, Jews, and the Holocaust', *The American Historical Review*, vol. 103, no. 3 (1998), p. 787.

4   See, for example, the objections voiced in October 1993 by Jerzy Kanal, chairman of the Berlin Jewish Community, to the phrase 'To the Victims of War and the Rule of Violence': 'The phrase lies along the Bitburg line; victims and perpetrators are placed on the same level.' See *Der Spiegel*, vol. 48, no. 40, 4 October 1993, p. 243. Kanal refused to attend the dedication ceremony in 1993. See Ladd, *The Ghosts of Berlin*, pp. 220–1.

5   Quoted in Kattago, *Ambiguous Memory*, p. 139. Koselleck's intervention was published originally in *Frankfurter Allgemeine Zeitung*, 23 August 1993.

6   Kattago, *Ambiguous Memory*, p. 133.

7   Alex King, *Memorials of the Great War in Britain: The Symbolism and Politics of Remembrance* (Oxford and New York, 1998), p. 249.

8   'Wilfred Owen's Poems', *Times Literary Supplement*, 6 January 1921, p. 6.

9   Quoted in King, *Memorials of the Great War in Britain*, p. 76.

10 *Marie-Claire*, supplement *Nos enfants* (July 1937). Quoted in Weber, *The Hollow Years*, p. 21.

11 Jay Winter and Antoine Prost, *The Great War in History: Debates and Controversies, 1914 to the Present* (Cambridge, 2005), p. 181.

12 See Annette Becker, *Les Monuments aux morts: patrimoine et mémoires de la grande guerre* (Paris, 1988), pp. 75, 89. This is not the only local French monument to the dead of the Great War that features this phrase. The same may be found in Equeurdreville, just outside of Cherbourg – a monument 'to the children of Equeurdreville who died during the war', with

the statue a mother and two children on a column on which is a list of the names of the fallen and the inscription 'Que maudite soit la guerre'.

13 Becker, *Les Monuments aux morts*, p. 76.

14 Wolfram Wette, 'Ideologien, Propaganda und Innenpolitik als Voraussetzungen der Kriegspolitik des Dritten Reiches', in Deist, Messerschmidt, Volkmann and Wette, *Das Deutsche Reich und der Zweite Weltkrieg, Volume 1*, p. 88.

15 Benjamin Ziemann, *Contested Commemorations: Republican War Veterans and Weimar Political Culture* (Cambridge, 2013), pp. 133–5. On French war memorials, see especially Antoine Prost, *Les anciens combattants et la société française 1914–1939, Volume 3, Mentalités et idéologies* (Paris, 1979), pp. 41–52; Annette Becker, 'Der Kult der Erinnerung nach dem Grossen Krieg: Kriegerdenkmäler in Frankreich', in Reinhart Koselleck and Michael Jeismann (eds.), *Der politische Totenkult: Kriegerdenkmäler in der Moderne* (Munich, 1994), pp. 315–24.

16 According to Annette Becker, there were only six war memorials in France that bore 'truly pacifist messages'. See Becker, 'Der Kult der Erinnerung nach dem Grossen Krieg', op. cit., p. 322. Becker notes that 'the supporters of pacifism were usually veterans who cursed the war' – which was not all that different from the case in Germany.

17 For the general argument, see Bessel, 'Violence and Victimhood', op. cit., pp. 228–44.

18 See Sabine Behrenbeck, 'Between Pain and Silence: Remembering the Victims of Violence in Germany after 1949', in Bessel and Schumann (eds.), *Life after Death*, pp. 37–64.

19 For an overview, see Richard Bessel, 'Leaving Violence Behind: Thoughts on the Development of Germany after 1945', *Historia 396*, vol. 2 (2012), pp. 181–95.

20 On this transformation generally, see especially Konrad Jarausch, *Die Umkehr: Deutsche Wandlungen 1945–1955* (Munich, 2004).

21 Gavriel D. Rosenfeld, *Munich and Memory: Architecture, Monuments, and the Legacy of the Third Reich* (Berkeley, Los Angeles and London, 2000), pp. 117–24.

22 Bundesministerium für Vertriebene, Flüchtlinge und Kriegsgeschädigte (ed.), *Die Vertreibung der deutschen Bevölkerung aus den Gebieten östlich der Oder-Neiße* (3 vols., Bonn, 1954–1960).

23 King, *Memorials of the Great War*, pp. 186–7.

24 Becker, *Les Monuments aux morts*, p. 76. For other examples, of both pacifist and patriotic French memorials to the dead of the First World War, see Secrétariat d'etat aux ancients combattants et victimes de guerre, *Monuments de Mémoire: Monuments aux morts de la Grande Guerre* (Paris, 1991), p. 32 (Fay-de-Bretagne, Loire-Atlantique), p. 37 (Plessé, Loire-Atlantique), p. 57 (Machecoul, Loire-Atlantique), p. 62 (Rosnay, Vendée), p. 65 (La Bourboule, Puy-de-Dôme), p. 69 (Sault-lès-Rethel, Ardennes), p. 70 (Attigny, Ardennes), p. 73 (Seuil, Ardennes).

25 Antoine Prost, 'Les cimetières militaires de la Grande Guerre, 1914–1940', *Le mouvement social*, no. 237 (2011), p. 140; Daniel J. Sherman, 'Bodies and Names: The Emergence of Commemoration in Inter-war France', *The American Historical Review*, vol. 103, no. 2 (1998), p. 447; Daniel J. Sherman, *The Construction of Memory in Interwar France* (Chicago and London, 1999), pp. 83–6.

26 Sherman, *The Construction of Memory*, p. 84.

27 Among the best known was the memorial for the fallen of the First World War in the architecturally stunning administrative building of Farbwerke Hoechst in Frankfurt am Main, designed by Peter Behrens and Richard Scheibe. See Ursel Berger, '"Immer war die Plastik die Kunst nach dem Kriege": Zur Rolle der Bildhauerei bei der Kriegerdenkmalproduktion in der Zeit der Weimarer Republik', in Rainer Rother (ed.), *Die letzten Tage der Menschheit: Bilder des Ersten Weltkrieges* (Berlin, 1994), p. 427.

28 www.cwgc.org/find-a-cemetery/cemetery/80800/THIEPVAL %20MEMORIAL; Gavin Stamp, *Memorial to the Missing of the Somme* (London, 2007).

29 www.cwgc.org/find-a-cemetery/cemetery/91800/YPRES%20(MENIN GATE)%20MEMORIAL. See also John Stephens, '"The Ghosts at Menin Gate": Art, Architecture and Commemoration', *Journal of Contemporary History*, vol. 44, no. 1 (2009), pp. 7–26.

30 Sassoon wrote:

Who will remember, passing through this Gate
The unheroic Dead who fed the guns?
Who shall absolve the foulness of their fate, –
Those doomed, conscripted, unvictorious ones?
Crudely renewed, the Salient holds its own.
Paid are the dim defenders by this pomp;
Paid, with a pile of peace-complacent stone,
The armies who endured that sullen swamp.
Here was the world's worst round. And here with pride
'Their name liveth for ever,' the Gateway claims.
Was ever an immolation so belied
As these intolerably nameless names?
Well might the Dead who struggled in the slime
Rise and deride this sepulchre of crime.

Siegfried Sassoon, 'On Passing the new Menin Gate', in Siegfried Sassoon, *Collected Poems, 1908–1956* (London, 2002), p. 172.

31 Quoted in John Stephens, '"The Ghosts at Menin Gate"' op. cit., p. 23.

32 Bruce Scates and Rebecca Wheatley, 'War Memorials', in Jay Winter (ed.), *The Cambridge History of the First World War, Volume III: Civil Society* (Cambridge, 2014), p. 553.

33 This point has been made by Sarah Farmer, *Martyred Village: Commem-*

orating the 1944 Massacre at Oradour-sur-Glane (Berkeley, CA, and London, 1999), pp. 7–11.

34 www.lidice-memorial.cz/default_en.aspx.

35 Farmer, *Martyred Village*, p. 14.

36 Sherman, 'Bodies and Names', op. cit., p. 444; Sherman, *The Construction of Memory*, pp. 66–7.

37 See Anne Bernstein, *Bath Massacre: America's First School Bombing* (Ann Arbor, MI, 2009); Monty J. Ellsworth, 'The Bath School Disaster' (first published in 1927 by the author), accessed: http://www.daggy.name/tbsd/tbsd-x.htm.

38 This comment may be found among the 'customer reviews' on the Amazon website devoted to the book, Grant Parker, *Mayday: History of a Village Holocaust* (Lansing, MI, 1990). Accessed: www.amazon.com/Mayday-History-Holocaust-Grant-Parker/dp/0960495800.

39 This formulation comes from Daniel Sherman's discussion of French war memorials after the First World War: Sherman, 'Bodies and Names', op. cit., p. 447.

40 Titchener introduced 'empathy' as a translation of the German term *Einfühlung* (feeling into) or *Einfühlungsvermögen* (sympathetic understanding). See 'Empathy', *Stanford Encyclopedia of Philosophy*, revised 14 February 2013, accessed: www,plato.Stanford.edu/entries/empathy/; E. B. Tichener, *Lectures on the Experimental Psychology of Thought Processes* (New York, 1909). The term subsequently was re-translated into German as '*Empathie*'.

41 'Remembering Victims of Violence', *Brant News*, 7 December 2012. Accessed: www.brantnews.com/news-story/4109902-remembering-victims-of-violence/.

42 'Remarks by the President at Sandy Hook Interfaith Prayer Vigil', 16 December 2012. Accessed: www.whitehouse.gov/the-press-office/2012/12/16/remarks-president-sandy-hook-interfaith-prayer-vigil.

43 'Trauerrede des damaligen Bundespräsidenten Johannes Rau', 3 May 2002. Accessed: www.amoklauf-in-erfurt.de/399-0-Trauerrede-des-damaligen-Bundespräsidenten-Johannes-Rau.html.

44 Bodo von Dewitz, 'Zur Geschichte der Kriegsphotographie des Ersten Weltkrieges', in Rother (ed.), *Die letzten Tage der Menschheit*, pp. 163–76.

45 Ernst Jünger, 'Krieg und Lichtbild', in Ernst Jünger (ed.), *Das Antlitz des Weltkrieges: Fronterlebnisse deutscher Soldaten: Mit etwa 2000 photographischen Aufnahmen auf Tafeln, Kartenanhang sowie einer chronologischen Kriegsgeschichte in Tabelle* (Berlin, 1930). Translation in Ernst Jünger, 'War and Photography', *New German Critique*, no. 59 (1993), p. 25.

46 Michael Wieck, *Zeugnis vom Untergang Königsbergs: Ein 'Geltungsjude' berichtet* (Munich, 2005), pp. 238–9.

47 Friedrich Wilhelm Nietzsche, *On the Genealogy of Morals* (New York, 1967), p. 61 (2nd essay, Section 3).

48 Report by Master Sergeant Jack Bessel, Sixth Army Group History, Section 1, Narrative, S. 350; (United States) National Archives, RG 332,

ETO, Historical Division Program Files, Sixth Army Group 1944–45.

49 Altogether, roughly 360,000 British Empire soldiers were listed as 'missing' in the First World War; nearly half of the Australian war dead – 25,000 of 60,000 – were 'missing'. See Stephens, '"The Ghosts at Menin Gate"', op. cit., p. 11.

50 Ralf Blank, 'Kriegsalltag und Luftkrieg an der "Heimatfront"', in Jörg Echternkamp, (ed.), *Das Deutsche Reich und der Zweite Weltkrieg, Volume 9/1: Politisierung, Vernichtung, Überleben* (Munich, 2004), p. 460; Dietmar Süß, *Tod aus der Luft: Kriegsgesellschaft und Luftkrieg in Deutschland* (Munich, 2011), pp. 478–9; Overy, *The Bombing War*, p. 483.

51 Overy, *The Bombing War*, p. 395.

52 The greatest number, roughly 700,000, died in Soviet captivity. See Bessel, *Germany 1945*, p. 251.

53 Ibid., pp. 67–9.

54 Neil Gregor, '"Is he still alive, or long since dead?": Loss, Absence and Remembrance in Nuremberg, 1945–1956', *German History*, vol. 21, no. 2 (2003), p. 184; Neil Gregor, *Haunted City: Nuremberg and the Nazi Past* (New Haven, 2008), pp. 85–7.

55 Doris Bergen, *War and Genocide: A Concise History of the Holocaust* (2003), p. 178.

56 Peter Longerich, *Holocaust: The Nazi Persecution and Murder of the Jews* (Oxford, 2010), pp. 340, 411.

57 Most notably, Eugen Kogon's book on the 'SS-State' as he had experienced it in Buchenwald: *Der SS-Staat: Das System der deutschen Konzentrationslager* (Munich, 1946).

58 Hugo Gryn (with Naomi Gryn), *Chasing Shadows* (London, 2001), p. 256.

59 Aharon Appelfeld, 'Buried Homeland', *New Yorker*, 23 November 1998, pp. 48, 51, 52, 54. Quoted in Gross, *Neighbors*, pp. 126–8.

60 Otto Dov Kulka, *Landscapes of the Metropolis of Death: Reflections on Memory and Imagination* (London, 2013), p. 41.

61 Quoted in Antoine Prost, *In the Wake of War: 'Les Anciens Combattants' and French Society* (Providence and Oxford, 1992), p. 10.

62 Quoted in Prost, *In the Wake of War*, pp. 10–11.

63 Edward Glover, *War, Sadism and Pacifism: Further Essays on Group Psychology and War* (London, 1947), pp. 251–2. Quoted in Joanna Bourke, 'Introduction: "Remembering" War', *Journal of Contemporary History*, vol. 39, no. 4 (2004), p. 477.

64 Therese Benedek, *Insight and Personality Adjustment: A Study of the Psychological Effects of War* (New York, 1946), pp. 55–6. Quoted in Bourke, 'Introduction: "Remembering" War', op. cit., p. 477.

65 E. B. Sledge, *With the Old Breed at Peleliu and Okinawa* (New York and Oxford, 1990), pp. xxi–xxii.

66 Ibid., pp. 116–7.

67 Quoted in Allan Young, *Harmony of Illusions: Inventing Post-Traumatic Stress Disorder* (Princeton, 1995), p. 238.

68   Ibid., p. 255. This veteran also stated in 1987: 'You know, I'm a 39-year-old man, and the last time I remember being happy was when I was eighteen.' (p. 254)

69   Doris Lessing, *A Small Personal Voice: Essays, Reviews, Interviews* (London, 1994), p. 94.

70   Ibid., pp. 92, 93.

71   Jones, 'Historical Approaches to Post-Combat Disorders', op. cit., p. 533.

72   Jay Winter, *Remembering War: The Great War Between Historical Memory and History in the Twentieth Century* (New Haven, 2006), p. 52.

73   Paul Lerner, 'Psychiatry and Casualties of War in Germany, 1914–1918', *Journal of Contemporary History*, vol. 35, no. 1 (2000), p. 18.

74   Joanna Bourke, 'Effeminacy, Ethnicity and the End of Trauma: The Sufferings of "Shell-Shocked" Men in Great Britain and Ireland, 1914–39', *Journal of Contemporary History*, vol. 35, no. 1 (2000), p. 57. See also generally, Bourke, *An Intimate History of Killing*.

75   'Combat Fatigue Lasts', *Science News Letter*, vol. 87. no. 22, 29 May 1965, p. 343.

76   This definition comes from the American Psychiatric Association, *Diagnostic and Statistical Manual of Mental Disorders* (3rd revised edn., Washington, DC, 1987), p. 247. Quoted in Alice Förster and Birgit Beck, 'Post-Traumatic Stress Disorder and World War II', in Bessel and Schumann (eds.), *Life after Death*, p. 17. See also Winter, *Remembering War*, pp. 43–5.

77   Young, *Harmony of Illusions*, p. 7.

78   This is how the 'National Center for PTSD' of the United States Department of Veterans Affairs describes PTSD. See www.ptsd.va.gov.

79   Derek Summerfield, 'The Invention of Post-Traumatic Stress Disorder and the Social Usefulness of a Psychiatric Category', *British Medical Journal*, vol. 332, no. 7278, 13 January 2001, p. 95.

80   Ibid.

81   Olaf Schulte-Herbrüggen and Andreas Heinz, 'Psychological Trauma in Soldiers – a Challenge for the German Armed Forces (Bundeswehr)', *Deutsches Ärzteblatt International*, vol. 109, no. 35–6 (2012), pp. 557–8; HU Wittchen, S. Schönfeld, C. Kirschbaum et. al, 'Traumatic Experiences and Posttraumatic Stress Disorder in Soldiers Following Deployment Abroad: How Big Is the Problem', *Deutsches Ärzteblatt International*, vol. 109, no. 35–6 (2012), pp. 559–88. See also the report about the film 'Willkommen Zuhause', transmitted by the public broadcaster ARD on 2 February 2009, and described as 'Germany's first Vietnam film': Peter Huber, '"Willkommen zuhause" (ARD): Deutschlands erster "Vietnam-Film"', accessed: www.diepresse.com/home/kultur/medien/tvkritik/449335/Willkommen-zuhause-ARD_Deutschlands-erster-VietnamFilm.

82   Catherine Merridale, 'The Collective Mind: Trauma and Shell-Shock in Twentieth-Century Russia', *Journal of Contemporary History*, vol. 35, no. 1 (2000), p. 53.

83   Martha Ramos, 'The Effects of War', accessed: www.vietnow.com/

ptsd-effects-of-war/.

84   Quoted in 'Combat Fatigue Lasts', op. cit., p. 343.

85   Transcript of discussion broadcast on 2 March 2005, 'Frontline: The Soldier's Heart', *Washington Post*. Accessed: www.washingtonpost.com/wp-dyn/articles/A50926-2005Feb24.html. Allan Young summarizes: 'Normally, cycling and processing continue until memory is metabolized, at which point it becomes part of the individual's inactive memory: in effect it is buried in the past. PTSD is exceptional in this respect, because its traumatic memory generates a high level of anxiety. Consequently, the engagement phase is brief and ineffective, and the memory cannot be buried. It lives on for decades, a source of suffering and socially and psychologically maladaptive behaviour.' See Young, *Harmony of Illusions*, p. 9.

86   Jones, 'Historical Approaches to Post-Combat Disorders', op. cit., p. 540.

87   Summerfield, 'The Invention of Post-Traumatic Stress Disorder', op. cit., p. 95.

88   'Interview Andrew Pomerantz', conducted on 4 October 2004, *Frontline*. Accessed: www.pbs.org/wgbh/pages/frontline/shows/heart/interviews/pomerantz.html.

89   See National Collaborating Centre for Mental Health, *Post-Traumatic Stress Disorder: The Management of PTSD in Adults and Children in Primary and Secondary Care* (Leicester, 2005). Accessed: www.nccmh.org.uk/downloads/pts)CG026fullguideline.pdf.

90   Summerfield, 'The Invention of Post-Traumatic Stress Disorder', op. cit., p. 96.

91   Robert Musil, 'Denkmale', in *Gesammelte Werke* (Hamburg, 1957), pp. 480–3.

92   Scates and Wheatley, 'War Memorials', op. cit., p. 554.

93   Farmer, *Martyred Village*, p. 205.

IX. Conclusion

1   For perceptive comments along these lines, see Jörg Baberowski, 'Gewalt verstehen', *Zeithistorische Forschungen/Studies in Contemporary History*, vol. 5, no. 1 (2008), p. 4. For the internet version, see: http:www.zeithistorische-forschungende/1-2008/id%3D4400

2   Christopher R. Browning, *Ordinary Men: Reserve Police Battalion 101 and the Final Solution in Poland* (New York, 1992).

3   Jörg Baberowski, 'Gewalt verstehen', op. cit., p. 1.

4   Ibid., p. 2.

5   For the development of this argument in the context of Germany after 1945, see Richard Bessel, 'The War to End All Wars: The Shock of Violence in 1945 and its Aftermath in Germany', in Lüdtke (ed.), *The No Man's Land of Violence*, pp. 71–99; Richard Bessel, 'Leaving Violence

Behind: Thoughts on the Development of Germany after 1945', *Historia 396*, vol. 2 (2012), pp. 181–95.

6   See Philip Gourevitch, *We Wish to Inform You that Tomorrow We Will Be Killed With our Families* (Basingstoke, 2000); Peter Eichstaedt, *Consuming the Congo: War and Conflict Minerals in the World's Deadliest Place* (Chicago, 2001); Jason K. Stearns, *Dancing in the Glory of Monsters: The Collapse of the Congo and the Great War of Africa* (New York, 2012).

7   See Julia Eichenberg and John Paul Newman, 'Introduction: Aftershocks: Violence in Dissolving Empires after the First World War', *Contemporary European History*, vol. 19, no. 3 (2010), p. 188. Their reference is to Baberowski, 'Gewalt verstehen', op. cit., pp. 5–17.

8   Gerlach, *Extremely Violent Societies*.

9   Timothy Snyder, *Bloodlands: Europe between Hitler and Stalin* (New York, 2010).

10   See Kate Brown, *A Biography of No Place: From Ethnic Borderland to Soviet Hinterland* (Cambridge, MA, and London, 2003).

11   Norbert Elias, *The Loneliness of the Dying* (Oxford, 1985), p. 8: 'Life grows longer, death is further postponed. The sight of dying and dead people is no longer commonplace. It is easier in the normal course of life to forget death.'

12   Ibid., p. 48.

13   As of 13 February 2014 there were 184,828 active soldiers in the German armed forces. See www.bundeswehr.de/portal/a/bwde/!ut/p/c4/Dcmx DYAwDATAWVgg7unYAAufc8kSWI4OMIesTXXm002D8SeWQy7jRStsh c-4p94L0hENCnXEGUvXXSuMKG8FwBd26TD9uIZiT/.

14   'Defence Statistics 1998', House of Commons Research Paper 98/120, 22 December 1998.

15   Thom Shanker and Helene Cooper, 'Pentagon Plans to Shrink Army to Pre-World War II Level', *The New York Times*, 23 February 2014.

16   Joanna Bourke, *Fear: A Cultural History* (London, 2005), p. 332.

17   See Bessel and Schumann (eds.), *Life after Death*.

18   Tony Judt, 'The Past is Another Country: Myth and Memory in Post-war Europe', *Daedalus*, vol. 121, no. 4 (1992), pp. 95–6; Judt, *Postwar*, p. 61.

19   Bessel, *Germany 1945*, pp. 396–7; Bessel, 'Violence and Victimhood', op. cit., pp. 229–44.

20   Baberowski, 'Gewalt verstehen', op. cit., p. 4.

21   Norbert Elias, 'Zivilisation und Gewalt: Über das Staatsmonopol der körperlichen Gewalt und seine Durchbrechungen', in Elias, *Studien über die Deutschen*, p. 225.

Bibliography

English-language books

Al-Rasheed, Madawi, and Shterin, Marat (eds.), *Dying for Faith: Religiously Motivated Violence in the Contemporary World* (London and New York, 2009)

Appleby, R. Scott, *The Ambivalence of the Sacred: Religion, Violence and Reconciliation* (Lanham MD, 2000)

Arendt, Hannah, *On Revolution* (New York, 1965)

Arendt, Hannah, *On Violence* (Orlando and London, 1970)

Audoin-Rouzeau, Stéphane, and Becker, Annette, *1914–1918: Understanding the Great War* (London, 2002)

Avalos, Hector, *Fighting Words: The Origins of Religious Violence* (Amherst, NY, 2005)

Baker, Carrie N., *The Women's Movement against Sexual Harassment* (New York, 2008)

Baker, Keith Michael (ed.), *The Terror, Volume 4: The French Revolution and the Creation of Modern Political Culture* (Oxford, 1994)

Bartov, Omer, *Murder in Our Midst: The Holocaust, Industrial Killing, and Representation* (New York and Oxford, 1996)

Bauman, Zygmunt, *Modernity and the Holocaust* (Cambridge, 1989)

Bayley, David H., *Police for the Future* (New York and Oxford, 1994)

Bedau, Hugo Adam, *The Death Penalty in America* (New York, Oxford, 1982)

Benedek, Therese, *Insight and Personality Adjustment: A Study of the Psychological Effects of War* (New York, 1946)

Benedict, Philip, *Rouen during the Wars of Religion* (Cambridge, 1981)

Bennett, John C., *Christian Ethics and Social Policy* (New York, 1946)

Bergen, Doris, *War and Genocide: A Concise History of the Holocaust* (Lanham, MD, 2003)

Berger, Peter L., *A Far Glory: The Quest for Faith in an Age of Credulity* (New York, 1992)

Berger, Peter L. (ed.), *The Desecularization of the World: Resurgent Religion and World Politics* (Washington, DC, 1999)

Bernstein, Anne, *Bath Massacre: America's First School Bombing* (Ann Arbor, MI, 2009)

Bessel, Richard, *Germany 1945: From War to Peace* (London and New York, 2009)

Bessel, Richard, *Germany after the First World War* (Oxford, 1993)

Bessel, Richard, *Political Violence and the Rise of Nazism: The Storm Troopers in Eastern Germany 1925–1934* (New Haven and London, 1984)

Bessel, Richard, and Feuchtwanger, E. J. (eds.), *Social Change and Political Development in Weimar Germany* (London, 1981),

Bessel, Richard, and Schumann, Dirk (eds.), *Life after Death: Approaches to a Cultural and Social History of Europe during the 1940s and 1950s* (Cambridge, 2003)

Bosworth, R. J. B., *Mussolini* (London, 2002)

Bourke, Joanna, *An Intimate History of Killing: Face-to-Face Killing in Twentieth-Century Warfare* (London, 1999)

Bourke, Joanna, *Fear: A Cultural History* (London, 2005)

Bourke, Joanna, *Rape: A History from 1860 to the Present* (London, 2008)

Brown, Callum G., *The Death of Christian Britain: Understanding Secularisation, 1800–2000* (London, 2001)

Brown, Kate, *A Biography of No Place: From Ethnic Borderland to Soviet Heartland* (Cambridge, MA, and London, 2003)

Brown, Richard Maxwell, *Strain of Violence: Historical Studies of American Violence and Vigilantism* (New York, 1975)

Browning, Christopher R., *Ordinary Men: Reserve Police Battalion 101 and the Final Solution in Poland* (New York, 1992)

Brownmiller, Susan, *Against Our Will: Men, Women, and Rape* (New York, 1975)

Bruce, Steve, *Religion in the Modern World: From Cathedrals to Cults* (Oxford, 1996)

Brundage, W. Fitzhugh, *Lynching in the New South: Georgia and Virginia, 1880–1930* (Urbana, IL, 1993)

Bussmann, K. D., *The Effect of Banning Corporal Punishment in Europe: A Five-Nation Comparison* (Martin-Luther-Universität Halle-Wittenberg, 2009)

Cane, Peter, and Conaghan, Joanne (eds.), *The New Oxford Companion to Law* (Oxford, 2008)

Bibliography

Carroll, Stuart, *Blood and Violence in Early Modern France* (Oxford, 2006)

Carroll, Stuart (ed.), *Cultures of Violence: Interpersonal Violence in Historical Perspective* (Basingstoke, 2007)

Carson, Clayborne, *In Struggle: SNCC and the Black Awakening of the 1960s* (Cambridge, MA, 1995)

Carter, Cynthia, and Weaver, C. Kay, *Violence and the Media* (Buckingham and Philadelphia, 2003)

Cavanaugh, William T., *The Myth of Religious Violence: Secular Ideology and the Roots of Modern Conflict* (Oxford, 2009)

Chesterman, Simon (ed.), *Civilians in War* (Boulder, CO, 2001)

Chickering, Roger; Förster, Stig; and Greiner, Bernd (eds.), *A World at Total War: Global Conflict and the Politics of Destruction, 1937–1945* (Cambridge, 2005)

Chickering, Roger; Showalter, Dennis; and van den Ven, Hans (eds.), *The Cambridge History of War, Volume IV: War and the Modern World* (Cambridge, 2012)

Corner, Paul, *Fascism in Ferrara 1915–1925* (Oxford, 1975)

Crew, David, *Town in the Ruhr: A Social History of Bochum, 1860–1914* (New York, 1979)

Cuklanz, Lisa M., *Rape on Trial: How the Mass Media Construct Legal Reform and Social Change* (Philadelphia, 1996)

Davies, Norman, *Europe: A History* (Oxford and New York, 1996)

Delap, Lucy; Griffin, Ben; and Wills, Abigail (eds.), *The Politics of Domestic Authority in Britain since 1800* (Basingstoke, 2009)

de Tocqueville, Alexis, *L'Ancien Régime* (trans. M.W. Patterson) (Oxford, 1962)

Dobash, Rebecca Emerson (ed.), *Gender and Crime* (Cardiff, 1995)

Dobash, Rebecca Emerson, and Dobash, Russell, *Violence Against Wives: A Case Against Patriarchy* (New York, 1979)

Dower, John, *War without Mercy: Race and Power in the Pacific War* (London and Boston, 1986)

Ebner, Michael, *Ordinary Violence in Mussolini's Italy* (Cambridge, 2011)

Echternkamp, Jörg, and Martens, Stefan (eds.), *Experience and Memory: The Second World War in Europe* (New York and Oxford, 2010)

Eichstaedt, Peter, *Consuming the Congo: War and Conflict Minerals in the World's Deadliest Place* (Chicago, 2001)

Eisen, Robert, *The Peace and Violence of Judaism: From the Bible to Modern Zionism* (Oxford, 2011)

Elias, Norbert, *The Civilizing Process: The History of Manners* (Oxford, 1978)

Elias, Norbert, *The Loneliness of the Dying* (Oxford, 1985)

Elman, R. Amy, *Sexual Subordination and State Intervention: Comparing Sweden and the United States* (Providence and Oxford, 1996)

345

Emsley, Clive, *Crime and Society in Twentieth-Century England* (London, 2011)

Emsley, Clive, *Gendarmes and the State in Nineteenth-Century Europe* (Oxford, 1999)

Emsley, Clive, *Hard Men: Violence in England since 1750* (London, 2005)

Emsley, Clive, and Weinberger, Barbara (eds.), *Policing Western Europe: Politics, Professionalism and Public Order, 1850–1940* (Westport, CT, 1991)

Epstein, Catherine *Model Nazi: Arthur Greiser and the Occupation of Western Poland* (Oxford, 2010)

Esdaile, Charles J., *The Wars of Napoleon* (London, 1995)

Evans, Richard J., *Rituals of Retribution: Capital Punishment in Germany, 1600–1987* (London, 1997)

Evans, R. J., (ed.), *The German Working Class, 1888–1933: The Politics of Everyday Life* (London, 1981)

Farmer, Sarah, *Martyred Village: Commemorating the 1944 Massacre at Oradour-sur-Glane* (Berkeley, CA, and London, 1999)

Ferguson, Niall, *The Pity of War* (London, 1998)

Ferguson, Niall, *The War of the World: History's Age of Hatred* (London, 2006)

Figes, Orlando, *A People's Tragedy: The Russian Revolution 1891–1924* (London, 1996)

Fink, Carole; Gassert, Philipp; and Junker, Detlef (eds.), *1968: The World Transformed* (New York, 1998)

Flannery, Daniel J.; Vazsonyi, Alexander T.; and Waldman, Irwin D. (eds.), *Cambridge Handbook of Violent Behavior and Aggression* (New York, 2007)

Flynn, Nick, *Introduction to Prisons and Imprisonment* (Winchester, 1998)

Fogelson, Robert M., *Big-City Police* (Cambridge, MA, 1977)

Foley, Robert, *German Strategy and the Path to Verdun: Erich von Falkenhayn and the Development of Attrition, 1870–1916* (Cambridge, 2005)

Forrest, Alan; Hagemann, Karen; and Rendall, Jane (eds.), *Soldiers, Citizens and Civilians: Experiences and Perceptions of the Revolutionary and Napoleonic Wars, 1790–1820* (Basingstoke, 2008)

Foucault, Michel, *Discipline and Punish: The Birth of the Prison* (New York, 1977)

Fox, Craig, *Everyday Klansfolk: White Protestant Life and the KKK in 1920s Michigan* (East Lansing, MI, 2011)

Foyster, Elizabeth, *Marital Violence: An English Family History, 1660–1857* (Cambridge, 2005)

Friedländer, Saul, *Nazi Germany and the Jews: The Years of Extermination, 1939–1945* (London, 2007)

Friedländer, Saul, *Nazi Germany and the Jews: The Years of Persecution 1933–1939* (London, 1997)

Friedman, Lawrence M., and Scheiber, Harry N. (eds.), *American Law and the Constitutional Order* (2nd edn., Cambridge, MA, 1988)

Bibliography

Fulbrook, Mary, *Anatomy of a Dictatorship: Inside the GDR 1949–1989* (Oxford, 1995)

Futrell, Alison, *Blood in the Arena: The Spectacle of Roman Power* (Austin, 1997)

Gatrell, Peter, *A Whole Empire Walking: Refugees in Russia during World War I* (Bloomington, IN, 1999)

Gatrell, V. A. C., *The Hanging Tree: Execution and the English People, 1770–1868* (Oxford, 1994)

Geary, Dick, *European Labour Protest 1848–1939* (London, 1981)

Geary, Roger, *Policing Industrial Disputes, 1893–1985* (Cambridge, 1985)

Gelles, Richard J., and Straus, Murray A., *Intimate Violence: The Causes and Consequences of Abuse in the American Family* (New York, 1988)

Gerlach, Christian, *Extremely Violent Societies: Mass Violence in the Twentieth-Century World* (Cambridge, 2010)

Gerwarth, Robert, and Horne, John (eds.), *War in Peace: Paramilitary Violence in Europe after the Great War* (Oxford, 2012)

Geyer, Michael, and Tooze, Adam (eds.), *Cambridge History of the Second World War*, (Cambridge, forthcoming)

Gildea, Robert, *France since 1945* (Oxford, 1996)

Gildea, Robert; Mark, James; and Warring, Anette (eds.), *Europe's 1968: Voices of Revolt* (Oxford, 2013)

Gill, Graeme J., *Peasants and Government in the Russian Revolution* (London, 1979)

Glover, Edward, *War, Sadism and Pacifism: Further Essays on Group Psychology and War* (London, 1947)

Gordon, Linda, *Heroes of Their Own Lives: The Politics and History of Family Violence, Boston 1880–1960* (New York, 1988)

Gossman, Patricia A., *Riots and Victims: Violence and the Construction of Communal Identity among Bengali Muslims, 1905–1947* (Boulder, CO, 1999)

Gourevitch, Philip, *We Wish to Inform You that Tomorrow We Will Be Killed With our Families* (Basingstoke, 2000)

Gray, J. Glenn, *The Warriors: Reflections on Men in Battle* (New York, 1970)

Gregor, Neil, *Haunted City: Nuremberg and the Nazi Past* (New Haven, 2008)

Gross, Jan, *Fear: Anti-Semitism in Poland after Auschwitz – An Essay in Historical Interpretation* (Princeton, 2006)

Gross, Jan, *Neighbors: The Destruction of the Jewish Community of Jedwabne* (Princeton and Oxford, 2001)

Gryn, Hugo, and Gryn, Naomi, *Chasing Shadows* (London, 2001)

Gurr, Ted Robert (ed.), *Violence in America, Volume 2: Protest, Rebellion, Reform* (Newbury Park, CA, 1989)

Halliday, Jon, and Cumings, Bruce, *Korea: The Unknown War* (London, 1988)

Hall Stewart, John, *A Documentary Survey of the French Revolution* (New York, 1963)

Hay, Douglas et al. (eds.), *Albion's Fatal Tree: Crime and Society in Eighteenth-century England* (New York, 1975)

Heitmeyer, Wilhelm; Haupt, Heinz-Gerhard; Kirschner, Andrea; and Malthaner, Stefan (eds.), *Control of Violence: Historical and International Perspectives on Violence in Modern Societies* (New York and London, 2011)

Hendrick, Harry, *Children, Childhood and Society, 1880–1990* (Cambridge, 1997)

Hendrick, Harry (ed.), *Child Welfare and Social Policy: An Essential Reader* (Bristol, 2005)

Hendrick, Harry, *Child Welfare: England 1872–1989* (London and New York, 1994)

Hendrick, Harry, *Child Welfare: Historical Dimensions, Contemporary Debate* (revised edn., Bristol, 2003)

Hewitt, Christopher, *Political Violence and Terrorism in Modern America: A Chronology* (Westport, CT, and London, 2005)

Hirschfeld, Gerhard; Krumeich, Gerd; and Renz, Irina (eds.), *Brill's Encyclopedia of the First World War, Volume I* (Leiden, 2012)

Hitchens, Christopher, *God is Not Great: How Religion Poisons Everything* (New York, 2007)

Holquist, Peter, *Making War, Forging Revolution: Russia's Continuum of Crisis 1914–1921* (London, 2002)

Horne, Alastair, *The Price of Glory: Verdun 1916* (Harmondsworth, 2007)

House, Jim, and MacMaster, Neil, *Paris 1961: Algerians, State Terror, and Memory* (Oxford, 2006)

Hull, Isabel V., *Absolute Destruction: Military Culture and the Practices of War in Imperial Germany* (Ithaca, NY and London, 2005)

Jackson, Kenneth, *The Ku Klux Klan in the City, 1915–1930* (New York, 1967)

Judt, Tony, *Postwar: A History of Europe since 1945* (London, 2005)

Kagan, Robert, *Paradise and Power: America and Europe in the New World Order* (London, 2003)

Kattago, Siobhan, *Ambiguous Memory: The Nazi Past and German National Identity* (Westport, CT, and London, 2001)

Kent, Peter C., *The Lonely Cold War of Pope Pius XII* (Montréal, 2002)

Kershaw, Ian, *Hitler 1889–1936: Hubris* (Harmondsworth, 1998)

Kershaw, Ian, *Hitler 1936–1945: Nemesis* (Harmondsworth, 2000)

Kershaw, Ian, *The 'Hitler Myth': Image and Reality in the Third Reich* (Oxford, 1987)

King, Alex, *Memorials of the Great War in Britain: The Symbolism and Politics of Remembrance* (Oxford and New York, 1998)

Koshar, Rudy, *From Monuments to Traces: Artifacts of German Memory, 1870–1990* (Berkeley, CA, and London, 2000)

Bibliography

Kramer, Alan, *Dynamic of Destruction: Culture and Mass Killing in the First World War* (Oxford, 2007)

Kulka, Otto Dov, *Landscapes of the Metropolis of Death: Reflections on Memory and Imagination* (London, 2013)

Kyle, Donald, *Spectacles of Death in Ancient Rome* (London, 1998)

Ladd, Brian, *The Ghosts of Berlin: Confronting German History in the Urban Landscape* (Chicago, 1997)

Lawrence, Bruce B., *Defenders of God: The Fundamentalist Revolt Against the Modern Age* (London, 1990)

Leed, Eric J., *No Man's Land: Combat and Identity in World War I* (Cambridge, 1979)

Lenin, V. I., *Collected Works, Volume 28: July 1918–March 1919* (Moscow, 1965)

Lessing, Doris, *A Small Personal Voice: Essays, Reviews, Interviews* (London, 1994)

Levene, Mark, *Genocide in the Age of the Nation State, Volume 2: The Rise of the West and the Coming of Genocide* (London and New York, 2005)

Lintott, Andrew W., *Violence in Republican Rome* (Oxford, 1968)

Linz, Juan J., and Stepan, Alfred (eds.), *The Breakdown of Democratic Regimes: Europe* (Baltimore, 1978)

Longerich, Peter, *Holocaust: The Nazi Persecution and Murder of the Jews* (Oxford, 2010)

Lüdtke, Alf (ed.), *The No Man's Land of Violence: Extreme Wars in the 20th Century* (Göttingen, 2006)

Lyttelton, Adrian, *The Seizure of Power: Fascism in Italy 1919–1929* (3rd edn., Abingdon, 2004)

Macleod, Jenny, *Reconsidering Gallipoli* (Manchester, 2004)

Mann, Horace, *Lectures and Annual Reports on Education* (Cambridge, MA, 1867)

Masur, Louis P., *Rites of Execution: Capital Punishment and the Transformation of American Culture, 1776–1865* (New York, 1989)

Mayer, Arno *The Furies: Violence and Terror in the French and Russian Revolutions* (Princeton and Oxford, 2001)

McGovern, James R., *Anatomy of a Lynching: The Killing of Claude Neal* (Baton Rouge, LA, 1982)

McLeod, Hugh, *Religion and the People of Western Europe 1789–1989* (2nd edn., Oxford, 1997)

McLeod, Hugh (ed.), *The Cambridge History of Christianity, Volume 9: World Christianities c. 1914–c. 2000* (Cambridge, 2006)

McLeod, Hugh, *The Religious Crisis of the 1960s* (Oxford, 2007)

Meyersfeld, Bonita, *Domestic Violence and International Law* (Oxford, 2010)

Mill, John Stuart, *The Subjection of Women* (London, 2001, first published 1869)

Mommsen, Hans, *The Rise and Fall of Weimar Democracy* (Chapel Hill and London, 1996)

Mommsen, Wolfgang J., and Hirschfeld, Gerhard (eds.), *Social Protest, Violence and Terror in Nineteenth- and Twentieth-Century Europe* (London, 1982)

Monkkonen, Eric H., *Police in Urban America, 1860–1920* (Cambridge, 1981)

Morgan, Jane, *Conflict and Order: The Police and Labour Disputes in England and Wales 1900–1939* (Oxford, 1987)

Mosse, George L., *Fallen Soldiers: Reshaping the Memory of the World Wars* (New York, 1990)

Mueller, John, *The Remnants of War* (Ithaca, NY, and London, 2004)

Nadelson, Theodore, *Trained to Kill: Soldiers at War* (Baltimore, 2005)

Nietzsche, Friedrich Wilhelm, *On the Genealogy of Morals* (New York, 1967)

Nussbaum, Martha, *The Clash Within: Democracy, Religious Violence, and India's Future* (Cambridge, MA, 2007)

O'Rourke, Shane, *The Cossacks* (Manchester, 2007)

Ortiz, Paul, *Emancipation Betrayed: The Hidden History of Black Organizing and White Violence in Florida from Reconstruction to the Bloody Election of 1920* (Berkeley, Los Angeles and London, 2005)

Ousby, Ian, *The Road to Verdun: World War I's Most Momentous Battle and the Folly of Nationalism* (London, 2002)

Overy, Richard, *The Bombing War: Europe 1939–1945* (London, 2013)

Panayi, Panikos (ed.), *Minorities in Wartime: National and Racial Groupings in Europe, North America and Australia during the Two World Wars* (Oxford and Providence, 1993)

Parker-Jenkins, Marie, *Sparing the Rod: Schools, Discipline and Children's Rights* (Stoke on Trent, 1999)

Payne, Stanley G., *Spain's First Democracy: The Second Republic, 1931–1936* (Madison, WI, 1993)

Pfeifer, Michael J., *Rough Justice: Lynching and American Society, 1874–1947* (Urbana, IL, 2004)

Pinker, Steven, *The Better Angels of our Nature: The Decline of Violence in History and its Causes* (London and New York, 2011)

Pipes, Richard, *Russia under the Bolshevik Regime 1919–1924* (London, 1995)

Potter, David, and Mattingly, David, *Life, Death, and Entertainment in Roman Society* (Ann Arbor, MI, 1999)

Preston, Paul, *The Spanish Holocaust: Inquisition and Extermination in Twentieth-Century Spain* (London, 2013)

Prost, Antoine, *In the Wake of War: 'Les Anciens Combattants' and French Society* (Providence and Oxford, 1992)

Pugh, Michael (ed.), *Regeneration of War-Torn Societies* (London, 2000)

Ramsden, John, *Don't Mention the War: The British and the Germans since 1890* (London, 2006)

Bibliography

Rebora, Giovanni, *Culture of the Fork: A Brief History of Food in Europe* (New York, 2001)

Rhodes James, Robert, *Gallipoli* (London, 1965)

Richards, Michael, *A Time of Silence: Civil War and the Culture of Repression in Franco's Spain, 1936–1945* (Cambridge, 1998)

Rohan, Marc, *Paris '68: Graffiti, Posters, Newspapers, and Poems of the Events of May 1968* (London, 1988)

Rosenfeld, Gavriel D., *Munich and Memory: Architecture, Monuments, and the Legacy of the Third Reich* (Berkeley, Los Angeles and London, 2000)

Rosenhaft, Eve, *Beating the Fascists? The German Communists and Political Violence* (Cambridge, 1983)

Roth, Randolph, *American Homicide* (Cambridge, MA, and London, 2009)

Ruff, Julius R., *Violence in Early Modern Europe 1500–1800* (Cambridge, 2001)

Rule, Wilma, and Noonan, Norma C. (eds.), *Russian Women in Politics and Society* (Westport, CT, and London, 1996)

Russell, Diana E. H., *Rape in Marriage* (revised edn., Bloomington and Indianapolis, 1990)

Russell, Diana E. H., *The Politics of Rape: The Victim's Perspective* (Lincoln, Nebraska, 2003)

Ryder, A. J., *The German Revolution of 1918: A Study of German Socialism in War and Revolt* (Cambridge, 1967)

Sagan, Eli, *Citizens and Cannibals: The French Revolution, the Struggle for Modernity and the Origins of Ideological Terror* (Lanham, MD, and Oxford, 2001)

Sassoon, Siegfried, *Collected Poems, 1908–1956* (London, 2002)

Schama, Simon, *Citizens: A Chronicle of the French Revolution* (London, 1989)

Schissler, Hanna (ed.), *The Miracle Years: A Cultural History of West Germany* (Princeton and Oxford, 2001)

Schopenhauer, Arthur, *Religion: A Dialogue and Other Essays* (New York, 2007)

Schumann, Dirk, *Political Violence in the Weimar Republic, 1918–1933: Fight for the Streets and Fear of Civil War* (New York and Oxford, 2009)

Schwartz, Regina M., *The Curse of Cain: The Violent Legacy of Monotheism* (Chicago and London, 1997)

Sher, Julian, *White Hoods: Canada's Ku Klux Klan* (Vancouver, 1983)

Sherman, Daniel J., *The Construction of Memory in Interwar France* (Chicago and London, 1999)

Singer, D. G., and J. L. (eds.), *Handbook of Children and the Media* (Thousand Oaks, CA, 2001)

Skidelsky, Robert, *Politicians and the Slump: The Labour Government of 1929–1931* (London, 1967)

Skocpol, Theda, *States and Social Revolutions: A Comparative Analysis of France, Russia and China* (Cambridge, 1979)

Sledge, E. B., *With the Old Breed at Peleliu and Okinawa* (New York and Oxford, 1990)

Smead, Howard, *Blood Justice: The Lynching of Mack Charles Parker* (Oxford and New York, 1986)

Smith, John R., *The War in the Pacific: Cartwheel – The Reduction of Rabaul* (Washington DC, 1959)

Snyder, Jack (ed.), *Religion and International Relations Theory* (New York, 2011)

Snyder, Timothy, *Bloodlands: Europe between Hitler and Stalin* (New York, 2010)

Sperber, Jonathan, *The European Revolutions, 1848–1851* (Cambridge, 1994)

Spierenburg, Pieter, *The Spectacle of Suffering: Executions and the Evolution of Repression; from a Preindustrial Metropolis to the European Experience* (Cambridge, 1984)

Sprinzak, Ehud, *Brother against Brother: Violence and Extremism in Israeli Politics from the Altelena to the Rabin Assassination* (New York, 1999)

Sprinzak, Ehud, *The Ascendance of Israel's Radical Right* (New York, 1991)

Stamp, Gavin, *Memorial to the Missing of the Somme* (London, 2007)

Stearns, Jason K., *Dancing in the Glory of Monsters: The Collapse of the Congo and the Great War of Africa* (New York, 2012)

Steinmetz, Suzanne K., and Straus, Murray A. (eds.), *Violence in the Family* (New York, 1974)

Sutherland, D. M. G., *Murder in Aubagne: Lynching, Law, and Justice during the French Revolution* (Cambridge, 2009)

Sutherland, D. M. G., *The French Revolution and Empire: The Quest for a Civic Order* (Oxford, 2003)

Thomson, Clare, *The Singing Revolution: A Political Journey through the Baltic States* (London, 1992)

Tilly, Charles, *The Politics of Collective Violence* (Cambridge and New York, 2003)

Titchener, E. B., *Lectures on the Experimental Psychology of Thought Processes* (New York, 1909)

Tolnay, Stewart E., and Beck, E. M., *A Festival of Violence: An Analysis of Southern Lynchings, 1882–1930* (Urbana, IL, and Chicago, 1992)

Tombs, Robert, *The Paris Commune 1871* (London, 1999)

Trotsky, Leon, *The History of the Russian Revolution* (London, 1934)

Ventresca, Robert A., *Soldier of Christ: The Life of Pope Pius XII* (Cambridge, MA, 2013)

Vital, David, *A People Apart: The Jews in Europe 1789–1939* (Oxford, 1999)

Vogt, Henri, *Between Utopia and Disillusionment: A Narrative of the Political Transformation of Eastern Europe* (New York and Oxford, 2005)

von Clausewitz, Carl, *On War* (trans. J. J. Graham) (London, 1977)

Bibliography

Watson, Alexander, *Enduring the Great War: Combat, Morale and Collapse in the German and British Armies, 1914–1918* (Cambridge, 2008)

Weber, Eugen, *The Hollow Years: France in the 1930s* (London, 1996)

Weldon Whalen, Robert, *Bitter Wounds: German Victims of the Great War, 1914–1939* (Ithaca, NY, and London, 1984)

Wellman, James K. Jr. (ed.), *Belief and Bloodshed: Religion and Violence across Time and Tradition* (Lanham, MD, 2007)

Westwood, J. N., *Endurance and Endeavour: Russian History 1812–1992* (4th edn., Oxford, 1993)

Wiese, Christian, and Betts, Paul (eds.), *Years of Persecution, Years of Extermination: Saul Friedländer and the Future of Holocaust Studies* (London and New York, 2010)

Wilson, Peter H., *Europe's Tragedy: A New History of the Thirty Years War* (London, 2009)

Wilson, Trevor, *The Myriad Faces of War: Britain and the Great War, 1914–1918* (Cambridge, 1986)

Winter, Jay, *Dreams of Peace and Freedom: Utopian Moments in the Twentieth Century* (New Haven and London, 2006)

Winter, Jay, *Remembering War: The Great War Between Historical Memory and History in the Twentieth Century* (New Haven, 2006)

Winter, Jay (ed.), *The Cambridge History of the First World War, Volume I: Global War* (Cambridge, 2014)

Winter, Jay (ed.), *The Cambridge History of the First World War, Volume II: The State* (Cambridge, 2014)

Winter, Jay, (ed.), *The Cambridge History of the First World War, Volume III: Civil Society* (Cambridge, 2014)

Winter, Jay and Prost, Antoine, *The Great War in History: Debates and Controversies, 1914 to the Present* (Cambridge, 2005)

Winter, J. M., *Sites of Memory, Sites of Mourning: The Great War in European Cultural History* (Cambridge, 1995)

Wittner, Lawrence S., *The Struggle Against the Bomb, Volume II: Resisting the Bomb – A History of the World Nuclear Disarmament Movement, 1954–1970* (Stanford, 1997)

Wood, James B., *The King's Army: Warfare, Soldiers and Society during the French Wars of Religion, 1562–76* (Cambridge, 1996)

Wright, Gordon, *Between the Guillotine and Liberty: Two Centuries of the Crime Problem in France* (Oxford, 1983)

Wuthnow, Robert, *The Restructuring of American Religion: Society and Faith since World War II* (Princeton, 1988)

Young, Allan, *Harmony of Illusions: Inventing Post-Traumatic Stress Disorder* (Princeton, 1995)

Ziemann, Benjamin, *Contested Commemorations: Republican War Veterans and Weimar Political Culture* (Cambridge, 2013)

English-language journals, newspapers, magazines and reports

The Advocate of Peace

Africa Action Africa Policy
  E-Journal

Albion: A Quarterly Journal
  Concerned with British Studies

The American Historical Review

The American Political Science
  Review

American Slavic and East European
  Review

American Sociological Review

Annals of the American Academy of
  Political and Social Science

Annals of the Association of
  American Geographers

Annual Review of Sociology

Anthropological Quarterly

The Arkansas Historical Quarterly

AsiaOne

Boston Review

Brant News

The British Journal of Sociology

British Medical Journal

The Catholic Historical Review

Central European History

Chicago Tribune

Child Abuse and Neglect

Contemporary European History

Crime and Delinquency

Crime and Justice

Daedalus

Detroit Free Press

Domestic Violence against Women
  Report

Economic and Political Weekly

European Journal of Criminology

European Sociological Review

Family and Conciliation Courts
  Review

The Family Coordinator

The Florida Historical Quarterly

Focus Historia

Forbes

Foreign Affairs

Foreign Policy

French Historical Studies

Furrow

Gender and Development

Gender and History

Gender and Society

German History

German Politics and Society

GHI Bulletin

Greece & Rome

The Guardian

Hansard

Historia 396

The Historical Journal

History of Education

History of Education Journal

History of Education Quarterly

International Affairs

International and Comparative Law
  Quarterly

The International History Review

International Journal of Middle East
  Studies

International Journal of Politics,
  Culture and Society

International Legal Materials

International Politics

International Review of the Aesthetics
  and Sociology of Music

International Security

Journal of American Folklore

The Journal of American History

Journal of Black Studies

The Journal of British Studies

The Journal of Conflict Resolution

Journal of Contemporary History

Bibliography

The Journal of Criminal Law and
   Criminology
Journal of Family Violence
Journal of Feminist Studies in
   Religion
Journal of Genocide Research
The Journal of Interdisciplinary
   History
Journal of Marriage and Family
The Journal of Military History
Journal of Modern European History
The Journal of Modern History
Journal of Peace Research
Journal of Social History
Journal of Southern History
Journal of the Early Republic
Kennebec Journal
Kritika: Explorations in Russian and
   Eurasian History
The Lancet
Latin American Politics and Society
Law and History Review
Law and Social Inquiry
Law & Society Review
Life
Liverpool Mercury
London Review of Books
Manchester Guardian
Military Affairs
The Modern Law Review
The New England Quarterly
New German Critique
New Republic
New Yorker
The New York Times
OAH Magazine of History
Off Our Backs
Past & Present
Philosophical Transactions: Biological
   Sciences
The Police Chief

Policy Review
Political Psychology
Polity
The Quarterly of Film, Radio and
   Television
The Review of Economics and
   Statistics
The Review of Politics
The Russian Review
Science
Science News Letter
Slavic Review
Slavonic and East European Review
Social Indicators Research
Social Forces
Social Problems
Social Science History
Sociological Forum
The Sociological Quarterly
The South Carolina Historical
   Magazine
Theory and Society
The Times (London)
Times Literary Supplement
Transactions of the Institute of British
   Geographers
Transactions of the Royal Historical
   Society
Trauma Violence Abuse
Victorian Studies
Violence against Women
Washington Post
Washington Post and Times-Herald
The Wilson Quarterly
Women's Studies International
   Forum
World Politics
World Report on Violence and Health
World Today
Yale Law & Policy Review

Foreign-language books

Afflerbach, Holger, *Falkenhayn: Politisches Denken und Handeln im Kaiserreich* (Munich, 1994)

Afflerbach, Holger, and Cornelißen, Christoph (eds.), *Sieger und Besiegte: Materielle und ideele Neuorientierungen nach 1945* (Tübingen and Basel, 1997)

Bahr, Eckhard, *Sieben Tage im Oktober: Aufbruch in Dresden* (Leipzig, 1990)

Bastian, Till, *Das Jahrhundert des Todes: Zur Psychologie von Gewaltbereitschaft und Massenmord im 20. Jahrhundert* (Göttingen, 2000)

Becker, Annette, *Les Monuments aux morts: patrimoine et mémoires de la grande guerre* (Paris, 1988)

Becker, Jean-Jacques, and Krumeich, Gerd, *Der Grosse Krieg: Deutschland und Frankreich im Ersten Weltkrieg 1914–1918* (Essen, 2010)

Brüggemeier, Franz-Josef, *Leben vor Ort: Ruhrbergleute und Ruhrbergbau 1889–1919* (Munich, 1983)

Bundesamt, Statistisches, *Justiz auf einen Blick, Ausgabe 2011* (Wiesbaden, 2011)

Bundesministerium für Vertriebene, Flüchtlinge und Kriegsgeschädigte (ed.), *Die Vertreibung der deutschen Bevölkerung aus den Gebieten östlich der Oder-Neiße* (3 vols., Bonn, 1954–1960)

Conzenius, Victor; Greschat, Martin, and Kochen, Hermann (eds.), *Die Zeit nach 1945 als Thema der kirchlichen Zeitgeschichte* (Göttingen, 1988)

Crouzet, Denis, *Les Guerriers de Dieu: La violence au temps des troubles de religion vers 1525–vers 1610, Volume 1* (Seyssel, 1990)

Deist, Wilhelm; Messerschmidt, Manfred; Volkmann, Hans-Erich; and Wette, Wolfram, *Das Deutsche Reich und der Zweite Weltkrieg, Volume 1: Ursachen und Voraussetzungen der deutschen Kriegspolitik* (Stuttgart, 1979)

Denizot, Alain, *Douaumont: 1914–1918: vérité et légende* (Paris, 1998)

Deutsches Historisches Institut Warschau, *Jahresbericht 2009* (Warsaw, 2010)

Deutschland-Berichte der Sozialdemokratischen Partei Deutschlands (Sopade) 1934–1940, Zweiter Jahrgang 1935 (Frankfurt am Main, 1980)

Echternkamp, Jörg (ed.), *Das Deutsche Reich und der Zweite Weltkrieg, Volume 9/1: Politisierung, Vernichtung, Überleben* (Munich, 2004)

Elias, Norbert, *Studien über die Deutschen: Machtkämpfe und Habitusentwicklung im 19. und 20. Jahrhundert* (Frankfurt am Main, 1994)

Elias, Norbert, *Über den Prozeß der Zivilisation: Soziogenetische und psychogenetische Untersuchungen* (Bern, 1969, reprinted Frankfurt am Main, 1976)

Elsner, Erich, and Steffen, Wiebke, *Vergewaltigung und sexuelle Nötigung in Bayern* (Munich, 2005)

Fourastié, Jean, *Les trente glorieuses, ou la révolution invisible de 1946 à 1975* (Paris, 1979)

Bibliography

Frevert, Ute, *Die Kasernierte Nation: Militärdienst und Zivilgesellschaft in Deutschland* (Munich, 2001)

Friedrich, Ernst, *Krieg dem Kriege!; guerre à la guerre!; War against War; oorlog an den oorlog!* (Berlin, 1924)

Fürmetz, Gerhard; Reinke, Herbert; and Weinhauer, Klaus (eds.), *Nachkriegspolizei: Sicherheit und Ordnung in Ost- und Westdeutschland 1945–1969* (Hamburg, 2001)

Furrer, Theresa, *Bedrohte Sicherheit: Untersuchungen zu einem fragmentierten Begriff* (Zürich, 2008)

Geyer, Martin H., *Verkehrte Welt: Revolution, Inflation und Moderne, München 1914–1924* (Göttingen, 1998)

Gilcher-Holtey, Ingrid (ed.), *1968: Vom Ereignis zum Gegenstand der Geschichtswissenschaft* (Göttingen, 1998)

Goebbels, Joseph, *Kampf um Berlin* (9th printing, Berlin, 1936)

Greschat, Martin, *Die evangelische Christenheit und die deutsche Geschichte nach 1945: Weichenstellungen in der Nachkriegszeit* (Stuttgart, 2002)

Greschat, Martin (ed.), *Im Zeichen der Schuld: 40 Jahre Stuttgarter Schuldbekenntnis, Eine Dokumentation* (Neukirchen-Vluyn, 1985)

Gumbel, Emil Julius, *Vier Jahre politischer Mord* (Berlin-Fichtenau, 1922)

Herbert, Ulrich (ed.), *Wandlungsprozesse in Westdeutschland: Belastung, Integration, Liberalisierung 1945–1980* (Göttingen, 2002)

Hessische Stiftung Friedens- und Konfliktforschung (ed.), *Faszination der Gewalt: Politische Strategie und Alltagserfahrung* (Frankfurt am Main, 1983)

Hirtenworte zu Krieg und Frieden: Die Texte der katholischen Bischöfe der Bundesrepublik Deutschland, der Deutschen Demokratischen Republik, der Niederlande, Österreichs, der Schweiz, Ungarns und der Vereinigten Staaten von Amerika (Cologne, 1983)

Holl, Karl, and Wette, Wolfram (eds.), *Pazifismus in der Weimarer Republik: Beiträge zur historischen Friedensforschung* (Paderborn, 1981)

Jarausch, Konrad, *Die Umkehr: Deutsche Wandlungen 1945–1955* (Munich, 2004)

Jeismann, Michael (ed.), *Mahnmal Mitte: Eine Kontroverse* (Cologne, 1999)

Jensen, Uffa; Knoch, Habbo; Morat, Daniel; and Rürup, Miriam (eds.), *Gewalt und Gesellschaft: Klassiker modernen Denkens neu gelesen* (Göttingen, 2011)

Joas, Hans, *Kriege und Werte: Studien zur Gewaltgeschichte des 20. Jahrhunderts* (Göttingen, 2000)

Jünger, Ernst (ed.), *Das Antlitz des Weltkrieges: Fronterlebnisse deutscher Soldaten: Mit etwa 2000 photographischen Aufnahmen auf Tafeln, Kartenanhang sowie einer chronologischen Kriegsgeschichte in Tabelle* (Berlin, 1930)

Jünger, Ernst, *Der Kampf als inneres Erlebnis* (Berlin, 1928)

Kaiser, Ingrid, *Gewalt in häuslichen Beziehungen. Sozialwissenschaftliche und evolutionsbiologische Positionen im Diskurs* (Wiesbaden, 2012)

Kaiser, Jochen-Christoph, and Doering-Manteuffel, Anselm (eds.), *Christentum und politische Verantwortung: Kirchen in Nachkriegsdeutschland* (Stuttgart, 1990)

Kippenberg, Hans G., *Gewalt als Gottesdienst: Religionskriege im Zeitalter der Globalisierung* (Munich, 2008)

Kogon, Eugen, *Der SS-Staat: Das System der deutschen Konzentrationslager* (Munich, 1946)

Köhler, Joachim, and van Melis, Damian (eds.), *Siegerin in Trümmern: Die Rolle der katholischen Kirche in der deutschen Nachkriegsgesellschaft* (Stuttgart, 1998)

Koselleck, Reinhart, and Jeismann, Michael (eds.), *Der politische Totenkult: Kriegerdenkmäler in der Moderne* (Munich, 1994)

Kurz, Thomas, *'Blutmai': Sozialdemokraten und Kommunisten im Brennpunkt der Berliner Ereignisse von 1929* (Berlin, 1988)

Lemke, R., *Die Preußische Exekutiv-Polizei: Wie sie war, wie sie ist und wie sie sein müßte* (Osnabrück, 1904)

Lisken, Hans, and Denninger, Erhard, *Handbuch des Polizeirechts* (3rd edn., Munich, 2001)

Longerich, Peter, *Die braunen Bataillone: Die Geschichte der SA* (Munich, 1989)

Lüdtke, Alf (ed.), *'Sicherheit' und 'Wohlfahrt': Polizei, Gesellschaft und Herrschaft im 19. und 20. Jahrhundert* (Frankfurt am Main, 1992)

Meinel, Reinhard, and Wernicke, Thomas (eds.), *Mit tschekistischem Gruß: Berichte der Bezirksverwaltung für Staatssicherheit Potsdam 1989* (Potsdam, 1990)

Michalka, Wolfgang (ed.), *Der Erste Weltkrieg: Wirkung, Wahrnehmung, Analyse* (Munich, 1994)

Michaud, Yves, *La violence* (Paris, 1986)

Ministerium des Innern: Kommission zur Erforschung und Ausarbeitung der Geschichte der Deutschen Volkspolizei (ed.), *Geschichte der Deutschen Volkspolizei, Band 2 1961–1985* (Berlin, 1987)

Müller, Rolf-Dieter, and Volkmann, Hans-Erich (eds.), *Die Wehrmacht: Mythos und Realität* (Munich, 1999)

Musil, Robert, *Gesammelte Werke* (Hamburg, 1957)

Pehle, Walter H. (ed.), *Der historische Ort des Nationalsozialismus. Annäherungen* (Frankfurt am Main, 1990)

Prost, Antoine, *Les anciens combattants et la société française 1914-1939, Volume 3, Mentalités et idéologies* (Paris, 1979)

Reichardt, Sven, *Faschistische Kampfbünde: Gewalt und Gemeinschaft im italienischen Faschismus und in der deutschen SA* (Cologne, Weimar and Vienna, 2002)

Reuter, Astrid, and Kippenberg, Hans G. (eds.), *Religionskonflikte im Verfassungsstaat* (Göttingen, 2010)

Richter, Michael, *Die Friedliche Revolution: Aufbruch zur Demokratie in Sachsen 1989/90, Volume 1* (Göttingen, 2009)

Riesebrodt, Martin, *Die Rückkehr der Religionen: Fundamentalismus und der 'Kampf der Kulturen'* (2nd edn., Munich, 2001)

Rother, Rainer (ed.), *Die letzten Tage der Menschheit: Bilder des Ersten Weltkrieges* (Berlin, 1994)

Secher, Reynald, and Meyer, Jean, *Le génocide franco-français: la Vendée-Vengé* (Paris, 2006)

Secrétariat d'etat aux anciens combattants et victimes de guerre, *Monuments de Mémoire: Monuments aux morts de la Grande Guerre* (Paris, 1991)

Süß, Dietmar, *Tod aus der Luft: Kriegsgesellschaft und Luftkrieg in Deutschland* (Munich, 2011)

Thoß, Bruno, and Volkmann, Hans-Erich (ed.), *Erster Weltkrieg Zweiter Weltkrieg: Ein Vergleich: Krieg, Kriegserlebnis, Kriegserfahrung in Deutschland* (Paderborn, Munich, Vienna and Zürich, 2002)

Ullrich, Klaus; Seifert, Peter; Müller, Brigitte; and Sauer, Horst (eds.), *Deutsche Demokratische Republik* (Leipzig, 1989)

van Dülmen, Richard, *Theater des Schreckens: Gerichtspraxis und Strafrituale in der frühen Neuzeit* (Munich, 1985)

Vigarello, L. Georges, *Histoire du viol* (Paris, 1998)

Wieck, Michael, *Zeugnis vom Untergang Königsbergs: Ein 'Geltungsjude' berichtet* (Munich, 2005)

Winkler, Heinrich August, *Von der Revolution zur Stabilisierung: Arbeiter und Arbeiterbewegung in der Weimarer Republik 1918 bis 1924* (Berlin and Bonn, 1984)

Foreign-language journals etc.

Annales: Histoire, Sciences Sociales

Archiv für Sozialgeschichte

Cahiers du Monde Russe

Der Spiegel

Deutsches Ärzteblatt International

Die Welt

Die Zeit

El País

Forschungsberichte aus dem Duitsland Instituut Amsterdam

Geschichte und Gesellschaft

Le mouvement social

Mitteilungsblatt des Instituts für soziale Bewegungen

Vingtième Siècle: Revue d'histoire

WestEnd: Neue Zeitschrift für Sozialforschung

Zeithistorische Forschungen

Zeitschrift für Geschichtswissenschaft

Index

Index

Index

Index

Index

Index